CALVINISM

D.G. Hart

Calvinism
A HISTORY

YALE UNIVERSITY PRESS
NEW HAVEN AND LONDON

For information about this and other Yale University Press publications, please contact:
U.S. Office: sales.press@yale.edu   www.yalebooks.com
Europe Office: sales@yaleup.co.uk   www.yalebooks.co.uk

Set in Arno Pro by IDSUK (DataConnection) Ltd
Printed in Great Britain by TJ International Ltd, Padstow, Cornwall

Library of Congress Cataloging-in-Publication Data

Hart, D. G. (Darryl G.)
   Calvinism : a history / D.G. Hart.
      pages cm
   ISBN 978-0-300-14879-4 (hardback)
1. Calvinism—History. I. Title.
   BX9422.5.H37 2013
   284'.209—dc23
                                                                2013003010

A catalogue record for this book is available from the British Library.

10 9 8 7 6 5 4 3 2 1

To Jim and Nancy Loux

Contents

Preface and Acknowledgments

'TIS THE SEASON OF Calvinist anniversaries. July 10, 2009 marked the 500th anniversary of John Calvin's birthday, an occasion that prompted the appropriate number of conferences, op-ed pieces, biographies, and anthologies. This year was the 200th anniversary of the founding of Princeton Theological Seminary, a United States institution with an international reputation for teaching and studying Calvinism. Next year will mark the 450th anniversary of the Heidelberg Catechism, a pedagogical device for the Reformed churches in the Palatinate that became a doctrinal standard for Calvinists around the world. We are still over ten years from the 500th anniversary of the start of the Protestant Reformation in Zurich, the first European city to check a religious identity box different from both Lutheranism and Roman Catholicism under Ulrich Zwingli's leadership.

This book is not designed to observe any particular anniversary but it almost coincides with half a millennium of Calvinist developments. It is an audacious undertaking in many respects. Putting so much history in so many places into one relatively small volume runs against the grain of academic history since it requires pronouncements on subjects and eras about which the historian has no professional competency. I am trained as a historian of the United States and have worked generally on subjects since the Civil War. The prospect of writing a paragraph, let alone a section of a chapter, on religious developments in sixteenth-century Poland is almost as scary as bungee jumping. But when an editor at Yale University Press asked me to consider a history of Calvinism that would cover its global dimensions I immediately accepted, maybe because the only legal excitement available to me is one that comes with landing a golf ball on a green surrounded by sand.

Readers will discover soon enough my rationale for organizing material from five different centuries and just as many continents. Finding a single narrative that could do justice to Reformed Protestantism without relying on parochial forms of denominational history was arguably the hardest challenge. But what was not difficult was the fascination that ensued from observing historical circumstances that saw a small group of churches in sixteenth-century Swiss cities gain a following throughout Europe, only to become a global phenomenon after 1600 through colonialism, migration, and missions. Just as the framers of the United States Constitution could not have fathomed that the republic they formed would be engaged 175 years later in a Cold War with Communists in eastern Europe, so John Calvin would never have imagined that Asian Christians in twenty-first-century Seoul, Korea, would identify with the interpretation of Scripture and church structures that he proposed in 1540s Geneva. Indeed, what makes a global history of Calvinism captivating is seeing how accidental and unexpected Reformed Protestant developments were. No leader of the Presbyterian or Reformed churches could have planned the way that Calvinism turned out. Some might even have been disappointed with the outcome. Whatever those expectations, the global history of Calvinism reveals a set of religious institutions caught up in the tumultuous developments of the modern era that saw Europeans (for good and ill) dominate affairs on Planet Earth.

I am grateful for the help and encouragement of many people during the writing of this book. Chief among them is Heather McCallum, my longsuffering editor at Yale, who patiently waited for drafts and provided useful direction once they arrived. Mark Noll, who has been my teacher and mentor for thirty years, and Philip Benedict, whose social history of Calvinism set the standard for Reformed Protestant studies, gave very helpful sets of comments that improved the book significantly. Colleagues at Hillsdale College, Richard Gamble, Matthew Gaetano, Paul Moreno, and David Stewart, reacted to ideas in conversations and informal presentations that let me know whether I was going in the right direction. Former colleagues at Westminster Seminary California, W. Robert Godfrey, David VanDrunen, Ryan Glomsrud, John Fesko, Bryan Estelle, Joel Kim, Michael Horton, and Charles Telfer, raised good questions during presentations at the school's Warfield Seminar. Ryan Glomsrud deserves special mention for being an important sounding board while he and I attended the 2009 Calvin conference in Geneva, and for giving useful guidance on Karl Barth.

From the time that I first submitted a proposal to the day when I finished revisions I experienced a number of personal challenges that go with the territory of human existence. My wife, Ann, and good friend, John Muether, were a limitless source of encouragement during these trials. But deserving special thanks are Jim and Nancy Loux, to whom I dedicate this book. In countless ways their friendship softened life's blows and lifted my spirits so that writing this book never became a burden but remained a pleasure.

Hillsdale, Michigan
September 17, 2012

Introduction

FOR CLOSE TO FIVE centuries, Geneva, the city that gave birth to Calvinism, has enjoyed an international influence. John Bale, a refugee to Geneva during the Reformation and a friend of the Scottish reformer, John Knox, marveled at the city's polyglot demographics. To see Spaniards, French, Scots, English, and Germans "disagreeing in speech, manners, and apparel, sheep and wolves, bulls and bears, being coupled with the only yoke of Christ," was a "wonderful miracle of the whole world."[1] What inspired Bale, though, was troubling to city officials and citizens, especially when Geneva needed to raise a militia against the emperor's soldiers. In 1557 Geneva's council thought better of holding a public inspection of all able-bodied men because the balance would likely tip in favor of refugees over citizens. Such an imbalance would fill the "strangers" with "undue pride."[2] Three centuries later, in 1863, Henry Dunant, a native of Geneva and disciple of the nineteenth-century revival of Calvinism in his home town, led the group of Genevan humanitarians responsible for launching the International Committee of the Red Cross. This organization solidified Geneva's reputation as home to international relief efforts that would inspire the League of Nations and the United Nations High Commission on Refugees. The close identification between the city and international humanitarianism lives on in the commonly and widely invoked Geneva Conventions.

Humanitarianism is not the first thought that comes to mind with Calvinism. John Calvin is best known for thundering against human depravity and promoting divine sovereignty such that only a predestined few escape eternal damnation. This constellation of beliefs prompted the American journalist, H. L. Mencken, to place Calvinism in his "cabinet of horrors," right next to cannibalism.[3]

But Mencken's was a minority perspective on Calvinism during the late nineteenth and early twentieth centuries. Scholars like Max Weber and Robert K. Merton were busy attributing to Calvinism the genius of modern civilization – from capitalism and democracy to natural science and freedom of inquiry. This was a different and more productive side of international Calvinism than Dunant's Red Cross. Instead of drawing the world's displaced and persecuted either to Geneva or to the local offices of the Swiss city's international organizations, the Calvinism praised by scholars and statesmen between 1860 and 1930 was a religion that migrated out from Geneva to change the world. Either way, Calvinism was a faith with international stature. Of course, other varieties of Christianity also possessed extensive networks of churches and agencies around the world. But none of them were as identified as Calvinism was with Geneva and its message of a better world.

This book explores a different side of Calvinism's global footprint. Instead of examining Calvinism's emergence as a model for humanitarianism or fuel for modernization, the ensuing narrative follows an expression of western Christianity that emerged in marginal cities in central Europe, gradually establishing a presence throughout Europe and eventually around the world. This story features less Calvinism's role in the forces of globalization than the unlikely ways by which it became a global faith. As many observers have noted, Reformed Protestantism did indeed circumnavigate the planet. It did so not by underwriting the political and economic forces of the modern West or by preaching humanitarian ideals, but through the ordinary – and often accidental – efforts of average pastors and lay people.

This narrative has three phases. In the first, Calvinism took root in settings where church reform was tethered to efforts to establish political autonomy. Although Reformed Protestant churches began across Europe, only those in Scotland, the Netherlands, England, and parts of Switzerland and Germany became home to the most enduring branches of Calvinism. Over time the entanglement of church and state in Europe's ecclesiastical establishments became a burden. In the second phase, Calvinists adopted new models for extending their beliefs. Some of these were intentional. Others were the consequence of setting up churches in colonial environments or evangelizing non-European peoples. In the last phase, Reformed Protestants adjusted once again, this time to the rise of secular political orders prompted by the revolutions of the eighteenth century. Among Calvinists arose several gifted leaders who successfully disentangled Reformed churches from the patronage of the state, becoming the inspiration for communions around the world. This is not a narrative abounding with episodes of power, heroism, and genius. Their absence makes the history of Calvinism all the more remarkable.

CHAPTER ONE

CITY LIGHTS

DURING THE WINTER OF 1522, a group of Christians in the city of Zurich met in the home of the printer Christopher Froschauer. Church teaching required Christians during the Lenten season to abstain from meat. In a bold act of defiance, comparable to flag burning today, the assembled ate the sausages served by the host. One of those present was the local priest, Ulrich Zwingli, who was surprised by the food and abstained from eating. Even so, Zwingli defended the choice of food the following month with a sermon entitled "On the Choice and Freedom of Foods." His reasoning was simple even if it captured a theme at the heart of the Swiss Reformation: if the Bible did not require a Lenten fast or specify foods to be avoided, then Christians were free to eat.

This principle became in turn the substance of the Twenty-Fourth Article (out of sixty-seven) adopted in November 1523 by the city council of Zurich: "That no Christian is bound to do those things which God has not decreed, therefore one may eat at all times all food, wherefrom one learns that the decree about cheese and butter is a Roman swindle." Reformed opposition to Roman Catholic requirements would become such a matter of conviction that in 1530 when the emperor, Charles V, requested Protestants in his lands to explain their culinary practices, Martin Bucer and Wolfgang Capito, ministers in the Imperial City of Strasbourg, followed Zwingli's lead and added a chapter to the Tetrapolitan Confession (1530) on "The Choice of Meats." It stated that the apostle Paul had called "the selection of meats prescribed for certain days" a "doctrine of demons." This did not mean that Christians should indulge in gluttony or avarice. It did mean that the church should not create rules that God himself had not revealed.

Fourteen years after the sausage-eating incident in Zurich, on May 25, 1536, the citizens of Geneva pledged to "live according to the Law of the Gospel and the Word of God, and to abolish all Papal abuses."[1] The apparent orderliness and consensus of that expression of popular sovereignty in Geneva could not hide the turmoil by which the Reformation had come to a city that, although not part of the Swiss Confederacy, would soon rival Zurich for leadership among Reformed Protestants. For the better part of a decade, the citizens of Geneva had been trying to gain independence from the House of Savoy. To do this Geneva needed the support of nearby Swiss cities, Fribourg and Bern. When the political autonomy of the 1520s led to religious reforms in the 1530s, political rivalries turned ugly. Fribourg officials, who were Roman Catholic, used the death of one of their citizens during a religious riot in Geneva in 1533 to pressure the Genevans back into the fold of Rome. But thanks to friendly relations with Protestant Bern, Geneva resisted Fribourg's intimidation. In turn, Geneva sponsored two public debates between Protestant and Roman Catholic representatives, one in January 1534, the second in June 1535. Both led to riots. They also increased Geneva's resolve regarding for political independence and the prerogative to establish the city's religious identity. By the time that Geneva's citizens vowed to submit to the word of God in the spring of 1535, the city had withstood intimidation from both Fribourg and Bern, and had informed its Roman Catholic clergy that they needed either to convert to Protestantism or leave.

In 1517 when Martin Luther nailed his famous Ninety-Five Theses to the door of Wittenberg's cathedral, no one had any idea, except for John Calvin's predestinating deity, what would become of a university professor's protest against the corruption of the Roman Catholic church. In the early sixteenth century Europe was already a society in flux, and evangelical preachers like Luther, Zwingli, and Guillaume Farel in Geneva, thanks to that social, economic, and political instability, had sufficient wiggle room to avoid martyrdom. None of these Protestants had a plan for reforming the church, much less for poking a hole through the sacred canopy that had united Christendom. Switzerland was an especially unlikely place from which to launch a comprehensive reform of the church. But like the rest of Calvinism's history, the trickle of protests and changes that emerged among the Swiss Confederacy's cities would overflow to drench practically all of Europe.

The Limits of the Holy Roman Empire

The Reformation happened mainly because it could. No matter how much the Holy Roman Empire connoted political stability, cultural coherence, and unity on matters of ultimate importance, this sacred regime, as opposed to the pagan one it emulated, was more intimidating on paper than in most cities or villages under its authority. The Holy Roman Empire may have had an emperor – Maximilian I until 1519 and Charles V until 1558 – yet by the end of Charles's rule Protestantism was an established reality for Europe. But below the emperor were a host of lesser nobles, church officials, and rulers of specific territories or estates, who elected the emperor, met in various assemblies to deliberate on his proposals, and ran the affairs of their own principalities. Of course, the monarchs of France and England, for instance, also needed the consent of the nobility to maintain their authority and so a king did not necessarily control his kingdom any more than the Holy Roman Emperor. But the Holy Roman Empire provided more nooks and crannies for dissenting Christians to gain a foothold than in France where the monarchy battled fiercely with the new Christians, or in England where Henry VIII himself functioned as head of the church.

The lands of Germany and Switzerland prove the point about political decentralization within the Holy Roman Empire, while suggesting why Protestantism took hold first in that part of Europe. Was it the case that the Roman Catholic church was most corrupt in those territories? If the Reformation depended solely on clerical abuse then those Italians closest to Rome should have produced a mass of souls ready and willing for Reformed Christianity. If commercial factors were responsible for the rise of Protestantism then the reforms of the sixteenth century could have taken hold in any number of cities throughout a European economy that generated significant wealth and a burgeoning middle class – the Italian city-states come to mind. Meanwhile, if education were a chief factor then Paris would have been more likely to produce a Reformation than Zurich. In other words, the Protestant Reformation depended overwhelmingly on political variables and the Holy Roman Empire provided as much variation as Europe could muster.

During the sixteenth century the Habsburg Empire, under Charles V, who ruled from 1519 to 1558, and his brother Ferdinand I, from 1558 to 1564, dominated European society in ways reminiscent of the Franks in the eighth and early ninth centuries under Charlemagne, who also claimed an empire of sacred and Roman proportions. Not only did the Habsburgs control the German estates, but through marriages and alliances amassed the lands of the Netherlands (1506), the Spanish kingdoms (1516), and then the Austrian lands with the 1519 election of Charles as emperor. Charles' brother, Ferdinand, controlled Austria for the emperor and added Bohemia and part of Hungary (1526) to the Habsburgs' domain. The Habsburgs also had designs on England. Charles' son Philip was married to Mary Tudor and became King of England for a brief period (1553–58), when England veered from Protestantism into fellowship with Rome. Meanwhile, Ferdinand's son Charles almost married Queen Elizabeth I, who restored the Church of England to a moderately Protestant identity. Eventually, through Philip, the Habsburgs in 1580 would take charge of Portugal and also commandeer that nation's explorations in the New World, thus adding to its colonial interests through Spanish and

Portuguese conquistadors. Charles V's great-grandfather, Frederick III, had claimed during his reign (1452–93) through the acrostic AEIOU in Latin that "the rule of the whole world is Austria's."[2] Under Frederick, an underachieving ruler, that line was far-fetched. For the Holy Roman Empire of the sixteenth century it gained plausibility.

And yet the Reformation happened on Charles V's watch rather than in France, the Habsburgs' constant rival, where Protestantism received its fiercest initial opposition. This difference says something about the capacity of rulers with inherent limits of time, energy, and talent to manage affairs of almost limitless detail. The task of confining and even defeating religious dissenters was relatively easier in one nation than across an entire continent. Whether owing to circumstance or providence, Protestants in the Holy Roman Empire had the benefit of a ruler whose ability to keep the new faith in check was akin, to use a biblical metaphor the Reformers would have appreciated, to old wine skins containing new wine.

At first, Martin Luther's objections to papal policy on the sale of indulgences that combined forgiving sin with fund-raising for St Peter's Basilica were little more than the personal opinions of a tormented monk who taught theology to university students. In fact, his famous Ninety-Five Theses, in which he disputed the pope's power to grant indulgences, was tangential in Luther's deeper doubts about his own standing before God, simmering since 1513 when he started to lecture on the Psalms. Soon after October 31, 1517, when Luther posted his views on indulgences, he engaged church officials in a series of debates, while responding to papal condemnations. Both sides dug in their heels, and on June 15, 1520, Pope Leo X threatened Luther with excommunication. The university had sixty days to calm the situation, but instead began to appeal to the German nobility to throw off the yoke of Italian hegemony. By the fall of 1520, the threat had become a reality and Charles V, only a year into his tenure as emperor, needed to confer in Cologne with Frederick the Wise, the Elector of Saxony and patron of the university where Luther taught. Charles petitioned Luther to defend his views before the Diet of Worms, which he did the following spring, in April 1521. Despite the rousing "Here I Stand" speech that would turn Luther into a hero of both zealous Protestants and modern individualists, he could not change the emperor's mind. The next month Charles placed Luther under imperial ban. Were it not for the protection of Frederick and a well-timed kidnapping after Worms that removed the reformer to Wartburg, Luther would likely have become another martyred forerunner of the Reformation, listed after John Huss and John Wycliffe.

These circumstances allowed Luther's colleagues back at the university, Andreas Karlstadt and Philip Melanchthon, to implement ecclesiastical reforms in the city of Wittenberg. Among their changes were marriage for clergy and making the sacrament of the Lord's Supper more accessible to the laity. Some of these reforms went farther than Luther desired. Even so, city officials had embraced a form of Christianity yet to be called Protestantism, and were reforming the local church. As Philip Benedict astutely observes, the reformation in Wittenberg set the pattern for the way other cities and principalities would institutionalize religious change: the preaching of evangelical priests stirred up a "sizable fraction" of the urban population and pressured city officials to enact the goals of reformation.[3] In early 1522 when Luther returned to the city he put the brakes on reform, partly because of differences with Karlstadt and partly to protect his political patron, Frederick. Luther was no radical and knew reform should not alienate sympathetic political patrons, a position that would become particularly and painfully evident during the Peasants' War two years later. But even if Luther knew the value of compromise, his political supporters took risks that made Protestantism possible.

A similar pattern obtained in other German principalities even without the presence of a figurehead like Luther or lieutenants like Melanchthon. To be sure, a combination of Luther's own arguments against the abuses of clergy and the papacy, as well as the longing of devout souls for guidance better than Rome's, was part of the appeal. Also assisting the spread of Protestantism was the printing press and university faculty, who under the influence of Renaissance humanism were willing to give Luther's appeal to the ancient texts of Scripture a hearing and who often felt a resonance with his calls for clerical reform. But without the patronage of local rulers Protestantism would never have spread beyond Saxony. Mark Greengrass explains that princes throughout the German territories "were well aware of the possible advantages to be gained from annexing neighbouring secularized bishoprics and lands."[4] At the same time, rulers needed to balance the consequences of supporting Protestantism with retaliation by the emperor and neighboring princes. Dynastic rivalries and financial gains, as well as conscientious religious devotion, were all factors in the spread of Protestantism. The growth of Protestantism (specifically Lutheranism) proceeded between the 1520s and the 1560s amid political intrigue, war, religious alliances, and ecclesiastical compromise, from the duchies of Hesse, Brandenburg, the Rhine Palatinate, and Bavaria, to numerous German principalities including East Prussia, Württemberg, and Neuberg, each with its own prince. Such an expansion was testimony to the limits of the emperor's power to control religious dissent, not to mention the papacy's dependence on secular authorities to enforce Rome's spiritual bonds.

If Protestantism could gain a foothold in the German portions of the Holy Roman Empire, the lands that constituted the Swiss Confederacy provided even more fertile soil for religious reform, thanks to a heritage of the Swiss people's commitment to independence, geographical isolation, and political savvy. The term Switzerland, first used in the sixteenth century, stood for a patchwork of territories, largely German speaking (but also including French and Italian), roughly four hundred miles southwest of Wittenberg. The confederation originated with the late thirteenth-century formation of a defensive alliance among the cantons of Schwyz, Uri, and Unterwalden. By the middle of the fourteenth century, Zurich had joined this original confederation along with three other cities or cantons. Two more joined in 1481, which proved to be the basis for Swiss independence – sometimes de facto and sometimes militarily achieved – from the Holy Roman Empire and other potential hegemons. The Swiss in 1499 defeated Emperor Maximillian I in the Swabian War, a battle in which Maximillian had hoped to teach the Swiss that they needed a master. Adding to the Swiss capacity to form alliances for mutual defense was the skill of its young men as mercenary soldiers. Providing fighters for foreign sovereigns such as the king of France or the pope was an important part of Switzerland's economic and political existence on the eve of the Reformation. The damage done to the Swiss people through mercenary service, as well as the defeat the confederation suffered to the king of France (Francis I) at the battle of Marignano in 1515, were matters much on the minds of preachers in Switzerland, who also had designs on reforming the church.

Within the Swiss cantons themselves residents witnessed a great deal of variety of local rule. What was true of the Swiss Confederacy itself at the level of European politics was true of individual territories and cities among the Swiss. Free townsmen and peasants worked out complex agreements that permitted access to land and mountain passes; they also met formally in confederation diets that facilitated local rule. Whether the experience of the Swiss would justify idealistic arguments about the virtues of spontaneous democracy and local government, it did prove how much autonomy was possible even within regimes that possessed titles like the Holy Roman Empire. Political independence was not simply coincidental with the Reformation; it was necessary for church reforms to become a reality. In fact, if one pattern applied to Protestant developments it was the need for political patronage. The variety of polity might differ – the ruler might be a king, a prince, or a member of a city council – but Protestant churches could not survive without the state's support.

The Reformation in Zurich

Zwingli (1481–1531) may not have been the Luther of the Reformed branch of Protestantism, and he was by no means acting alone in the work of evangelical preaching and church reform, but he did bolster the Swiss reputation for independence by establishing a variety of Protestantism distinct from Lutheranism. Zwingli was born only six weeks after Luther, in the village of Wildhaus in the territory of St Gallen. His father was a wealthy peasant who held a position in the ruling class of the local republic, a circumstance that likely endeared Zwingli to rulers in Zurich and that predisposed him to regard highly the usefulness of magistrates in church reform. Thanks to the family's resources, Zwingli received a good education that took him eventually to the universities of Vienna and Basel. The rigors and formalities of medieval scholasticism dominated his official education but while serving as a priest in Glarus he began to read the works of humanists who lauded the study of ancient Greek and Latin sources. By 1516 Zwingli had discovered Erasmus, and wrote a letter in which he identified with the humanist's program of reinvigorating the church, and personal devotion through disciplined study and renouncing worldliness.

Thanks to his later skirmishes with Luther, Zwingli tended to speak of his own Protestant convictions as having emerged independently of the German reformer. Zwingli maintained that he had become a preacher of the Protestant gospel as early as 1516. A more likely date for the change in his preaching and identity was between 1519 and 1521, by which time he was a priest in Zurich and had begun to read Luther. Also notable for the change in Zwingli was his preaching on the depths of human sinfulness and the sinner's absolute dependence on divine grace for salvation in ways that echoed the apostle Paul and Augustine. Prior to that Augustinian shift, Zwingli had been deeply influenced by Erasmus' quip about war – "war is sweet to those who do not know it"[5] – and opposed the Swiss penchant for trafficking in war. He had accompanied his parishioners from Glarus into Italy for bloody battles in 1513 and saw the ravages of the momentous Swiss defeat in 1515 at Marignano. Zwingli's 1516 poem, "The Labyrinth," echoed Erasmus' brief against war. For counseling Swiss mercenaries against fighting for the French, Zwingli received a stipend from the papacy. This remuneration coincided with Leo X's strategy of undermining France's military expansion into parts of Italy. When the town of Glarus signed another pact that committed Swiss soldiers to assist the French, Zwingli renounced his stipend and moved to Zurich. This constellation of influences between 1516 and 1521 – humanism, opposition to Swiss mercenaries, church corruption, and Luther's teaching – moved Zwingli to a conviction about Scripture alone as the final and supreme authority in the life of the church. This formed the backbone for his critiques of church customs and traditions which included prohibitions against eating sausage during Lent. Zwingli's Reformation was not dependent on Germany. Neither was Zwingli an original.

The differences between Lutheran and Reformed initiatives were evident in each tradition's critique of Rome. Whereas for Luther the doctrine of justification by faith alone became the centerpiece for correcting the church's abuses, for Zwingli the guiding light was the sufficiency of Scripture as the rule for church teaching and believers' devotion. For instance, when in 1523 Zwingli prepared the Sixty-Seven Articles to be debated by Zurich's officials, he introduced them with the affirmation that he had preached these doctrines solely on the basis of Scripture and was prepared "to be instructed and corrected, but only from the aforesaid Scripture."[6] Among the propositions he defended was one on good works in which Zwingli echoed Luther: because Christ is the believer's righteousness, "our good works are good in so far as they are of Christ; in so far as they are our works they are neither righteous nor good" (Art. 38). At the same time, while Zwingli also sounded Lutheran in teaching about the freedom of the Christian, he went farther by drawing out the implication that where Scripture was silent Christians could not be bound by church authority. So when it came to prohibiting certain foods, "no Christian is bound to perform works which God has not commanded; he is free to eat all foods at any time." In fact, the church's rules for fasting were "a Roman fraud" (Art. 39).

In point of fact, the final authority of Scripture was the condition for Zwingli to participate in public debates during 1523, called by Zurich's city council. The occasion for state intervention came late in the previous year when Zwingli and other local clergy requested permission from the bishop of Constance to marry. Bishop Hugo almost nonchalantly conceded the existence of errors in the church, but because they had stemmed from good intentions and because uprooting them would disrupt the church's stability and order, he declined the petition by appealing to the dictum: "a universal error has the force of right."[7] This misstep by an unpopular authority gave the city council the chance to orchestrate reforms along lines more congenial to them than to the loose-lipped bishop. In January 1523 they assembled six hundred clergy and lay people to debate in German, as opposed to the church's lingua franca, Latin, the differences that were emerging in Zurich. The moderators also specified that debaters could appeal only to Scripture, which, as Steven Ozment observes, settled a number of issues in advance and turned the debate into a "charade."[8] Still, the outcome of the debate was a victory for Zwingli and reform. The city council instructed its pastors to preach only from Scripture, a rule that in 1523 effectively made Zurich a Protestant city.

But preaching continuously through a book of the Bible (instead of the biblical text assigned by the lectionary) was only a small part of the change that Zwingli desired. The party of reform in Zurich also wanted to end the Mass and remove images from the churches. Acts of iconoclasm by more radical elements among the emerging Protestant faithful prompted another public disputation in October of 1523. Zwingli was again successful in convincing the city council that Scripture required further reform. Officials resolved to abolish the Mass and remove images from the churches, but they also wanted to avoid disorder and so delayed implementing these reforms. In June of 1524 the city oversaw a gradual removal of images; the abolition of the Mass had to wait until April 1525. Meanwhile, the city confiscated the houses of the Dominicans and Augustinians. Remaining monks had to take residence with the Franciscans.

Compared to Luther's efforts, which both encouraged and suffered from the major convulsions of the Peasants' War (1524–25),[9] the Reformation in Zurich was remarkably peaceful. But frictions did develop, and the last years of Zwingli's relatively short life were filled with battles against other Protestants and Roman Catholics. The first came soon after the second disputation in Zurich and involved a break between Zwingli and Conrad Grebel, the ostensible founder of Anabaptism, and one of those who in 1522 had eaten the forbidden sausage. Part of the difference between these Protestants concerned the issue of moderation and compromise for the sake of long-term reform. From Grebel's perspective, Zwingli lacked courage, leading him to comply with the city's gradual reforms and tolerate practices that he knew to be unbiblical. On the other side, Zwingli could not adopt Grebel's notion of a voluntary church composed entirely of believers; Zwingli still believed in the corporate ideal of Christendom, and the reality of one faith and practice for all people in a city, territory, or kingdom. The most significant difference concerned infant baptism. For Anabaptists, infant baptism was another indication of the church's impure cooperation with the state because it was the entry point for those newly born into the life both of the church and the civil polity. It also smacked of political coercion, since all infants were required to be baptized. Just as Grebel wanted a voluntary church in which true believers withdrew from the world and gathered with the faithful, so he desired a form of baptism freely chosen by followers of Christ, which meant adult baptism. For those baptized as infants, rebaptism (hence "ana" baptist) was necessary. For Zwingli, baptism replaced circumcision as the New Testament sign of entry into the community of faith, and just as circumcision was intended for all male babies in Israel, so baptism was the norm for all children of Christians. In addition, an infant's dependence and passivity in baptism reinforced the idea of a person's utter powerlessness in salvation.

The controversy between Anabaptists and Reformed Protestants broke out in January 1525, when the city was gradually implementing church reforms. Grebel performed his first adult baptism, a rebaptism of George Blaurock on January 21. This was a capital offense. Two months later, four Anabaptists in Zurich were executed, and families who refused to submit their children for baptism had eight days to comply or face expulsion from the city. By 1529, not only did Roman Catholics, Lutherans, and Reformed Protestants oppose Anabaptism, but Emperor Charles V revived a dated Justinian law that made rebaptism a capital offense throughout the empire. Over the next century at least 850 (and perhaps as many as 5,000) Anabaptists died in the face of widespread persecution. Grebel himself was imprisoned by Zurich's authorities, along with Felix Manz. Grebel and Manz delayed their execution by escaping from prison, but in 1526 the former died while evading the law; in 1527 the latter was recaptured and executed by drowning.

If Anabaptism represented a threat to Reformed Protestantism in taking reform farther than Zwingli believed either legitimate or wise, Roman Catholicism posed another obstacle to Zurich's reformation. The city was one of the strongest within the confederation and had a history of using its economic and political muscle to influence other Swiss cantons or cities. This was no less true in religion, and Zwingli himself wanted to see evangelical preaching prosper throughout the confederation. But the interior or forest cantons, traditionally jealous of their independence from Zurich, determined to resist Protestantism by holding their own debates and conferences to decide the religious question. In 1526 the Roman Catholic cantons sponsored a debate at Baden and established ground rules beforehand that were favorable to Rome, such as starting the gathering with the Mass and forbidding Protestant preaching. Zwingli refused to debate under such conditions, but Johannes Oecolampadius, a Protestant minister from Basel, did join the debate. To no one's surprise, the conferees decided in Rome's favor.

Roman Catholic opposition did not deter the spread of Protestantism, however. Among the Swiss cities to follow Zurich down the road of reformation were St Gallen (1526), and eventually Basel (1530). To respond to the Roman Catholic conference at Baden, Protestants gathered in 1528 at the city of Bern, where they had recently become the religious majority. There they hammered out a consensus position of desired reforms. Ministers from Basel, Zurich, Strasbourg, Constance, Schauffhausen, and Bern attended and debated with Roman Catholic priests and theologians sufficiently courageous to participate. Both sides debated the Ten Theses of Bern, one of the first Reformed confessional statements after Zwingli's articles, and the result was an overwhelming vote – 235 to 46 – by Bern's authorities in favor of Protestantism. This was a major coup for Zwingli and the progress of reform. Bern was one of the confederation's largest cities, with a substantial hinterland that extended into French-speaking lands, and with important political and economic ties to Neuchâtel, Lausanne, and Geneva. Because of Bern's decision, many communities in the vicinity adopted the Protestant faith.

Despite victory, Protestants could never forget about Roman Catholicism and the threat of ecclesiastical or political retaliation. Philip of Hesse was one such prince, who believed that unity between Lutherans in Germany and Reformed Protestants in Switzerland was crucial for reformation to survive military reprisals from the emperor. Philip had converted through the teaching of Philip Melanchthon, and no matter what his political ambitions he was well versed in theology and knew what was at stake with the rise of Protestantism. He was also aware of a growing divide between the two wings led by Luther and Zwingli. In June of 1529, Lutherans had proposed the Schwabach Articles as the basis for Protestant union. But the articles were decidedly hostile to Zwingli's understanding of the Lord's Supper and became a source of friction in south German and Swiss cities. At the same time, Luther was growing more cantankerous thanks to challenges from the peasants, Anabaptists, and assorted humanists. He was in no mood to receive counsel from Zwingli, whose view of the Lord's Supper sounded too mystical to be any good. From his side, Zwingli needed to tread carefully with Luther's sacramental theology since a concession to Luther's teaching might bring political challenges to Zurich from Roman Catholic cantons in the Swiss Confederacy.

To break the stalemate, Philip invited Zwingli and Luther to his castle in Marburg for three days in the fall of 1529. Also attending was Oecolampadius from Basel, perhaps to take the rough edges off the other participants. From one angle, the conference was a success because all parties were able to agree on all but one out of fifteen points. But they continued to trip over the Lord's Supper. Given the emerging divisions within Christendom and their sometimes radical consequences, this much Protestant unity should have been encouraging. But consensus was impossible on what would become for Luther the non-negotiable article of Christ's real, as opposed to spiritual, presence in the Lord's Supper. For Zwingli, eating the bread and drinking the wine in the sacrament were synonymous with believing. So a Protestant in Zurich who participated in the Lord's Supper was eating merely physical bread while feeding through faith on the spiritual body of Christ. As such, when Christ instituted the sacrament and said, "this is my body," for Zwingli this actually meant, "this signifies my body." Zwingli held that because of Christ's ascension into heaven, Jesus' resurrected physical body was no longer present on earth; as such, during the period between the ascension and the Second Coming, Christ could not be present physically in the sacrament. Also at work in Zwingli's understanding was a denial that physical or material objects could convey or contain spiritual truths or divine grace. Zwingli's faith was a spiritualized one.

Luther understood Zwingli's point about the location of Christ's body after the ascension, but defended his position by countering that Christ's physical body could be ubiquitous just like his divine nature (i.e. *communicatio idiomatum*). Because Christ was omnipresent in his divinity, he could also be physically present everywhere. Luther raised the stakes when he also insisted that wherever Christ was present in his divine nature, he was also physically present. At the same time, Luther had an aversion to Zwingli's spiritualized faith. For Luther, it smacked of the medieval trend to locate the glories of Christianity in heaven and sever it from life in this world. He believed that Roman Catholic teaching had so emphasized Christ's eternal rule that it had failed to do justice to his participation in the messiness of human, earthly existence. Not only were Luther and Zwingli clashing over sacramental theology, it was also a conflict between different kinds of devotion: one that reveled in the physical; the other that tried to sublimate the earthly.

Although Philip prevailed upon both sides to issue the fourteen-point Marburg Articles as a sign of Protestant unity, the good will was more theoretical than real. A year later Lutherans and Reformed Protestants existed in distinct churches, separated by different creeds. For Lutherans the Schwabach Articles remained in force, while Zwingli had rallied with other Reformed cities – Strasbourg, Constance, Memmingen, and Lindau – behind the Tetrapolitan Confession, a statement written largely by Strasbourg's Martin Bucer. Creedal division also meant political separation. Only for a brief time during 1530 would Strasbourg sign on to Lutheran creeds, for the sake of protection from the Lutheran princes who had formed the Schmalkaldic League.

Meanwhile, the Reformation provoked war among the Swiss. Fears of Protestant expansion and older resentments of Zurich's influence, combined with Zwingli's own political miscalculations, led the Roman Catholic cantons to form an alliance in 1529 with Archduke Ferdinand of Austria. The threat of Turkish assaults on Habsburg lands in the East nullified the potential power of such an alliance, but the Roman Catholic Swiss soldiers were strong in their own right. In 1529 their Christian Alliance (Luzern, Uri, Schwyz, Unterwalden, and Zug) fought the Protestant-oriented Christian Civic Union (Zurich, Bern, Basel, St Gallen, Strasbourg, Mühlhausen, and Schaffhausen). The cause of war was the Roman Catholic execution of a preacher (Jacob Kaiser) who was teaching Protestant doctrine in the Roman Catholic territory, Schwyz. Zwingli and others had wanted the freedom to extend Protestantism into other cantons if those churches and governments were so persuaded. But Roman Catholics wanted Protestants contained. The First Kappel War lasted only sixteen days in 1529, avoided bloodshed, and produced a peace that recognized the legitimacy of Roman Catholic and Protestant cantons each within their own cities and territories (*cuius regio, eius religio*).

The terms of peace deeply disappointed Zwingli, who had hoped for a defeat of Roman Catholicism and a vindication of the Protestant cause. He wanted Protestant pastors to have the freedom to take their message everywhere throughout the confederation. His domestic policy included plans for bringing the rural cantons under the sway of Bern and Zurich, and he interpreted the terms of peace as Roman Catholicism's acknowledgment of Protestantism's legitimacy, thus opening the way for Reformed preaching throughout the confederation. Bern urged caution and Zwingli was initially content with the use of economic policies (i.e. blockades on foodstuffs) to combat Roman Catholic intransigence. Zwingli's own stubbornness only increased Roman Catholic fear and resolve. In response, Roman Catholic territories sponsored an army of seven thousand soldiers to attack Kappel, a Protestant city about thirty miles south of Zurich on the border of Zug, a Roman Catholic canton. Zurich attempted to defend the besieged city but could only muster an army half the size, even needing to enlist pastors in the battle. The war of 1531 lasted only a day and Zurich suffered five hundred casualties, among them twenty-five pastors. Zwingli was one of the clergy to lose his life at Kappel. So deep was the resentment against him and his work that the victorious soldiers quartered and burned the Reformed pastor's corpse before mixing his ashes with cow dung.

By 1531, Reformed Protestantism had established an identity different from Lutheranism. But the loss of Zwingli and the defeat at Kappel were huge blows to the Reformed cause. The situation was compounded by the death of Oecolampadius, Basel's influential pastor, only five weeks after Zwingli's. Reformed Protestantism was small and on the ropes. Its influence was confined largely to the cities of the Swiss Confederacy, and hopes for freedom to preach beyond the Swiss Protestant territories, let alone to expand beyond Switzerland into the capacious Holy Roman Empire, were meager. Even the reinforcements soon to come from Geneva were initially of little help to the Swiss Confederacy. For Geneva to gain the stature that it would among the Reformed churches, the city's rulers would need the support of Switzerland's larger and more powerful cities. Admitting that need was not easy.

Geneva and Calvin

Unlike Saxony and Zurich where religious reforms either led to political revolt or solidified political independence, in Geneva the sequence was the opposite: politics were the precondition for ecclesiastical reform. At the beginning of the Reformation Geneva was not part of the Swiss Confederacy. It was a French-speaking episcopal city, ruled by a bishop who was an arm of the Duchy of Savoy. This feudal order dated back to the tenth century. The prince-bishop ruled over all civil and criminal cases, and the bishop's self-selected vicar presided over the city council. Despite the autonomy of the House of Savoy in Geneva and the region south of Lake Léman, during the early sixteenth century the Swiss cities north of the lake were expanding their influence southward, much like Zurich was on the north side of the confederation. Not only were

Fribourg and Bern increasingly active in Geneva, but the city's businessmen were dependent economically on these cities and so were inclined to reject the House of Savoy in favor of a Swiss alliance.

Before 1528, when Bern enlisted in the Protestant cause, religion was a minor factor in Geneva's politics. For a brief time in the 1510s, about the same time that Luther was posting theses on the Wittenberg cathedral door, Geneva was pursuing an alliance with Fribourg, which would remain decidedly Roman Catholic. The Savoys managed to counter Geneva's resistance to their control, but by the 1520s the prince-bishop, Pierre de la Baume, was no longer able to withstand Swiss expansion. In 1525 Lausanne, a nearby city, like Geneva, under the Savoys' dominance, allied with Bern. Charles III, the Savoyard Duke, registered a preemptive strike with Geneva and ordered the Genevans to reaffirm their allegiance to the prince-bishop. The city complied, but Genevan exiles, led by Besançon Hugues – the name formerly supposed to be the basis for "Huguenot" (i.e., French-speaking Protestants) – was negotiating an alliance with Fribourg and Bern.[10] In 1526 that hoped-for alliance, despite some intimidation by Charles III and a brief extraction of loyalty from the Genevans to Savoy, became a reality, and Geneva formally joined the Swiss Confederacy. Meanwhile, the city government was divided between two aristocratic assemblies, the Council of Two Hundred and the Little Council, which was an executive body consisting of twenty-five members, sixteen of whom were selected by the Two Hundred.

Church reform in Geneva could not have happened without these political developments. In fact, the city's alliance with the Swiss Confederacy preceded the appearance of Protestantism in Geneva by several years. Although Luther's writings had circulated in the city as early as 1524, signs of discontent with the Roman Catholic church did not become evident until 1532, thus putting Geneva in the position of a baby brother among the Protestant cities of Zurich, Basel, and Bern. Preachers delegated from Bern did not arrive in Geneva until 1533. The pastor who became a lightning rod for the Reformation was Guillame Farel. But the spread of Protestantism to Geneva was not smooth. The canton of Fribourg was part of the Swiss Confederacy, was closer to Geneva, and had helped with Geneva's political independence. Fribourg's officials remained staunchly Roman Catholic and did not take lightly the spread of Protestant heresy within Geneva. Consequently, as soon as Geneva established independence from the House of Savoy, the city found itself almost completely dependent on its new Swiss allies.

Between 1534 and 1536 the Genevans sorted through the interests of Bern and Fribourg with the disputes between Roman Catholics and Protestants at the forefront. The public debates that ensued (mentioned at the beginning of the chapter), and that prompted the citizens of Geneva to vote to become Protestant, were a manifestation of the irony involved in the city's assertion of its autonomy and simultaneous reliance on the muscle of Bern to do so. But by the time of the decisive vote in May 1536, when citizens pledged to "live according to the Law of the Gospel and the Word of God, and to abolish all Papal abuses," Geneva did achieve independence, and with it a Protestant identity.

All of these political and religious developments transpired before Calvin had even set foot in Geneva. Geneva was arguably the last place in Europe where Calvin wanted to work and, more importantly, study. Born in Noyon in 1509 – twenty-five years after Luther – Calvin was steeped in French literary and religious culture as a boy and young man. His father worked in an advisory capacity for the bishop of Noyon and endeavored mightily to direct his son toward a position of responsibility. At the age of eleven, Calvin obtained through his father a benefice at the Cathedral church in Noyon, the stipend from which helped to pay for Calvin's education at the Collège de la Marche in Paris, begun when he was fourteen. In Paris Calvin acquired familiarity with the new ideas that typically went hand in hand at the time: humanistic education and church reform. He also studied at the Collège de Montaigu, an institution that had a reputation for being strictly orthodox and academically conservative. From Paris he moved in 1528 to study law at Orléans. This coincided with Gérard Cauvin's excommunication by the church owing to questions surrounding his record keeping and administration of church funds. The father now planned for the son to become a lawyer, not a churchman. Calvin complied, completed his studies by 1532, and received a doctorate in civil law. As part of his studies he wrote a commentary on Seneca's *De Clementia*. In many respects, Calvin's first published writing showed conventional humanistic elements: an interest in reform, good Latin, and respect for and dependence on the ancients. By the time Calvin turned twenty-three he showed no real interest in Protestantism and did not seem to be headed for work in the church.

Calvin was an extremely private person, and so determining the point at which he converted to Protestantism has left biographers guessing. Sometime between 1532 and 1534 Calvin gave signals that he was rejecting the Roman Catholic church. An indication of his religious resolve came during a visit in 1534 to his home in Noyon, where he relinquished church benefices that had paid for much of his education. Around the same time, Calvin visited the noted French humanist Lefèvre d'Étaples, who likely showed the young scholar that reforming the Roman churches from within was largely pointless. Still, despite the apparent resolve of Calvin's new convictions, it was less clear how he could pursue a life of learning.

One thing that Calvin could do was write. Between 1534 and 1536 while he traveled through France and Italy, he produced the first edition of *The Institutes of the Christian Religion*, arguably the most important survey and overview of Reformed teaching to emerge in the first half of the sixteenth century. The first edition, published in 1536, was short; by the time Calvin had finished revising it with the 1559 edition, it had expanded into a weighty textbook of Reformed theology. Sometimes regarded as the urtext of Reformed Protestantism, Calvin's aims were fairly simple and ordinary. As Richard Muller, one of the foremost interpreters of Reformed Protestantism, argues, Calvin was writing primarily as a pastor who wanted to explain the Nicene Creed to church members.[11] Although the content and structure of the *Institutes* had grown by the time of its final edition, thanks in part to the importance of Calvin's study of the New Testament (especially the Epistle to the Romans) and his interaction with Philip Melanchthon, the basic content remained the same. When Calvin's teaching veered from other Protestants – as it would, for instance, over predestination – the differences had much more to do with specific contexts and the appropriation of biblical and medieval sources than with efforts to arrive at a single system of theology for all Protestants. Calvin even recommended caution about the idea with which he is most associated, that of God's eternal decree to choose some for salvation and let the rest of the human race be damned (i.e. predestination):

> The predestination of God is indeed in reality a labyrinth from which the mind of man can by no means extricate itself. So unreasonable is the curiosity of man, however, that the more perilous the examination of a subject is, the more boldly he proceeds, so that when predestination is discussed he cannot restrain himself within due limits, thus he immediately through his rashness plunges himself, as it were, into the depth of the sea.[12]

In fact, the prominence of predestination in Calvin likely stems directly from his following Paul's Epistle to the Romans for the structure and content of theology.

Not only did Calvin explain Christianity according to Protestant teaching, but he also showed interest in the cause of reform in his native land by addressing the *Institutes* to Francis I, the king of France. Still, Calvin knew that his days in France were numbered given the opposition to French Protestants that was emerging in the 1530s. Consequently, he decided to visit Paris one last time in 1536, dispose of some family business, and then head for Strasbourg and a life of scholarship.

The war between France and the Holy Roman Empire forced Calvin to take a detour en route to Strasbourg by way of Geneva. He arrived there in August of 1536, only three months after the city had publicly affirmed its Protestant identity. Because of his emerging reputation Calvin was an appealing recruit for Guillaume Farel, who was in Geneva during the summer of 1536 attempting to execute Bern's wishes for reforming Geneva's ecclesiastical life. Calvin was reluctant. His temperament ran much more in the direction of scholarly than pastoral work. But Farel was belligerently persistent and threatened Calvin in ways reminiscent of the Old Testament prophets. According to Calvin's own account:

> Farel detained me at Geneva not so much by counsel and exhortation as by a dreadful curse which I felt to be as if God had from heaven laid his mighty hand upon me to arrest me. . . . He proceeded to utter the imprecation that God would curse my retirement and the tranquility of my studies which I sought if I should withdraw and refuse to help when the necessity was so urgent. By this imprecation I was so terror-struck that I gave up the journey I had undertaken.[13]

Farel may have succeeded with Calvin but the Protestant pastors' initial efforts in Geneva included more reform than Genevans could handle. Between 1536 and 1538 Calvin produced a catechism for the city along with ordinances for church government. Residents recognized that church reform was going to demand moral integrity. Meanwhile, the city's magistrates learned that reform would involve a struggle between state and church officials over power, specifically, over which institution was responsible for excommunication. One indication of the authority that Calvin desired for the church was a proposal for all city officers to make a public profession of faith so that citizens themselves would take a similar religious oath. For a city that had only recently won its independence, the thought of being subject to the Protestant junta of Reformed pastors was too much. By April 1538, the Council of Two Hundred rejected Calvin's proposals and dismissed him from the city, along with Farel.

Given Calvin's initial resistance to Farel's request, the city's release brought a welcome return to the scholarly life. Initially he planned to go to Basel and study at the university. But Martin Bucer had other plans and, in a manner akin to Farel, threatened Calvin with the fate of Jonah if he would not assist reforms in Strasbourg. Calvin complied, and between 1538 and 1541 resided in Strasbourg under Bucer's supervision. He lectured at the university and became pastor to French refugees. Calvin also completed a revised edition of the *Institutes*. And with advice from Bucer and Farel he found a wife, Idelette de Bure, the widow of an Anabaptist whom Calvin had led into the Reformed and less radical version of Protestantism. Calvin's hopes for a wife were as free from romantic idealism as his faith was averse to flights of enthusiasm:

I am none of those insane lovers who embrace also the vices of those they
are in love with, when they are smitten at first sight with a fine figure. This
only is the beauty which attracts me: if she is chaste, if not too nice or fastid-
ious, if economical, if patient, if there is hope that she will be interested about
my health.[14]

Geneva had not forgotten about Calvin, even though his reforms had pushed
too hard too soon. In 1539, the bishop of Carpentras, Jacopo Sadoleto, took
advantage of Calvin and Farel's absence to tempt Geneva back into fellowship
with Rome. The city council turned to Calvin for a response to Sadoleto's
letter, which contained theological objections to Protestantism as well as
questioning the reformers' motives. Calvin responded in one of the clearest
statements of Reformed Protestantism to date, and once again proved to be
invaluable to Geneva even if he came with baggage. Changes in the composition
of the city council the following year – more opposition to Bernese control –
created a political climate more congenial to Calvin. Even so, for the better part
of a year he weighed whether to return. Farel was as urgent as ever; he even
traveled to Strasbourg to twist Calvin's arm. Bullinger in Zurich also applied
pressure by arguing for Geneva's strategic importance to the Reformation. For
Calvin, the thought of going back was terrifying: "There is no place under
heaven of which I have greater dread," he wrote.[15]

Despite such misgivings, in 1541 Calvin returned to Geneva, and would
remain there for the rest of his life (until 1564). Within six weeks he had proposed
another round of ecclesiastical ordinances, many of which had prompted his
1538 exile. But given the circumstances, Calvin sensed a mandate to push forward
with reforms. One letter to the council while negotiating the terms of his post
indicated Calvin's self-understanding:

If you desire to have me for your pastor, correct the disorder of your lives. If
you have with sincerity recalled me from my exile, banish the crimes and
debaucheries which prevail among you. I cannot behold without the most
painful displeasure ... discipline trodden under foot and crimes committed
with impunity. I cannot possibly live in a place so grossly immoral. ...
I consider the principal enemies of the Gospel to be, not the pontiff of Rome,
nor heretics, nor seducers, nor tyrants, but bad Christians ...[16]

That confrontational style would characterize Calvin's time in Geneva for
most of his career, though by the time he gained citizenship in 1559 his call for
consistency between institutional reforms and personal conduct had just begun
to take shape. The antagonism between Calvin and Genevans went deeper than

the initial skirmishes between the city's magistrates and their pastors, both sides of which were dealing with an unprecedented situation in church–state relations. Calvin's reforms included supervisory positions for lay officers in the church (i.e. elders) which involved overseeing the affairs of city residents with a measure of scrupulosity unheard of outside (or even inside) the most devout monastery. For supporters such as the Scottish Reformer John Knox, Calvin's order made Geneva a harbinger of the New Jerusalem. For critics, such oversight granted Calvin dictatorial powers.

The reform of church life in Geneva included not simply doctrine but also worship and church polity. In worship, the biggest change was the elimination of images, colorful vestments, choirs and organs, the pageantry of the Mass, and a stress upon Scripture, particularly in the form of sermons that carefully explained sections of the Bible. The stress on the Word of God was particularly evident in Calvin's insistence as early as 1537 that congregational singing in Geneva use the Old Testament Psalter. Not only did Reformed Protestant worship involve the laity in ways dramatically different from the medieval church, but the creation of the Geneva Psalter, the production of which involved metrical translations from Clément Marot and tunes composed by Louis Bourgeois, established psalm-singing as the pattern for Protestant worship outside Lutheran and Anabaptist circles that would prevail for at least three centuries (in some places five).

In church government, Calvin prescribed ecclesiastical officers responsible for moral oversight of the congregation (and the city by virtue of religious establishment). These elders (or presbyters) were key to the success of Geneva's reforms and in other places that followed Calvin's church order. The resistance to his reforms by citizens who may have objected to the hypocrisy of the Roman Catholic clergy was natural when the contradiction between their own religious oaths and undisciplined conduct became the subject of pastors and elders. Likewise, the opposition to Calvin from older aristocratic Genevans who saw their city and positions challenged by a new set of ecclesiastical elites and an influx of Protestant refugees was not surprising, even if resistance to the new church order did make for juicy stories about their chief pastor's tyrannical ways. One of the juiciest, of course, was the 1553 execution of Michael Servetus, whose heretical views by both Roman Catholic and Protestant standards made him an outlaw throughout Europe. But as famous or infamous as Calvin's work in Geneva would be, he was not a theocratic tyrant who forced the city into his mold. Even while he worked out the implications of Protestant theology for the practice of the church and her members through fairly elaborate systems of church government, pastoral accountability, ministerial training, and prescriptions for worship, Calvin's reforms were always contested and partial. The reason stemmed directly from his dependence, just like Luther and Zwingli, on the patronage of state or city rulers.

Calvinist or Reformed?

Reformed Christianity existed before Calvin became a Protestant, and so calling the churches to which he belonged Calvinist is anachronistic. Before Geneva became a home for Protestantism, several cities in the Swiss Confederacy, Zurich chief among them, had initiated reform. At the same time, Geneva was a late addition to the Swiss Confederacy and always dependent on stronger Swiss cities. This meant that in addition to the struggles Calvin faced in his adopted city, he also encountered resistance and sporadic opposition from the other Reformed churches in Switzerland. His difficult dealings with the other pastors make all the more ironic the later identification of Reformed Protestantism with Calvinism. For instance, in 1554, around the time that Calvin was facing stiff opposition in Geneva from old-time aristocrats who fought the new spiritually-inspired regulations of city life, the government of Bern banned Calvin's writings from the lands under its authority and ordered that they be burned. Burning books was what Roman Catholics were supposed to do with Protestant texts, but here was a Reformed city judging Calvin's teaching beyond the pale. In point of fact, the opposition to Calvin from the Bernese officials had less to do with theology than politics; Geneva was an upstart city that seemed to be acting independently of Bern and so the Bernese wanted to teach the Genevans a lesson. As one biographer argues, this treatment of Calvin's writings said more about the personalities involved than the intricacies of double predestination or any other contested point of doctrine.[17] Still, the incident is instructive for remembering Calvin's status among the Reformers and their civic patrons in Switzerland.

The Geneva pastor's need to take cues from other Swiss cities and churches was also true when it came to theology, where Calvin may have been closer to the Lutherans than to Zurich. Calvin did not affirm the ubiquity of Christ's humanity in his treatment of the Lord's Supper, as Luther had. But even if Christ was not physically present in the sacrament, he was for Calvin spiritually present, and this position on the Supper put him at odds with the churches of Zurich that emphasized the symbolic nature of the bread and wine. This strain of thought was responsible for lingering animosity between Lutherans and Zurich, and Calvin did not want it to jeopardize good relations among the Swiss. In 1549 he traveled to Zurich to work on a mediating position that would prevent a breach. The result was the Consensus Tigurinus, a creed that initially was entirely acceptable to Bullinger and the pastors in Zurich, but lacked many of the features of Calvin's sacramental teaching such as the Supper as a means of grace and the importance of the physical elements.

Calvin's willingness to let Zurich set the terms of the Consensus did not sit well with him, and he soon drafted two articles on the Lord's Supper more congenial to Geneva to be inserted into the statement. Bullinger accepted these additions, but primarily because Calvin had reassured him that the resulting creed would allow for different interpretations. As such, the Consensus Tigurinus was not a hollow statement. Indeed, by reconciling Zurich and Geneva, the Consensus was a significant development in consolidating the Swiss Confederacy's cities as the font of Reformed Protestantism.

Even so, the church's relationship to the magistrates prevented the Consensus from accomplishing the unity among Reformed churches for which Calvin and Bullinger hoped and on which all Protestant pastors depended. For instance, on the eve of the Consensus, Calvin and Bullinger had been unable to agree on how to assist Protestants in France. Henry II, the recently inaugurated French monarch, had solicited help from the Swiss Confederacy in his ongoing conflicts with Charles V and the Holy Roman Empire. As a Frenchman, Calvin was clearly inclined to support the new king in hopes that Henry would look favorably on his Protestant subjects. But deep-seated hostility in Zurich to France's use of Swiss mercenaries prompted a different reaction to Henry's request. One of Calvin's reasons for traveling to Zurich to work on the Consensus Tigurinus was to persuade Bullinger to change his attitude toward the French monarchy. Calvin failed. The best he could do was a statement on the Lord's Supper that he would later need to revise.

Meanwhile, the other major Reformed centers, Basel and Bern, did not ratify the Consensus Tigurinus. Although each of these cities was inclined to lend some assistance to the French, primarily owing to the need for an alliance against the designs of the emperor, the two cities had political reasons for refusing to endorse the compromise between Geneva and Zurich. Tensions owing to early disagreements between Bucer and Zwingli were still responsible for reserve, if not suspicion, among Basel's pastors toward Bullinger and Zurich. In Bern the pastors were favorably inclined toward the Consensus but would not sign it because of resentment toward Zurich. The magistrates in Bern regarded Geneva as one of its clients, generally viewed Calvin as presumptuous in his handling of reform, and were suspicious of Zurich expanding its influence into Bernese districts. For that reason, only Geneva and Zurich could reach a fragile consensus on key elements of Reformed Protestantism, some three decades after Luther's initial protest.

As difficult as the relations among Swiss Protestants were, the gains for the Reformed churches outweighed the losses. For one thing, the Protestant churches within the Swiss Confederacy agreed on far more than they let on.

Granted, all of the Reformers had grown up within the Roman Catholic church and shared understandings about God, sin, salvation, and the church that even if translated into Protestant idiom registered similar points about human sinfulness, the holiness of God, the need for grace, and the work of the church in ministering to fallen humanity. Once the Reformers had broken fellowship with Rome, they could have rejected far more of Roman Catholic teaching than they did. The Anabaptists were testimony to the drastic – even radical – change that could come when ties to Rome were severed. Meanwhile, individual idiosyncrasies stemming from temperamental, educational, cultural, and generational differences did account for disagreements even among those within a similar communion of churches. Even here many pastors were willing to downplay matters of personal opinion for the sake of the greater good within a city and wider body of churches. One additional feature of note about the Reformed churches circa 1550 was that pastors like Calvin and Bullinger were still alive. They had and would not suffer the fate of those who had previously attempted reform, such as Jon Huss or John Wycliffe, who either lost their lives or had their views condemned for defying Rome. A significant factor in the level of agreement among the Reformed churches and for the well-being of their pastors was the patronage of magistrates who combined political and religious interests to create space for Protestantism to take root and even flourish.

Equally important was the relief that this form of Christianity brought to believers who could no longer find sustenance from Roman Catholicism. Undoubtedly, the motives of rulers were mixed. But the magisterial melange of worldly cunning and heavenly-mindedness, of vice and virtue, was incidental to a deeper substance: the faith and practice of the Roman Catholic church were creaking under the weight of devotion that was increasingly implausible. Even the hierarchy of the Roman church acknowledged the problem; when the Bishop of Constance responded to the initial reform measures of Zurich in 1522, he issued the following concession:

> We have for some time now . . . heard reports that there are, almost throughout Germany, those who cry out day and night that the people of Christ have been wrongfully oppressed . . . with hard and burdensome regulations, observances, and ceremonies. . . . In this "golden age," as they call it . . . they believe the gospel is at last beginning to shed its light upon mankind and they see themselves leading . . . the people back to the freedom of the gospel.

The bishop not only heard these reports but acknowledged that many of the church's requirements were an imposition. What he could not concede was that removing the warts of the church could be performed without maiming

Rome's holy countenance, as if removing the tares would not also destroy the wheat.

> Granted even that the whole body [of the church] was wrong in establishing
> ... a ceremonial system which has been thus far maintained and that, as is the
> portion of human ignorance and frailty, some things have become mixed with
> the Christian religion which are not altogether in harmony with the gospel
> and Holy Scripture, still Christian piety .... demands that ... we make
> some allowance for those who err with good intentions ... rather than expose
> everything to manifest uproar and rebellion.[18]

One response to the church's weakness was to argue for the status quo and hope that wayward practices would not accelerate. But when scholars began to dissect the church's woes, whether through the insights of humanism or the ideas that Martin Luther's judicial proceedings popularized, the case against Rome became more plausible and the need for reform more obvious than at any point in the period since the Avignon papacy (1309–78),[19] when the contradiction between Rome's claims and actions were patent. As such, not only were bishops willing after 1520 to concede the unwholesomeness of ecclesiastical conditions but scholars and churchmen began to propose solutions. Once that happened, the entire system of piety upon which the Roman church depended began to unravel.

The practice of indulgences, the occasion for Luther's initial complaint, underscores the inherent weakness and burden of the Roman Catholic faith. On the one hand, it was a spiritual remedy for sensitive souls. On the other, it became a source of revenue for acquisitive church leaders. The medieval believer who sought relief from the guilt of sin – which came from a host of directions – had tremendous difficulty finding comfort in Rome's scheme of salvation. The penitential system – confession, absolution, and works of satisfaction – provided only temporary relief but no peace of conscience or personal assurance. Of course, this was Luther's own problem as he earnestly sought ways to answer the charges of guilt that haunted his soul. The sacrament of penance could manage the immediate pain of imperfection, but it could not prevent the punishment for sin that believers would have to endure in purgatory. In this case, indulgences became a way for the papacy to lighten the load of future punishment, by dispensing the merits of Christ to the deceased through the contributions of the living.

The search for a remedy to sin became even more earnest when devout believers grappled with different kinds of wickedness and the accompanying degrees of punishment. Much of the church's teaching took the chaste and celibate life of monastics and priests as the norm for lay piety and consequently doled out prescriptions for average believers' failing to measure up to priestly ideals. Over time, the conviction that lay life should conform to clerical models sapped the ordinary believer's vitality. What once had been an inspiration had become a burden, even to the point of criticism and derision. The disparity need not have been the product of hypocritical monks or priests, who surely existed. It was, as Steven Ozment points out, the increasing disparity between "clerical ideals of obedience and sexual purity" with an "increasingly literate, socially mobile urban laity, who prized simplicity, directness, and respectful treatment in all spheres of their lives."[20]

The Protestant remedy to these conditions was not necessarily radical but did constitute a significant break. Protestants (along with humanists) sought ways to make clergy conform to the ways of the world, especially civil laws, and not hide behind sacred rank. They were attracted to a conciliar theory of church government that presumably offered more accountability than the monarchical pattern of Rome and the papacy. The Reformers wanted to restore simplicity to church devotion and worship while also recognizing the legitimacy and value of secular work and responsibilities. Furthermore, Protestants made the sermon the heart of worship both to reflect the importance of Scripture and to supply needed instruction to Christians whom the Roman church had neglected through its preoccupation on separation from the world and its insistence on the Mass as the centerpiece of worship.

These modifications were not specified in the earliest Protestant literature. As the churches that grew up around Luther and Zwingli took shape, Lutherans and Reformers would reveal significant differences in terms of worship and theology. Consequently, although the initial case for reform was plausible thanks to Rome's inadequacies, the nature of reform was not. Zwingli himself testified to the widespread sense that reform was necessary when in 1525 he contrasted the true religion of Scripture with Rome's false article:

> Faithfulness demands, first, that we learn from God in what way we can please Him, in what manner serve Him. Next, it demands that we should add nothing to what we have learned from Him, and take away nothing. . . . The things . . . on which faith hinges should be brought out without delay, but the things that militate against it need to be demolished with skill, lest they do harm in their downfall and bury the little that has already been built.[21]

Even if this conception of Christianity did not predict the shape that Reformed Protestantism would take, it did tilt heavily away from Rome's devotion, which depended on objects, artifacts, and rites (physical representations of revealed truth), toward a form of worship based on ideas and dispositions (expressions of faith not discerned by the eye). This meant that rallying the pious who were discontent with the existing forms of Christianity to abandon icons and the Mass would be a much easier task than the alternative of cultivating a new worship and form of devotion that could replace Rome's elaborate, revered, and hoary – if flawed – piety.

Zurich and Geneva were the two most important cities, and representative of Reformed Protestantism's early attempts to change the European churches. The teachings and especially the new ways of conducting church life in these cities became models for Christians elsewhere, but what those Reformers could not pass on to other Protestants were the city councils that supported reform. In fact, the realities of European politics would prevent the Swiss examples from being readily exported. Switzerland was unique in its isolation and independence. Meanwhile, the dynamics of city politics were distinct from those of Europe's kingdoms, territories, and empires. Those differences would invariably determine the success and failure of Calvinist initiatives elsewhere.

CHAPTER TWO

GOD'S FICKLE ANOINTED

IN THE FIRST QUARTER of 1547 the ruling class of Europe lost two members who each had a stormy relationship with church reform. The first was Henry VIII of England, who died on January 28, 1547, in all likelihood from symptoms related to obesity and gout. (Later stories about syphilis gratified those who disapproved of his womanizing and revolving marriage bed but were likely untrue.) The second loss from Europe's royal ranks was Francis I, king of France, who died on March 31 at the age of thirty-two, the husband of only one wife. Both kings had dabbled in the trappings of learning and the arts made attractive to European nobility through the extension of humanism to northern Europe. Henry and Francis also had first-hand experience with the new teachings and practices that pastors and theologians like Luther, Zwingli, and Calvin were proposing in cities and territories within their jurisdiction. Despite different consequences for the churches in their realms, their religious policies reflected a sensible political strategy of maintaining stability.

After 1519 Luther's writings crossed the Channel and began to sell well in England. Henry VIII took an immediate dislike and commissioned a group of theologians to write under his name *The Assertion of the Seven Sacraments* (1521). This book was so effective in rejecting Lutheran teaching that it not only earned for Henry from the pope the title Defender of the Faith, but also signaled to the king's subjects how serious the Protestant heresy was. Throughout the 1520s the number of executions for heresy in England plummeted to zero thanks to the regime's ban and the exodus of leading dissenters, such as William Tyndale and John Frith, to the Continent. But by the 1530s the demands of the Tudor dynasty and Henry's need for a male heir would force him to change course. Unable to secure from Rome an annulment of his marriage to Catherine of Aragon, Henry looked for help from scholars who could argue that the king of England was the most superior ruler on the planet. The legend of King Arthur provided some of the intellectual calculation, while Thomas Cromwell, a former staff member of Cardinal Thomas Wolsey, supplied the legal rationale for Henry's declaration in 1534 that the king was the head of the Church of England. Henry's determination had no precedent; he was the first king in Europe to sever ties with the pope. As archbishop, Thomas Cranmer, at first hostile to Lutheranism and then a committed Protestant, became the king's agent of reform. Cromwell drove domestic policy (especially the dissolution of monasteries) under the spell of reform, while Cranmer worked to implement changes within the church proper. Only when resistance to reformation took the form of open rebellion did Henry begin to listen to Cromwell's opponents and opt for a "middle way." On July 28, 1540, Cromwell was executed on charges of treason and heresy, and two days later three Roman Catholic loyalists and three Protestants followed Cromwell's fate. Cranmer was able to evade Henry's displeasure, and in so doing insured a Church of England that had a more Protestant than Roman Catholic tilt.

Across the Channel, Francis I had less room to maneuver than Henry thanks to domestic, international, and personal relations. He was able to reach agreement with the papacy in 1516 to limit Rome's interference in French affairs (Concordat of Bologna), but the theologians in Paris were among the most conservative of churchmen in Europe and were no fans of the consolidation of royal power. Even if the pope gave Francis greater freedom than Paris' theologians did to defend the faith, the king was powerless in 1525 to do anything when taken prisoner by the Habsburgs after France's defeat in the battle of Pavia. During his absence, Francis' queen, Louise of Savoy, instituted heresy proceedings against Protestants in the village of Meaux, a town where the local bishop had begun to implement reforms. Among the persecuted was Guillaume Farel, who with other Protestants sought refuge in Strasbourg. Francis, not a prisoner for long, was inclined to tolerate the reformers and allowed Protestants to return. One explanation may be the king's close relationship to Marguerite d'Angoulême, his sister, who put him in touch with the writings and arguments of French humanists who were initially attracted to Luther's arguments. But soon protests against Roman Catholicism became violent and threatened social order. In 1528, Parisians smashed a statue of the Virgin Mary on a street corner, and from this point Francis paid greater heed to counselors who warned about the threat of Protestantism. Then the Affair of the Placards in the fall of 1534 prompted the king to crack down. The display of posters in prominent places throughout the kingdom which objected to the Mass was a turning point for France. (It was also the incident that forced Calvin into exile.) Despite a brief dalliance in 1536 with German Protestants to form a political alliance against the emperor, Reformed Protestantism under Francis would be a clandestine affair.

The examples of England and France indicate again that the success of the Reformation initially depended on the disposition of ruling authorities. In eastern and western Europe Luther's ideas received a warm reception from the usual suspects of academics and conflicted religious leaders. As the Protestant leaders in Zurich, Geneva, Basel, and Strasbourg circulated their own ideas about church reform and developed relationships with churchmen in other lands, the Reformed model of church government and worship became more attractive than Lutheranism to local Protestants. Historians estimate that the number of Reformed church adherents in Europe increased from roughly half a million in 1554 to as many as ten million by 1600, in places as diverse as Britain and Transylvania. In some cases, such as England and France, opposition from rulers to the new faith was a boon to Reformed Protestantism's appeal; in those same instances the nature of the opposition from the monarchy would produce a different kind of resolve among the adherents of the new faith. In other situations, such as in Poland–Lithuania and Hungary, local nobles could stand up to a weakened monarch by asserting religious independence; at the same time, without political order the new churches, as the example of eastern Europe attests, could easily verge into disorder.

In effect, the Reformed church became a vehicle for political dissent. At the same time, restricting or abolishing the faith of Protestants could be a way to preserve a regime's stability. In other words, among Europe's kings and nobility, Calvinism would face a markedly different environment than Switzerland's cities. Some kingdoms were supportive, some hostile, and some equivocated. Either way, Reformed Protestantism could not live without the state's support. Even so, beneath political maneuvering the spread of Reformed Protestantism reflected genuine desire for a more accessible and less arbitrary form of Christianity than Rome's apparently bloated and worldly faith. The test for the growth of Reformed Protestantism was to adjust the changes in church life, initiated by Zwingli and developed by Bullinger and Calvin, to diverse political and cultural settings.

The Reformation Comes to France

The initial French interest in church reform, naturally enough, came through the circulation of Luther's writings. Humanists concerned about defects in church practices, especially regarding the sacraments, read Luther's early writings enthusiastically and began to study the Church Fathers as part of an effort to recover a more pristine and less complicated Christian expression than Rome's. Although books were expensive and not printed in large quantities, Luther's works sold well in Paris. As many as six Frenchmen also traveled to Wittenberg to study with the reformer. A further sign of Protestantism's appeal around 1520 was a Grenoble priest's advocacy of administering the Mass in a way that would enable the laity to receive both elements (i.e., wine in addition to bread). He also promoted marriage for clergy. In Meaux, a village about halfway between Paris and Noyon (Calvin's hometown), the bishop Guillaume Briçonnet also appointed a number of priests who were inclined to reform.

By 1524 this group in Meaux had turned for advice and support to the Reformed Protestant leaders in Switzerland, Zwingli and Oecolampadius. One reason for consulting them instead of Luther may have been the University of Paris' 1521 condemnation of the German's works. (Thanks to linguistic barriers and state regulations, only 22 editions of Luther's were published in France during his lifetime, compared to 2,946 editions in Germany.) A related consideration is that the French authorities were generally unaware of Swiss developments. Either way, the French who would be Protestant gradually opened their intellectual horizons to leaders of reform. The refuge that Switzerland provided to persecuted French Protestant exiles was also significant. Guillaume Farel, one of those initially within the circle of reform-minded French humanists and a member of the circle of evangelicals at Meaux, escaped to Basel in 1524 when Francis I began to restrict religious dissent. Farel studied with Oecolampadius before conducting evangelistic work between 1526 and 1529 on the east side of Lake Léman, with the town of Aigle as his base of operation. During this time he also composed a *Summary and Brief Declaration* (1529), a work that was the best outline of Protestant convictions in French before Calvin's *Institutes*. Farel showed the influence of Zwingli and Oecolampadius by rendering the Lord's Supper more as a symbolic representation of Christ's death than an instance, as Luther had it, of Christ's real presence.

French Protestants benefited from Francophone Switzerland as an outlet even if political exile did nothing for reforming France's churches. The number of heresy trials in France for heterodox views (which could include more than Protestantism) increased steadily between the 1520s and 1540s. The Parlement of Toulouse, the jurisdiction of which accounted for about one-fifth of the nation's population (roughly 13 million), conducted 8 heresy trials in the 1520s, 121 in the 1530s, and 257 in the 1540s. At the time of France's greatest political instability after the death of Francis I, the 1550s, the number jumped to 684. For the Parlement of Paris, which oversaw the rest of France, the 1540s witnessed the greatest number of heresy trials – 797 – a figure that declined to 290 a decade later. In addition to legislative and judicial proceedings against Protestants, Francis I called for the Sorbonne faculty to draft articles of the faith that specified the boundary between Roman Catholic orthodoxy and its false upstart. The statement of faith affirmed transubstantiation and papal supremacy, and rejected

Reformed teaching in a manner and wording that likely informed the later condemnation of Protestantism at the Council of Trent.

This opposition underlined regional differences in the French contest with Protestants. On the one hand, the Parlement of Paris was most effective in countering Protestantism in northern and central France, thus making a city like Geneva appealing as a place of refuge. By 1549 the city of Geneva did, in fact, establish procedures for keeping track of all the refugees. On the other hand, the increase of heresy trials conducted by Toulouse indicates that Protestantism was spreading relatively successfully in the semi-circle of regions in southern France between La Rochelle, Montauban, and Nîmes. Differences between the two French *parlements* also reveal divergences in rates of execution for bad faith. Of those tried in Paris, 14 percent received the death penalty; the same was true for 6 percent of those prosecuted in Toulouse. If Paris was twice as hard on Protestant crime as the French authorities in the South, French Protestants would be more inclined to leave the northern and central parts of the kingdom and settle either in French cities closer to Geneva or simply to leave the country altogether. Whatever inferences these statistics allow, political repression of Protestantism did not make it go away. In 1525 approximately ten cities experienced instances of the Protestant heresy; by 1540 the new faith was attracting followers in every part of France, except for Brittany (northwest) and Auvergne (south central) where Protestant convictions were sparse.

From 1540 to 1555 efforts to give stability to Protestant convictions took different forms. In 1546 the Protestants in Meaux, who sought to emulate Calvin's worship, decided to start their own services. They designated a wool carder known to be well versed in Scripture to preach and administer the sacraments, and met clandestinely in a private home. Because as many as four hundred believers participated in services that were supposed to be secret, this group could hardly escape notice. Local officials eventually put a stop to the proceedings and arrested sixty Protestants, fourteen of whom received the death penalty.

More typical than gathering for public worship was the decision by Reformed adherents to meet for Bible study and mutual edification. Two notable examples emerged in 1551 in Lyon. One met privately while members still went through the motions of attending Roman Catholic services. The other, composed of artisans, was more public and showed defiance of traditional religion by marching through the streets while singing psalms. The policies of government officials insured that the best chance for Protestantism to survive was through clandestine meetings. For espousing the wrong religious ideas Protestants would only need to confess guilt publicly to escape the death penalty. The more defiant were their actions, such as iconoclastic destruction of images or statues, the greater their chance of execution.

Only around 1555, with Calvin's approval, did Protestants begin to create congregations and move beyond undercover operations. In Paris and Poitiers, Reformed believers established churches according to the forms that Calvin had prescribed for Geneva: a ruling body of elders as the consistory, a minister, and the regular administration of baptism and the Lord's Supper. By 1559 Protestants in seventy-two other French cities or towns followed suit. One explanation for Protestant boldness during this time was the monarch's (Henry II, 1547–59) preoccupation with war against the emperor in Italy. The king's death during a jousting match in 1559 threw the French government into additional turmoil as Henry's teenage sons succeeded him to the throne. The first, Francis II, a sickly fifteen-year-old, ruled for only eighteen months between 1559 and 1560. His brother, Charles IX, a ten-year-old, lasted until 1574. The instability of the monarchy created rivalries among France's elites for control of the young monarchs. It is no coincidence that the Reformed churches in the country during this period were beginning to proliferate and establish national structures of ecclesiastical assemblies. Between 1555 and 1570, over 1,200 churches were formed. Meanwhile, Protestant literature, mainly from francophone Switzerland, gained a wide distribution. Geneva sent as many as 220 pastors to help the Reformed cause. One of Calvin's closest colleagues, Pierre Viret, left Geneva to pastor in Nîmes, Lyon, and Béarn. Calvin's successor in Geneva, Theodore Beza, visited France periodically to offer advice.

The most visible evidence of Geneva's influence and the most vigorous effort of the French was the first national assembly of Reformed churches, held in 1559 in Paris. At this synod the French church, with small revisions, adopted the Gallican Confession, "in one accord by the French people, who desire to live according to the purity of the gospel, of our Lord Jesus Christ."[1] The creed, written in Geneva with significant input from Calvin, started with affirmations about the sufficiency of Scripture and the Trinity before moving on to standard Protestant assertions about salvation and the church. In Article Eighteen, for instance, the French churches confessed that "all our justification rests upon the remission of our sins, in which also is our only blessedness," and rejected "all other means of justification before God, and without claiming any virtue or merit [other than] the obedience of Jesus Christ." The article that distinguished the true from the false church stressed the necessity of teaching only the word of God and administering baptism and the Lord's Supper. It also condemned "the papal assemblies" since "the pure Word of God is banished from them, their sacraments are corrupted, or falsified, or destroyed, and all superstitions and idolatries are in them" (Art. 28).

But even in less obvious ways than this creed, the French Reformed followed the practices of Protestants in and around Geneva, though not without introducing distinct local variations. The French used the catechisms and worship of Geneva, and also followed in general the presbyterian form of government that Calvin had developed, with four distinct ecclesiastical offices (pastors, teachers, elders, and deacons), and individual congregations grouped in regional patterns with the respective ministers ruling as a body over the member churches. But when establishing patterns for unity and governance, the French churches set up a system of parity among all the congregations. This differed from Switzerland, where in the regions of Geneva and Zurich the expectation was for rural churches to follow the lead of the urban pastors. The French also instituted regular meetings of regional church officers, both lay and clerical, as a court of appeal for doctrinal and polity questions. This presbyterian system of church government delegated authority to regional associations of churches rather than to individual congregations. Church power was, obviously, independent of the civil authorities.

The new organized French Reformed church, according to the best estimates, attracted approximately 10 percent of France's population (approximately fifteen million). The churches were strongest in Nîmes, Montauban, and La Rochelle, where Protestants were in the majority, while in Rouen, Orléans, and Lyon they constituted a sizable minority. The Christians drawn to Reformed teaching and worship were overwhelmingly urban and literate, irrespective of wealth or social standing. Literacy suggests a capacity to read Scripture apart from traditions established by the Roman Catholic church. This pattern seems to account for a certain disproportion between men and women in the Protestant churches; because women were less likely to read than men, they were also less likely to join the Reformed fold.

The Protestant cause was also remarkably strong among the nobility and aristocrats (in ten regions the Reformed churches attracted anywhere between 10 percent and 40 percent of elites). The reasons for worshiping in the new churches, as suggested by the most popular literature and folklore from the era, invariably involved frustration with the Mass and the papacy. On the former, many found incredible the Roman Catholic teaching that the bread and wine became the actual body and blood of Christ, and were growing tired of measures to support this doctrine. In the case of the papacy, many Protestant recruits had long tired of the apparent hypocrisy of Christ's representative on Earth participating in affairs and living in a style more typical of the Jewish and Roman officials responsible for the crucifixion than of Christ himself. For people who viewed the church as a corrupt institution, the new message of justification by faith alone, a simpler manner of worship, and a renewed respect for biblical teaching provided relief for pent-up frustrations.

Because the church was an established institution throughout Europe, hoary with ceremony, cathedrals, and vestments, ecclesiastical reform was not simply a matter of changing beliefs or worship. The Reformation also depended upon rulers who were willing to challenge the papacy's status both as one of Europe's sovereigns and as the sole provider of Christendom's holy unction. As the Reformed churches grew both numerically and institutionally in France, a show-down with the monarchy was unavoidable. Adding to the inevitability was the spread of iconoclastic activities between 1557 and 1561, where Reformed pastors and laity removed images from churches and destroyed statues of saints. In some cases, city or town governments, such as Montpellier, Castres, Bazas, Nîmes, and Montauban, actually promoted these efforts to purge local churches of idolatry. Elsewhere, spontaneous reactions erupted from people frustrated by Rome's seeming indifference.

After Francis II's death, Catherine de'Medici took the lead in the government of Charles IX, the second of her sons to succeed to the throne. She was interested in a moderate reform of the church and peace within the nation, and sought reconciliation between Protestants and Roman Catholics. To this end she spon-sored a meeting at Poissy in 1561 between the bishops and Reformed leaders, which included Beza from Geneva and Vermigli from Zurich. Rapprochement failed but Catherine still hoped for social stability, and in 1562 issued the Edict of St Germain, which decreed religious toleration and gave Protestants freedom to worship anywhere except within walled towns. But this legislation only heightened the religious antagonism because of a growing sense among Protestants that the Reformation was about to supplant Roman Catholicism in France. Within three months of this edict, civil war broke out, and for the remainder of the century under the rule of Charles and Henry III, Protestants would see their ranks thin and their religious freedoms substantially curtailed. After 1562, outnumbered by Roman Catholics almost ten to one, the best Protestants could hope for were pockets of Reformed faith and practice in cities such as La Rochelle, Nîmes, and Montaubon. These locations were no more tolerant of Roman Catholics than was the reverse true elsewhere. A stalemate allowing the faith of the local nobility to determine the identity of the local church provided Protestants some space. But war also undermined the appeal of Reformed Protestantism by apparently vindicating the Roman Catholic claim that the new faith nurtured anarchy.

Among the civil wars that punctuated French history between 1562 and 1598, the events surrounding the Saint Bartholomew's Massacre of 1572 are legendary. After a failed assassination of the Protestant leader, Admiral Gaspard de Coligny, in Paris, who was in town for the Protestant wedding of Henry, king of Navarre, to Marguerite, daughter of Catherine de'Medici, the Royal Council

advised Charles IX to strike preemptively against the Reformed dignitaries still
in Paris. On Sunday, August 24, 1572, soldiers rounded up and executed
Protestant leaders in the capital city. When news spread outside Paris, Roman
Catholic partisans followed the king's example and used similar tactics against
ordinary Protestants throughout France. Estimates suggest that as many as 5,000
Huguenots were slaughtered in the weeks after the initial purge in Paris. Many
others were humiliated into renouncing Protestantism. What had been a vigorous
French minority with certain strongholds between Poitou and Dauphiné was
now reduced to a bitter faction.

This was the context for the rise of Reformed resistance theory and the hard-
ening of French Roman Catholic opposition to Protestantism (with a good deal
of encouragement from a politically interested and religiously motivated Spain).
Caught between Huguenot appeals to the rights of lesser magistrates to disobey
tyrannical rulers and Roman Catholic insistence that only someone loyal to the
pope could accede to the throne, Henry III (1574–89) attempted a policy
of toleration. He succeeded Charles IX, who had died apparently guilt-stricken
by the brutality shown to Protestants. But hardline Roman Catholics who in
1576 had formed the Catholic League would have none of Henry's moderation.
The reality of a Protestant successor (Henry of Navarre) to the crown was
undoubtedly a factor. When in 1588 Henry III tried to stand up to Roman
Catholic pressure (and to Spanish meddling), he resorted to having two Roman
Catholic nobles killed. This led to a backlash that took Henry's life, when a
disgruntled Dominican friar assassinated him in August of 1589.

This precipitated the ascension of Henry of Navarre as Henry IV. To the
disappointment of Protestants, some of whom regarded the new king as the
second coming of Israel's King David, Henry converted to Roman Catholicism
with the oft-repeated quip, "Paris is worth a Mass."[2] As flippant as the remark
may sound, Henry IV did realize that the only way he could rule in a predominantly Roman Catholic country was by satisfying the demands of his least-
supportive subjects. At the same time his identification with Rome became the
basis for attempting to grant toleration to his Protestant subjects, thereby
restoring peace and order to the realm. His Edict of Nantes (1598) ended
another round of civil wars and granted Protestants terms that were the best
available in a politically tense atmosphere. It specified places for worship, and
granted Protestants political rights, social standing, and even legitimate control
of military forces. Clearly, Protestants had suffered at the curious policies of the
French crown. But France's monarchy had no easy time trying to reconcile two
versions of Christianity vying for the same polity.

Whatever the disposition of France's unreliable kings, French Protestantism
bore the unmistakable fingerprints of Geneva. The Protestant churches in

France would lead a wedge of ecclesiastical reform that would extend northward into the Low Countries and wreak further havoc in the Holy Roman Empire. The Huguenots taught an important lesson, namely, that political opposition and defeat could be as consequential for later successes as the support of magistrates inclined to identify with Protestantism.

Top-Down Reform

Compared to France, England was less overtly hostile to ecclesiastical reform once Henry VIII saw the advantage of independence from Rome. Even before his assertion of royal supremacy in 1534, the instances of legal suppression of heresy were meager. After enjoying a measure of popularity in the early 1520s, Luther's ideas generated legal opposition and those holding Lutheran sympathies fled to the Continent, among them Robert Barnes and William Tyndale. In fact, these English clergy and scholars visited Wittenberg. Like France, iconoclasm was decisive in England for prompting formal suppression of Protestantism. The reasons had less to do with religious devotion than with threats to the social order. Still, by 1530 only one person had been executed in England for harboring Lutheran (as opposed to Lollardian) views. At the same time, Reformed Protestantism in England never became as coherent and resolute as in France, and again this phenomenon owes much to the shifts within the Tudor monarchy's policies as well as cultural and regional ties. One lesson seems to be that sustained persecution and martyrdom deepened evangelical convictions in ways that fickle monarchs did not.

Although Lutheranism enjoyed the initial attention of English Protestants, once the king established a national church, reform became the object of Henry's chief advisor, Thomas Cromwell. A member of Cardinal Thomas Wolsey's staff and a gifted administrator, Cromwell was also a committed Protestant who used his delegated authority to secure a decidedly Protestant identity for the Church of England. Of the ten bishops to leave office between 1532 and 1536 – mostly due to death – seven of the replacements were known to advocate reform. Wolsey also enjoyed the support of Henry's second wife, Anne Boleyn, who was a patron to several of the newly appointed bishops as well. The chief among them was Thomas Cranmer, a professor at Cambridge who was able to keep his head during the tumultuous and volatile years of Henry's reign by following a wise course of moderation that sometimes appeared to show cowardice. Even so, Cranmer's judiciousness, tainted as it may have been, allowed him to preside over the English church all the way up until the reign of Mary Tudor, who tried to restore England's ties with Rome.

The most visible part of the English Reformation during the 1530s was the dissolution of the monasteries and friaries and the destruction of images in and around the churches. As much as this policy became a newfound source of income for the crown, the loss of monks and friars undercut significantly traditional Roman Catholic piety. Members of the orders had been some of the best preachers, and the statues and images in churches had functioned as the basis for pilgrimages and financial contributions. These direct attacks on Roman Catholic devotion prompted uprisings in northern England in 1536 and 1537 known as the Pilgrimage of Grace for the Commonwealth. Henry responded with cunning and force, putting down the rebellion handily. But the persistence of Roman Catholic piety among the laity was a hedge upon the extent and speed of reform.

The theologians and churchmen who gathered in 1537 to give coherence to the new church refused to press Henry beyond where he felt comfortable. Their deliberations reaffirmed medieval teaching and piety, while deploying Protestant tactical expressions regarding justification and the authority of Scripture. They also ratified a decision to destroy images and statues. But with Henry refusing to abandon the ways and teachings of the old church, reform was going to be piecemeal. Indeed, in 1538 Henry reaffirmed Roman Catholic teaching on transubstantiation, vows of chastity, clerical celibacy, and auricular confession. Soon Cromwell's status with the king was shaky. Having orchestrated charges of treason and the execution of Anne Boleyn in order to arrange for the king's third marriage, this time to Jane Seymour (who did produce a male heir but died shortly after giving birth), Cromwell then helped Henry marry for a fourth time. Anne of Cleves may have been a smart choice to give England an ally in case France and the Holy Roman Empire decided to join forces against Henry, but dubbed by the king as the "Flanders Mare," she was no match for his sexual appetite. Cromwell's inability to please the king through this alliance made plausible the criticisms of his enemies at court. In 1540 Cromwell suffered the fate of so many that were part of the king's inner circle: he was executed on charges of heresy and treason. Without the patrons of Protestantism at court, some of the reform-minded bishops resigned and some left for the Continent. One of the earliest English reformers, Robert Barnes, died at the stake for opposing the king's failure to break decisively with the old Roman Catholic faith.

If not for Henry's mercurial disposition, the Protestant cause might have depended solely on the cautious Cranmer and his ability to gain the king's favor. But in 1546, a year before Henry's death, missteps by nobles and high-ranking clergy of Roman Catholic persuasion prompted the king to form a regency council for his young son, Edward, composed primarily of those who supported reformation, most notably Edward Seymour, the duke of Somerset, an uncle to Henry's son. After Henry's death in 1547, Edward VI, with guidance from his regency council, turned the Church of England onto a Protestant course. This change was too abrupt for some, and uprisings stemming from religious and economic grievances hobbled the new government. The duke of Somerset literally lost his head in 1549, because of poor performance during the rebellions of 1548 and 1549. But his successor as chief advisor to the young king, John Dudley, duke of Northumberland, was also decidedly Protestant. Among Somerset, Northumberland, Edward, and the cautious Cranmer, the English church moved steadily into the Reformed column.

Protestant ideas and devotion in England prior to 1547 drew upon Lollard, humanistic, Lutheran, and Reformed sources, but thanks to a number of historical circumstances took a particularly Reformed path during Edward's reign. Very shortly after Edward's ascension Charles V defeated Lutheran forces (i.e. the Schmalkaldic League) and imposed the Augsburg Interim, a resolution of religious conflict that sought a compromise on devotional practice while holding off on doctrine until the conclusion of the Council of Trent. The terms of peace drove many Protestant pastors and theologians on the Continent into exile, with England under a Protestant king providing a relatively safe haven. Very important for the development of English Protestantism was the arrival of Peter Vermigli and Martin Bucer from Strasbourg, and Jan Laski from Emden. Vermigli took a position at Oxford University, where he trained at least six students who would become bishops in the English church. His eucharistic teaching generated controversy while introducing a strain of doctrine more akin to Zurich than Wittenberg. Bucer soon followed and became a professor of theology at Cambridge University. Although he died after only two years of work, Bucer was widely popular and he too trained many future English church leaders. Laski came to England to serve as pastor of the London Church for Refugees. His ministerial and worship practices provided a model for church reform. Laski also served, along with Vermigli and Bucer, on the king's ecclesiastical commission and made recommendations on ecclesiastical policy.

As much as the new government appeared to support Reformed Protestantism, the reforms of the institutional church in England were gradual. By 1548 the Church of England's teaching on salvation began to affirm justification by faith alone and the practices of the parishes reflected Reformed objections to images and the Mass. By 1549 Parliament had approved a new Book of Common Prayer composed by a committee overseen by Cranmer. The prayer book introduced worship in the vernacular, reduced the sacraments from seven to two (baptism and the Lord's Supper), and eliminated the practice of elevating the host during the administration of Communion. At the same time, the new prayer book was intentionally conservative. Church leaders did not want to lose touch with many churchgoers. The aim was not to complete but to begin reform. The moderate character of the new liturgy and the initial reforms upset some, like John Hooper, one of the bishops who went into exile when Henry VIII had reaffirmed traditional Roman teaching. He questioned the continued use of vestments in the church, as well as the practice of kneeling when receiving the elements of the Lord's Supper. Bucer and Vermigli believed these matters were of little consequence and counseled Hooper to cooperate. Laski thought otherwise.

Either way, this disagreement, which was a harbinger of Puritanism, was inconsequential. In 1552 Cranmer led the completion of a second Book of Common Prayer and the following year drafted Forty-Two Articles of faith for the English church. The revised liturgy was designed to allow less room for priests and bishops who continued to follow Roman Catholic forms. It significantly modified the Communion service, simplified the priest's vestments, exchanged bread for wafers, and replaced the altar with a table. Thanks to the Black Rubric, which explained the meaning of a worshiper's posture in the Lord's Supper, communicants still kneeled while receiving Communion. But the clarification, designed by government officials in the Privy Council to mollify objections by the Scottish reformer John Knox, insisted that this posture did not signify adoration of the elements. Meanwhile, the Forty-Two Articles of 1553 adopted Reformed teaching, but not aggressively so. They affirmed predestination (God's choosing before time the elect) but avoided reprobation (God's eternal judgment of the rest of humanity), and taught a real spiritual presence of Christ in the Lord's Supper while denying the Lutheran position on the ubiquity of Christ's body. At the same time, the prayer book allowed practices with Roman Catholic associations that Reformed churches on the Continent would not countenance. Meanwhile, the polity of the Church of England, with the king as supreme head and the church hierarchy of bishops intact, saw no change during Edward's reign. From Calvin's perspective, the English church lacked a desirable level of purity. He also believed its defects were permissible.

One reason that reformation only went as far as it did was that when Edward died in 1553 his successor was Mary Tudor, the offspring of Henry VIII's first marriage (to Catherine of Aragon). She was a committed Roman Catholic, and even though uncomfortable with her own position as head of the Church of England, she reinstituted the Mass and promoted the reinstallation of altars in parishes. The number of ordinations increased. And aside from a minor uprising, the Wyatt Rebellion, most of the English accepted Mary's changes amicably. In fact, the protest that took Thomas Wyatt's name stemmed primarily from opposition to the queen's plan to marry Philip of Spain. Whether owing to religious or political considerations, English Protestants had no interest in being subject to a Roman Catholic king of foreign descent.

While restoring Roman Catholic practices in England, Mary also sought the elimination of Protestantism, including those who held Protestant convictions, earning her the nickname "Bloody." Her government executed more than 280 Protestants, including the bishops Cranmer, Hooper, Latimer, and Ridley. But the list of martyrs included lay people, overwhelmingly urban, young, and from the southern part of England. At the same time, as many as eight hundred Protestants left the country as religious refugees. Here the Reformed cities of Emden, Wesel, Frankfurt, Strasbourg, Zurich, Basel, and Geneva proved to be more accommodating than Lutheran territories, an important factor in turning English Protestantism further in a Reformed direction. For those who had wanted Cranmer to go farther in reforming the English church than he had – John Knox was among them – Geneva proved to be the most hospitable place of exile.

Mary's reign was short-lived, and so was the English Church's return to Roman Catholic practices. Her successor, Elizabeth I (the daughter of Anne Boleyn), who lived the longest of any of Henry VIII's children, ruled from 1558 to 1603 and generally restored the church to its Protestant and Reformed character under Edward. For good measure and to reassure European rulers that the English church was not too different from its peers, Elizabeth avoided the rigor and simplicity of Reformed worship, and allowed for vestments and wording in the Lord's Supper that Roman Catholics could interpret favorably. As governor, rather than supreme head, of the church – to reflect the truth that Christ was the only true head – Elizabeth also modified the church articles, reducing them from forty-two to thirty-nine. At the same time, she appointed many of the returning Marian exiles as bishops. Her first two archbishops, Matthew Parker and Edmund Grindal, had been greatly influenced by Bucer. The Geneva Bible, published in 1560, which contained strongly Calvinist teaching, was used widely. Meanwhile, the works of John Calvin enjoyed their greatest popularity among publishers between 1578 and 1581. His successor in Geneva, Theodore Beza, also emerged as one of the Elizabethan church's favorite authors. The English church may not have followed the Reformed Protestants on the Continent on the precise matters of church polity and worship, but its general tenor for much of Elizabeth's reign drew inspiration from Geneva and Zurich.

While the Church of England's leaders were taking cues from Reformed Protestants on the Continent, the queen herself kept her own convictions private and initially pursued ecclesiastical policies that were decidedly ambiguous, charitably interpreted as a *via media* between the extremes of Roman Catholicism and Protestantism. The result was tension between Elizabeth's moderation and calls from churchmen for greater reform. The word applied to these advocating further reformation was Puritan, a term first used in 1567 as one of opprobrium to those most zealous to rid the church of compromise and corruption. During the first decade of Elizabeth's reign these puritanical elements within the church sought to revise the liturgy, reduce the number of holy days, eliminate vestments, abolish kneeling for Communion, and remove organs from churches. The reactions from Swiss church leaders were unfavorable. Bullinger in Zurich detected a "contentious spirit in the name of conscience," while Beza in Geneva compared the situation in England to that of Babylon.[3]

After 1570 the instances of Puritanism assumed a higher degree of importance, if only because Elizabeth, in response to threats to her authority from within England as well as from the papacy, adopted a clear religious policy. She required subscription to the Thirty-Nine Articles, oaths of loyalty to the crown, and use of the prayer book. In response, Reformed-minded ministers during the 1570s proposed a revision of the English church's government along the lines of presbyterian councils rather than episcopalian hierarchy. The proponents of these measures looked to the churches in France and Switzerland as models, but their views were unwelcome and some were imprisoned while others escaped punishment through exile. Another reform initiative arose during the 1580s, again drawing on presbyterian convictions, though this time picking up support from reformers to the north, in Scotland. A proposal came to the English Parliament in 1584 that would have replaced the Book of Common Prayer with the Geneva Liturgy and overhauled the system of church government in presbyterian fashion. Another came in 1586, after local conferences of priests had begun to organize themselves in a presbyterian pattern of regional and national assemblies of church officers. Both initiatives failed, which in turn led to more radical efforts at reform, with some pastors founding separatist congregations. Religious authorities cracked down on the Puritans by breaking up the conferences and imprisoning their leaders. Some of the beleaguered escaped to the Netherlands during the 1590s, and were the origin of the Pilgrims who fled to North America three decades later.[4]

Instead of reforming the Church of England, the effort to purify hardened the Anglican policy of moderation. John Bridges, for example, published a work in 1587 that defended episcopacy, an unusual argument among the many versions of church reform in the sixteenth century. Even more ambitious were Richard Hooker's *Laws of Ecclesiastical Polity* (1593) and subsequent writings, which justified the Church of England as a golden mean between the extremes of Rome and Geneva (in contrast to Reformed Protestant leaders, who saw Geneva and Zurich as a middle ground between Roman Catholicism and the Anabaptists).

The consolidation of the English church's legitimate calling as a distinct expression of the Christian religion turned efforts for greater reform (among Puritans) from external to internal methods. After 1590, instead of relying upon the discipline supplied by ecclesiastical structures, those dissatisfied with the Church of England cultivated voluntary and informal means for reforming the lives of ordinary Christians and preserving sound instruction from Scripture. In other words, the culmination of the English Reformation in the Elizabethan settlement proved to be especially frustrating (though the persecution of Protestants was not as grave in England as in France). Like church reform in France, English Protestants also drew inspiration from Geneva. But as in France, the English monarchy, even if supportive of Protestantism, proved a barrier to true reform. The tension between Calvinist ideals and English politics was a potent combination that England's imperial ambitions would unwittingly extend throughout the colonial world. Although reform might hit a wall in the mother country, English colonists would enjoy a variety of settings, fairly far removed from the crown, in which to experiment with Reformed Protestant ideals. At home, however, Protestants who wanted a thorough reformation could sound like over-scrupulous zealots incapable of adjusting to the limits of a fallen world.

Reformed Prospects in Eastern Europe

The kingdom of Poland and the grand duchy of Lithuania, a joint monarchy more than twice the size of France, under the rule of the Jagiellon dynasty, was Europe's largest political power measured by land mass. At the beginning of the sixteenth century, the Jagiellons also ruled the kingdoms of Hungary and Bohemia. These territories experienced the brunt of Turkish expansion, and the cruel defeat of Hungary at Mohács in 1526 significantly weakened the Jagiellons' ability to govern this vast domain. But the region had known diversity – especially religious diversity – even before the events of 1526 altered Poland–Lithuania's political landscape. The kingdom was situated literally between centers of western and eastern Christianity. As such, in addition to twenty-one dioceses under Rome's oversight, a significant portion of Lithuania's population looked for spiritual direction from the Orthodox archbishop in Kiev. At the same time, the Jewish portion of the kingdom enjoyed a legal status that in 1549 would result in its recognition as a fifth estate, alongside clergy, nobility, burghers, and peasantry. If Poland–Lithuania could handle such religious diversity, how difficult would Lutherans or Reformed Protestants be to accommodate? Indeed, Lutheranism spread to German-speaking cities in the kingdom. It also attracted a following among the Lithuanians, and Luther's short catechism was the first book printed in the Lithuanian language (in 1547).

Such religious diversity meant that the Jagiellon kings would need to tread carefully amid the rival claims of Roman Catholics and Protestants. Adding greatly to the monarchy's caution were the powers and privileges of lesser nobles who were used to protecting their status and eventually acquired authority to elect the Polish kings. The Jagiellons may have supported Rome throughout most of the sixteenth century, but their assistance was largely passive. Sigismund I himself remained loyal to Rome and opposed the reformers' teachings. As early as 1520 he issued a decree forbidding Luther's writings, and three years later followed with the threat of death to anyone guilty of harboring Protestant convictions. But the political diversity and the jealousy of lesser Polish nobles for their own prerogatives, not to mention the king's own sympathy for humanism and many of the changes in church life associated with the new learning, prevented Sigismund's edicts from producing any Protestant martyrs. His son, Sigismund II, who ruled in Lithuania from 1529 and succeeded his father as king of Poland in 1548, was open to Protestantism, thanks in part to his correspondence with the likes of John Calvin. In fact, in 1549 Calvin dedicated his commentary on Hebrews to the new Polish king, so hopeful were Reformed Protestants of a favorable reception of their faith in the East. Meanwhile, lesser nobles throughout Poland–Lithuania advocated Protestantism for a variety of reasons, both genuinely religious and for political leverage against the monarchy.

Throughout the 1530s and 1540s Lutheran and Reformed Protestant writings circulated in Poland–Lithuania without a particular pattern, aside from the obvious linguistic links (German), academic interests, and urban settings. Cracow and Königsberg were two cities where Protestant ideas gained a following. Legend has it that one graduate from the university in Cracow in 1546 appeared before the local Roman Catholic bishop to answer an accusation of heresy. When asked if he held Calvin's views, the young man replied this was the first time he had heard the Geneva pastor's name. After evading the charge, the accused proceeded to procure several of Calvin's books and eventually became a Reformed Protestant advocate. By the late 1540s, modifications in worship along Swiss lines began to take hold in the small Polish region between Cracow and Lublin. In 1550, an Italian Protestant exile, Francesco Stancaro, had implemented reforms at a church in Pińczów through his *Canons of the Reformation of the Polish Church*. By 1553, worship was also following Reformed pattern in Lithuania. In most cases, the religious changes stemmed from a local nobleman who had become the patron of a Protestant pastor, who in turn implemented the new doctrines and worship.

In practically all of these cases Protestants were acting illegally, but Polish and Lithuanian rulers were unwilling to enforce prohibitions. Often the noblemen, even of Roman Catholic faith, preferred to defend the rights of citizens against bishops' authority; for instance, in Pozna, when three burghers were sentenced to death in 1554 for adhering to the new faith, one escaped and armed nobles sprung the others not only from prison but also spared them from execution. A similar fate attended a cobbler convicted of Protestantism. When nobles rallied to the cobbler's defense, the bishop naturally inquired why members of the upper ranks of society would defend a common artisan. The response was: "it's not that we care about the cobbler, but we realize that if you got your way with him, you might do the same tomorrow to [us]."[5] Eventually the Sejm (the Polish parliament) revoked ecclesiastical jurisdiction over the laity. But the crown retained the right to determine religion in the royal cities. Since the king usually needed the support of local nobility for war and other political purposes, aristocrats sympathetic to Protestantism possessed leverage to contravene the crown's wishes.

Church reforms conducted locally were gratifying for Protestants in Poland–Lithuania but many reformers hoped for a national Protestant church. Fueling this optimism and desire was knowledge that Sigismund II, inaugurated in 1548, read Protestant literature and had Protestant advisors. One of the king's counselors had actually visited Geneva to purchase Protestant literature. He also encouraged Calvin to initiate correspondence with the Polish king. By 1555 the Sejm of Piotrków gave Sigismund power to determine religion in the realm and called for a national council to address such ecclesiastical reforms as worship in the vernacular, communion in both elements, and clerical marriage. Some Polish Protestants also petitioned Geneva for help, hoping that Calvin himself might visit Poland, or at least send one of his pastors. The Frenchman declined but he did commend Jan Laski, a native Pole, who was part of the Reformed resurgence in England during Edward VI's reign. Laski relocated to Poland in 1556 and proceeded to organize the first national synod. He endeavored to create as broad a consensus as possible to corral the various Protestant streams, including Lutheran and Czech Brethren currents, that were swirling through the kingdom.

Laski added a calming presence to Polish Protestantism, but it was short-lived. He died in 1560, and the timing was untoward since just before his death a division had emerged within the Polish churches. Thanks largely to the Italian Protestants exiled to Poland, a strain of anti-Trinitarianism emerged. Even Francesco Stancaro, who had originally led the reform of worship, embraced heretical views and propounded them persuasively. Laski fought these developments. Meanwhile, Calvin and Bullinger wrote treatises on behalf of the Trinity precisely for the Polish situation. During the 1560s the Polish churches split along anti-Trinitarian and orthodox lines, with the majority of pastors taking the former position and the nobles adhering to traditional beliefs about Christ's deity. By 1565 the anti-Trinitarians had established their own synod and churches.

Despite the rise of anti-Trinitarianism, Reformed Protestantism during the second wave of the Reformation had succeeded in establishing churches throughout the Polish kingdom. Little Poland witnessed the most success. At one point, as many as 265 Reformed congregations gathered for worship, no matter how briefly in some cases, compared to approximately 100 of the anti-Trinitarian version. In Lithuania, Reformed Protestantism accounted for another 229 congregations at any one time, despite cultural and linguistic affinities with German Lutheranism. In Greater Poland, where Lutheranism enjoyed a large presence, Reformed Protestantism produced only fifteen congregations. A major factor in the success of Reformed Protestantism was the patronage of nobility. Estimates suggest that one-sixth of the elites embraced the Reformed faith. But elite support was also a weakness. Without a following from the lower ranks, Reformed churches lacked a stable population of believers to endure beyond the lives of their patrons.

In Hungary, where in 1526 the young king, Louis Jagiellon, died in the battle of Mohács, the cause of church reform appeared to be more a question of expediency than principle. Some Hungarians interpreted the Ottoman victory as a form of divine judgment on Rome's faith. But the way church reform developed in the Habsburg and Turk-controlled region might also have prompted the arresting conclusion that the Muslims were on the side of the evangelical faith.

Prior to 1526, Luther's writings circulated among academics and learned Hungarian nobles and carried the same appeal as elsewhere in Europe. But the threat of the Ottoman armies and the papacy encouraging the rest of Europe's rulers to defend Hungary against the infidel also bred caution about the consequences of embracing church reforms. The defeat of Hungary at Mohács split the kingdom politically and religiously. The Habsburgs retained control of the northern and western borders of the old Hungarian kingdom while the Ottomans controlled the rest. The defeat also cost the church dearly: seven of the its sixteen bishops died during the struggle and many priests fled. As a result, four-fifths of the parishes in the Ottoman-occupied territories were vacant. An additional consequence of the 1526 defeat was Rome's alienation of nobles in parts of Hungary outside Habsburg rule. John Sigismund Zápolyai, one of the claimants to the Hungarian monarchy, had arranged with the sultan to retain control of the southeastern sector of Hungary as a tribute-paying vassal. The papacy excommunicated Zápolyai for this decision and in turn the Ottoman authorities rejected Rome's assistance in establishing order in their new lands. When the Turks looked for religious authorities to help with administration they granted Protestant preachers great liberty to proselytize and conduct worship as long as they respected the Ottomans' sovereignty. Protestantism, consequently, spread almost without resistance in the Muslim quarter of Hungary. For instance, Mihály Sztárai, an itinerant Protestant evangelist, in 1551 wrote to one of his correspondents that he had been preaching freely for seven years and in the course of those efforts he and other Protestants had established roughly 120 congregations.

Fluidity generally characterized reform efforts in Hungary until 1550. Doctrinal reflection drew upon Erasmian humanism, Lutheranism, and Reformed Protestantism. Formal church structures received more definition than doctrine, with Hungarian Protestants adapting the existing ecclesiastical framework to form districts that spanned from Royal Hungary in the East to Transylvania in the West, over each of which a superintendent – designated bishop – presided. The Christian part of Hungary had as many as six districts. The Ottoman sector had one. A controversy over sacramental theology in the town of Debrecen during the late 1540s, however, furthered the definition of Hungarian Protestantism. By the 1560s Transylvanian district synods had adopted Theodore Beza's confession of faith and the Heidelberg Catechism, a teaching device used by German Reformed Protestants in the Palatinate. At roughly the same time, synods embraced Beza's confession and Calvin's catechism. The anti-Trinitarianism that afflicted the Reformed churches in Poland also tormented Transylvania. Controversies over these views throughout the 1560s led to a broad policy of religious toleration in western Hungary, which made room for Reformed churches, Roman Catholics, and anti-Trinitarians.

Such religious toleration took longer to form in Royal Hungary in the East. From 1550 until the end of the century, the Habsburg rulers essentially refused to enforce Roman Catholicism. But by the time of the revival of war against the Ottomans (1593–1606), accompanied by military success and Roman Catholic pressure on the Habsburgs, Protestants lost churches and pastorates to priests. The nobility in many royal towns resisted these changes and the Habsburgs decided to implement a loosely worded policy of religious tolerance. This concession acknowledged the dominance demographically of Protestantism in Hungary. In the upper house of the Hungarian diet, all but three out of thirty-six magnates were Protestant. In the population as a whole, Protestantism accounted for approximately 75 percent, with Reformed Protestantism constituting the largest religious body in Hungary (40 percent of the people). By adopting the creeds developed in Geneva and Zurich, the Hungarian churches revealed both the primacy of the Swiss churches for Reformed Protestantism as well as a working consensus among Reformed believers in western and eastern Europe.

The Difference a Monarch Makes

Diarmaid MacCulloch observes that in its initial phases the Reformed branch of Protestantism prospered in cities where political authority was in the hands of a city council. But when proponents of church reform needed to convince monarchs to side with the new faith, the barriers grew higher. The leaders of the major "European dynasties would need a good deal of persuading that Luther, Bullinger, or Bucer were any safer investments than Caspar Schwenckfeld or Melchior Hoffman" – two noted radical Protestants (also known as Anabaptist).[6] Aside from Charles V, the hardest case of all, the Holy Roman Emperor, Francis I of France, Henry VIII, and Sigismund I of Poland each saw the spread of Protestantism and responded in ways that had as much to do with politics (both domestic and international) as with personal convictions. One important factor for each monarch was his relationship to Rome. The further removed from papal pressure, the more willing was the king to live with ecclesiastical experimentation.

The lesson that Reformed Protestants learned in places like France, England, Poland–Lithuania, and Hungary was that, although appealing, the new faith would only go as far as rulers would allow. Not to be missed in the politics of these settings was the tremendous appeal of Reformed Protestantism. Its leaders produced a body of ideas that circulated widely and became a handy guide to church life and biblical instruction among those educators and social leaders who were dissatisfied with Rome's performance. At the same time, its adherents possessed a vigor that assisted its spread well beyond cultural and linguistic ties (e.g. Poland–Lithuania). One last attractive feature was a perceived plan for addressing the specific failings of the Roman churches; ecclesiastical orders that provided blueprints for maintaining integrity among the clergy and instilling godliness among the faithful were an obvious boon for those frustrated with Christendom's hypocritical clergy and the second-class status of ordinary church members who did not belong to a holy order.

At the same time, Reformed Protestantism could not overcome the obstacles of rulers who remained unconvinced. The new faith would spread in remarkable ways across all of Europe; but it would only take root in those kingdoms where the monarchy determined that more could be gained by tolerating some form of Protestantism than by opposing it altogether. For this reason, monarchy was the least fertile soil for orderly and sustainable reform. It was responsible for martyrs (France), zealots (England), or stillborn Calvinists (Poland–Lithuania). In practically all of these settings the Reformed churches benefited from gifted churchmen and theologians; those Calvinists wound up being only as influential as their monarchs would let them.

CHAPTER THREE

TO REBEL AND TO BUILD

IN 1559, FREDERICK III became the prince-elector of the Palatinate, a small German-speaking territory within the Holy Roman Empire. As was typical throughout the Germanic parts of the empire, he inherited a Protestant church that had been reformed along Lutheran lines. Granted, the Lutheranism in Frederick's hometown, Heidelberg, was not the high-octane variety that some, known as gnesio-Lutherans, were advocating. These conservative Lutherans regarded the form of Lutheranism cultivated by Philip Melanchthon (one that inspired hopes in places like Geneva for unity between Lutherans and the Reformed) as betraying Luther's original insights. Still, the Palatinate church had a reputation even before Frederick's succession for taking stances that resembled Reformed practices, for instance, by prohibiting the use of images in worship. The commercial ties between Heidelberg and imperial cities to the southwest like Strasbourg, where Reformed teaching took root, accounts for some of Heidelberg's ecclesiastical character and its openness to Reformed ideas.

By the time Frederick assumed his princely duties, he had experienced a reformation of his own faith. Born in 1515, Frederick grew up a devout Roman Catholic. But his marriage to Maria of Brandenburg-Ansbach changed his outlook. Maria was a committed Lutheran, and in 1547 he followed her into the Protestant fold by adopting her church. Frederick's faith did not determine his political alliances, however. In Charles V's war against the Schmalkaldic League (1546–47), an alliance of Lutheran princes, Frederick backed the emperor. Naturally, the Lutheran princes regarded Frederick as an enemy, an animosity that likely colored their suspicions of Reformed teachings in the Palatinate a decade later.

Whatever the personal dimensions of Frederick's loyalty to Lutheranism, his responsibilities as elector of the Palatinate forced him to confront the escalating tensions among Lutherans as well as the differences between Reformed

Protestants and Lutherans. He determined to study the reasons for Protestant divisions, not simply for the good of his territory but because of his own devotion. He called for a disputation among leading Lutheran theologians while continuing his own reading, especially Luther's writings against Protestants who opposed Christ's real presence in the Lord's Supper. After these initial lines of investigation, Frederick decided that Reformed interpretations were closer to biblical teaching than the Lutheran position. The prince had help, since one of the Lutheran theologians to participate in the debates, Pierre Boquin, was leaning toward Reformed Protestantism himself.

Once Reformed convictions began to leak within Frederick's domain, Heidelberg experienced a torrent of Reformed initiatives. The faculty at the city's university became the home for some of the most able theologians in the Reformed camp, among them Zacharias Ursinus, Kaspar Olevianus, Petrus Dathenus, and Girolamo Zanchi; in the process Heidelberg supplanted Geneva as the leading provider of Reformed theological training. Frederick's understanding of the Christian faith extended beyond university classrooms to the religious life of Heidelberg. He approved laws that required church attendance, and that punished blasphemy and superstition. Frederick also oversaw the creation of a liturgy and church order according to the practices prevailing among Reformed churches, as well as the production of one of Reformed Protestantism's instructional jewels, the Heidelberg Catechism. The catechism clearly showed the Reformed identity of the city's prince and churches, and became the doctrinal standard for Reformed churches in German-speaking territories.

Because it was immediately translated into Dutch, the Heidelberg Catechism also became an important part of the Reformed churches in the Low Countries. So helpful was Heidelberg's instruction in the Reformed faith that Bullinger called it "the best catechism ever published."[1] Its first question and answer may explain Bullinger's judgment since it rivaled in clarity and devotion any other catechism produced in the era:

Q.: What is thy only comfort in life and death?

A.: That I with body and soul, both in life and death, am not my own, but belong unto my faithful Saviour Jesus Christ; who, with his precious blood, has fully satisfied for all my sins, and delivered me from all the power of the devil; and so preserves me that without the will of my heavenly Father, not a hair can fall from my head; yea, that all things must be subservient to my salvation, and therefore, by his Holy Spirit, He also assures me of eternal life, and makes me sincerely willing and ready, henceforth, to live unto him.

The second question was no less exemplary for letting catechumens know what they were in for:

Q.: How many things are necessary for thee to know, that thou, enjoying this comfort, mayest live and die happily?

A.: The first, how great my sins and miseries are; the second, how I may be delivered from all my sins and miseries; the third, how I shall express my gratitude to God for such deliverance.

One additional example, question sixty, summarized effectively the basic conviction of Protestantism:

Q.: How are thou righteous before God?

A.: Only by a true faith in Jesus Christ; so that, though my conscience accuse me, that I have grossly transgressed all the commandments of God, and kept none of them, and am still inclined to all evil; notwithstanding, God, without any merit of mine, but only of mere grace, grants and imputes to me, the perfect satisfaction, righteousness and holiness of Christ; even so, as if I never had had, nor committed any sin: yea, as if I had fully accomplished all that obedience which Christ has accomplished for me; inasmuch as I embrace such benefit with a believing heart.

Lutheran reactions to Heidelberg's reformation did not exhibit the same levels of enthusiasm as Bullinger. The imperial diet in 1566 summoned Frederick to defend his churches since Heidelberg's reforms appeared to violate the Peace of Augsburg. Frederick replied that Geneva's and Zurich's teaching had not influenced him; what had were the simple teachings of the Bible. What is more, Frederick argued that he had signed the Augsburg Confession and approved of subsequent Lutheran developments. His defense satisfied alarmed Lutheran princes who also knew that another division within Protestant ranks could aid Roman Catholic opposition to the new churches.

Frederick's church in the Palatinate demonstrated a recurring feature of Protestantism during the second wave of reformations after 1550. Reformed Protestantism extended its influence across Europe, while Lutheranism remained confined to German-speaking parts of the empire. Consequently, as Protestantism entered kingdoms like Scotland or would-be nations like the Netherlands, local pastors, nobles, and lay people embraced the Reformed faith instead of Lutheranism. The temptation is to attribute this Reformed hegemony to the genius of the doctrine and practices that the churches in Zurich and Geneva originally developed. But just as important – and likely decisive – is that

Lutheranism by mid-century was experiencing considerable internal strife, while Reformed Protestantism was continuing to work out its distinct identity and demonstrating considerable flexibility in doing so. This was indeed Frederick's experience in Heidelberg. And although Scottish and Dutch Protestants would experience circumstances less dependent on the piety of the prince, Scotland and the Netherlands would emerge along with the Palatinate as places where Reformed Protestantism's success would rival the Swiss cities' achievements. In fact, the Scottish and Dutch experiences indicate that an important factor in the establishment of a Reformed church was the capacity of ecclesiastical figures to create structures independent of the state for overseeing and determining religious affairs. Once these institutions gained stability, they became the basis from which to export Calvinism. Indeed, what Switzerland was to the first fruits of Reformed Protestantism in Europe, Scotland and the Netherlands were to Calvinism in the New World.

Kirk and Covenant

If Reformed Protestants possessed a board of advisors responsible for developing a strategic plan for advancing church reform, Scotland would not have been high on their list. The kingdom north of England was poorly populated, politically decentralized, and agriculturally impoverished. It was a place where men often attended church carrying weapons for self-defense. In addition, Scotland's rulers had close political alliances with France, a tie that predisposed the Scottish monarchy to view Protestantism with suspicion. Scotland's cultural backwardness was indeed responsible for the late arrival of Luther's writings among the Scots. Only in 1525 did authorities pass a law against Protestantism, one indication that the Reformation was becoming a live concern. Iconoclasm, another sign of Protestant presence, did not surface until 1533. Before 1560 Scotland produced only twenty-one martyrs for the Protestant faith.

   Although prospects for church reform looked grim, political developments within Scotland conspired to make Protestantism a useful tool for ambitious rulers. James V's death in 1542 inaugurated a period of monarchical instability in which the church became a pawn within a larger contest for control of the kingdom. James' immediate successor was his daughter Mary Stuart, who was only five days old at the time of the king's death. James Hamilton, second earl of Arran, emerged as the leading figure in the regency government and was responsible for opening the door to Scottish Protestantism. He legalized an English Bible and appointed two Protestant chaplains, Thomas Gwilliam and John Rough, who preached widely and gained many converts, including John Knox, who would emerge as Scotland's John Calvin. But such religious developments could not proceed independently of political maneuvering. Henry VIII in England hoped to attach Scotland to his kingdom through an arranged marriage between his son Edward and Mary Stuart. Henry's attention in turn prompted Scots to look to France as an ally to prevent England's advances. Mary of Lorraine, the queen mother, gained the ascendancy within the regency government. Consequently, church reform and evangelical preaching took a back seat to the Roman Catholic loyalty necessary to placate the French. Throughout the 1540s Scotland experienced a civil war between those who favored the patronage of the Roman Catholic French and others who looked to the Protestant English. Between 1547 and 1549, St Andrews, where John Knox became a vigorous preacher, went back and forth between Roman Catholic and Protestant control. Knox himself became a galley prisoner of French soldiers, the penalty for trying to secure St Andrews for Protestants.

Affairs of state may have restrained the initial burst of church reform during the 1540s, but those same considerations once again provided openings for Protestants. Mary of Lorraine's desire to preserve Scotland's independence was in fact crucial to the growth of Reformed Protestantism. Although the succession of Mary Tudor to the English throne in 1553 witnessed a resuscitation of Roman Catholicism – an outcome Mary of Lorraine favored on religious grounds – she opposed an alliance between England and the Habsburg dynasty through the marriage of the English queen to Philip II of Spain. When Reformed preachers began to seek refuge in Scotland during the 1550s, Mary of Lorraine recognized the advantage of the new faith to her political designs. She also needed to maintain a delicate balance within a nation that had a significant Protestant population that would have objected to her own efforts to form an alliance between Scotland and France through marriage. These conditions made possible a Protestant presence in Scotland even though the nation was still officially Roman Catholic.

Knox was one of those Protestants who returned to Scotland under conditions favorable to reform. John Willock was likely more prominent at the early stages of the Scottish Reformation than Knox, but Willock left no writings and Knox wrote the first history of Scotland's church reforms, thus insuring his fame. Knox' strategy for reform, such as it was, lacked the judiciousness and restraint that Calvin had encouraged among the Huguenots. Knox was slow to form congregations under the oversight of elders but preferred to rely on local bands of believers who covenanted together to uphold the true faith and support and defend faithful ministers. By 1559 Scotland had only seven organized Protestant congregations, and in contrast to Reformed developments in Geneva and France these Scottish churches had yet to form presbyteries or synods to insure stability and order. Knox also lacked political tact but made up for it in temerity. While ministering in Frankfurt he had already compared the emperor to Nero, and back in Scotland he directed his invectives at the Protestant queen Elizabeth of England, in his infamous *First Blast of the Trumpet against the Monstrous Regiment of Women*. Knox not only faulted the English female monarchs for restoring the Mass (Mary Tudor) but also for contradicting divine will (Mary and Elizabeth). The only solution was male rule. In other publications addressed to Scottish authorities, he even contended that if the magistrate did not comply with his (or her) divine obligation to reform the church and its worship, ordinary citizens could take matters into their own hands. Knox was capable of doing what he suggested as only a possibility for the people. In 1559 his preaching provoked iconoclastic melees at different sites. This was the sort of militancy of which Reformed leaders looking on from Geneva and Zurich disapproved.

Mary of Lorraine attempted to bring the Protestants to heel, but religious and political divisions among the nobility prevented prosecution of the evangelical faith. Mary's hand grew stronger when in 1559 her son-in-law, Francis II, succeeded to the French throne along with a sympathetic majority on the king's council. France's involvement in Scotland's affairs was not a welcome development for England, so with English assistance, Scottish nobles rose up in armed opposition, not only to oppose the designs but also the authority of Mary. They invoked the venerable liberties of the Scottish people to be protected from foreign powers, pointed out Mary's failure to consult with Scotland's nobility, and condemned her refusal to uphold the true religion and suppress idolatry. This Protestant show of force received divine blessing when Mary's attempt to respond failed to materialize. At first, storms in the winter of 1560 prevented French soldiers from reaching Scotland. By the time the weather improved, Francis II faced political difficulties within his own kingdom that made him reluctant to intervene in Scotland. And then in June of 1560 Mary of Lorraine died. Rather than defending the wishes of his mother-in-law, Francis II in July 1560 agreed to a treaty in which he would withdraw all French troops from Scotland and a select council would determine the future of Scotland's government. The religious settlement would await the next meeting of the Scottish parliament.

In August of 1560, the said parliament met and formally implemented the reformation of the Scottish church. One of the body's first acts was to abolish the Roman Catholic Mass and, in vague language, all other forms of "idolatry." Parliament adopted a confession of faith which was noticeably silent about predestination but fulsome about the duties of the civil magistrate to promote and defend the true religion. On the contentious matter of Christ's presence in the Lord's Supper, the Scots followed Geneva more than Zurich by stressing that

Christ really was present, though in a spiritual manner. The 1560 parliament also approved the First Book of Discipline as the polity responsible for ordering the church's government. The reformation of worship would await the work of the church's future assemblies.

Parliament's task in the Book of Discipline was to take charge of an existing national church rather than establish what had emerged independently as a rival to Rome. The new order did away with church institutions like monasteries and left standing only parish churches and related schools (even specifying that each parish implement a Latin and grammar school). To fund these institutions the Book of Discipline retained the system of tithes and glebe lands that were already in place for the older Roman Catholic structures. The Book of Discipline also called for the appointment of superintendents, one in each of twelve regions, to oversee the churches and ministers in their territory. This feature of the Scottish polity combined elements of episcopacy – one superintendent responsible for a given region – with a presbyterian system that granted ministers in a region the power to call their superintendent and to gather regularly and instruct each other in the correct interpretation of Scripture. Within each parish the Book of Discipline granted the congregation authority to elect its pastor, pending the approval of elders and ministers from nearby churches. Each parish also elected elders, who assisted pastors in the work of discipline.

The Scottish Book of Common Order, originally devised while Knox was ministering to other British exiles in Frankfurt, relied on Calvin's liturgical reforms in Geneva. The influence of Calvin was also evident in the publication of the Geneva Catechism in practically all editions of the Book of Common Order. The service was plain. It featured readings from Scripture, preaching, and prayer, with congregational singing punctuating worship. The Book of Common Order also provided prayers and forms for different elements of worship. Because the First Book of Discipline established a liturgical calendar based on Sunday worship services as opposed to the traditional Christian holidays, the Scottish church lacked instruction or directives for rites or ceremonies on days other than the Sunday. The Book of Discipline did encourage a regimen of daily prayers and family worship, and it specified that the Lord's Supper was to be observed quarterly (and not on Easter Sunday). With the Book of Common Order establishing a simple service and the Book of Discipline regulating the pattern of Sunday worship, the Scottish churches took a major step in overturning what many reformers regarded as the abuses and idolatry of Rome's liturgical traditions.

As pleasing as these reforms may have been to Reformed leaders, their reception in Scotland more generally was mixed. On the one hand, the church government, liturgical reforms, and disciplined clergy that Geneva's churches inspired in Scotland provided a set of mechanisms for taking Protestantism beyond political debates in parliament to the ordinary lives of parishioners. Records of sessions suggest that Reformed Protestantism provided a substantial alternative to Roman Catholicism's sacramental system of holy days, liturgical mysteries, and monastic ideals. At least in certain territories, especially among the urban populations in the region from Stirling to St Andrews (in Edinburgh rates of communion suggest a different outcome), weekly sermons (twice each Sunday), catechesis, and relief to the poor readily filled in for the evaporation of the old religious order. Especially effective were the elders' and pastors' regular meetings with parishioners to address sexual offenses, drunkenness, marital disputes, and town quarrels. These instances of church discipline replaced older forms of penance with a different method for resolving conflict and restoring fellowship. Communion seasons (quarterly), which included days of preaching services before and after the observance of the Lord's Supper, also became a ritualized manner for observing the sacrament. One last noteworthy aspect of Reformed Protestant piety was congregational singing, which featured the metrical psalter. The simplicity and repetition of tunes in the Scottish Psalter meant that one "section of the scriptures could easily be learned by heart without the need for literacy."[2] Jane E. A. Dawson even contends that psalm-singing in the vernacular and simplified forms of the Kirk, though previously associated with monastic daily worship and complex musical settings, became for the laity a "marker of a distinctly Scottish Reformed identity."[3]

On the other hand, even if church reform caught on with the laity the crown's response would continue to be decisive, as it was throughout European society. Upon her return to Scotland after trying to arrange for a second royal husband (after Francis II's death in 1560), Mary Stuart decided momentously to accept the Protestant program of church reform. Since many of the inner workings of church government, though codified, had yet to be implemented, the Scottish Reformation at the time was very much a work in progress. Mary's acceptance of Protestantism, consequently, may have been intended as only part of a negotiation process. What the queen did specify was that she retain the right to a Roman Catholic Mass wherever her court was in session. This was only the first of a series of missteps, which included her retaining a claim to the English throne (in violation of the Treaty of Edinburgh), and a contested marriage to Lord Darnley in 1565. Between 1560 and 1567 Mary managed to alienate most of the Scottish nobility and nurture the mistrust of the English. In 1567 the Scots forced her to abdicate the throne, thus prompting a period of intermittent civil war between those who supported the legitimacy of Mary's rule and the advocates of James VI, her infant son.

Mary's plight would continue for almost two decades, until her cousin Elizabeth I could no longer tolerate her schemes, but the uncertainty of royal succession in Scotland naturally affected church life. Indeed, without a strong central authority, Scotland's ensuing three-cornered struggle among leading nobles, the monarchy, and the church prevented the Scottish Reformation from achieving stability. On the one side, the Scottish church faced constant meddling from local nobles, who for their own purposes sought to control ecclesiastical revenues from benefices and property. On the other side, the crown, through its regency, looked upon the Church of England, with the supremacy of the monarch over the church and a system of episcopal hierarchy, as a model for the church in Scotland. The Scottish ministers' lone outlet for articulating and maintaining their prerogatives was the General Assembly, a body composed of the three estates in the manner of the Scottish parliament. During the period of the earl of Morton's regency (1572–78), church and crown attempted a compromise between presbyterianism and episcopacy by stipulating that the offices of bishop and archbishop in Scotland be subordinate to the Assembly. Morton, who had required that all benefice holders subscribe the Scottish Confession, was firmly in the Protestant camp. But his understanding of a reformed church owed more to a strong monarchy presiding over the church than it did to a vigorous set of ministers responsible for the spiritual health of the nation. By following Geneva's model of ecclesiastical authority over spiritual matters in a manner independent of civil government, the Scottish reformers posed a "jurisdictional rival" to the Stuart monarchy that had not been nearly so vexatious with an episcopal system. In effect, the conflict over presbyterianism and episcopacy was a debate over the degree to which the Kirk's "potential power in the realm . . . should exist independently from the crown and other reins of authority running through the kingdom."[4]

The debate over episcopacy and the monarchy's supremacy prompted the Scottish authorities to solicit advice from Geneva. Although Calvin and Beza had expressed toleration for episcopacy during England's Reformation, by the 1570s Beza had soured on bishops as part of the church's government. He explained that a parity of ministers was much better than episcopacy for the good order of the church and disapproved of bishops retaining standing within parliament. Ministers in Zurich got wind of Geneva's advice and indirectly offered a counter-proposal. Their advice favored the mixture of ecclesiastical and civil authorities within parliament as well as the king's supremacy over the church. But Geneva's recommendation prevailed and the Scottish church sought to implement the pattern of Calvin's church government. The Genevan orientation of the Scottish church was evident in the Second Book of Discipline (1578). Not only did the new form of government follow Calvin by delineating four ecclesiastical offices – pastors, doctors (teachers), elders, and deacons – but it also implemented the presbyterian structure of graded church courts, from session within the local congregation, to presbyteries for the regional churches, and synods and general assemblies at the provincial and national levels. On matters that had specifically bedeviled the Scottish church, the Second Book eliminated bishops and superintendents, while it also condemned any diversion of church revenue for non-church use.

Even as the Second Book brought Scotland into line with Geneva, it was a further fillip to Scottish politics. Parliament and the advisors to the king saw the new church government as an affront to their authority. Between 1582 and 1590, the young King James was caught between a Presbyterian faction that insisted on the church's authority to govern its own affairs, and an anti-presbyterian group that insisted upon the supremacy of the king over the church. With the assistance of Andrew Melville, the minister who succeeded Knox as the leader of the Scottish clergy, James devised a compromise that implemented much of the Second Book of Discipline while also retaining bishops (who also needed to minister within a specific parish). The compromise may not have pleased those pastors most eager for Presbyterianism, but James himself deemed the 1590 General Assembly "the sincerest Kirk in the world." Parliament in turn gave its blessing in 1592 by recognizing the power of synods and presbyteries to approve and call their own candidates for ministry (though secular patrons would still play a role in ordination and have access to church income).[5]

The politics of the Scottish Reformation succeeded in the main in establishing a Reformed church, but hurt the reform of church life at the local level. By the 1560s most of the congregations throughout Scotland were following a Protestant form of worship. But the training of Reformed clergy lagged behind significantly. By the end of the sixteenth century, only approximately half of the nation's parishes had trained clergy. Meanwhile, pockets of Roman Catholic practice remained. Consequently, while the reformation of Scotland's church put in place the bones of a Reformed church, the flesh on the skeleton was thin. Philip Benedict puts it well when he writes that the Scottish Reformation created "not an ordered, puritanical society, but a political culture in which the language of the godly magistrate, the obligation of the ruler to combat idolatry, and the pretensions of the clergy to moral guardianship over the society all gained substantial resonance."[6] This was an all-encompassing Calvinism that would inspire the descendants of Scottish Protestantism to hope for and promote a godly ruler who would carry out in the civil realm what ministers and elders undertook within the church. That the churches themselves had trouble executing the Calvinist ideals did not dissuade Presbyterians from either such optimism or sense of guardianship.

Dutch Political Independence and Modest Church Reform

The Reformation in the Netherlands was contemporaneous with the one in Scotland, but it had been building for a much longer period. Another instance of the second wave of Reformed Protestantism to wash across Europe, the Reformation in the Low Countries produced the most Protestant martyrs of any nation and demonstrated how brutal the Holy Roman Empire's religious policies could be without the buffer of strong, independent nobles. For this reason, although Protestant ideas had reached the Netherlands in the 1520s (before Geneva), the establishment of a Dutch Reformed church would have to wait for the United Provinces to establish political independence from Spanish rule. As such the Dutch Reformation was more politically disruptive and even less religiously comprehensive than Scotland's. When Luther's ideas began to circulate, the Low Countries were seventeen disparate provinces within the Holy Roman Empire under the rule of the Habsburg overlord, Charles V, a native of the Flemish city of Ghent. Charles cultivated the Netherlands as a separate political entity and a center of commercial activity. The emperor's personal attachment to the Netherlands was an important factor in the early opposition to Protestant ideas and ministers. His son, Philip II, king of Spain, gained the reputation of an absentee ruler with little sympathy for the provinces. Philip's detachment would make his religious policies against the Protestant heresy aggravating to the point of instigating political rebellion by nobles who wanted to protect legal prerogatives even more than they cared about Luther's or Calvin's ideas.

Although Protestant convictions gained a hearing among the literate and urban sectors of Netherlands society, the emperor's response was even more commanding. Luther's works received Dutch translations early and circulated much more widely in the Low Countries than in England or France. Augustinian monasteries in Antwerp and Tournai produced Protestants who as early as 1523 began to meet for instruction. Unlike other parts of the empire, Charles did not have to rely on ineffective lords or city councils to weed out heretical views; he could act directly. Between 1520 and 1545 the emperor established a highly disciplined state-run inquisition to supplement existing ecclesiastical measures to discover and punish heretics. The offending monastery in Antwerp was leveled and three of the monks accused of heresy were executed (two in 1523, the other in 1528). Part of the imperial animus against Protestantism stemmed from the popularity not only of Lutheranism but also the threat of Anabaptist politics. The result was the execution of more than 1,300 Dutch heretics between 1523 and 1566 (compared to roughly five hundred in France with nine times more inhabitants, and twenty-one in Scotland with one-third of the Netherlands' population); by 1555 the Netherlands had produced more martyrs for the Protestant cause than any other European country. Only after 1560 did persecution temporarily decline, thanks partly to widespread recognition that the system of paid informants, trials, and executions was good neither for society nor commerce. Even so, the prosecution of heretics did not deter but legitimized the Protestant cause.

The early Protestant influences were by no means uniform, and Reformed Protestantism was not dominant in the Netherlands until the 1560s. From 1521 to 1544, the total number of persons accused of harboring Protestant beliefs was 186 (160 Lutherans and 26 Anabaptists); from 1545 to 1565 the total jumped to 1,332 (989 Reformed Protestants and 343 Anabaptists).[7] John Calvin's books did not show up on the index of forbidden books until 1546, and not until 1550 was the Geneva pastor included in Charles V's edict against heresy. Anabaptism was strong in the Low Countries thanks to the leadership of Menno Simons. Other mystical or spiritual forms of Christianity – which drew upon objections to the seemingly magical and ornate nature of Roman Catholicism – also appealed to believers enduring opposition from church and political authorities. Lutheran teaching circulated widely through translations of German works into Dutch. Meanwhile, Reformed influences circulated primarily through personal contacts among reform-minded Dutch clerics and Reformed pastors in other cities. The initial input came primarily from Strasbourg, first with Martin Bucer and then with Pierre Brully, a former Dominican priest from a part of France near Luxembourg, who pastored the French-speaking congregation previously occupied by Calvin. Brully evangelized throughout regions of the Low Countries around Tournai before inquisition authorities caught and executed him. As the case of Brully indicated, the Inquisition was effective in preventing Protestantism from gaining an institutional base. But it was also very unpopular. Some trace the decline between 1530 and 1560 in the observance of Roman Catholic practices, such as indulgences and pilgrimages, to the people's opposition to inquisitorial measures.

By the 1550s, when Charles abdicated his rule and transferred power to Philip (1555), the center of Reformed strength was in the southern Low Countries, particularly the provinces of Brabant, Hainaut, Walloon Flanders, and Zeeland. Only in the 1560s would the northern provinces become Calvinist strongholds, thanks in part to the migration of Dutch and French Protestant refugees to religiously tolerant territories. In the middle of the 1550s, Antwerp in the province of Brabant became home to several Reformed congregations. To escape detection many of these churches divided followers into units of eight to twelve members, with each group assigned particular times to attend preaching services led by ministers who were often in town only to conduct the service before returning to a safe place (most likely Emden). Within a decade, sixteen congregations had been formed, including the cities of Tournai (Flanders) and Valenciennes (Hainaut). Thanks to the persecution of the Huguenots in France, these Dutch congregations included French refugees who gave a strong French Protestant flavor to the emerging Dutch Calvinist identity. And much like the Protestants in France, Calvinists in the Low Countries would depend initially on itinerant preachers and clandestine congregations.

Giving a measure of coherence to these piecemeal efforts was Guy de Bray, a native of Mons (in the south of the Spanish Netherlands), who took the lead in establishing churches near Tournai. He had studied at Geneva and Lausanne between 1557 and 1558. De Bray produced a confession of faith for the Low Countries that relied heavily on the French Confession of Faith (1559). After receiving approval from other ministers, the creed, known as the Belgic Confession, was published first in French (1561) and then Dutch (1562). This was another effective statement of Reformed convictions and in its comparative brevity represented trends among sixteenth-century churches to arrive at relatively simple affirmations of faith, such as Belgic's Second Article, on "the means by which we know God":

We know him by two means:

First, by the creation, preservation, and government of the universe, since that universe is before our eyes like a beautiful book in which all creatures, great and small, are as letters to make us ponder the invisible things of God: his eternal power and his divinity, as the apostle Paul says in Romans 1:20.

All these things are enough to convict men and to leave them without excuse.

Second, he makes himself known to us more openly by his holy and divine Word, as much as we need in this life, for his glory and for the salvation of his own.

A further indication of solidarity and organizational presence among the Dutch Reformed came in 1563 with efforts by Antwerp church leaders, following the French again, to form synods that would oversee congregations. Oversight included requiring church members to subscribe the Belgic Confession.

Whatever strides the Reformed churches may have made thanks to lesser nobles who looked the other way or to the influx of Huguenots, the cause of ecclesiastical reform was difficult to spot during the 1560s as the Spanish Inquisition grew increasingly unpopular. Opposition to Spain's tactics was not the same as ecclesiastical reform. Executions of heretics began to spark riots in the late 1550s. Then leading members of the Council of State – among them William of Orange – called for moderation. The king's plans for new bishoprics in 1561, with Antoine Perrenot (Cardinal de Granvelle) at the top of the hierarchy in the newly created diocese of Mechelen, suggested a refusal by Philip to hear from his nobles. Even so, persistent maneuvering by the Dutch nobility, along with periodic episodes of iconoclasm, forced Granevlle's withdrawal in 1564. At this point, religious motivations rivaled political frustrations. Protestant preachers circulated widely in open-air meetings, adherents who gathered sang psalms, and hearers were encouraged to compare what they heard to the actual contents of Scripture. One contemporary observed that only four or five sermons were sufficient to change views held for almost four decades.[8]

Under pressure, in early 1566 Margaret of Parma, Philip's sister and regent in the Low Countries, negotiated the Compromise of the Nobility with Dutch lesser rulers (roughly 300 in all), a petition to the king that called for moderation of the Inquisition. Philip refused. The king's decision was a major factor in the iconoclastic riots that broke out in August of 1566. Some of this destruction of statues, images, and structures was spontaneous, some orchestrated by Reformed pastors and local nobles. In west Flanders alone rioters sacked 400 churches and convents. Margaret made further concessions and granted freedom of worship to Protestants in areas where it was already taking place but nowhere else. Although many Protestants and ruling elites mistrusted the government's new policy, it did allow for full worship by Reformed Protestants (and some Lutherans) in Antwerp, Tournai, and Ghent.

A situation fraught with uncertainty and peril prompted Philip to act decisively by sending Don Fernando Álvarez, duke of Alba, to the Netherlands to quiet the turmoil. According to Geoffrey Parker, this decision was a "Rubicon" for Spanish imperialism and a turning point in European history.[9] Before Alba arrived in the summer of 1567 – marching over ten thousand Spanish soldiers from Lombardy to the Netherlands in a politically contested Europe was no easy feat – Margaret had managed to regain control through an aggressive military campaign in December of 1566. In this warfare, Reformed pastors and consistories raised funds to pay soldiers who fought the government's army. Rebel forces were significantly outnumbered. By April of 1567 the Spanish government had ousted Reformed pastors and their fighters from the southern Low Countries. Reformed worship ceased and the pastors responsible for the services either fled for safety or lost their lives. The latter was the fate of Guy de Bray, the preacher at Valenciennes, a town that fell in 1567; he was executed for proclaiming the Reformed faith as publicly as he had when he wrote a confession of Protestant faith addressed to Philip.

Although Margaret informed Philip that Alba's troops were no longer needed, the duke had already begun the journey and could not be called off. In August, when Alba arrived in the Netherlands and informed Margaret of his mission to pacify the territory, the regent resigned her post. From here it was a short route to Alba's iron-fisted policies. Most notable was the establishment of the Council of Troubles, a tribunal designed to ferret out all rebels and anyone who had given them aid. The Council tried over twelve thousand people, nine thousand of whom lost either some or all of their property. Over one thousand were executed for treason. Under these conditions, the Reformed churches reverted to clandestine practices. They maintained solidarity through synods that met outside the Netherlands in nearby Germany at the cities of Emden and Wesel. When the 1571 synod convened, it calculated that twenty-eight fugitive Dutch Reformed churches were gathered in Germany and England, while sixteen congregations persisted under the threat of persecution.

William of Orange (1533–84) had by now emerged as the leader of Dutch opposition and the prince in whom Protestants hoped. Those hopes were not uniform since William, a Lutheran in upbringing, had converted to Roman Catholicism upon taking up political duties in the Low Countries. But his opposition to Spanish rule was consistent and based on a defense of the traditional rights of nobles. To avoid Alba's muscle, William went into exile but did so to gear up for a counter-attack. In 1568 the prince invaded but Alba's forces turned back the rebels. William spent the next several years trying to raise military support for another attack. In 1572 he rallied again. Despite the failure of Huguenots to assist thanks to the Saint Bartholomew's Day Massacre, this time the prince was successful. In addition to William's army, the so-called Sea Beggars, a body of Dutch pirates whose business was to raid Spanish merchant ships in the English Channel, contributed another layer to the rebellion. The Beggars had planned to stock up at the Spanish garrison in the town of Brill. But when they found no Spaniards there and experienced a welcome reception from the city's inhabitants, the Beggars decided to change course and liberate nearby towns. They were successful in all of the provinces' cities except for Amsterdam, Middelburg, and Goes. In July, the provinces of Holland, Zeeland, and Frisia appointed William the general governor and lieutenant king over Holland. Alba rebuffed the prince temporarily but by October William had returned with reinforcements to defend his lands and repel the Spanish.

The existence of the new independent political entity in the Low Countries was tentative at best. William had tried to consolidate power throughout the Low Countries, with a policy of toleration for both Roman Catholics and Protestants. But Calvinist leaders objected and the policy foundered. In the provinces of Holland and Zeeland in particular, authorities replaced Roman Catholic priests with Reformed pastors, even though the majority of the population was Roman Catholic. Reformed aggression was also on display when Holland and Zeeland took the lead in the Union of Utrecht (1579), a treaty that bound together as one province the states of Holland, Zeeland, Utrecht, Frisia, Gelderland, and the Ommelanden and that prohibited Roman Catholicism. With Rome banned in the new union, ruling nobles in the southern provinces

Walloon Flanders, Hainaut, and Artois turned to the Spanish for support through the Union of Arras (1579). The emerging wedge between the Protestant Dutch Republic and the Roman Catholic southern provinces provided a platform for Alessandro Farnese, the duke of Parma, to try to reconquer the Low Countries. In 1583 the United Provinces lost the leadership of William of Orange to an assassin. By 1589 the duke had reconquered most of the southern Netherlands and had even successfully retaken the entire eastern half of the United Provinces, going as far north as Groningen. The future of Dutch independence looked bleak as did the hopes for a Reformed church. Dutch nobles looked unsuccessfully to Henry III in France and Elizabeth in England to support the United Provinces in the capacity of a protectorate. Despite its fragility the Dutch Republic survived and by 1594 had recovered most of the territory lost to Parma. Conflict with Spain came to end in 1609 with the Twelve Years' Truce, at which point the Spanish formally recognized the Dutch Republic.

Through the warfare and political maneuvering of an independent Dutch state, support for Protestantism was mixed and unreliable, making the establishment of a Reformed church almost as difficult as resisting Alba. Participation in Reformed services was small at the outset of the rebellion, and would remain so even after Dutch independence. But animosity to Spanish rule and the Roman Catholic establishment ran so deep that the provinces' initial policy of toleration for Protestants and Roman Catholics drew strong opposition from many Dutch who desired an outright ban on Roman Catholicism. In 1573 the United Provinces turned over the parishes to Reformed congregations with provisions for Protestant ministers to receive support from ecclesiastical revenues. This was the same year that William of Orange joined a Reformed congregation.

Reformed ministers may have been encouraged by these developments but they were still powerless to implement the reforms that many had experienced as refugees, whether in Germany or Geneva. The 1574 Synod of Dort's decision to empower consistories and classes (the Reformed version of the presbyterians' sessions and presbyteries) to call and ordain ministers was not popular with the laity or local elites, many of whom did not resonate with the spare contours of Reformed worship, or wanted input if not power in the selection of a pastor. An additional wrinkle for the Dutch churches was the disagreement among ministers about the power of church assemblies. Several controversies bedeviled the Dutch churches during the 1570s and 1580s, stemming from recalcitrant ministers who refused to comply with the Synod's directives.

The Dutch Reformed churches reached a novel form of compromise to adjust ministers' expectations to the realities of a population and ruling class that was hardly enthusiastic about Calvinism. At first, the Dutch Republic tried to appropriate the Reformed churches as the national church, a civic institution that included all citizens. In 1574 its religious policy stipulated that church consistories needed the approval of town councils or provincial assemblies for their affairs. In 1576 the proposed church order allowed for all citizens to participate in the Lord's Supper whenever it was administered (four times each year). But church leaders, partly through the influence of Geneva and the Huguenots, balked at the ideal of including indifferent or unbelieving persons in the sacrament. They argued that church discipline should restrict participation to those who adhered to the Reformed faith. The way through the impasse between a civic church and a disciplined congregation was to sever the public and private aspects of church membership. The resulting Dutch religious policy would allow the Reformed churches to maintain high levels of ecclesiastical discipline, but limit their spiritual authority to persons who qualified as church members. At the same time, no law would require church attendance, and citizens wanting to marry could opt for either a church ceremony or a civil observance. In effect, the Dutch Reformed church's membership was a subset of the Dutch Republic's population. In fact, between 1580 and 1600 church membership in some locales was no more than 10 percent of the population.

This arrangement gave citizens the option of attending church without being under the oversight and discipline of the pastor and elders. In 1579, for instance, of Leiden's twenty-eight magistrates, only five were full members of the church. The situation, as Philip Benedict observes, cultivated a "brand of personal Christianity that did not include regular observance [at church] of any form."[10] It also generated creative approaches to include all citizens under the umbrella of the church, such as one attempted in 1578 by the Utrecht pastor, Hubert Duifhuis. With the approval of the city's magistrates, Duifhuis admitted into full communion everyone who desired to be. He also decided to remove any obstacles that might prevent people from joining the church. His ministry included no body of elders (consistory) and no catechism. Duifhuis' practice did not escape the notice of Reformed ministers who appealed to church authorities to intervene and remedy the novel and flawed situation in Utrecht. The controversy over Duifhuis precipitated a division among the local ministers between the Reformed of the consistory (anti-Duifhuis) and the preachers of the Old and New Testaments (pro-Duifhuis).

The Duifhuis conflict, which simmered for a generation, was a reflection of the Reformed churches' ambiguous status within Dutch society. On the one hand, the theocratic option of a church stipulating religious policy was impolitic, since anti-Catholicism, which many Reformed ministers would have supported, could revive Spanish military aggression. On the other hand, an Erastian arrangement where civil authorities defined the church's function was unworkable since Reformed pastors were effective in using ecclesiastical assemblies to get rid of latitudinarian ministers favored by the ruling class. The result was an awkward entente in which church and state recognized each other as valuable allies while refusing to give ground on disputed matters.

Odd though it was, compared to the Spanish Netherlands, the original site for Calvinist strength in the Low Countries where Reformed Protestantism was prohibited, the Dutch Reformed churches looked as vigorous and resilient as Geneva under Calvin. The limits of reform in the Dutch republic may have been frustrating but, like Puritanism in England, it yielded a productive tension that made Dutch Calvinism one of the most dynamic centers of Reformed convictions. Zeal for reform fueled later efforts among Dutch Protestants and their cousins overseas to complete what the Low Countries had begun when establishing political and ecclesiastical independence.

The other German Reformation

Although the Germanic portions of the Holy Roman Empire where Protestantism succeeded were generally Lutheran, during the second half of the sixteenth century, as the Reformation spread, Reformed Protestantism also took root in German-speaking territories and developed some of its strongest advocates. An important factor in the growth of Reformed Protestantism within the area of Lutheranism's greatest influence was controversy among Lutherans themselves. From the 1550s until the adoption of the Formula of Concord in 1577 Lutherans feuded from within two camps: the Philippists (after Philip Melanchthon) and the gnesio-Lutherans. The former adapted many of humanism's insights to give Lutheran piety a strong sense of personal holiness and moral zeal. Gnesio-Lutherans stressed following Luther, especially on the nature of Christ's presence in the Lord's Supper and the Christological doctrines that supported the real presence. Because of the friendship between Melanchthon and Calvin, and owing to Melanchthon's willingness to regard Christ's presence in the sacrament as largely spiritual, gnesio-Lutherans accused Philippists of crypto-Calvinism. In the 1550s and early 1560s Lutherans engaged in a heated dispute over the Lord's Supper. Then during the 1570s, leading up to the Formula of Concord, the elector of Saxony imprisoned leading Philippists for harboring heretical views; not helping the Philippist defense was a fairly extensive correspondence between the Philippists and Reformed pastors in Geneva and Heidelberg. To celebrate the victory over heresy, the elector of Saxony hung Calvin publicly in effigy.

The harsh treatment of Reformed Protestantism as well as the sometimes brutal regime of Lutheran orthodoxy had the effect of turning Reformed Protestantism into the faith of the underdog within the empire. As debates so often do, the controversy also unintentionally popularized the teachings of the

Reformed. For Protestant Germans, most specifically princes who either had hoped for a consensus between Lutherans and Reformed, or who had assisted the armed conflicts of Protestants in France or the Low Countries, the Reformed faith was a worthy cause and became a local option. Part of the reason stemmed from the Reformed presence that had existed from the earliest days of the Reformation. The imperial city of Strasbourg was one of the first sites for Reformed Protestantism to blossom. Although the city's church would become Lutheran, it retained a Reformed presence at least through the efforts of individuals. Other cities within the empire also demonstrated a Reformed influence: Alsace looked to Basel during the 1570s for assistance in reforming the church; Bremen went back and forth during the second half of the sixteenth century between Reformed and Lutheran dominance; Jülich, Cleves, and Berg, locations lower on the Rhine near the Netherlands, with ties to Emden, a German Reformed stronghold, were also receptive to Reformed teaching and practice.

One of the more notable sites in the northern portion of the empire near the Low Countries to welcome Reformed Protestantism was the territory of Nassau-Dillenburg, which did so during the 1560s and 1570s under the rule of Count John VI. A significant influence on John was the assistance he gave to his older brother, William of Orange, in resisting Spanish tyranny in the Netherlands. Prior to the conflicts of the 1560s, John had a general disdain for Reformed Protestants, but his experience in the Low Countries prompted him to see these believers as persecuted, in need of assistance, and possessing an admirable faith. During the 1570s John looked for ways to introduce Reformed Protestantism within his territory. The reforms were minor at first; they involved small adjustments to the celebration of the Lord's Supper, a doctrinal testimony that accommodated predestination and affirmed the Augsburg Confession as long as it agreed with "the confessions of the other evangelical reformed churches outside Germany," and a system of church government modeled on the presbyterian system that had developed in France.[11] By 1581 the territories of Nassau-Dillenburg, Wittgenstein, Solms-Braunfels, and Wied, under John's encouragement and instruction, had adopted the rudiments of a Reformed church. The changes in church life were unpopular at the parish level, but John continued his support. In fact, he lent important assistance to the Reformed cause and provided a place for Calvinist refugees from other territories in Germany under threat from Lutheran reprisal.

One of the regions to produce Reformed exiles was the Palatinate, originally the most important expression of Reformed Protestantism within the German-speaking territories of the empire. During the 1560s, Frederick III, the elector of the Palatinate, was successful in withstanding Lutheran pressure to conform and oversaw the consolidation of a Reformed church order and system of instruction. His appearance before the Lutheran imperial diet in 1566 to answer for his religious views was, in fact, a significant factor in establishing a pan-Reformed identity across Europe. Not only did Reformed church leaders from Switzerland, England, France, and the Netherlands send letters of support; but to bolster Frederick's case, Heinrich Bullinger reproduced a confession he had originally written for the Swiss Protestant cities, the Second Helvetic Confession, to give creedal solidarity to Reformed churches as far and wide as Poland, Scotland, France, and Switzerland.

As initially encouraging to other Reformed churches as Frederick was, his reforms ran into two obstacles that revealed the flaws of a prince-led church. The first was a major controversy over the rival claims of church power and state authority in the work of ecclesiastical discipline (specifically excommunication). This controversy was essentially a contest between the Geneva system, which granted the church autonomy in exercising discipline, and the pattern in Zurich, where a joint body consisting of city and church officials was responsible for excommunication. In 1568 a student from England, George Withers, had proposed for debate at the University of Heidelberg a thesis asserting that the power of excommunication was necessary for a church to be legitimate. Taking the opposing view was a professor of medicine, Thomas Erastus, who also served in a lay capacity within the Reformed church at Heidelberg. A year later Erastus produced the *Explanation of the Weighty Questions Concerning Excommunication*, in which he argued for state control of the church (including the duties of church discipline). At the theoretical level he regarded the possibility of two heads within one body as recipe for disorder and saw the potential for ecclesiastical tyranny within a system that granted the church powers of excommunication. Erastus also had concrete reasons for his position. In a city where only 30 percent of the population was qualified to receive communion, the church as separate agency of discipline could easily create two classes of citizens.

The controversy over discipline had repercussions for the Reformed churches throughout Europe, but was particularly revealing of the long-standing differences between Zurich and Geneva. These cities' respective theologians weighed in on the debate in Heidelberg, with Bullinger (Zurich) supporting Erastus' position and Beza (Geneva) providing a refutation. Heidelberg's authorities were evenly split on the matter, and the disagreement was so intense that the advocates of the Geneva position considered banning Bullinger's *Treatise on Excommunication* from the Palatinate. Yet, as heated and revealing as the Heidelberg controversy was, the idea of state control of the church became synonymous with Erastus (i.e. Erastianism) because cooler heads within the Swiss churches did not want an open breach between the oldest cities of Reformed Protestantism.

Frederick himself found the position of church responsibility for discipline more compelling than Erastus' argument. The church order implemented after 1570 was a compromise but leaned toward church control. Each congregation would have a body of elders responsible for disciplining members. The consistory could meet privately with wayward Christians, and should the desired reform of personal conduct and attitude of remorse not surface, the elders could suspend church members from the Lord's Supper. If the offender still proved recalcitrant, then the church would hand over the disobedient member to the city council, which had the power to excommunicate. The aim was not simply the reform of church members' lives. The church order also called for regular meetings of ministers, grouped regionally, for mutual encouragement and critique.

Frederick may have successfully introduced Reformed Protestantism into the Palatinate, but he was less successful with his family. His oldest son, Ludwig, was already a professing Lutheran when Frederick determined to join the Reformed effort. Ludwig never renounced his Lutheran convictions, and when he succeeded Frederick as elector in 1576, after his father's death, the son reinstated Lutheranism in Heidelberg, a process that meant a complete overhaul of the clergy and university professors. Among the theologians at Heidelberg who had to find new university positions were Zacharias Ursinus and Girolamo Zanchi, who both relocated to the university at Neustadt an der Weinstrasse under the patronage of John Casimir, Frederick III's third son. Ludwig's efforts did not last, and in 1583 when Frederick IV succeeded him as elector, John Casimir appointed Reformed advisors to serve the young ruler, which in turn led to the restoration of Reformed church order in Heidelberg and the Palatinate.

Although the Palatinate and Nassau-Dillenburg would become the most important centers of Reformed Protestantism within the German-speaking portions of the empire, the faith and practice started in the cities of Switzerland would find other outlets over the course of the sixteenth century. Especially after 1580, religious and political factors prompted German princes to embrace Reformed Protestantism. The proposed Formula of Concord by Lutherans, along with another round of harsh treatment by Lutherans of the Reformed church, pushed some rulers away from Lutheran orthodoxy and its sometimes heavy-handed tactics. Meanwhile, Roman Catholic military threats to Protestants both within and outside the empire were a catalyst for princes to form alliances with Reformed Protestants, and to implement appropriate reforms in church life to reinforce those coalitions. In Saxony in 1586, for instance, a young prince of Reformed inclinations, Christian I, assumed the throne and subsequently conducted a series of personnel changes in the churches and university that saw Reformed Protestants and Philippists replace staunch Lutherans. Christian also forged an alliance with the Palatinate, Brandenburg, Hesse, and Anhalt to support Huguenots and encourage the new French Protestant monarch, Henry of Navarre (IV).

Saxony's status as a stronghold of Reformed Protestantism was short-lived thanks to the premature death of Christian in 1591, but the Protestant alternative to Lutheranism made additional inroads within the empire. Among the territories to enter the alliance to aid the Reformed cause in France, Anhalt and Hesse implemented significant reforms. In the former, John George I introduced liturgical changes such as eliminating exorcism from the baptismal rite, which culminated in the 1596 reforms that included the elimination of images, and the adoption of the Heidelberg Catechism and liturgy used by Reformed Protestants in the Palatinate. In Hesse, the elector Maurice came to Reformed convictions through conflict with Roman Catholic Spain and a marriage to Juliana of Nassau. In 1604 he introduced reforms similar to those of Anhalt: the elimination of images and the use of the Heidelberg Catechism. Around this time further changes of a Reformed flavor took place in the small territories of Bentheim-Steinfurt-Tecklenburg, Zweibrücken, and Lippe. For similar reasons, having to do with political alliances against Roman Catholic rulers and resentment of orthodox Lutheran tactics, rulers in these regions introduced measures that leaned toward the Reformed side of the Reformation.

By the second decade of the seventeenth century, the spread of Reformed Protestantism within the empire had stopped. The territory of Brandenburg exemplified the factors that ended Reformed influence. John Sigismund, elector of Brandenburg from 1608 to 1619, as a young man found the Reformed faith to be more plausible than Lutheranism, at least on the Lord's Supper; he then discovered the politics of the Lutheran princes to be despotic, thus encouraging his affinity for the Reformed. When he ascended to the position of elector, he surrounded himself with Reformed political and ecclesiastical advisors and planned the reform of his churches. John's directions followed the pattern of other Reformed churches in the German-speaking territories: changes in the observance of baptism and the Lord's Supper; a new form of church government; and the replacement of Lutheran faculty at the university with Reformed professors. But as was also true elsewhere in the empire, the changes met with popular opposition. In 1615 an attempt to eliminate idolatrous aspects from the Berlin cathedral's furnishings led to a Lutheran minister renouncing the reform and a subsequent uprising in support of the Lutheran protest. At one point the crowd yelled at a city official, "You damn black Calvinist, you have stolen our pictures and destroyed our crucifixes; now we will get even with you and your Calvinist priests!"[12] The rocks that accompanied this rant were likely more intimidating than the religious slur but the point was well taken. Soon the estates of Brandenburg produced a compromise with John that granted tolerance for Lutherans and barred the elector from arrogating "to himself dominion over consciences" or imposing "any suspect or unwelcome preachers on anyone," even in places where he had the right of patronage.[13] What had happened by the early seventeenth century, as this incident in Berlin suggests, was that the people had become so accustomed to the first stages of church reform that they objected to further disruptions of their received (even if recent) religious ways.

By 1620, after Reformed Protestantism had run its course in the empire, Lutheranism was by far the larger Protestant presence among German speakers but the Reformed churches had done remarkably well in the land of Luther. Twelve state churches in different territories within the empire, led by the conversion of princes, were Reformed. Five imperial cities – Emden, Bremen, Wesel, Mulhouse, and Colmar (Lutheran and Reformed) – had also instituted ecclesiastical practices patterned on the Reformed churches. Aside from these state-approved reforms, Reformed Protestantism also found outlets in a number of small congregations throughout the empire, and some formed associations in territories that tolerated both Lutherans and Reformed Protestants. The estimated population of Reformed Protestants at the beginning of the seventeenth century was one million (out of a total population of sixteen million). At the upper echelons of imperial politics, two of the seven electors were adherents of the Reformed faith. In the halls of learning the Reformed accounted for four of the empire's twenty-six universities: Heidelberg, Frankfurt, Marburg, and Herborn.

The appeal of Reformed Protestantism to German speakers, however impressive, was also constrained by imperial politics. Unlike Scotland or the Netherlands where church reforms were part of an emerging national consciousness, in the empire the blend of imperial and local princely rule contained Reformed Protestantism to areas or cities that depended on the patronage of an elector. As such, Reformed churches developed in relatively isolated pockets and often had their own regional character. If German Reformed churches did achieve a uniform identity it was more the case before 1585 than after. Prior to the 1580s, as happened in the Palatinate, Reformed Protestants included the structures and justification for church government that characterized Reformed churches among the French, Scottish, and Dutch. After 1585, however, the extent of church reform within the empire involved mainly liturgical modifications and the adoption of the Heidelberg Catechism. Nowhere among the German Reformed did the commitment to a reformation of manners and civic life emerge the way it did in Zurich, Geneva, Scotland, and England. The loose nature of German Reformed church life would be an important factor in the way that these Protestants would carry their faith to the New World. German

Calvinism would not yield the busybodies that Scottish Presbyterianism and Dutch Calvinism produced. The Germans were sober, diligent, resilient, and content to let others experience the headaches and excitements that came with running things.

Weak Strongholds

The institution of Reformed churches in German-speaking portions of the Holy Roman Empire outside Switzerland testified to the appeal of a wing of Protestantism initiated in Zurich. After the initial wave of church reform in Wittenberg and Zurich, Protestantism became a lively cause throughout Europe, from the British Isles to Transylvania. In fact, during the 1550s and 1560s a so-called Second Reformation began to play out in places such as Scotland, the Netherlands and the Palatinate. In most cases, the second phase of reformation depended on energy supplied by church models and teaching originated not by Lutherans but Reformed Protestants. Aside from the religious appeal of Reformed faith and practice, political factors were significant. As was true in Switzerland, France, England, and Poland, the post-1550 round of church reforms depended on political circumstances, where magistrates or ruling bodies emerged as patrons of the changes that Reformed Protestants proposed and implemented.

As obvious as this political dimension of Reformed Protestantism's success may be, given the realities of a European society in which religion and politics were intimately intertwined, the Reformed faith offered a political theology that could readily justify the decisions of pious magistrates. On the one hand, Reformed Protestantism prompted a zeal for reform that refused compromise with the perceived idolatry and errors of Rome, thus motivating church leaders and nobility to resist rulers who were hostile to the new faith. On the other hand, even while implicitly endorsing political resistance – and in some cases, revolution – the Reformed version of Protestantism, especially as practiced in Zurich, supplied a rationale for rulers to exert control over the church in the appointment of clergy and the act of excommunication. Meanwhile, the Reformed understanding of church government through the rule of pastors and elders and a series of ecclesiastical assemblies linked churches not only within a nation but also throughout Europe. These networks in turn informed the foreign policy decisions of Protestant monarchs and nobles, who often rallied to the side of another Protestant ruler who was facing political opposition. In sum, the Reformed churches would be the strongest not simply where their existence was bound up with political resistance. They also developed ecclesiastical structures that generated stability and coherence within the churches themselves.

These institutional forms insured that Reformed Protestantism would not be a momentary phenomenon but a form of Christianity that could endure and multiply.

For that reason, as insignificant as the reformations in Scotland, the Netherlands, and the Palatinate seemed compared to the glories of emperor and pope, those Reformed churches would turn out to be remarkably consequential for the future of the faith launched in Switzerland. In fact, the Scottish, Dutch, and German expressions of Reformed Protestantism would be the most influential in Calvinism's growing global presence. During the seventeenth, eighteenth, and nineteenth centuries, these varieties of Calvinism would become the chief exporters of Reformed Protestantism to lands outside Europe. Through colonialism, immigration, or foreign missions, the Scots, Dutch, and Germans would be decisive in establishing patterns and orders for Reformed churches in other parts of the world. The irony, perhaps, is that the Swiss churches of Zurich and Geneva, the original Reformed communions, would have little direct influence on the character of Reformed churches in other societies. But since the reforms in Scotland, the Netherlands, and the Palatinate could not have happened without the spadework of Zwingli or Calvin, the expansion of Reformed Protestantism globally would always have Swiss fingerprints. That Calvinism would succeed in relatively weak nations was indicative of the difficulty involved in overturning the established ways of a powerful kingdom or empire.

CHAPTER FOUR

SHAKING THE FOUNDATIONS

THE ORIGINS OF THE earliest Reformed churches defied a general pattern. Individual clergy came to Protestant convictions through circuitous routes, members of city councils calculated the spiritual, political, and economic benefits of reform, and the combined efforts of clergy and magistrates produced reformations that bore the imprint of local settings. To be sure, Luther's struggle with Rome and the reforms promoted by humanists functioned as banks to channel the surging waters of reform. But the idiosyncratic character of Reformed Protestantism's beginnings meant that new churches lacked common characteristics that could identify them, at least initially, as a distinct version of Christianity. Ironically, the very political circumstances that could have ended reform also required Protestant ministers to explain their efforts to magistrates, kings, and emperors in ways that would supply the coherence that the diversity of local settings could not.

The Tetrapolitan Confession (1530) was one of the earliest Reformed declarations of a Protestant identity distinct from Lutheranism. Its very name indicated that it was the statement of faith for four cities – Strasbourg, Canstance, Memmingen, and Lindau, all of them imperial – in preparation for the 1530 meeting of the Imperial Diet of Augsburg. Unlike prior Reformed statements, such as Zwingli's Sixty-Seven Articles, or the Ten Theses of Bern, the Tetrapolitan Confession spoke for a set of churches beyond one location, and hence achieved a working theological, liturgical, and ecclesial consensus. The particular occasion for this confession written primarily by Martin Bucer along with Wolfgang Capito – both from Strasbourg – was the need to arrive at a Protestant alternative to the Lutheran position affirmed in the Augsburg Confession (also prepared for the approaching imperial diet). For this gathering of Germany's rulers, Zwingli also prepared a separate statement. The pastors of the four imperial cities were not satisfied with either Lutheran or Zwinglian teaching and so proposed their own.

Although the members of the diet rejected both Zwingli's statement and the Tetrapolitan Confession, and even though the four cities responsible for the latter would be forced in 1531 to adopt the Augsburg Confession, these Reformed cities produced the first confession to speak for multiple locations that was Protestant but not Lutheran. As such, the Tetrapolitan Confession articulated themes that were foundational to Reformed Protestantism. At the heart of these concerns was a new understanding of the sufficiency of Christ for salvation, which in turn elevated Scripture alone as the rule for faith.

One of the apparently most unusual aspects of the Tetrapolitan Confession was the devotion of four chapters – out of a total of twenty-two – to the question of food. Of course, the Reformation in Zurich had begun with the consumption of sausage on a Friday during Lent as an act of defiance against Rome's prescription of fasts and holy days. Observers of Protestantism might have chalked up such activity to immaturity or foolish zeal. Instead, that consumption of meat was a principle that captured one of Reformed Protestantism's chief features, namely, that the church could only require of Christians not what pious clerics thought best but what Scripture itself required. In a chapter devoted to "The Choice of Meats" the Tetrapolitan Confession appealed to the teaching of the apostle Paul, who condemned those in the early church who insisted on abstaining from meat offered to idols. According to Paul, such teaching was the doctrine of demons, because it denied the goodness of everything God had created and granted a power to the church – to bind consciences – that belonged only to God (Art. 9). As the Tetrapolitan Confession testified in its chapter on "The Commanding of Fasts," churchmen went beyond Scripture in commanding abstinence from certain foods on specified days. In turn, the effort of reformation was to free the "necks" of Christians from these "snares" (Art. 8). Reformed Protestants were not opposed to fasts per se. In fact, the confession complained that Rome's fasts were superficial in teaching abstinence from a specified list of foods rather than teaching the value of "chastising the flesh" by denying all "dainties" for a time (Art. 9). Still, fasting could not merit salvation. "We must fast, that we may the better pray and keep the flesh within duty, not that we may deserve anything for ourselves before God" (Art.10).

By the time Reformed pastors felt compelled (primarily by politics) to draft another statement, justifications for sausage were absent but food was still important, particularly the characteristics of the bread and wine at the Lord's Supper. Geneva and Zurich maintained at times an uneasy alliance owing to different emphases regarding the nature of Christ's presence in the sacrament.[1] In 1549 the churches of Zurich and Geneva wrote the Consensus Tigurinus to overcome disputes about the Lord's Supper. The occasion was Calvin's own effort, along with Bucer, to secure a working agreement among Reformed and

Lutherans. Lutherans themselves were divided between the gnesio-Lutherans (following Luther) and the Philippists (following Melanchthon). By the mid-1530s Luther and Melanchthon had been able to come to terms, and because Reformed ministers such as Calvin and Bucer had been cordial with Melanchthon, the hope was to overcome the differences between Zwingli and Luther. Ministers in Zurich, however, were leery of Geneva's overtures to the Lutherans. For the sake of maintaining solidarity among the Swiss, Calvin went to Zurich in 1549 to write the Consensus Tigurinus with Heinrich Bullinger's input and approval. It eventually received affirmation from the churches at Bern.

The document was devoted almost exclusively to the Lord's Supper. Of the twenty-six articles, all but the last six addressed a general framework for understanding the nature and purpose of both baptism and the Lord's Supper. True to its name, the Consensus came with compromises on each side. It was flexible enough to allow for Geneva's teaching about a physical eating of a spiritual reality through faith by the operation of the Holy Spirit. It also permitted Zurich's contention that the spiritual reality of the Lord's Supper was more (or less) independent of the physical elements. Even if rapprochement depended more on the physical text than on the spirit behind the words, the Consensus was important for outlining a sacramental theology that was distinct from both Rome's and Wittenberg's.

Zurich was at the center of another effort to arrive at a Reformed consensus only a few years after Calvin's passing (1564). This time the creed that emerged was the Second Helvetic Confession (1566), Bullinger's statement of faith from the early 1560s that he intended for Zurich's city council to use as his will (a plague was threatening the city at the time). Within five years, having survived the plague, Bullinger sent the Confession to Frederick III of the Palatinate to explain to the rest of Germany's electors the nature of the Christianity that was taking root in Heidelberg. The Second Helvetic also circulated to other Reformed churches throughout Europe and gained their approval. Given its wide reading and approval, the Second Helvetic Confession was the "most authoritative statement" of Reformed Protestantism for the second generation of reformers.[2] It also became the standard theological basis for ordination among the Swiss Protestant churches.

Although the Reformation's political uncertainties were still pressing, the Second Helvetic Confession used less space than previous creeds to explain differences to confused and alarmed magistrates. Instead, it summarized positively and comprehensively the teaching, worship, and polity of Reformed Protestants. For all of its positive content, the Second Helvetic Confession was not silent on the practices and underlying theories that had prompted opposition to Rome. It devoted a chapter to prayer, which included congregational singing, public prayers, and canonical hours. Earlier objections to Rome's requirements on fasting also received a separate chapter that identified Sunday as the holy day and rejected Rome's church calendar. These Reformed convictions looked less antagonistic than earlier creedal formulas, however, because they ran alongside other chapters on practical religious duties, such as catechesis, comforting the sick, adiaphra (i.e. matters not governed by Scripture), church property, human sexuality (marriage and celibacy), and the duty of the magistrate. Neither was the Confession silent on the contested matter of Christ's presence in the Lord's Supper. Here Bullinger softened the most objectionable (to Luther) features of Zwingli and almost came round to Geneva's position.

The last of the sixteenth century's comprehensive efforts to define the boundaries of Reformed Protestantism was the Harmony of Confessions, published in 1581 in Geneva. The occasion was a gathering of Reformed leaders from France, Hungary, Poland, and the Netherlands, called in 1577 by John Casimir of the Palatinate and Wilhelm of Hesse. Initially, Girolamo Zanchi and Zacharias Ursinus drew the assignment to draft a confession that could unite Reformed churches in a way that the Lutheran Formula of Concord had for Protestants in Germany. Instead of writing a new confession, Reformed pastors compiled an index of the various Protestant creeds that shared a similar doctrine of the Lord's Supper. This catalogue of confessions included the Augsburg (1530), Tetrapolitan (1530), Basel (1534), First (1536) and Second (1566) Helvetic, Saxony (1551), Wirtemberg (1552), Gallican (1559), and Belgic (1561) Confessions, the Thirty-Nine Articles (1562), and the Bohemian Confession (1573).

The editors of the Harmony of Confessions arranged the contents in a conventional order. Although not using a uniform table of contents, the selected creeds generally began with affirmations about Scripture and the Trinity, proceeded to Creation and the fall of man, devoted numerous chapters to Christ and the means of salvation, elaborated the nature of the church, its unity, officers, and ministry – particularly the sacraments – and finished with questions regarding civil government, marriage, and areas in which believers enjoyed liberty (adiaphra). The Harmony followed this pattern. The only real suspense was which confessions would make the final cut. For instance, in the chapter on predestination – a teaching that was initially controversial among Reformed Protestants but became one of the chief differences between the Reformed and Lutherans – the Harmony republished only five of the eleven creeds: the First Helvetic, Gallican, Belgic, Scottish, and Basel. In contrast, in the chapter on the fall and human sinfulness, the Harmony included all of the creeds except for the Tetrapolitan Confession, which lacked the fuller exposition of later creeds.

The most surprising aspect of the Harmony was the inclusion of Lutheran teaching on the Lord's Supper. In the fourteenth section, not far from the First Helvetic, a creed of decidedly Zwinglian sentiments, the editors printed the Augsburg Confession's affirmation of the real presence. The way around this oddity, of course, was the handy editorial device of a footnote in which the editors explained that "the body of Christ is not really present in, with, or under the bread" other than in a "sacramental manner." The reason for the note was that Christ's body, "being circumscribed in its local situation," had "truly ascended" to heaven.[3] The Harmony added further explanations that would have likely drawn dogmatic fire from inveterate Lutheran divines. Yet, as shallow as the Protestant unity may have appeared because the Lutheran presence in the Harmony was only on paper, this Reformed statement reflected a genuine attempt at the end of the sixteenth century to create a united Protestant front. The churches and pastors responsible for the Harmony were convinced that Protestant unity should extend ideally to Lutherans. This communion was not merely creedal. Reformed churches in Geneva and France followed policies for admitting Lutherans to the Lord's Supper on the basis of both groups' adherence to fundamental articles of the faith. Roman Catholics, in contrast, needed to repent publicly before being able to commune in a Reformed church.

Only the Reformed churches in France, the Netherlands, and Bremen adopted the Harmony. But the statement was indicative of the need for Reformed Protestants to explain themselves, both to other branches of the movement and to rulers who functioned as patrons of the churches. These sixteenth-century creeds were, in effect, precursors to the precise and elaborate statements that Reformed churches produced during the seventeenth century's period of high orthodoxy. According to Richard A. Muller, orthodox or scholastic Reformed Protestantism stood in "double continuity" with both the Reformation and the scholastic methods of the medieval church.[4] The purpose was to synthesize the theology of the Reformed tradition and distinguish it polemically from both Roman Catholicism and other Protestants. Particularly notable in this regard were the efforts of the Dutch churches at the Synod of Dort (1618) and the English and Scottish divines who gathered in war-besieged London during the 1640s at Westminster. Ironically, however, the clearer the Reformed churches became in their teaching, the more prone those same churches were to defection from within and hostility from without. During the seventeenth century, Reformed pastors, like their predecessors when producing statements like the Tetrapolitan Confession or the Second Helvetic, needed to explain their views to headstrong and sometimes hostile rulers. This made the seventeenth century an era of consolidation and definition as Reformed polemicists distinguished Calvinism from both Roman Catholicism and Lutheranism. It was the culmination of the original sixteenth-century reforms. At the same time, Calvinists also elaborated their convictions in the context of answering dissenters within their own ranks – therefore, the era of Reformed orthodoxy was not a golden age of church life but indicative of deep turmoil.

Victories, Defeats, and Ties

Reformed Protestants entered the early seventeenth century in remarkably good shape but would soon find that the task of consolidating and ordering church life was much more difficult than reform itself. Despite the variety of expressions in different locales, in 1600 Reformed churches across Europe possessed a well-developed and relatively stable ecclesiastical, doctrinal, and liturgical tradition. Between 1610 and 1680 these churches would be put severely to the test. The most immediate threat came from the same hand that had fed church reform: princes and kings. In fact, where Reformed churches were most dependent on their standing among the aristocracy of a country or region, the more vulnerable they were. Poland and Hungary illustrate the point. In the former, the decline of Reformed Protestantism occurred even before the seventeenth century. As early as the 1560s the work of the newly founded Jesuits was paying dividends when their schools became the favorites of Polish nobility – even Protestants. Jesuits also gained the ear of King Sigismund III, who increasingly favored Roman Catholic appointments during his lengthy tenure from 1587 to 1632. Roman Catholic influence found a favorable climate thanks to the Warsaw Confederation of 1573, which granted nobles the power to determine the religion within their territory. As such, Poland gradually turned back to Roman Catholicism through nobles who ended Protestant worship and priests who aggressively sought legal sanctions against infidels. By 1650 Poland had only 40 Reformed churches compared to 265 in 1570. Reformed Protestantism persisted a little longer in Lithuania. But the Second Northern War (1655–60), which witnessed invasions by Russia and Sweden, weakened the Reformed churches significantly. By 1700 conversions to Protestantism were illegal, and Protestant nobles could only worship in their personal churches.

In Hungary the trajectory of Reformed Protestants followed a similar course. In the territory controlled by the Habsburgs, rulers and Roman Catholic leaders conspired to roll back Protestant gains. Prior to the Thirty Years War (1618–48), Habsburg kings appointed officials and granted privileges explicitly on the basis of Roman Catholic identity. During the war, while Hungary took a back seat to Habsburg governance, Péter Pázmány, a former Reformed Protestant who switched churches under the influence of the Jesuits, introduced the Council of Trent's own efforts to reform the church. Pázmány founded three Jesuit seminaries and one Roman Catholic university in Hungary, while also writing a number of important controversial and devotional works that became influential in making Rome attractive again to Hungarian elites. After the Thirty Years War, Hungarian authorities imposed Roman Catholicism on churches that had been Protestant. During the reign of Leopold I (1658–1705), who attempted to reconstitute Hungarian law and restore religious unity, Protestant ministers started to be suspected of rebellion and disloyalty. The government rounded up as many as 750 ministers and freed only those who renounced Protestantism or converted to Rome. The others were imprisoned and sent to the galleys. When forty of those in galleys were forced to march to Naples in 1675 and a year later were liberated thanks to Dutch intervention, these Hungarian Protestants became a cause célèbre throughout Europe. Hungarian nobles, jealous to preserve their rights, reacted against Leopold's repression of Protestantism and instigated a religious war that enlisted support from the French, who always looked for ways to check the Habsburgs. By 1681 the hostilities had ceased and Leopold agreed to revert to a 1670 agreement that had granted religious freedom to Protestants. But this did not stop his efforts to undermine Protestantism in Hungary. By 1700 Reformed Protestants comprised roughly a third of the popu-lation, down from between 40 percent and 45 percent at the beginning of the seventeenth century.

In France, Protestant dependence on the favors and faith of the aristocracy during the sixteenth century became a flimsy platform for stability in the next. The Edict of Nantes (1598) that had granted Huguenots limited but definite forms of toleration and protected freedom of conscience became increasingly contested after 1620. Louis XIII (1610–43) not only attempted to impose Roman Catholicism on Protestant outposts, such as Béarn, but also through political and economic perks wooed French nobles to return to Rome. Although the memory of the St Bartholomew's Day Massacre made plausible their defen-sive strategies, the Huguenots did not ingratiate themselves to a system of toler-ance when their militancy – both religious and political – could readily be construed as treasonous. Over time, aristocrats who had been Protestant reverted back to Rome. By the time of Louis XIV's active reign in 1661 (until 1715), the kingdom's attitude toward Protestants hardened into outright opposition. At first, the king established institutions to insure that Protestant churches complied with the finest points of the Edict of Nantes. Laws forbidding Reformed churches from receiving converts from Roman Catholicism followed. The most objectionable of these laws was a rule that removed children above the age of seven who desired to join a Roman Catholic church from their Protestant homes, and placed them with Roman Catholics families at the expense of their parents. Finally, in 1685 Louis XIV revoked the Edict of Nantes and established an active campaign to force Protestant conversions. As many as 400,000 Protestants abjured their faith and fearfully affirmed Rome's. Those who would not renounce their faith – about half as many – left France. Many settled in the Netherlands, England, Switzerland, and Brandenburg, and smaller numbers migrated to the British colonies in North America.

Defeat, however, was not the only outcome that Reformed Protestants experienced during the seventeenth century. In Transylvania, for instance, rulers who supported Reformed churches remained in power throughout most of the century. At first, Transylvania might have appeared to be following the pattern of Roman Catholic recovery on the heels of Protestant gains. But when Gábor Bethlen secured the crown from Sigismund Báthory in 1601, Transylvania became a hospitable even if somewhat isolated outpost for Calvinists. Bethlen and his successors established schools that inculcated Reformed teaching, sent aspiring scholars to universities in the empire and the Netherlands for training to teach in the kingdom's schools, and sided with Reformed ministers in conflicts with both anti-Trinitarians and Roman Catholics.

Even more impressive were the results of Reformed activity in the Netherlands where the contours of Reformed orthodoxy received their first significant post-Reformation codification. Against the backdrop of a theological conflict over election and human depravity, seventeenth-century Dutch Reformed Protestantism gave to Calvinism its memorable mnemonic TULIP (i.e., Total depravity, Unconditional election, Limited atonement, Irresistible grace, Perseverance of the saints), also known as Calvinism's five points.[5] Alongside the Dutch contribution to Reformed theology was a British-inspired rejuvenation of practical piety, called the Nadere Reformatie (i.e. further reformation), that infused among the churches a sense of purpose and commitment to godliness like that which had characterized Puritanism at turn of the seventeenth century. Willem Teellinck (1579–1629), the leader of this movement, had studied law in England, admired the zeal he witnessed in Puritan churches, and sought to model the Dutch churches after the Puritans, especially in the matter of Sabbath observance, by prohibiting recreation and business on Sundays.

Teellinck's teaching received sporadic and informal support in different Dutch settings during the seventeenth century but the chief development among the Dutch Reformed churches was the theology of Arminianism. This was the designation for controversial teaching that grew out of the thought and career of Jacobus Arminius (1560–1609), a Reformed pastor in Amsterdam and later a theology professor at the University of Leiden, who had learned Reformed theology both in the Netherlands at Leiden and in Geneva through studies with Theodore Beza. Arminius' time in Geneva was significant for developments in the Dutch church because he studied during a period when Beza's teaching on predestination began to receive critical scrutiny. Calvin's own view on God's sovereign determination to save the elect was not without its critics. But as difficult as Calvin's doctrine was, he treated it in the context of the divine power necessary for salvation and so argued that predestination should be as much a source of comfort as a subject that required delicacy. In contrast, his successor in Geneva, Beza, developed the notion that God had predestined those whom he would save and those whom he would condemn before the beginning of time. For Beza, predestination had more to do with the plan of salvation (i.e. soteriology) than with the nature and power of God. Beza's teaching also elicited criticisms, and during the 1580s church leaders in Germany, England, and Switzerland called for conferences to address predestination. In 1588 the city of Bern hosted one of those debates.

Discussions of predestination during the late sixteenth century were inconclusive but generated the sort of doubts that Arminius himself would express. His questions went beyond predestination to the atonement, and whether or not Christ underwent a sacrificial death only for the elect, chosen before time, or for the entire human race who were then responsible either to trust Christ or reject his saving work. Another consideration was whether a believer could lose salvation through infidelity, or would saints persevere in faith thanks to divine sovereignty? Arminius began to speculate and publish on these subjects, and in 1603 when the faculty at Leiden appointed him as professor of theology his views took on added significance. Franciscus Gomarus, one of Arminius' colleagues at Leiden, scrutinized the new professor's views and engaged him in public debates. Quickly these disagreements spread to other quarters of the Dutch churches and many ministers started to call for a national synod.

The Arminian controversy not only trickled down from the university's ivory tower to the church's rank and file but also rekindled older disputes between ministers and magistrates over the ultimate final authority in ecclesiastical affairs. Thanks to his own convictions and personal connections – Arminius was married to the daughter of a family prominent in Amsterdam politics – he took the position, associated with Erastianism, that the state was the final arbiter of church matters. One of Arminius' greatest defenders, Johannes Uytenbogaert, the pastor to the stadtholder, Prince Maurice, wrote *On the Office and Authority of a Higher Christian Government in Church Affairs* (1610) to resolve the political dispute that accompanied Arminius' contested theology. On the other side, Arminius' pastoral opponents argued for autonomy from the state; they insisted that church classes and synods were not only competent but responsible to oversee and correct the witness and work of the Dutch church. Related to questions surrounding the relative powers of church and state was the status of the creed or the church's official doctrine. Arminius claimed that his views were compatible with the Heidelberg Catechism and the Belgic Confession but also believed that if a national synod were convened these doctrinal statements should be reconsidered to see if revision were necessary. Without surprise, opponents of Arminius took the opposite view, insisting that these creeds had not only given theological coherence to the Dutch churches for four decades but had summarized the faith of Protestants who had sacrificed their lives.

Arminius died in 1609 but the dispute over his views lived on, as his supporters, known as the Remonstrants, leaned heavily on civil authorities, while the Counter-Remonstrants held a majority of pastors. A year after Arminius' death, the Remonstrants, now led by Uytenbogaert, issued a petition that identified their chief religious convictions: that those who believed in Christ and persisted in their faith were the elect; that Christ had died for the entire human race; and that people had the power to resist divine grace. The statement also declared the state's authority over the church, and called for a revision of the Belgic Confession. In 1611, the Counter-Remonstrants, led by Arminius' rival at Leiden, Gomarus, responded with a declaration of their own about the particular nature of Christ's death – that it was only for the elect – and the impossibility of believers losing their salvation. The state, led by Johan van Oldenbarnevelt, an influential regent of Holland, contributed to the growing animosity and unintentionally hurt the Remonstrants' cause by imposing a system of tolerance for all views within the church. The intention was to calm the hostilities, but the proposal included controversial sermons or classical or synodical actions against erroneous views. When Counter-Remonstrant pastors persisted in exposing the dangers of Arminianism, the state in some cases intervened and removed the contentious ministers from their pulpits. Meanwhile, Lutherans, Anabaptists, and Roman Catholics, under religious tolerance afforded by the Dutch government, were conducting services without opposition. In effect, by seeking the aid of the state, the Remonstants appeared to be guilty of inconsistently using political repression to enforce tolerance for their views. Ironically, this move turned the foes of tolerance, the Counter-Remonstrants, into victims of political oppression.

The situation almost completely reversed itself once Maurice of Nassau, the leader of the House of Orange, decided to support the Counter-Remonstrants. In the summer of 1617 he began to worship in The Hague with Counter-Remonstrants, led by a minister whom city officials had dismissed. Oldenbarnevelt regarded this as an act of defiance against the existing religious order and at his direction the States of Holland empowered all local governments to hire mercenary soldiers to counter such disobedience. This action only emboldened Maurice, who had legitimate control over all soldiers, to establish his authority, disband the mercenaries, and dismiss all local officials who were sympathetic to Oldenbarnevelt. Maurice also had Oldenbarnevelt arrested and condemned to death for disrupting Dutch society and undermining the true faith.

The intervention of Maurice was the political backdrop to the Synod of Dort, which met in November 1618 to address the doctrines originally taught by Arminius and then advanced by the Remonstrants. The assembled pastors and university professors included representatives from British, German, and Swiss churches. (Invitations went out to all the Reformed Churches in Europe.) These delegates met for over six months, first examining individual Remonstrants who were more interested in synodical procedures than in explaining their views. Under the tight control of Counter-Remonstrants, the Synod then turned to the printed works of Remonstrants and predictably found Arminianism wanting. At the same time, the Synod avoided the dogmatic speculation that sometimes afflicted discussions of divine sovereignty and predestination, and instead adopted a series of positions designed to combine doctrinal clarity and pastoral guidance. The Five Points of Calvinism that Dort formulated stressed divine sovereignty but in ways designed to console believers rather than to answer philosophical speculation. For these commissioners, human beings were incapable of doing anything that could merit God's favor, but such sinfulness could not withstand the gracious intervention of God to initiate faith in Christ and a life of good works. This Christian life depended on Christ's merits, particularly his sacrificial death to pay the penalty of sin for those whom God had elected to save. This grace, in turn, because it did not depend on the believer's goodness, could not be lost and believers, once saved, would continue in a life of faithfulness no matter how imperfect.

The Synod's decision received approval from the States-General, which in turn sent the articles to all of the provincial church bodies for their ministers' signature. As many as two hundred Remonstrants refused to sign. The penalty for defiance was removal from office and loss of income. Forty of the recalcitrant eventually reconciled their views with the Synod's teaching; seventy remained within the country and lived as private citizens. The most vociferous Remonstrants went into exile. Some of these regrouped in Antwerp and established a Remonstrant Brotherhood, complete with their own creed, which was unsurprisingly critical of predestination and the imposition of creeds on ministers and church members. Under Dutch laws the assembly was illegal.

The decrees of Dort also drew affirmation from other Reformed churches. In France, the 1623 National Synod required the churches to accept the Dutch declaration; ministers who did not lost their offices. As late as 1647 Geneva's Company of Pastors still required subscription to Dort from all its members. The churches in Scotland and German-speaking Switzerland, though not requiring formal affirmation, greeted the 1618 Synod's findings with approval.

The Synod of Dort did not end questions surrounding predestination, however. The most famous instance of lingering disputes took place among the French, thanks to the teaching of Moyse Amyraut (1596–1664), professor of theology at the Reformed Academy of Saumur. His book, *Brief Treatise on Predestination* (1634) outlined another approach to the difficult implications surrounding divine election, namely, hypothetical universalism. Amyraut hoped to avoid the errors of Arminius by arguing that Christ's sacrificial death was effective for all people as long as they trusted in him. He also opposed the Arminian notion that believers, by summoning up the necessary belief, played an active role in their salvation. This modified understanding of election attempted to soften the apparently arbitrary treatments of divine sovereignty by stressing the possibility of grace for all people.

Amyraut's peers, however, did not regard his revisions as an improvement. Pierre Du Moulin, the most gifted Huguenot theologian of the seventeenth century, judged that Amyraut was guilty of at least two-thirds of Arminius' errors. In 1637 Amyraut successfully defended his views before the national synod that met in Alençon. Although he escaped formal censure, the synod's deliberations registered significant doubts about the Saumur professor's soundness. Within a decade his teaching became the object of another dispute that involved the faculty at Leiden; to his opponents Amyraut appeared to be heading in the same direction that had landed Arminius outside the bounds of Reformed orthodoxy (even though his views were remarkably similar to Richard Baxter – see Chapter Nine, below – who escaped condemnation). The ongoing controversy prompted churches in Switzerland and France either to bar students from studying at Saumur or to prohibit the school's graduates from ordination. Finally, in 1649 France's Reformed churches arrived at a compromise that put an end to the controversy and left Amyraut in his position at Saumur. But outside the northern parts of France, where Amyraut's teaching had its greatest support, his views continued to be suspect and his influence meager.

United Kingdom, Divided Church

The experience of Reformed churches was arguably more explosive in the British Isles than anywhere else in Europe. Thanks to the British Empire's expansion overseas during the seventeenth century, those explosions would have ramifications for the future of Calvinism in the New World. In England frustrations over the failure to reform the Church of England thoroughly – especially in matters of church government and worship – led Reformed ministers to cultivate informal and personal methods of godliness outside the institutional church. In Scotland, the ink was barely dry on the harmonization of episcopal and presbyterian polities within the Kirk when the king responsible for the agreement, James VI, succeeded Elizabeth as James I of England and replaced the House of Tudor with that of Stuart. A common monarch for Scotland and England meant that the existing tensions in those respective nations now had the potential to multiply. Adding to this recipe for turmoil was a monarch who believed in the divine right of kings and needed to resist an understandable temptation to impose order on his ministers for the good of his kingdom.

Even before the religiously inspired tensions that developed during the Stuart dynasty, English churchmen had grown frustrated with political road-blocks to reform and proposed an alternative. Unable to convince Elizabeth and her advisors of either the biblical warrant or practical benefits of presbyterian government in the English church, an important strand of Puritanism began to look away from the church's formal structures to the inner and personal aspects of believers' lives and experience. These writers became known as the Puritan "physicians of the soul" and traced their intellectual and institutional lineage to Cambridge University, where the likes of Richard Greenham, Richard Rogers, Arthur Dent, and William Ames pursued a vein of introspective piety that William Perkins had opened a generation earlier when he searched for evidence of predestination in the interior life of Christians. Lewis Bayly, an Oxford churchman, was also an important contributor to Puritanism's practical divinity. This school of Reformed Protestantism sublimated Puritanism's zeal for a thor-oughly reformed church into a project for personal reformation by supplying methods – from prayer and Bible reading to Sabbath observance and strenu-ously moral behavior – for individual godliness. What Reformed Protestants achieved elsewhere through pastors and elders overseeing the lives of parish members, advocates of practical divinity accomplished through believers attending to their own experience and practice.[6]

An important theme in the literature of English practical divinity was the call for Christians to make their election sure by charting the progress of holiness in of daily affairs. As popular as this strain of piety became – both in England and in parts of the Netherlands – it also placed significant strain upon the adherents of Reformed Protestantism. On the one hand, critics objected that practical divinity turned free grace into moralism by suggesting that saints could prove their salvation through moral effort. On the other hand, it also encouraged some – later Baptists and Congregationalists – to dispense with the older pattern of devotion that presumed infant baptism and a process of gradual identification (on the part of young people) with the teachings and practices of the church.

Another unintended consequence of Puritan zeal for personal holiness was a high-church, sacramental Anglican reaction under James I that was explicitly opposed to the precision of Reformed practical divinity. Puritans who were zealous for experiential devotion did not get off to a good start with James I when they confronted him, soon after his inauguration, with the Millenary Petition, a proposal for modifications in worship, doctrinal fidelity, and church government along the lines of other Reformed churches. In opposition to this petition a party within the Church of England emerged that championed sacraments and rites and adopted the name, Arminian, at least out of objections to Reformed teaching on predestination. These English churchmen, sometimes called Formalists or Laudians (named for Archbishop William Laud), viewed Reformed Protestants suspiciously as sectarians who were alienating people from the church with an overly strict piety and a hopelessly high standard for institutional purity.

If James I did not identify with the Formalists' understanding of the church, like them he was suspicious of zealously scrupulous presbyterian types after his experiences with the Kirk in his homeland. As a result, James opposed any effort to overturn episcopacy or yield the crown's supremacy over the church. He also resisted Puritan attempts to implement strict Sabbatarian observance by overseeing the publication of the Book of Sports, a guide that determined the approved forms of Sunday recreation outside the hours of worship and included archery and dancing. James also hurt his standing with Puritans and strict Presbyterians with the Five Articles of Perth (1618). This statement was designed to bring the Scottish church into closer uniformity with England by prescribing kneeling at worship, confirmation by bishops, the church calendar and holy days, and by permitting private communion. Even so, James was not opposed to Reformed zeal in the way the Formalists were. He affirmed predestination, supported the Synod of Dort by sending English and Scottish delegates, and silenced English critics of the Synod's canons. Overall, James steered a moderate course between the extremes of personal religion and sacramentalism, and the politics of two national churches.

Once his son, Charles I, ascended the throne in 1625, however, the balance of ecclesiastical power shifted decidedly toward the Formalists. William Laud was not only an important advisor to the new king but in 1633 became Archbishop. In turn, Laud became the king's enforcer of ecclesiastical uniformity. The Caroline Divines, all high-church Formalists, claimed, contrary to the Puritans and Presbyterians, that they were recovering the original themes of English Protestantism and preserving the church from sectarians and schismatics. The most committed Reformed Protestants who looked to Geneva and Zurich for inspiration and who maintained close ties to the Dutch churches took an opposite view. For the Puritans, Charles and his Archbishop were steering the English church back toward Rome. Those who worried most about the fate of the church and the threat of impending divine judgment left England. Some settled in the Netherlands, others left for the New World to begin the experiment of transplanting Puritanism to New England.[7]

For Scotland, Charles was no less provocative in his ecclesiastical policies. Not only did the king enforce the Five Articles of Perth, but he essentially ignored the compromise between episcopacy and presbyterianism that his father had crafted; Charles decided to increase the civil responsibilities of Scottish bishops without seeking input from the General Assembly. Charles' major offense was to call for a new prayer book in 1636 for the Scottish church. It not only contained many features that Presbyterians rejected as Roman Catholic, but the six-month interval between the king's decision and the service book's introduction gave critics ample time to let fears worsen and prepare a response. On July 23, 1637, when the dean of Edinburgh's St Giles cathedral finally used the book in services, the people revolted by shouting and throwing stools in an outburst that some believed to have been well orchestrated. Scottish officials responded to continued demonstrations against the prayer book by forbidding all gatherings for protest as treasonous. The Scottish faithful retaliated by entering into a national covenant to preserve the true religion. Covenanting was a practice with deep roots in Scotland and the 1637 instance called upon the king and parliament to remember and uphold the National Covenant of 1581, administered at the time of James VI's accommodation of zealous Presbyterians, in which the nation determined to use its political institutions to abolish Roman Catholicism. The reiteration of the covenant in 1637 to challenge James' son, Charles, drew widespread support in the Lowlands from the people, clergy, and nobles.

To counter the Scottish uprising, the king was prepared to use force but called for a general assembly before rousing the militia. Charles hoped to diffuse the situation through the Scottish religious institution by stacking the deck of participants and agenda, and thereby overturn the Presbyterian challenge. But the opposition to his religious policies was so fierce that opponents themselves were able to influence the selection of delegates and topics for debate. When the assembly met in Glasgow in 1638 it defied the king and proceeded to condemn the Five Articles of Perth and the prayer book, and to abolish episcopacy. Charles tried to bring the Scots into compliance through force, but in two successive wars the Scottish military proved superior to English units that were underfunded and lacked motivation. The king's failed requests to the English parliament for funding only heightened tensions in England. Meanwhile, the Scottish Kirk witnessed the triumph of a party committed to true Presbyterianism, the national covenant, and ending episcopacy in Scotland. Approximately one-tenth of the Kirk's ministers, not sharing these convictions, lost their posts during the 1640s.

The antagonism between Charles and the English parliament not only erupted in 1642 in civil war but also wound up involving the Scots. In the background of this conflict was the religious question and Charles' poor handling of the English and Scottish churches. Parliament was by no means unified on church matters and members ranged between a small group still inclined to a modified episcopacy, and others who favored presbyterianism, congregationalism, or even independency. Where the English officials agreed was in the opposition to Laud. In 1640 parliament impeached and imprisoned the archbishop along with several of his colleagues. Five years later Laud would be executed for treason. Also obvious to parliament was Charles' failure to uphold the liberties of Englishmen and the prerogatives of parliament.

Since parliament agreed in the main that Charles' religious policies were untenable, members called in 1642 for an assembly of ministers and theologians to meet at Westminster and devise a new church order. Because the war against the king was going badly, parliament solicited support from the Scots, who agreed on condition that the English also enter into a national covenant. In 1643 the Scots and English ratified the Solemn League and Covenant which committed England to the same principles of the true religion (read "Presbyterianism") to which the Scots had subscribed. In turn, this covenant recast the agenda for the Westminster Assembly. In addition to recommending a new church order, the British Divines would draft a new confession of faith, a directory for worship, and catechetical aids, all designed to ensure uniformity of faith and practice in England.

The majority of delegates to the assembly, which along with Dort constituted the high point of seventeenth-century Reformed orthodoxy, adhered to a presbyterian form of church government, but English politics prevented them from prevailing. The assembly's greatest concession was specifically on the matter of church government. Thanks to the success of Oliver Cromwell's New Model Army against the king's forces, the proponents of independency and Erastian views about the state were more successful in promoting their ideas at the assembly. The result was a church polity that favored presbyterianism while carving out room for independence and conceding church matters to the state. The assembly's work on liturgy again reflected a compromise that owed greatly to the alliance of the Scots and Cromwell in the war against Charles. The Directory for Public Worship struck a balance between the Scottish desire for a set order of worship and the independents' opposition to fixed prayers; the directory only supplied detailed outlines for public prayer. The Directory, along with the Confession of Faith, also incorporated themes from English practical divinity with continental Reformed teaching. The Westminster Divines favored many of the devotional practices that had developed among Puritans for half a century, such as Sabbatarianism, the elimination of holy days and festivals, and prescriptions for family worship. The influence of English practical divinity was also evident in the Confession of Faith, where the assembly explored in greater detail the order of salvation and the personal appropriation of grace. At the same time, the assembly followed Dort on the atonement, the sovereignty of the spirit in regeneration, and the impossibility of the elect falling from grace. But the Divines did avoid taking sides in the debates over predestination. One area where the assembly showed no innovation was in the production of a metrical psalter for public worship. Francis Rous, a member of parliament, proposed his own metrical psalter but the Scottish commissioners preferred the version by William Muir. Parliament had the last word when the Lords authorized the Rous edition for the English churches.

Although the Westminster Assembly relied on compromises to carry out its agenda, the reception of the Divines' work would reveal even wider gaps between Reformed ideals and British realities. During the Civil War the English churches resisted many of the prescriptions of Westminster, especially rules for a presbyterian church government. After the execution of Charles I on January 30, 1649 and the institution of the Commonwealth under Cromwell, religious bedlam prevailed, with parliament switching from laws that required weekly attendance at the established church's services to regulations that merely required attendance at some gathering of religious observance. Tolerance of all views was not an option, thanks to a Committee of Triers charged with overseeing the ordination of Baptists, Independents, and Presbyterians; England would not turn a blind eye to Ranters or Quakers. But expectations for a uniform religious order were gone, ironically under the devout Puritan Cromwell. Paths to the ministry were now available through Anglican or presbyterian routes, or through the official Committee of Triers. In congregations, the orders of services varied widely. The shift in England from an ecclesiastical establishment (under Laud) that imposed uniformity (1640s), followed by a parliament-sponsored and Puritan-informed debate over the best church order (1640s), to religious chaos (1650s) was arguably the most dramatic change in seventeenth-century European church life.

The consequences of the English Civil War were almost as convulsive for the Scots as the English. True to their covenant with the king and wary of England's inability to embrace presbyterianism, the Scots in 1646 had entered into negotiations with Charles in which they considered supporting him if he would agree to uphold the Solemn League and Covenant. Although Charles never signed the

Covenant, his response led the Scots to be encouraged. In turn, the nobility, who dominated parliament, came to the king's defense. Cromwell's eventual defeat of Scottish forces created a political vacuum in Edinburgh that ministers zealous for the Covenant (and opposed to defending Charles because of his failure to sign it) filled. After Charles' execution, these Covenanters negotiated with his brother, again seeking the king's endorsement of the Covenant in return for military support from the Scots. This alliance, however, proved disastrous for the Covenanters, whom Cromwell subjected to a humiliating defeat at Dunbar in 1650. In the aftermath of this battle, the Scots continued to be divided: the majority regarded the next Stuart monarch as the best means toward a presbyterian order in Scotland, while a minority, led by Samuel Rutherford, believed that defeat was a sign of God's judgment. The split mattered little after 1652, since Cromwell ended Scotland's independence and allowed the religious disorder of England to seep northward.

The end of the interregnum and the restoration of the monarchy under Charles II in 1660 returned ecclesiastical order to both England and Scotland. In England the monarchy initially insisted on the Book of Common Prayer and episcopacy, and renounced the Solemn League and Covenant. The Clarendon Code that established these policies only lessened in its severity after a decade, when in 1672 Charles II issued a Declaration of Indulgence to allow public worship for Protestant dissenters (Nonconformists), such as Presbyterians, Independents, Congregationalists, and Baptists. In Scotland the Restoration prompted parliament to recognize episcopacy as a better means to control the church than presbyterianism. Scotland followed England also in repudiating the Solemn League and Covenant. Those Presbyterian ministers who had been most committed to the Covenant lost their posts after refusing to submit to the oversight of bishops. These Covenanters in turn mounted various forms of protest, using gatherings in the fields as conventicles for worship and inspiration. Between the 1660s and the 1680s these uprisings met with armed suppression and the execution of offenders.

The Glorious Revolution that ushered to the throne William and Mary in 1688 finally put an end to almost a century of religious upheaval, but only then did British Reformed Protestants enjoy the blessings of monarchical supremacy. In England the adherents of Reformed theology, scattered among the Protestant dissenters, received legal protection to conduct their own services, while the Church of England lost touch with the currents that had connected the English and Scots to the Reformed churches on the Continent. In Scotland, the support for William came generally from those sympathetic to presbyterianism, which in turn led to the restoration of a presbyterian Kirk. But this was not satisfying to Scottish episcopalians, who eventually formed their own synods and parishes, independent of the national church. These episcopal bodies did not become legal until 1712. Meanwhile, those presbyterians most committed to the old covenants – known as Covenanters or Cameronians – refused the privileges and auspices of the Kirk, choosing to remain separate and continuing the tradition of gathering in conventicles. The cause of Reformed orthodoxy was hardly responsible for seventeenth-century British convulsions, but it hardly soothed them either.

Doctrinal Retrenchment and Intellectual Experimentation

Back on the Continent, Reformed church leaders faced divisions that were by no means as grave as those in England and Scotland but still revealed the difficulty of maintaining the logic and motivation that had launched their churches. In 1674 the pastors of Switzerland's Protestant cantons, led by Basel and Zurich, met to respond to several of the theological disputes and challenges that had plagued the Reformed churches since the rise of Arminianism. They produced a statement, the so-called Helvetic Consensus, deemed "the highest statement of high Reformed orthodoxy ever adopted by a major ecclesiastical gathering."[8] Among the participants was François Turretini (1623–87), a pastor and theologian from Geneva who solidified the city's reputation for sound theology and whose works would later be translated and circulated widely in various Reformed churches. The Consensus took aim specifically at new scholarly approaches to Scripture and lingering doubts about predestination, election, and the extent of the atonement. On the former topic, the Swiss Divines affirmed the reliability of the extant Hebrew manuscripts down to the text's vowel points and blamed scholars who highlighted discrepancies among the various manuscripts as bringing the foundation of faith "into perilous danger." On predestination and the atonement, which accounted for twenty-two of the Consensus' twenty-six canons, the pastors reaffirmed the positions that the Dutch had elaborated in 1618 at Dort; the Swiss condemned both Arminian and Amyrauldian teachings that were obviously continuing to find outlets. In that spirit, Canon IV declared: "[God] elected a certain and definite number to be led, in time, unto salvation in Christ, their Guarantor and sole Mediator. And on account of his merit, by the mighty power of the regenerating Holy Spirit, he decreed these elect to be effectually called, regenerated and gifted with faith and repentance."

That the Swiss pastors needed to respond to errors almost seven decades old was an indication of the failure of other attempts to settle the debates of the seventeenth century. In point of fact, the questions that Arminius raised at the beginning of the century established a pattern of critical inquiry that would create a countervailing undertow beneath the waves of orthodox Reformed doctrinal formulations at Dort and Westminster. In addition to the debates swirling around the eternal decrees of God, Reformed theologians faced intellectual challenges as abstract as the first principles of philosophy and as particular as the study of Hebrew vowel points. René Descartes' philosophical and scientific arguments, which featured knowledge of God and the self based on doubt and a mechanistic conception of the natural world, were one source of worry for Reformed academics. Because Descartes lived in the Netherlands for the better part of two decades (1628–49), his views gained a hearing and drew vigorous opposition from the great defender of Reformed orthodoxy, Gisbertus Voetius (1589–1676), who taught at the University of Utrecht. In France, the scholarship of Louis Cappel (1585–1658), who taught Hebrew at the Academy of Saumur, questioned the reliability of the most widely used manuscripts for the Old Testament. His doubts about textual variations did not go as far as whether Moses wrote the Pentateuch. But Cappel did introduce an interpretive method that highlighted differences between ancient Israel and contemporary Europe, such that anyone hoping to base modern statecraft on King David's policies would be guilty of anachronistic argumentation. Adding to Cappel's biblical scholarship was the work of Johannes Cocceius (1603–69), a theologian and Hebrew scholar from Bremen who had studied at German universities before taking a post at the University of Leiden. His covenant theology, which stressed the difference between the covenant of works and the covenant of grace, and between Israel and the church, was yet another challenge to received methods and conclusions of biblical interpretation. Like Descartes, Cocceius drew fire from Voetius and prolonged disputes among the Dutch Reformed churches. Unlike the Arminian controversy, this one never split the Dutch church. But Cocceius contributed to a trend in seventeenth-century academic circles that undermined literalistic readings of Scripture, especially those attempts to find in the pages of the Israelites' laws and prophets the norms for the Christian church.

In many cases, Reformed scholars and the churches that looked to them for the training of ministers absorbed these challenges without great hardship. But in some instances, the path of accommodation also involved significant drift away from the precise formulations of Reformed orthodoxy. This shift was nowhere more evident than in Geneva and the generational succession between François Turretini and his son, Jean-Alphonse (1671–1737). The elder Turretini died when his son was sixteen, thus freeing Jean-Alphonse to mature intellectually in ways that ran afoul of his father's orthodox convictions. His studies took him to several European universities where he became familiar with the new philosophy and methods advanced by Descartes and Isaac Newton. The tension between the new learning and Reformed orthodoxy, however, did not prevent

Jean-Alphonse from securing his father's post at the Geneva Academy. He began in 1701 as rector and within four years was lecturing where his father and Calvin had before him. An important theme in Jean-Alphonse's teaching was the elevation of reason as an independent source of knowledge about God and his ways. His 1735 work, *Treatise of the Christian Religion*, developed this point by attempting to prove, contrary to deism, that Reformed orthodoxy was fully reasonable. Jean-Alphonse's teaching was one consequence of the dilemmas faced by a century of theological debate; knowing how to handle the mysteries of predestination and election would make or break the proponents of Reformed Protestantism. Even those Geneva pastors who were closer to the senior Turretini than to Jean-Alphonse, such as Benedict Pictet, the author of the popular *Christian Theology* (1696), avoided dogmatism about predestination and preferred to promote practical guidance for believers instead of precise doctrine.

By the end of the seventeenth century, changes in Geneva church life were emblematic of disputes among the Reformed churches and political antagonisms within Protestant kingdoms. In 1690 the old psalter, a staple of Reformed worship among French speakers, made way for a modernized version which incorporated contemporary linguistic styles. Soon thereafter the Geneva pastors approved the introduction of services on Christmas afternoons, which led to the observance of other holy days from Rome's liturgical calendar. In 1707 the Company of Pastors approved a Lutheran minister to conduct worship services for the city's German-speaking residents. Within a few years they admitted the Lutheran pastor to their membership. Of course, the pastors in Geneva had historically sought unity with Lutherans, but not at the expense of indifference to those teachings and practices that had divided the two wings of Protestantism.

A Century's Worth of Conflict

In most histories of seventeenth-century Europe, religion occupies center stage, at least during the period from 1618 to 1648 when the Thirty Years War demonstrated the discrepancy among the ideals of Christendom, the reality of three rival Christian churches (Roman, Lutheran, and Reformed), and the power cravings of rulers. In point of fact, the Reformed churches largely escaped the ravages of those religious wars. But even without experiencing the continental European conflicts directly, Reformed Protestants confronted turmoil and division that was almost as traumatic.

The one Reformed stronghold to experience the brunt of the Thirty Years War was the Palatinate, where the ruler, Frederick V, allowed his awkward succession to the throne of Bohemia to distract from turmoil in his hereditary lands. Not only were his efforts to protect Protestant interests against the new emperor, the Roman Catholic Ferdinand II (1610–37), a colossal failure of statecraft and diplomacy, but they left the Upper Palatinate vulnerable to attacks initially from Spain and then decisively from Maximilian of Bavaria. By 1628, Protestantism in the Palatinate (which included Reformed Protestants and a large population of Lutherans, especially among the nobility) was illegal and Roman Catholicism was the official religion. Pastors lost their charges and Reformed adherents received a mandate either to convert or leave the territory. In 1631, a year after King Gustavus Adolphus of Sweden became the hero of Protestants by intervening successfully against Maximilian, Lutheranism, thanks to the Swedish monarch, became the Palatinate's official faith. Roman Catholics would gain the upper hand within the territory once more during the Thirty Years War, but they only managed a policy of toleration. Part of the reality behind this concession was that by the late 1630s the war had lost its explicitly religious character and had descended into political rivalry. The Peace of Westphalia (1648) restored the Palatinate to its pre-war status and thus returned the churches to their Reformed identity. But in 1685 when the electorate passed to the Roman Catholic side of the ruling family, the Palatinate experienced a competitive equilibrium among Reformed Protestants, Lutherans, and Roman Catholics. Reformed adherents were in the majority numerically, but often were forced to share buildings with Roman Catholics and hold separate services at specified times.

Even without war of the kind experienced in the Palatinate, during the seventeenth century the Reformed churches endured a series of conflicts, both internal and external, that proved how difficult the task of carrying out reform would be. In Hungary, Poland–Lithuania, and France, Reformed Protestants suffered enormous defeats. In Diarmaid MacCulloch's fitting description, by 1700 the frontier of Protestantism in Europe "had retreated hundreds of miles north," "from the borders of Italy to the Germanic middle territories of the Holy Roman Empire."[9] He adds that these changes in geographical distribution left Geneva in the south as "a lonely outpost." This left northern Europe as the political and intellectual center of Reformed Protestantism, with the Netherlands, the British Isles, and the Protestant parts of Switzerland as the strongest churches. But even in the areas of Reformed vitality, the seventeenth century had not been kind on churches, where important moments of theological definition took place alongside significant innovations. As Muller writes, Reformed orthodoxy after 1725 was "less secure in its philosophical foundations," "less certain of its grasp of the biblical standard, and often (though hardly always) less willing to draw out its polemic against other 'orthodox' forms of Christianity." In a word, while the seventeenth century saw the confessionalization of Europe, the eighteenth century reversed the trend with its own version of "deconfessionalization."[10]

The irony of the seventeenth century is that it was both the period when Reformed Protestants gained sufficient clarity to establish orthodox boundaries and when their churches showed the first strains of liberal theological trends. Perhaps just as ironic is that the achievements of national churches in bodies such as the Synod of Dort and the Westminster Assembly took place at the same time that a significant element within Reformed Protestantism was turning inward, away from the formal mechanisms of the institutional church to the personal and intense pursuit of personal holiness. The Reformed churches had emerged in the 1520s with great vigor and resiliency, thanks in part to able leadership and the support of sympathetic magistrates. Then during the middle decades of the sixteenth century the reforms begun in Zurich and Geneva took root, notably among the Scots, Dutch, and, to a lesser extent, Germans. Although part of the political establishment, Reformed churches still faced internal dissent and intellectual dilemmas that made necessary the defining synods of Dort and Westminster. Even with the aid of these confessional affirmations, the Reformed churches generally lacked the mechanisms, political and ecclesiastical, to enforce orthodoxy. That deficiency helps to account for the seventeenth-century decline of Calvinism among the Swiss.

By 1700 the future of Reformed churches in Europe did not look propitious. If Reformed Protestantism were going to experience revitalization, it needed new settings and vehicles even as it depended on the genius and energy of the Scots, Dutch, Germans, and their New World settlements.

CHAPTER FIVE

TAKING THE WORD TO THE WORLD

THE REFORMATION ERA WAS also the Age of Discovery. Even before Luther instigated challenges to Rome or Zwingli contemplated eating meat on Friday, Spanish and Portuguese sailors had discovered parts of the world formerly unknown to Europeans. Although the discovery of new lands and Protestant beliefs were part of a general challenge to Christendom's received ways, these developments were not directly linked. Explorers like the Italian Christopher Columbus and his royal patrons, King Ferdinand and Queen Isabella of Spain, were devout Roman Catholics and their interests in exploration included at least the extension of Rome's true religion throughout the world, whether flat or not. Although Roman Catholic countries, monarchs, and sailors opened the door of globalization, Protestants soon experienced the benefits (and sometimes the hardships) that came with life in the New World.

One of the first Protestant groups to realize the possibilities generated by the Age of Discovery was the Huguenots. Through the patronage of Gaspard de Coligny (1519–72), the French nobleman and admiral who would later become a champion of Protestantism in France and whose assassination triggered the St Bartholomew's Day Massacre in 1572, Nicolas Durand de Villegaignon (1510–75) in 1555 led a fleet of two ships that carried six hundred French to a small island in Brazil across the bay from modern-day Rio de Janeiro. Villegaignon, an admiral and military commander, like Coligny was sympathetic to the Huguenots, whose faith fell under the penalties of existing anti-heresy statutes. Although the Portuguese had arrived almost fifty years earlier, at first they left the French colonists alone on the island of Serigipe. Two years later the French received an infusion of assistance, both material and human, with the arrival of three ships that carried approximately eighty soldiers and two hundred people, among them Reformed pastors sent from Geneva, Pierre Richier and Guillaume Chartrier. The French colony was short-lived and succumbed to internal divisions even before the Portuguese decided to expel the Huguenots and their military defenders. Within a year of their arrival, the Reformed pastors ran afoul of Villegaignon, who could not abide the ministers' overly scrupulous views on the Lord's Supper. He quickly grew tired of theological disputes and expelled the pastors and their most ardent adherents, some of whom found passage back to France in 1558. By 1560 the Portuguese had ousted all the French.

The French colonial experiment in Brazil was not Coligny's only attempt to secure a safe haven for the Huguenots in the New World. In 1562 Jean Ribault with another group of Reformed Protestants crossed the Atlantic and settled in Charlesfort (modern-day Charleston, South Carolina). Within a year most of the exiles abandoned the project and sought to return to Europe, only to endure without adequate provisions a wretched voyage in which survivors were reduced to cannibalism. Another Huguenot expedition sponsored by Coligny sought refuge in the Spanish territories in Florida. In 1564 the French established Fort Caroline, a relatively strong fortress that kept the Spanish at bay for a year. But a year later the Spanish prevailed, and captured the French inhabitants. In a move that adumbrated the fate of Huguenots on St Bartholomew's Day, the Spanish forces executed the several hundred French Protestants on charges of heresy.

Although sixteenth-century Huguenots failed to establish colonies in the New World, their experience foreshadowed Reformed Protestantism's growth beyond Europe to the New World and eventually around the globe. In some cases, Reformed Protestants left their homes in Europe under political threat or legal penalty and hoped for a place free from religious strife. In other instances, the establishment of Reformed churches was part of state-sponsored exploration and colonial development in lands formerly unknown to Europeans. In still others, Reformed Protestants turned inward to discover the resources for a personal and intense devotion. In other words, the Great European migration was the setting for Calvinists to test their powers of adaptation and accommodation. Because the Netherlands and Great Britain were societies where Reformed Protestants enjoyed establishment status, and because as naval powers the Dutch and English were significant rivals of the French, Portuguese, and Spanish in the exploration of North America, churches that traced their spiritual roots to Zurich and Geneva would often be transplanted to uncertain religious soil by British and Dutch merchants. Sometimes that ground would prove to be rocky, as in the case of the Huguenots' experience in Brazil. But usually it was not.

For Calvinism to survive, it would need to find alternatives to European expectations. The colonial Calvinist churches were the beginning of a new age of religious discovery, a time when New World vigor contrasted sharply with Old World timidity.

Dutch Exploration and Church Planting

Coincident with the Arminian controversy was the inauguration of the golden age of Dutch cultural life and economic expansion. Not only was it a time that saw the remarkable accomplishments of Rembrandt, Hugo Grotius, and Spinoza, but it was also a period, beginning with Henry Hudson's 1609 voyage, when the Dutch, by virtue of a superior navy, established colonies around the world in a remarkable manner given the size of the Netherlands' population: 1.5 million (compared to England's 5 million. By 1670 the Dutch employed 120,000 sailors and shipped more goods than Spain, England, and France combined.) The Netherlands' commercial success was partly a result of its decentralized government, which encouraged a relatively diverse population through a policy of religious toleration. As such, the Netherlands was the Ellis Island of seventeenth-century Europe, receiving Huguenots, Iberian and German Jews, and philosophers (Spinoza, John Locke, and René Descartes), all yearning to breathe freely.[1]

One of the keys to Dutch success within such a short period after its independence from Spain was to maintain competition with Europe's powers on the high seas. Consequently, where the Spanish or Portuguese established commercial enterprises the Dutch followed and took advantage of their rivals' weaknesses and markets. This strategy accounts for the presence of Dutch colonies in Indonesia and Africa, and was also responsible for the Dutch supplanting the Portuguese as the carriers of spice and silk from Asia to Europe.

One colony that developed serendipitously was New Netherland in North America. As its name indicated, the East India Company's chief interest in this colony was to bolster trade with Asia. They employed the English admiral, Hudson, to find a quicker route. What he discovered instead was the east coast of North America; Hudson explored both the Chesapeake and Hudson bays before returning to Europe. Favorable reports about the new territory and possibilities for trade prompted the Netherlands to lay claim to the land between the Delaware and Connecticut rivers and to grant a charter, in 1614, to the New Netherland Company to explore the entire region between the French colony in Quebec and the English in Virginia. Makeshift trading posts and forts followed, along with colonists working for the newly chartered West India Company (1621). In the hope of attracting as many colonists as possible, both to increase commerce and to ward off European rivals, New Netherland attracted a diverse population: one French priest reported after visiting the colony that he had heard eighteen different languages. French, Flemish, Walloons, Germans, and Swedes were all well represented, many of whom had first migrated to the tolerant Netherlands, and then to the colony to comprise close to half the population. If Max Weber was right, the Dutch colony developed from Reformed Protestants seeking to justify their status as the elect through economic activity; more likely, the sailors, colonists, and directors of the West India Company knew little about the doings of Dort's Synod or the debates over Arminianism as they sought to establish a viable commercial venture.

To assert that religion was an afterthought in New Netherland is to overstate the situation, but provisions for the first pastor took almost a decade after the permanent settlement at Fort Orange (1614). (This contrasts significantly with the Puritan enterprise in Massachusetts Bay; another notable difference is that the Dutch lacked the missionary motive that was clearly present – no matter how sincere – in English, French, and Spanish ventures.) At the same time, the first directors in New Netherland were conventionally devout and sought to provide for colonists' spiritual needs. With the selection in 1626 as the colony's director-general of Peter Minuit, a Walloon whose Protestant family had migrated to the Netherlands to escape Spanish religious suppression, New Netherland's colonial administration transferred to Manhattan for greater security, at which point spiritual life received attention. Lay readers had performed basic religious services, such as leading services and visiting the sick; worship consisted of singing psalms, readings from the law and creeds, and sometimes the reading of approved sermons.

Finally in 1628 Jonas Michaelius (1577–1638?) arrived as the colony's first pastor. A graduate of Leiden University, and ordained in 1600 by Classis Enkhuizen, Michaelius had pastored in Holland and Brabant for nearly two decades. His interest in colonial life took him in 1624, with his family of five, toward San Salvador, Brazil, a city recently acquired through Dutch expansion into the New World. But before he arrived, the Portuguese would prove to be as effective in blocking the Dutch Reformed as they had been with the Huguenots. Without a parish in Brazil, Michaelius in 1625 went to Guinea on the coast of Africa to serve as chaplain to another West India Company venture. He lasted two years. In 1627 the West India Company appointed him, with the approval of Classis Amsterdam, for work in New Netherland. He sailed from Amsterdam on January 24, 1628. Colonial ministry took its toll on Mrs Michaelius, who died within two months of the family's arrival.

The original congregation (today's Collegiate Reformed Church) had roughly fifty members, among them the Company's director, Minuit, who had served as a deacon and became an elder. Church members were received on the basis of certificates from congregations in the mother country. Those who lacked papers received privileges on the basis of other settlers' testimonies. This was the first formally organized Reformed church in North America, and was ambiguously under the oversight of Classis Amsterdam. No single classis in the Dutch national church had been overseeing responsibilities for the colonies until Amsterdam became the center of the Netherlands' commercial enterprises and Classis Amsterdam became the default governing ecclesiastical body; in 1636 the pastors in Amsterdam created a special committee for the colonial congregations. Michaelius typically preached in Dutch, but sometimes in French to accommodate the Walloon members of the settlement. In a widely cited letter to Dutch ministers about conditions in New Netherland, Michaelius observed that the Europeans were "rough and unrestrained" but he complimented them for showing "love and respect." The natives were "savage, wild, and strangers to all decency."[2] Michaelius complained about the tenuous financial support for his labors. The Company had allotted land for him to work, but without servants or livestock the prospects for sustenance were grim. In 1631 Michaelius returned to the old country. Six years later he expressed an interest in returning, but the directors of the West India Company vetoed Classis of Amsterdam's recommendation.

New Amsterdam would be without a pastor for a couple of years before Everardus Bogardus assumed ministerial responsibilities in the colony. Born in 1607, he was another graduate of Leiden, and like Michaelius had also served, though only in the capacity as a comforter of the sick, in the colonial church on the Guinea coast of Africa. Bogardus was ill-suited to adjust to the poor decisions of the colony's leadership. He and one of New Netherland's governors, Wouter van Twiller, carried on a heated dispute in which the pastor called the governor a "child of the Devil, an incarnate villain," and in retaliation the governor drew his sword and chased Bogardus through the streets of New Amsterdam.[3] Their differences were so pronounced that they agreed to return to the mother country to find a resolution. They left New Netherland in the summer of 1647, but their vessel sank on September 27, off the coast of England. The pastor and governor did not survive. Bogardus' chief contribution had been to oversee the construction in 1642 of a church building, called St Nicholas, a facility that served its members and pastors until 1693.

Bogardus' successor was Johannes Cornelissen Backerus, who lasted only two years (1647–49) before Johannes Megapolensis (1603–70) arrived. He ministered in New Amsterdam until his death, and gave the churches stability. Megapolensis had been a pastor at Fort Orange (near today's Albany) since 1642. In 1648, governor Peter Stuyvesant persuaded Megapolensis against the pastor's will to remain in North America and minister to the two hundred church members in New Amsterdam. By 1652 Megapolensis' duties had become so onerous that the classis of Amsterdam sent a second minister, Samuel Drisius, then serving Dutch immigrants in London. Drisius remained until his death in 1673.

The West India Company had difficulty attracting colonists, and finding ministers to pastor their congregations was not any easier, because salaries were unreliable.[4] As settlements began to spread out – particularly on Long Island – new congregations also emerged. Brooklyn (1646), Flatbush (1651), New Utrecht (1657), and Bushwick (1660) put further strains on limited financial resources. In 1654 the Classis of Amsterdam glumly responded to a request for additional ministers with the observation that "no one desires to undertake such a journey on such a small salary."[5] Taxation became the preferred method for paying for ministers' services (1,040 guilders per year), but tax coffers were rarely full. At one point Stuyvesant himself committed 250 guilders of his personal wealth to pay the pastor in Brooklyn on the condition that he would also conduct services at Stuyvesant's personal chapel on Manhattan Island.

As scattered and as impoverished as the Dutch churches were, they maintained a monopoly on religious life in the colony. In the mother country religious toleration prevailed but colonial governments were free to determine most aspects of their societies. After 1650, when the West India Company tried to encourage additional settlers to join the enterprise, New Netherland began to attract Protestants from outside Reformed churches. In 1653 Lutherans in the colony planned to call their own minister. Quakers and Anabaptists presented another dilemma, since neither group had professional clergy and each member of the group could potentially conduct services. Megapolensis and Drisius repeatedly petitioned the Classis of Amsterdam to pressure the directors of the colony to forbid worship that was not Reformed. (They also actively opposed religious freedom for Roman Catholics and Jewish colonists.) Not only did the pastors in Amsterdam support the colonial ministers but Stuyvesant himself, the son of a minister, sided with his clergy. In 1656 he prohibited all "public or private conventicles and meetings, except the usual and authorized ones, where God's Word, according to the Reformed and established custom, is preached and taught in meetings held for the religious service of the Reformed, comformably to the Synod Dort . . ."[6] When a Lutheran pastor arrived in the colony in 1657 he could not conduct services. He eventually returned to Europe. Even so, the directors of the Company back in the Netherlands worried about the consequences of such strictness, and persuaded the colonial pastors to accommodate Lutherans at least by revising the baptismal formula.

The colonial clergy were also on the lookout for the moral failings of church members. In fact, the novel setting of colonial life prompted Dutch pastors to try to reform morals and manners in ways that the mother country would not abide. Settlers in New Amsterdam, many of them single males without the domesticating influences of marriage or home life, tended to behave the way young bachelors perennially have. Records indicate fines and warnings for stealing, fighting, drunkenness, and failure to pay debts. Megapolensis experienced the threat of a knife from one disgruntled colonist, and also lost a significant portion of his possessions to a thief. In response, pastors petitioned the Classis of Amsterdam in 1648 to persuade the Company's directors to close New Amsterdam's taverns. If this policy were implemented, "much evil and great offense would be removed." One pastor described the difficulty of ministering to settlers:

> There are many hearers, but not much saving fruit.... The people are rather reckless... [and] the taverns and villainous houses have many visitors.... The Company says that the congregation must pay the preacher. But they prefer to gamble away, or lose in bets, a ton of beer at twenty-three or twenty-four guilders, or some other liquor. I will say nothing against the better class; but of these there are too few to make up the salary.[7]

With support from Stuyvesant, pastors tried to preserve Sunday as a day of worship and rest. The governor regularly issued decrees, at the instigation of clergy, to prohibit ordinary farming, constructing, and hunting or fishing on Sundays. Playing games or dancing during worship or between the morning and evening services was illegal.

In the end, moral reform in New Amsterdam was not as difficult as fending off the English. Thanks to the lack of settlers and diminished resources, New Netherland was vulnerable. In 1664, the English, who had never acknowledged the Netherlands' claim to the territory between the Chesapeake Bay and New France, initiated a hostile annexation of the Dutch colony; the conflict lasted until 1667, when the Dutch signed a peace treaty. (For a brief time in 1673 the Dutch regained control, but again lost to stronger English forces.) Megapolensis advised Stuyvesant to surrender rather than try armed defense, a piece of counsel for which the Company's directors never forgave the pastor; they faulted Stuyvesant for "lending an ear to preachers and other chicken-hearted persons."[8] Nevertheless, the Dutch were in no position to defend themselves and the pastor's advice to preserve lives had merit.

The Dutch Reformed pastors faced uncertainty in a colony now named New York. One question was whether the ministers could still work in an English colony under the authority of a Dutch church body. The Duke's Laws of 1665 appeared to resolve this conundrum by granting to the Dutch churches religious toleration and the right to worship publicly. On the positive side, this meant that the Dutch could continue their religious work; the downside was legal toleration for all religious groups. In 1683 New York's Charter of Liberties and Privileges reinforced the religious freedoms granted in the Duke's Laws and also revealed that the English king – now James II – was likely less interested in personal liberties than in populating the colony with as many people as possible for commercial ends. The English government also resolved – not flawlessly – the question of ministers' salaries. The new government established wardens in each community to maintain church buildings. Each town would also pay taxes to support the local minister. Because the Dutch ministers were already settled in many towns, the public funds naturally went to them, that is, if residents paid their taxes.

The transition from Dutch to English rule was generally smooth but the Reformed churches experienced several snags. In 1688, when the Glorious Revolution ended James II's reign and left uncertain the oversight of the English colonies in North America – further complicated by Boston's arrest of Edmund Andros, the colonial governor – Jacob Leisler, a captain in the militia, took the reins of power in New York. Leisler was popular among the middle and lower ranks of New York society but the upper class and the pastors opposed him. For the two years of his tenure, Leisler harassed the Dutch clergy. Meanwhile political conflict divided the churches along class lines. Leisler's eventual execution for failing to yield to the royally appointed governor ended disputes in the short run. But the churches still faced a significant gap between elites and commoners that raised doubts about the public's willingness to support the colony's pastors.

An obvious challenge to the Reformed churches was the English government's allegiance to their national church. Although the Society for the Propagation of the Gospel in Foreign Parts did not begin until 1701, at which point the Church of England started to plant churches in the colonies, New York's governors sometimes sought Anglican priests for the colony. For instance, one of Andros' first acts as governor in 1674 was to appoint Nicholas Van Rensselaer, a son of the Reformed church in the Netherlands who became a deacon in the Church of England while working in London, to minister in the Reformed church in Albany. Reformed ministers in New York eventually prevailed upon Van Rensselaer to conduct services according Dutch norms. A similar conflict emerged under the colonial governor Lord Cornbury in the early eighteenth century, when the English official was not simply hostile to the Reformed churches but also attempted to appoint Anglican priests to Reformed congregations. The conclusion of Cornbury's tenure as governor in 1708 brought the controversy to a close. The subsequent governor, John Lovelace, followed the terms of the charter that the Reformed churches had secured in 1696 with the English government. That agreement granted the Dutch colonial churches to worship "according to the constitutions and directions of the Reformed churches in Holland, approved and instituted by the National Synod of Dort."[9]

Despite notable differences, the experience of Dutch Reformed pastors in South Africa was not decidedly different from that of their counterparts in North America. Tensions with the native population, negotiations with colonial authorities, responsibilities to church bodies in the mother country, and difficult relationships with settlers characterized the establishment of Reformed churches in the Dutch colony of Cape Town. Originally the Dutch presence in South Africa involved establishing a place of refreshment for vessels sailing between the East Indies and Northern Europe. The Cape Colony began in 1652 as part of the East India Company's commercial venture. Over time this halfway stop and administrative port blossomed into an agricultural colony with a settled European presence. Thirty years would pass before the colony was agriculturally self-sustaining. The first settlement consisted of ninety members living in tents. Religious provision for the colonists initially involved the work of the comforters of the sick. During the first thirteen years of Cape Colony's history the settlement went through four of these workers; Willem Wylant was the first. In 1665 the colony finally received its first Reformed pastor, Johan van Arckel. With the ministers' presence also came a consistory. The pastors and elders were accountable in religious matters to the Classis of Amsterdam and in secular affairs to the Company's directors and governor. Maintaining this distinction was never easy.

The first governor of Cape Town was Jan van Riebeeck (1619–77), the son of a surgeon and a native of the Dutch village of Culemborg. He joined the East India Company at the age of twenty and served in the East Indies, initially as an assistant surgeon. At the time of the decision to establish a port in South Africa, the directors of the Company gave the responsibility to van Riebeeck. From all appearances, the governor was devout and supported the Reformed churches. He was also known to rule with a heavy hand but set a good example by attending services regularly. But van Riebeeck's policies would eventually conflict with the Reformed pastors' designs. Instead of following the Dutch Reformed practice of holding two services each Sunday, van Riebeeck allowed only one, since two would have been onerous for the hard-working colonists.

Although services were chiefly about the colonists' religious needs, they also served a communal purpose. Like services in the Netherlands, worship in Cape Town followed a simple pattern. An invocation started the service, followed by the Decalogue, the creed, Scripture reading, and prayer. Congregations sang metrical psalms only, which sometimes allowed for the collection of an offering. Sermons generally lasted an hour. Pastors gave careful attention to biblical texts and used the sermon more for instruction than exhortation or inspiration. Churches administered the Lord's Supper six times each year, which came after the sermon. The service closed with a prayer and benediction. The afternoon services, though not as elaborate, featured sermons devoted to the Heidelberg Catechism, and when pastors administered baptisms, they took place in the second service. In addition to worship, attendees heard news about the colony. Before the morning services, after the second of three peels of the bells, readers announced marriages, the arrival of new settlers, and changes in church membership.

The growth of the churches was slow, thanks again to the lack of incentives for Europeans to settle in the colony. Another factor was the initial reluctance of the colony's governors to establish in South Africa anything more than a refreshing station for ships sailing to and from the East Indies. But in 1688 the Cape Colony received an influx of Huguenot refugees, a consequence of the revocation of the Edict of Nantes in 1685. Approximately 150 French men and women settled in the South African districts of Drakenstein and Stellenbosch. The minister to accompany them was Pierre Simond, considered South Africa's first author owing to his metrical version of the Psalms, published in 1704. He became so popular with church members that in 1700 when he requested permission to return to Europe, the congregation refused. He remained, even though he had already sold his possessions, until 1702 when the next pastor arrived.

Simond was not so popular with the colonial officials. When his congregation petitioned for the creation of a separate church with its own ruling body, the Council on Policy refused and informed the French settlers that such requests were a waste of time. The decision must have confused the Huguenots since the colony's governors had already approved the formation of separate Walloon congregations in Batavia, which was also the practice in the mother country. The Council on Policy's handling of the French request was not necessarily indicative of Dutch chauvinism. The Council regarded all the churches as extensions of the secular authorities; consequently, this body resisted policies that might have suggested the autonomy of clergy to govern ecclesiastical affairs, whether Dutch or French. As a result, the start of new congregations and the development of ecclesiastical structures were slow in coming. After the establishment of the first three congregations at Cape Town (1665), Stellenbosch (1686), and Drakenstein (1691), the next congregation would not be formed until Rhoodezand (1743). Likewise, the formation of church assemblies would have to wait until 1716 when congregations in Stellenbosch and Drakenstein first received permission to deliberate on church business. Not even the Classis of Amsterdam, to which the South African pastors belonged, bothered to challenge the situation.

Despite important differences between colonial life in North America and South Africa, Reformed Protestantism could not have come to New World locations without being part of the baggage that Europeans packed on their way to commercial adventure. For the short run, the colonial experience meant that Reformed churches would be more or less an appurtenance to the primary work of exploration and commerce. In the long run, Reformed churches would establish an independent existence and prosper in places like South Africa and North America in ways that the first colonists could never have imagined. Indeed,

Calvinism's colonial outposts would rival and eventually overtake Europe's national churches in the maintenance and promotion of a self-conscious Reformed Protestantism.

The Holy Colony at Massachusetts Bay

Not all colonial enterprises were primarily commercial, and the English Puritans who migrated to North America between 1620 and 1641 constitute the best example of godly motivation propelling political and economic development in a new land. During these two decades 21,000 devout English men, women, and children (among them seventy-six ordained ministers) left behind the comforts of familiar places for the perils of native populations, unproductive soil, and harsh weather. But these migrations were simply the mid-point in a century's worth of developments among the wing of Puritanism that would take the form of Congregationalism (i.e. a gathered body of saints who ruled within their congregation free from diocesan or synodical oversight).

Although examples of congregationalism appeared earlier, the first significant expression came in the 1580s when Robert Browne, a minister with Puritan convictions, established a separate congregation in the English town of Norwich. An act that could have been punished by execution, it demonstrated the frustration that some Puritans felt over the limits on reformation within the Church of England. Browne, like many Puritans, had studied at Cambridge and would eventually turn down an offer to minister within a parish in the university town. Ordination by a bishop would violate Browne's principles. His church in Norwich eventually drew the attention of civil authorities, and in 1581 Browne moved to the Low Countries (Middelburg), where he and Robert Harrison could implement their Puritan ideals of a covenanted group of believers. In the Netherlands, Browne wrote several treatises that defined the basic contours of Congregationalism, the most notable of which was that, as a body set apart from the world, the church should be comprised only of true believers, unlike the state church that included unbelievers and nominal Christians. Browne and Harrison eventually came to different convictions, and the former moved to Scotland. But the Scottish authorities would not be as tolerant as the Dutch and so Browne returned to England. Ironically for the history of Congregationalism, in 1586 Browne made his peace with the Church of England and served as a priest for the remainder of his life.

Although Browne's views on church government were unusual – among those Puritans who dissented from episcopacy, Presbyterianism was the preferred polity – his desire for a pure and spiritual expression of Christianity was the norm, especially in the last decades of the sixteenth century when the

Elizabethan Settlement adopted a course of moderation. An example of Puritan piety was John Winthrop (1588–1649); he had trained as a lawyer but at the age of twenty-four was assisting his father in running the family manor. Winthrop had always been interested in religion, but when he turned eighteen his devotion became intense and he sought to tame the residual wickedness of his soul. He did so by regulating his diet, singing psalms, and reading spiritual handbooks. Even so, he often complained that he was too occupied with worldly affairs even as he understood the value of ordinary work. After dreaming that he had seen Christ during a night's sleep, Winthrop recorded in his journal, "I was so ravished with his love to me . . . that being awakened it had made so deep an impression in my heart, as I was forced to unmeasurable weepings for a great while."[10]

During the first two decades of the seventeenth century, earnest souls such as Winthrop practiced a de facto form of congregationalism. In a manner similar to serious-minded Dutch Calvinists, many Puritans opted out of the national church to meet in conventicles where the faithful could gather among like-minded believers. In areas such as Essex and Northamptonshire, gentry could afford to support ministers with Puritan convictions, thereby providing a safe haven from the regulations of suspicious bishops. Others with a similar understanding of the church and spiritual life, such as William Bradford (1590–1657), were forced to carry out their ideals in exile. At the age of twelve Bradford first heard the preaching of a Puritan pastor in Yorkshire, whose call for a purified church captured the boy's devotion. The meetings of likeminded saints in Scrooby that ensued ran afoul of church and civil authorities. The archbishop of York had followers arrested; others were fined. This prompted the Scrooby group in 1607 to leave for the Netherlands and settle in Leiden. Historians have repeatedly attempted to distinguish among non-separating, semi-separatist, and separatist Puritans. What may make as much sense as any religious principle is political circumstance; when authorities threatened with legal penalties, they paved the way to separatism.

Whatever the differences among Puritans who doubted the merits of ecclesiastical hierarchy, the ones sympathetic to congregationalism were most likely to settle in the New World. The first group to settle was the Pilgrims, led by Bradford. After a decade in the Netherlands, their leaders were worried that their children would grow up more Dutch than English. Between 1617 and 1620 the Pilgrims negotiated a territory in North America and sought funding for the journey and colony. The final plan had them settling in land controlled by the London Virginia Company at the mouth of the Hudson River. After a treacherous voyage on board the *Mayflower*, 102 passengers arrived in New England on November 9, 1620, at New Plymouth north of Cape Cod, some distance from the planned destination. More bad weather during an attempt to sail to the

Hudson River sent the immigrants back to New Plymouth, where the Pilgrims remained. During the first winter, half the colonists died. But a successful harvest the next year became the occasion for a thanksgiving celebration (which became a United States holiday in the nineteenth century). With the arrival of two more ships in 1623, Plymouth Colony grew to three hundred colonists by 1630 and became the first permanent Puritan settlement in North America.

John Winthrop led the second group of Puritan settlers, a move premised on political developments in England that agitated non-separatists to opt for separation from the mother country. In 1625, Charles I succeeded James I as king of England. Married to a Roman Catholic, Henrietta Maria of France, Charles seemed to Puritans to be intent on turning back the ecclesiastical clock. His religious policies favored decorum, formality, and uniformity. Not only were the king's instincts virtually the opposite of Puritans, but his archbishop, William Laud, enforced Charles' policies by initiating the prosecution of Nonconformists. The triumph of the sacramentarian wing of Anglicanism led some Puritans not only to despair for the cause of church reform but to fear for their lives. So destructive and iniquitous were Laud's rules that in Puritan minds God could respond in judgment. To save their lives and preserve the true faith, in 1630 roughly a thousand joined Winthrop to sail for a colony overseen by the Massachusetts Bay Company.

Even before the immigrants who accompanied Winthrop left for the New World, John Endecott oversaw developments and made preparations for the colonial enterprise (he would also succeed Winthrop as governor in Massachusetts after Winthrop's death). Salem was the original center of the colony as well as the site of the first congregation, originally pastored by Samuel Skelton and Francis Higginson. A graduate of Cambridge University and disenchanted with the Church of England, Higginson (1588–1630) readily accepted the opportunity to minister without the restrictions imposed by the Stuarts or their archbishop. He also drafted the first rudiments of church order for the colony, which, in good congregationalist fashion, granted church members the power to select and ordain pastors and required members to subscribe to a church covenant. Part of this vow included a pledge to "give our selves to the Lord Jesus Christ and the word of his grace, for the teaching, ruleing and sanctifyieing of us in matters of worship and conversation, resolving . . . to oppose all contrarie wayes, cannons, and constitutions of men in his worship." The typical Puritan church covenant also stated:

> Wee do . . . promise . . . to endeavor the establishment amongst ourselves of all holy ordinances which [Christ] hath appointed for his church here on earth, and to observe all and every of them . . . opposing to the utmost of our power

whatsoever is contrary thereunto, and bewailing from our hearts our own neglect thereof in former tyme, and our polluting ourselve with any sinful intentions.[11]

Soon enough the original settlers of Salem would see a display of the sinfulness they had vowed to avoid. Some of the colonists objected to the organization and worship of the congregation for departing significantly from the Church of England. In particular, the Browne brothers, Samuel and John (no apparent relation to Robert Browne), believed that the pastors were separatists and in danger of Anabaptism. Bringing John Browne into line was a challenge since he was also on the Company's board of directors. But when he and his brother began to hold separate meetings that followed the Book of Common Prayer, Endecott ordered the Brownes back to England where they registered their complaints with the Company, which still included John Winthrop who had yet to depart for the New World. The matter did not find a resolution.

At roughly the same time, and perhaps owing to this dispute in the Salem congregation, the company's charter had changed in ways remarkably hospitable to the Puritans. The Puritans who signed up for the venture would have the opportunity to buy stock in the Company, thus turning the settlers into the Company's governors, but the Company's charter did not specify where stockholders should meet. This left the residents of Massachusetts free from the oversight and tinkering of directors and governors in London.

Whatever freedom the colonists may have enjoyed by virtue of the quirks in their charter, Winthrop constrained them with his speech, "A Model of Christian Charity," likely written on board the *Arbella* for the group of Puritans who sailed to North America. Uncertainty about the text's origins extends to whether Winthop actually delivered his remarks to his fellow travelers. Even so, the speech described the colonists' purpose unambiguously according to Puritan ideals. The famous conclusion, in which the governor used the language of Christ's "Sermon on the Mount" and described the Puritans' colony as a a "city on a hill" for all the world to see the integrity of their zeal, was actually a minor theme compared to the overwhelming concern for sharing wealth and looking after the physical needs of all the settlers. Indeed, Winthrop devoted most of the discourse to the disparity of financial resources and social standing that characterized these colonists. He feared significant physical hardships upon arrival and knew about the experience of the Pilgrims at Plymouth Plantation. In which case, the purpose of Winthrop's "Model" was chiefly to call upon those with more to care for those with less, and to do so under the logic of Christian charity. Not only did he refute objections to sharing the wealth based on notions of private property and personal responsibility, but he also prescribed how Puritans were to provide for each other. Winthrop closed his "Model" with Moses' instructions to the Israelites as they were about to enter the Promised Land. By invoking this moment in Israel's history, Winthrop was not simply hoping to inspire but also to remind settlers of their covenant with each other and their God, and the redemptive significance of their undertaking in the New World. "[I]f our hearts shall turn away, so that we will not obey, but shall be seduced, and worship other Gods, our pleasure and profits, and serve them," Winthrop warned, "we shall surely perish out of the good land whither we pass over this vast sea to possess it." "Therefore let us choose life," he implored, "that we and our seed may live, by obeying His voice and cleaving to Him, for He is our life and our prosperity."[12]

In addition to exhibiting charity, the Puritan errand was consequential to Winthrop because of what the Bible taught about a holy society. Although the English Protestants who preceded the Puritans had drawn inspiration from Reformed churches on the Continent, especially Calvin's Geneva, circumstances in the New World enabled this group to establish reforms of both the church and the state without interference from civil or ecclesiastical authorities and precedents. For civil polity the Puritans took cues from the laws and regulations of the Old Testament; for the church the New Englanders developed the relatively novel rules of Congregationalist polity. In other words, here was a blank canvas upon which Puritans, as heirs of Reformed Protestantism, could paint their ideal church, state, and society. At the same time, even though Massachusetts Bay would present an alternative to the corruptions of Old England, its settlers could not help but persist in traditional English ways. One example of this was the high regard that Puritans placed upon an educated clergy. Within the first decade the colonists in Massachusetts had made provision for a college (Harvard in 1636) that would continue to rely on knowledge of Greek and Latin antiquity as the basis for a godly ministry (as well as other professions).

The Puritan settlements at Plymouth and Massachusetts were not the only instances of Congregationalism in the British North American colonies. In 1636, a hundred settlers from Massachusetts Bay moved south to form the Colony of Connecticut. Thomas Hooker (1586–1647) was chiefly responsible for creating a new outlet for Puritanism. A graduate of Cambridge University, Hooker had served as a priest in the Church of England until some of his Puritan practices (in this case, lectures) ran afoul of Archbishop Laud. In 1626 he fled to Rotterdam, and seven years later he found passage to Massachusetts Bay, where he was the first pastor of the parish in Cambridge. Hooker's objections to restrictions on suffrage in Massachusetts were a factor in his decision to establish another Puritan experiment. In *Survey and Summe of Church Discipline* (1648), one of the most important early defenses of Congregationalism, Hooker advocated extending voting privileges in civil as well as ecclesiastical matters to all church members. Even so, Hooker's departure from Massachusetts did not signal a break with his former Puritan colleagues. He continued to meet with Boston clergy to settle controversies and to seek ways for better coordination. The Colony of Connecticut would eventually absorb two other Puritan settlements in the territory south of Massachusetts. One was the Saybrook Colony founded in 1635 by John Winthrop, Jr (1606–76), partly as a home for prominent Puritan politicians, among them Oliver Cromwell, who were contemplating leaving England. When these plans fell apart in 1644 the colony merged with Connecticut. The other colony was New Haven, founded in 1636, where the pastor John Davenport (1597–1670) led his flock after arriving in Boston and sensing the need for more freedom to implement his ideals. A vigorous rivalry between New Haven and Connecticut ended in 1662 after the Restoration of the English monarchy, when James II altered the terms of the Royal Charter. By 1665 New Haven was part of Connecticut.

Yet one more Puritan group to separate from Massachusetts, though not voluntarily, was the flock of saints to follow Roger Williams (1603–83) in 1636 to the colony of Rhode Island. In some ways the most consistent of Puritans, Williams had refused after training at Cambridge University to minister in the Church of England. For the sake of its integrity, the church needed to be free from the inevitably corrupting influences of civil patronage. After migrating to Boston in 1631, Williams refused a call to one of the town's parishes because he regarded the Puritan claim to be a Reformed expression of the English ecclesiastical establishment as nothing more than a subterfuge. Instead he ministered among the Pilgrims, for whom separatism was a mark of honor. Over the course of the next several years, Williams' public disapproval of the Massachusetts clergy, the king, and the terms of Puritan society made him a liability. In 1636, after being banished by Massachusetts authorities, Williams bought land from the Narragansett Indians to form a new colony. He was also rebaptized as a Baptist. But instead of turning Rhode Island into a political order dominated by Baptist churches, the colony became a release valve for believers who could not measure up to Puritan standards. The colony's policy of religious freedom resulted in an experiment in religious diversity, at least for religious groups on bad terms with civil authorities (such as the Quakers).

The availability of land to accommodate various strains of Puritan Congregationalism – unlike the options available to Dutch Reformed pastors to the south – proved to be particularly beneficial in 1636 when the saints in Massachusetts experienced a major theological controversy. On the surface the Antinomian Controversy of 1636–38 appeared primarily to be a challenge to congregational polity by pitting assertive laity against church officers. The case featured Anne Hutchinson, the wife of a successful Boston merchant who was also a respected member of the town's congregation. Anne, who was a disciple of John Cotton, the associate pastor in Boston, held popular weekday meetings in the Hutchinson home to discuss the previous Sunday's sermons. These conversations eventually revealed a tension between Cotton and Boston's other pastor, John Wilson, over the place and function of good works in a Christian's life: were they signs of saving grace to the point of reassuring against doubt or did certainty of salvation come inevitably from faith itself? Over time, Hutchinson's comments in private meetings became pointed as she pitted Wilson against Cotton, at least in her own mind. The most troubling aspect of her opinions was also the most challenging to clergy – but also to the laity as it turned out – namely, her insistence that a believer could discover religious certainty through invisible and internal means (e.g. through experience of the Holy Spirit). Because her faith appeared to be indifferent to outward behavior, Hutchinson's views could mean that even external observance of the colony's laws and church duties was irrelevant to genuine Christianity. With important officials in the colony implicated in the controversy by virtue of their membership in the Boston congregation, Hutchinson's views had potential to unravel the Puritan enterprise. A synod of ministers met at Newtown in 1637 to adjudicate the matter, and forbade private religious meetings like those hosted by Hutchinson. They also banned disrespectful questioning of established pastors. A year later the Boston church excommunicated Hutchinson and she sought refuge in Rhode Island with Roger Williams.

One of the lessons taught by the Hutchinson affair was that the independence and sovereignty of individual congregations hampered the ability of other pastors and other churches to intervene in a difficult situation. For some, the lesson of the Antinomian Controversy was the prudence of Presbyterianism compared to congregational polity. In 1641 John Eliot, pastor at Roxbury in Massachusetts Bay Colony, advocated a presbyterian form of church government, and his reasons stemmed from the debates over Hutchinson. Not only did the rule of elders and pastors look more appealing after the indiscretions of assertive laity, but the possibility of one congregation intervening in the affairs of another would have proved a wholesome check upon the isolationism inherent in congregational autonomy. Eliot's private remarks about the value of Presbyterianism found support from pastors at Hingham (Peter Hobart) and Newbury (Thomas Parker and James Noyes). Adding to the Presbyterian momentum was the complexion of the Westminster Assembly meeting in 1643 in London. Although New England Puritans clearly supported parliament and welcomed its call for an ecclesiastical assembly, they were not so enthusiastic about the strength of presbyterian views among the Westminster Divines. The mild controversy over Presbyterianism that ensued in New England was difficult to end thanks to the very autonomy that Congregationalism was supposed to guarantee. But the colony's General Court prevailed upon the ministers to convene a synod at Cambridge in 1646 that attempted to define Puritan church government.

The resulting Cambridge Platform, ratified in 1648 by churches both in Massachusetts and Connecticut, was ambiguous and indecisive on the matter of ecclesiastical authority, and so did more to confirm the existing autonomy of congregations and the power of the laity than it did to check the dangers of Congregationalism. On the one hand, the declaration affirmed the integrity of "particular churches" and found biblical warrant from the New Testament habit of addressing Christians in specific cities or towns (Chap. IV.2). It also reaffirmed the need for all church members to enter into a covenant with each other that followed the pattern of oath-taking in the Old Testament; without such a congregational covenant, the Platform explained, "we see not otherwise how members can have church-power over one another mutually" (Chap. IV.3). Even after the difficulties with Antinomian laity, the drafters held that true churches may exist "without any officers." This did not prevent rules for the appointment of pastors, elders, teachers, and deacons after Calvin's original four-fold model (Chap. VI.1). Still, the possibility of churches without officers indicated the degree to which these Puritans were turning their backs on all forms of church hierarchy. Consequently, even if the procedure of convening clergy to establish the Standing Order for the Massachusetts churches implied an emerging clericalism, in fact, the Platform ended up codifying and preserving the authority of the laity in ways that had only been tacit and informal during the colony's first twenty years.

While Puritans in New England worked through tensions in their own affairs, they could not ignore developments in the mother country, especially when these had the effect of undermining the Puritan *raison dêtre*. The Puritan ascendancy in parliament, a civil war with the New Model Army led by the Puritan statesman Oliver Cromwell, and the convening of an assembly of Puritan clergy to determine religious policy for England – all of these circumstances altered New England Puritans' perceptions of the society they had rejected and left behind. When parliament issued a call in 1640 for colonists in New England to return to the mother country, as many as a hundred responded. William Bradford himself estimated that half of New England's intellectual elites returned to England during the heady days of the Puritan ascendancy. England's parliament appealed to John Cotton to return so that he could assist with a defense of Congregationalism during debates about church polity. Cotton declined, but did write *The True Constitution of a Particular Visible Church*

(1642) to make up for his absence. The authorities in Massachusetts also assisted the cause in England in 1641 by dispatching Hugh Peter, William Hibbins, Thomas Weld, and John Winthrop, Jr, along with forty or so other New Englanders, to aid in the political struggle. Peter, who vowed to return to New England, became a chaplain in parliament's army and a close associate of Cromwell. So strong was the pull that when Peter wrote to John Winthrop (the Elder) to go back to England, residents of Massachusetts feared that if the governor left he would be elected to parliament and never return. The problem of reverse migration was also on the minds of the ministers who gathered to draft the Cambridge Platform. The document specifically addressed circumstances that would allow church members to forsake their congregation's covenant. Members who joined by consent "should not depart without consent." A "pretended want of competent subsistence" was not a sufficient ground for a settler to leave church and community (Chap. XIII).

Puritans in England who shared Congregationalist convictions looked to New England for help because they were outnumbered in parliament by Presbyterians and Independents (a position defined more by opposition to church hierarchy – episcopal or presbyterian – than affirmation of Congregationalism as the biblical norm). In fact, only five of the Westminster Divines advocated Congregationalism. After the Westminster Assembly and the Civil War, England's government under Cromwell was comprised of a coalition dominated by Independents. This arrangement was not inherently hostile to Congregationalists since one of their number, John Owen, became one of the most influential pastors and theologians in England. But the religious chaos that characterized the Interregnum was responsible for turning English Congregationalists in a politically and ecclesiastically conservative direction. In 1658 at the Savoy Assembly, roughly a hundred English Congregationalists set down their convictions to distinguish themselves from other Protestants. Their doctrinal affirmations mainly followed the teachings of the Westminster Assembly. For church government Savoy relied upon New England's Cambridge Platform. The hope was for a religious settlement that would allow Presbyterians and Congregationalists to co-exist. Restoration of the monarchy in 1660 ended those hopes. Within two years the Act of Uniformity would force most Congregationalists (and Presbyterians) into the status of religious dissenters.

At roughly the same time that Congregationalists were gathering at Savoy in England, those in New England were experiencing further difficulties thanks to strains within the Puritan ideal. An important consequence of the Congregational decision to limit church membership to those who could prove an experiential acquaintance and appropriation of the gospel was to raise doubts about the practice of infant baptism. Over time New England's churches included adults who had been baptized but could not exhibit the same dedication that characterized the original settlers' demanding piety. On top of the problem of knowing what to do about the status of these church members was the question of their children: could those who were baptized but unconverted submit their children for baptism? The Cambridge Synod had addressed this question in its Platform and upheld the Puritan practice of limiting baptism to the children of those in full communion – parents who had experienced true religion and owned the covenant. But this policy did not fit the reality that many ministers increasingly faced. During the 1650s another standard of church membership arose – one in which the children of baptized adults could be baptized regardless of whether their parents had shown sufficient devotion to enter into full communion.

In 1662 the Massachusetts General Court summoned ministers to another synod, this time to address the conflict over baptism and membership. The remedy was the so-called Halfway Covenant, which permitted congregations to expand the requirements for membership by extending baptism to children of baptized parents who had not had a conversion experience. But instead of fixing the problem, the 1662 synod merely paved the way for greater diversity within New England's ecclesiastical order. Thanks to the policy of congregational autonomy, each church could (and did) employ a different standard for full communion. As a result, ministers and lay persons found themselves on both sides of the proposed changes to the Puritan way. As James F. Cooper, Jr observes, the original Puritan project in New England "relied more on spirit than upon a carefully crafted set of rules and regulations." But establishing churches and a society to sustain them forced Puritans in the New World to try to codify their religious spirit. After the Halfway Covenant, "cooperation, mutuality, and a willingness to forgo immediate goals in the larger cause of harmony" no longer functioned as the "glue" that held the Puritan project together.[13]

For that reason, the anguish that the English government provoked in 1684 when England's Court of Chancery revoked Massachusetts Bay's charter only formalized what had been an emerging reality ever since 1650 when the colony's Standing Order began to totter. The reasons for this change in Massachusetts' status were overwhelmingly economic and political and had little to do with the religious policies of Charles II. Even so, the establishment of New England as a dominion under royally appointed governors revoked the independence that had allowed the Puritans to implement their religious ideals. The reality of this change became all too clear in 1687 when Sir Edmund Andros, the second governor of New England, gave Anglicans the priority of meeting for worship at Boston's Third Church. Efforts to secure a new charter were successful in 1692, but the terms provided that the crown would appoint New England's governors. This also meant that royal governors would oversee church life in Massachusetts, much like in New York. England's Toleration Act of 1689, which granted freedoms to Protestant dissenters to worship publicly, now applied to New England as well, though governors like Andros had leeway in providing support for colonial churches. Technically, the Act would have prevented the kind of establishment Puritans enjoyed in Massachusetts throughout most of the seventeenth century. But of greater significance was the loss of the original charter. This change opened not only the colonial administration but also church affairs to persons who knew little or cared much about the Puritans' vision of personal, social, and ecclesiastical reform.

For almost a century the Congregationalist stripe of Puritanism, inspired in part by the sort of godly society engineered in Geneva, had provoked important ecclesiastical and social experiments on both sides of the Atlantic Ocean. In the case of England, Puritans proved to be a revolutionary force that toppled a huge part of the nation's regime. In New England the effects of Puritanism were not revolutionary per se but they did involve unprecedented ecclesiastical and political experiments. In neither case was the Puritan ideal of reformation successful in establishing a sustainable order. In fact, the Puritan understanding of reform and godliness, which regarded compromise as a kind of infidelity, carried the Congregationalist wing of Puritanism farther way from the Reformed churches in Scotland, the Netherlands, Switzerland, and Germany than Puritans were when they first objected to the Elizabethan settlement. The failings and excesses of Puritanism would be significant factors later in the decline of Calvinism in Old and New England. The reason is that the ideal of a pure church constantly ran up against the frailty and depravity of clergy and lay people. As a result, the devotional literature of the Puritans would stay in print. It provided great inspiration to later generations of Calvinists. But it also sowed seeds of high expectations that produced the fruit of discontent. The closest that Puritanism would come to forging a godly church or society would be in the lives of pious persons who through informal networks or separately would follow Puritan prescriptions for practical holiness.

The Mixed Blessing of Colonial Churches

The good news for Reformed Protestants, though no one knew it at the time, was that Europe's colonial expansion into the New World also extended Reformed churches to parts of the world unknown to the pastors who originally took up the cause of reform. Not only did the colonial churches give the Reformed faith a global footprint, but they would also blossom into some of Reformed Protestantism's sweetest fruit; unlike the European churches that limped along under the impediments imposed by chary civil authorities, churches in North America and South Africa would eventually enjoy unparalleled freedoms to develop their religious identities in ways that may have even delighted John Calvin himself.

Even before establishing independence from European states and the national Reformed churches, the Dutch Reformed in North America and South Africa, and Puritans in New England experienced a measure of new freedoms that would be common to later generations. Colonial governments could either provide for greater religious uniformity than the mother country (e.g. New Netherland) or they could allow Protestants to use the colony as a laboratory for further reform (e.g. Massachusetts). The greater liberty that colonial Reformed churches enjoyed was not without its disadvantages; simply having fewer obstacles, such as state laws and procedures or rival Christian churches, did not guarantee a truly reformed church. Puritan ideals about a church comprised of true believers ran up against the realities of the second generation's indifference, and the Dutch Reformed monopoly on public funds in New Netherland did not result automatically in generously or promptly paid pastors. Still, colonial conditions provided Reformed pastors and their flocks with an alternative model for church life, one less beholden to Christendom and more open to a voluntary arrangement.

That said, greater freedom to practice Reformed ideals could not hide the reality of dependence upon economic backers and civil patrons. In the colonial environments, that patronage may have grown to add commercially minded overseers to the existing apparatus of state control; but this was no less an indication of the deep dependence of Reformed Protestants upon lay authorities. Without the support of kings, princes, and mayors, Reformed churches could not have started, and without the expansion of Europe's nations into foreign lands, the Reformed churches could not have established a global presence.

CHAPTER SIX

NEW COMMUNITIES IN THE LAND OF THE FREE

JOHN PHILIP BOEHM ARRIVED in Pennsylvania in 1720, when he was almost the same age as the British colony that William Penn had established in 1682 on the western side of the Delaware River. Born in 1683 to a Reformed pastor, Philip Ludwig Boehm, in the territory of Hesse-Kassel, John Philip pursued work similar to his father but without crossing the threshold of ordination; in 1708 the son took a position as teacher in the Reformed parish of Worms. Salary disputes led Boehm in 1715 to take a similar position at Lambsheim but the new home did not end worries over back wages owed by town officials and the need to provide for his wife and a young family of eight children (four by his first wife, who had died prematurely). These circumstances led Boehm to look favorably on invitations from Penn's colony for German settlers. Upon disembarking at Philadelphia he followed the road already traveled by previous German immigrants toward German Town and then beyond to the Perkiomen Valley.

When Boehm settled in Pennsylvania he found a group of immigrants, scattered ten to twenty miles from Philadelphia's ports on the Delaware River, who were doing what they did best: farming. These German settlers had come primarily from Europe, but some had relocated from New York and New Jersey. Under William Penn's Quaker ideals, Pennsylvania provided the freedom and – perhaps, just as important – the land that attracted those looking for a place to make a living without onerous oversight. In fact, Pennsylvania's administration of the colony was so loose that the colony's governor, William Keith, reported to the provincial council with some surprise that "foreigners from Germany, strangers to our Languages and Constitution," were dispersing throughout the colony without any documentation to prove their status. This led to a colonial policy that required all ship captains to provide a list of all their passengers. Reports from ministers in Philadelphia would confirm what ship captains knew, namely, that the German immigrants were from both Lutheran and Reformed backgrounds. By 1710 the Reformed contingent in the settlement around Skippack numbered as many as twenty, and sometimes gathered for worship in the vicinity of White Marsh. For baptism services these farmers employed a local Dutch Reformed pastor. When they felt compelled to partake of the Lord's Supper they would travel all the way to Philadelphia, where the Presbyterian pastor, Jedediah Andrews, admitted them to fellowship. Otherwise, they had no one to lead worship and sometimes would even meet with Quakers on Sundays, whose "good morals and blameless conduct" were agreeable and whose formless worship was better than "none."[1]

Boehm's arrival brought to the German community the presence of a pastor's son with book learning: he was a natural choice to conduct services even though he lacked credentials. In 1725, when the German Reformed adherents had grown to over fifty households, the farmers implored Boehm to conduct services for them. Even then Boehm only overcame reservations about the ministry once he saw how desperate the farmers were. As he later recalled, the request from local settlers was so touching "that our hearts melted together in tears." Adding to Boehm's burden was having to answer for his decision on Judgment Day. Did Boehm have the "courage" to leave these souls "without help and scattered among all kinds of sects, of which this country is filled?" He preferred to continue to support himself by farming, but with a pledge that he would be paid for his services, Boehm consented "to be persuaded to this work."[2]

The new pastor, still not ordained formally, had ample reason for resisting the settlers' petitions. Soon after his acceptance he determined the scope of the Germans' religious needs. He divided the Reformed population into three separate congregations, one at White Marsh (twenty-four members), another at Skippack (thirty-seven), and the third at Falkner Swamp (forty). Each congregation followed by calling Boehm as its pastor, and in late fall of 1725 he began to conduct services by preaching and administering the sacraments. This was the beginning of formal German Reformed church life in the New World.

Boehm's experience as the organizing pastor of immigrants who lacked direct ecclesiastical ties to mother churches in the old country was another important vehicle for the expansion of Reformed Protestantism from Europe to North America. Not only did the Great European Migration extend Reformed churches under the auspices of colonial governments that sought to provide for the spiritual welfare of their members, it also carried individuals and families from Reformed backgrounds to frontier settings where no church existed. These immigrants, in turn, became the basis at first for Reformed and Presbyterian congregations and, over time, for a kind of ecclesiastical organization unknown in Europe, namely, voluntary denominations. Instead of relying on political patrons, these immigrants, both lay and clerical, depended on the good will of Calvinists to join, support, and submit to the church's ministry. As different as this model of church life was from Old World patterns, the voluntary church would become the most successful model for establishing Reformed Protestantism in the New World and even for reinvigorating Europe's Calvinists.

First a Trickle, Then a Stream

The experience of Francis Makemie (1658–1707), the organizing pastor of Presbyterianism in the New World, was not so different from that of Boehm, except that the Scots-Irish immigrant departed for North America with clerical credentials in hand. The son of Scottish immigrants to County Donegal, in Northern Ireland – the exact date of his birth, like much of his childhood, remains obscure – Makemie embodied one of the chief tributaries of American Presbyterianism, namely, Scottish Presbyterians who had migrated to the Ulster Plantation and then sought comfort and livelihoods in North America. The Scots-Irish, in fact, demonstrate the accidental ways in which Reformed Protestantism moved to different parts of the world, sometimes with the direct blessing of the magistrates who patronized Protestantism, and sometimes as an unintended consequence of a ruler's political strategy.

England's Ulster Plantation was part of a strategy, initiated by Henry VIII, to secure a border land – Ireland – that England's Roman Catholic enemies could not use to oust the Protestant monarch. (The threat posed by the Spanish Armada in 1588 illustrated the plausibility of Henry's fear of an Irish alliance with European powers.) Like many colonial endeavors, the establishment of Ulster involved the same tensions that afflicted English endeavors in the New World: differences between the crown and colonial governments, inconsistencies between religious and commercial motives, and difficulty in recruiting settlers. Ulster's uniqueness stemmed from its proximity to England and Scotland, and its strategic importance to England's national defense. But like the colony at Jamestown, Ulster was difficult sell to would-be English settlers. Although the Irish colony had started to take shape during Henry's reign, by the early seventeenth century it was able to offer only the same bleak conditions that colonists in Virginia experienced.

James I began to remedy the situation by recruiting his native Scots. Although the migration of Scots to Ireland was centuries old, it became part of an official plan to establish an English-run Protestant beachhead across the Irish Sea. Between 1608 and 1610, forty-five adventurers, largely nobles solicited by James from the lowlands of Scotland, had visited Ireland to develop settlements in the Ulster Plantation. The people recruited to take up residence in the colony included both the devout and the undesirable. According to one of the former class of Scots – a Presbyterian minister – among those whom God had sent to Ireland were "several persons eminent by birth, education, and parts; yet the most part were such as either poverty, scandalous lives, or at the best, adventurous seeking of better accommodation had forced thither." The result was that "the security and thriving of religion was [sic] little seen to by those adventurers. . ."[3] But this did not prevent Scottish ministers from migrating to Ulster, which some did as early as the 1570s when James VI was considering policies to establish episcopacy in Scotland. Although the churches were often in disrepair, by 1622 as many as twenty Protestant ministers were serving approximately 2,500 parishioners in Northern Ireland. And despite reports of the ruffians who settled in Ulster, other comments suggested that the Scots-Irish had their pious moments, such as the pastor who remembered, in 1630, that the people would come from many miles away for the communion season of services, from Saturday through Monday, "not troubled with sleepiness" by the last sermon. "In those days," he added, "it was no great difficulty for a minister to preach in public or private, such was the hunger of the hearers."[4]

Over time, the Stuart policies that had made Ulster attractive to Scottish ministers would also send them from Ireland to the North American colonies. Under Charles I, Archbishop Laud first tried in the 1630s to introduce greater regularity in worship in Northern Ireland. Robert Blair, a minister from Scotland, tried to leave for New England in 1636 with forty others, but uncooperative winds brought them back to Belfast, and he subsequently returned to Scotland. The revolt of Irish Roman Catholics in 1641 against their English overlords (and against Protestants more generally) introduced an eleven-year period of religious conflict that took as many as twelve thousand lives and significantly undermined the life of Presbyterian congregations. Oliver Cromwell punctuated this era with sieges in September and October of 1649, of Drogheda and Wexford respectively, where soldiers and citizens of royalist persuasion were killed. Estimates put the number of civilians massacred at Wexford at roughly 1,500, and at approximately 800 at Drogheda. Although many Irish loyal to the crown were Roman Catholic, Presbyterians who thought they could cut a better deal with Charles than with parliament were also the victims of Cromwell's military campaign. By 1653, after the lord protector was finished with Ireland – which included teaching the Scots a lesson for siding with Charles I – only six Presbyterian ministers remained in Ulster. By 1663, that number had increased to seventy, but the restoration of the crown in 1660 had also restored the Anglican establishment as the Church of Ireland. Given the vicissitudes of British politics and the uncertainty of Ulster's future, young Presbyterians like Makemie looked to the North American colonies for opportunities.

When Makemie arrived in Maryland in 1683, he had left behind his parents, two brothers, and one sister; he was the only one of his family to leave Ireland. Only seven years prior to his trip he had enrolled at the University of Glasgow, where the registrar noted his blue eyes, brown hair covering "an intellectual forehead," and "the dignified mien of a true Irish gentleman."[5] Makemie studied divinity, and in 1680 started the process of ordination with his home Presbytery of Laggan. The Stuart monarchy's religious policies were again responsible for a gap from 1680 to 1691 in the presbytery's records during the time of Makemie's ordination. Charles II provided a modicum of support for the Irish Presbyterian Church, but this did not prevent periods when the its meeting houses were closed and Presbyterian worship prohibited. Under James II, the plight of Irish Protestants became more alarming thanks to the king's intentions to restore the Roman church in England and Ireland. James' administration purged Protestants from positions in the civic administration of Ulster and many Scots-Irish either moved back to Scotland or looked for homes in England. Under these unsettled conditions, the Presbytery of Laggan ordained Makemie, either in 1681 or 1682, and soon thereafter Makemie boarded a ship for North America. He took with him a commission from the presbytery to plant churches among the British colonists. Beyond that mandate, he had the freedom to channel the energies of a twenty-five-year-old into a productive pastorate; he also had no financial provisions beyond his own ingenuity.

Makemie left for the New World before the largest influx of Scots-Irish to the British colonies in North America. In the 1710s an initial wave of Scots-Irish looked to New England because of religious affinities, but historic ethnic differences repeated themselves and the Irish immigrants were forced to look for more hospitable places. Pennsylvania would prove to be one of the most attractive sites to Scots-Irish, and to other Europeans looking for land and religious freedom. By the 1720s the ports on the Delaware River and Bay had become the destination for most Scots-Irish migrants. But even before these later patterns of migration, Makemie and those with whom he traveled were settling in colonies around Chesapeake Bay, with Maryland's policy of religious toleration (especially to Roman Catholics) being especially attractive. Scots-Irish had arrived in Maryland as early as 1649, but significant numbers did not settle there until 1670. An important factor was a dearth of English indentured servants on tobacco plantations; merchants turned to Ireland for replacements. Even if Maryland was a frontier territory when Makemie arrived, Presbyterians made up the majority of settlers on the eastern and western shores of the Chesapeake. This Presbyterian presence explains the 1680 petition that Colonel William Stevens, an English settler in Maryland with ties to the Church of England, sent to the Presbytery of Laggan on behalf of his Scots-Irish neighbors for a pastor to the Presbyterian communities on the Eastern Shore. Makemie was not the only minister to respond to Stevens' request. Accompanying him in the work of establishing congregations in the Chesapeake region were William Trail and Thomas Wilson, also from the Presbytery of Laggan, along with Samuel Daves, whose background is unknown.

If nineteenth-century Methodist itinerant evangelists would emerge in American lore as the quintessential horseback-riding preachers, they were repeating the example of Presbyterian pastors like Makemie a century earlier. He spent his first four years traveling throughout Maryland, Virginia, Delaware, Pennsylvania, New Jersey, and even Barbados, conducting religious services for the settlers and encouraging the formation of congregations. Makemie's preaching in Philadelphia was likely responsible for the first congregation in the city that would become the unofficial capital of American Presbyterianism. In 1687 he finally settled, and married Naomi Anderson, the daughter of a merchant and planter in Virginia. They made a home in nearby Accomack County, and Makemie served the local congregation. But domestic life did not stop his travels: he made two trips to London, in 1689 and 1704, in the hope of recruiting ministers to work in the North American colonies. In 1695 Makemie also took an extended trip to Barbados, where his duties included business interests and church work. His most storied journey occurred in 1707, when he and another Presbyterian minister traveled north to Boston to recruit pastors. On the way, Makemie preached in New York in violation of Lord Cornbury's policies. After a brief imprisonment, Makemie's case went to trial; although exonerated, he still had to pay all his legal fees. The Presbyterian cleric would have the last word when he published a narrative of the incident and lodged in the minds of New World Presbyterians a link between Reformed Protestantism and resistance to tyranny.

Makemie's trip to Barbados in 1695 lasted for three years and suggests that in addition to working as a pastor he was also part of his father-in-law's commercial enterprise. This may account for Makemie's ability to sustain himself and his family when support for Presbyterian pastors was meager; it also likely explains why Makemie emerged as the leading pastor among colonial Presbyterians. His interest in commercial development was particularly evident in one of Makemie's most insightful books, *A Plain and Friendly Persuasive to the Inhabitants of Virginia and Maryland for Promoting Towns and Cohabitation* (1705), where he noted the dependence of sustainable congregations on stable and productive communities. He wrote:

> . . . in remote and scattered Settlements we can never enjoy so fully, frequently, and certainly, those Privileges and Opportunities as are to be had in all

Christian Towns and Cities; for by reason of bad Weather, or other Accidents, Ministers are prevented and People are hindered to attend, and so disappoint one another: . . . it is a melancholy Consideration, how many came very ignorant of Religion to the Plantations, and by removing to remote Settlements, have been neglected by others, and careless of themselves, continue grossly ignorant of many necessary parts of the Christian Religion; and many Natives born in ignorant Families, and by distance, seldom hear a Sermon, which would be more common, and frequently attended, if we had Towns and Cohabitation.[6]

The establishment of the first presbytery in the New World in 1706 proved Makemie's point. Philadelphia was the place Makemie chose to hold the first presbytery meeting. The city also supplied the name for the first Reformed ecclesiastical assembly outside Europe – the Presbytery of Philadelphia. At the time, the city founded and run by Quakers was still in its infancy, and home to almost 4,500 residents who represented the greatest cultural and religious variety of any British colony in North America. The Quakers' religious toleration created a congenial environment for many religious groups, including Presbyterians, who lacked the financial support and administrative backing from a colonial government.

At the time of the presbytery's founding, Philadelphia had only one Presbyterian congregation. Its pastor, Jedediah Andrews, had been found on one of Makemie's recruiting trips. Born in 1674, in Hingham, Massachusetts, Andrews had graduated in 1695 from Harvard before relocating in 1698 to Philadelphia to organize and pastor the first Presbyterian congregation in the city. When he arrived he ministered to a motley assortment of Protestants. As many as nine of the group were Baptists, and others came from Scotland and Wales. Some were transplants from New England, like Andrews himself; still others were from Sweden, the legacy of the Swedish monarch's short-lived colonial venture at the beginning of the seventeenth century in the Delaware Valley. Andrews did not impress observers of the Presbyterian congregation. One Anglican dismissed him by remarking on how low the standards were for Presbyterians: "In Philadelphia one pretends to be a Presbyterian, and has a congregation to which he preaches." By 1706, the Presbyterians, led by Andrews, had their own meeting house, but another neighbor predicted that "they are not likely to increase here."[7]

Thanks to the efforts of Andrews and Makemie, Presbyterians did prosper. The work of the first presbytery was small. Seven ministers, mostly from Northern Ireland, Scotland, or England – Andrews was the lone New Englander – had gathered to ordain John Boyd, who was planting a congregation in East

Jersey. Beyond this initial reason, according to Makemie, the ministers would meet yearly, or more often "if necessary," for advice and encouragement on "the most proper measures for advancing religion and propagating Christianity in our various stations, and to maintain such a correspondence as may conduce to the improvement of our ministerial abilities." They would also assign texts for members to preach at the meetings and evaluate each other's performances.[8] Because the presbytery was responsible for ordaining new ministers and receiving those who transferred, it was more than a pastor's conference. Still, not until 1714 did it require congregations to maintain records. By 1716 elders were required to attend. All along, the presbytery had minimal clout in running the infant colonial Presbyterian church.

In 1717, when the community of Presbyterians grew large enough to form its first synod, Philadelphia was again the center of the church's activities. The newly constituted Synod of Philadelphia included three presbyteries and sixteen ministers, with the bulk of Presbyterian congregations located near the Delaware Valley in Pennsylvania and New Jersey, or the Chesapeake Bay in Maryland and Virginia. The Presbytery of Philadelphia had remained almost the same size as at the time of its founding; it included six ministers (Makemie had died in 1707), working in nine different congregations. Of these, two were from England, one was from Wales, one from Scotland, one from Northern Ireland; Andrews remained the lone New Englander. The Presbytery of New Castle (Delaware) had absorbed the short-lived Presbytery of Snow Hill (Maryland) and included eight ministers, four with Scots-Irish backgrounds, three from Scotland, and one Welshman. The youngest presbytery, formed in conjunction with the constitution of the Synod of Philadelphia, was the Long Island Presbytery. It had two ministers, one from New England and one from Northern Ireland. Given its proximity to New England, the Long Island Presbytery would absorb the greatest number of ministers from English Puritan backgrounds. Between 1717 and 1729, the Synod of Philadelphia ordained twenty-seven new ministers, eleven of whom came from New England and accepted charges in New York, New Jersey, and Delaware.

If Reformed Protestants in Europe could not readily achieve unity among themselves with the head start supplied by a common language and national history, American Presbyterians were pressed even harder to establish coherence within their infant church. But try they did, and in 1729 the Synod of Philadelphia approved the American church's first constitution and also adopted the Westminster Confession of Faith and Catechisms as its doctrinal rule. This was by no means an easy decision. Throughout the 1720s two tendencies in the American church had emerged, one opposing creedal subscription as a violation of freedom of conscience, the other favoring subscription in order to prevent men with questionable views from obtaining ministerial credentials. Each position sought to draw on the experience of other churches. The anti-subscriptionist perspective derived from ministers who had grown up in or received their training in New England where Puritan congregationalism nurtured a spirit of autonomy. The pro-subscription argument stemmed from a desire to avoid doctrinal defections that had plagued Presbyterians in Ireland. The latter argument prevailed with the Adopting Act of 1729, in which the synod unanimously affirmed the teachings of the Westminster Assembly and also collectively took exception to the Confession's teaching on the civil magistrate, which included Erastian provisions for the magistrate that made no sense in the environments of colonial Pennsylvania, New Jersey, Delaware, and Maryland.

The upshot of 1729 for American Presbyterians was the use of the Westminster Standards for licensure and ordination. The Adopting Act stipulated that "all the Presbyteries within our bounds shall always take care not to admit any candidate of the ministry into the exercise of the sacred function, but what declares his agreement in opinion with all the essential and necessary articles of said Confession," either by subscription or verbal assent. To be sure, the Act granted presbyteries the power of ordination and so allowed for varieties of conformity. It also complicated the desire for doctrinal uniformity by invoking the somewhat vague idea of "essential and necessary" doctrines within the Standards, thus implying a core set of convictions that should be distinguished from Westminster's peripheral teachings. In effect, the Adopting Act was a compromise statement that sailed between the Charybdis of strict subscription and the Scylla of freedom of conscience. Synod's effort to keep a lid on divergent strands of Reformed Protestantism came through in the preamble to the formal language of the Act. Members agreed that "none of us will traduce or use any opprobrious terms of those that differ from us in these extra-essential and not necessary points of doctrine, but treat them with the same friendship, kindness and brotherly love as if they had not differed from us in such Sentiments."[9]

Despite these brotherly efforts, colonial Presbyterians could not avoid controversy or even a split. In addition to differences between the practices and attitudes of Presbyterians with backgrounds in either New England or Ireland, the zealous devotion and controversial measures introduced by revivalism furthered emerging antagonisms.[10] At first the revivals broke out sporadically under the ministry of pastors who feared the deadening effects of disengaged church members who were going through the motions of worship. An additional factor was the question of influence in the training of prospective clergy. William Tennent, Sr, who was likely a native of Ireland, came to North America by way of a degree at Edinburgh and ordination into the Church of Ireland. He established a school for training ministers, the Log College, which supplied pastors who promoted revivals. Tennent's sons, especially Gilbert and William, Jr, were also forceful figures in Presbyterian debates, spreading the techniques and message of revival. Opponents of the awakening preferred ministerial candidates to study either at historic universities in Scotland (Edinburgh, Glasgow, or St Andrews) or at established colleges in New England (Harvard and Yale). Then came the phenomenon of George Whitefield, an Anglican itinerant evangelist who catalyzed all colonial Protestants, including Presbyterians, into pro- and anti-revival camps. In 1741 colonial Presbyterians divided between the Synod of Philadelphia (anti-revival and Old Side) and the Synod of New York (pro-revival and New Side). These separate bodies reunited in 1758 with a plan of union that recognized rights and wrongs on both sides. The terms that ended hostilities allowed that the revivalists had violated church order at numerous points and that the anti-revivalists were right to uphold the rules of Presbyterian procedure; on the flip side, the proposal affirmed that revivalists had engaged in a truly divine work and that the anti-revivalists had been wrong to quench the work of the Holy Spirit by insisting on Presbyterian procedure.

Adding to the peace supplied by the 1758 Plan of Union was the arrival of another immigrant from the Old Country (in this case Scotland). In 1768 John Witherspoon (1723–94) came to America formally to preside over the College of New Jersey, an institution inspired by Tennent's Log College and founded in 1746 by the leaders of the pro-revivalist party among colonial Presbyterians. A son of a Church of Scotland minister, Witherspoon also became a pastor and served in two Scottish parishes before accepting an invitation to preside over the College of New Jersey. As a Presbyterian minister, he had established a reputation as an conservative especially through his book, *Ecclesiastical Characteristics* (1753), a parody of the Moderate leadership within the Kirk.[11] In addition to his defense of orthodoxy and careful exegetical preaching, Witherspoon became acquainted with College leaders in 1754 during a fundraising trip that took Gilbert Tennent and Samuel Davies to Scotland. As a Scot, Witherspoon was able to gain the confidence of the former Old Side wing of the American church. He was not exactly a compromise choice but American Presbyterians on both sides of the Awakenings saw in him reasons for further cooperation.

The new arrival proved to be much more than a college administrator. Witherspoon threw himself into the colonies' political affairs and achieved fame for being the only minister to sign the Declaration of Independence, which he did as a representative from New Jersey to the Continental Congress. But as much time as he devoted to the "sacred" cause of liberty, Witherspoon also became a tireless churchman and worked actively to give the American church greater organizational unity than it had enjoyed as a colonial enterprise. During the 1780s he served on committees to write a constitution for the first General

Assembly of the American Presbyterian church. This scheme was partly a response to declining levels of participation at the synods of Philadelphia and New York among ministers and elders. Some of this inactivity was understandable during the War of Independence. But Witherspoon and other leaders were concerned about a trend toward isolation among Presbyterian congregations and hoped to supply the new national church with a structure that would invite more participation in an efficient manner. The committees looked to Scottish patterns of governance and worship. The culmination of these plans was the 1789 General Assembly, which met in Philadelphia.

Unlike Scottish precedents where the General Assembly preceded and held greater power than the presbyteries, in the American church the new ecclesiastical structure would preserve the priority and prerogatives of the presbyteries. The Plan of Government adopted by the church, now named the Presbyterian church in the United States of America, reflected fears of centralization and hierarchy. The new order insured that congregations and presbyteries would remain free to set many of their own rules. Sessions would determine criteria for membership and congregations would be able to adapt Presbyterian polity to their own situations. Presbyteries retained all of their previous powers over the licensure and ordination of ministers. The Plan of Government did include recommendations for theological education of pastors, standards of piety, and doctrinal norms. But it provided great flexibility to accommodate the practices and expectations of the synods and presbyteries. The Directory for Worship proposed to and ratified by the Assembly was indicative of the new body's relative powers. It included suggestions about the administration of the sacraments, the officiation of funerals and weddings, and even about the conduct of worship in the home, much like the Westminster Assembly's directory. But the American directory was only advisory and left great latitude for pastors, sessions, and congregations to adapt according to taste and conviction.

Almost a century after Francis Makemie had set out to minister among the scattered Scottish and Scots-Irish settlers in the Chesapeake Bay region, the churches and presbytery he had helped to organize had formed a national body, complete with a General Assembly. At the time of its first assembly, the American Presbyterian Church consisted of four synods: New York and New Jersey, which included four presbyteries; Philadelphia, with five; Virginia, with four; and the Carolinas, with three. The Assembly recorded that 177 ministers and 111 licentiates belonged to the communion, with total of 420 congregations (only 215 of which had pastors). Underneath the organization and numbers, however, existed a communion that had grown not from central planning but as a result of the accidents of migration, economic opportunity, and quirks in colonial government. The American Presbyterian church was a daughter church of neither the

Scottish Kirk nor the Presbyterian Church of Ireland. It had received no financial support from the Old World communions and had instituted its own local forms of oversight. The American church did, of course, depend on the ministers and church members who left the British Isles in search of work and homes in the New World. But like the nation included in its name, the Presbyterian Church USA was an independent expression of Reformed Protestantism. American Presbyterianism's eventual emergence as a leader within international Calvinism owed as much to the fortunes of the nation whose name it bore as to the genius of its colonial founders.

The Palatinate in Pennsylvania

According to Joseph Henry Dubbs, who wrote the one of the first histories of German Reformed Protestants in America, "[t]he religious condition of the Germans of Pennsylvania in the earlier part of the eighteenth century was certainly deplorable."[12] As undesirable as those conditions may have been, they were not worse than what German Protestants in the central and southern German-speaking territories faced during the seventeenth century. Residents of this section of Europe endured multiple layers of violence, from attacks upon homes and the loss of property to the burning of entire villages, thanks to resentments and ongoing warfare that ravaged central Europe after the Thirty Years War. The War of the Grand Alliance, for instance, which lasted from 1689 to 1697, involved France, Ireland, England, Spain, and the League of Augsburg in a struggle for political succession in the Palatinate. Under these circumstances, parts of the German-speaking population migrated to Britain and North America. By 1710 between two thousand and three thousand German immigrants had settled in the Dutch and Swedish colonies of the Hudson and Delaware valleys. At the time of the first United States census (1790), residents of German descent accounted for 7 percent of the American population (approximately 280,000). The highest number of emigrants from Germany came in the years 1749–55, when approximately thirty thousand arrived in Philadelphia. This only added to the significant numbers of Germans living in Pennsylvania. In 1745 they numbered as many as 45,000 in Pennsylvania alone; at the time, Philadelphia's population was roughly 15,000, and the colony was only a little more than twice the size (approximately 100,000) of the contingent of German speakers that Quaker officials welcomed to Pennsylvania.

The Reformed Protestants among these settlers found a church that was still very much in flux. Because many of these German speakers hailed from Switzerland – perhaps even a majority before the arrival of John Philip Boehm, the former school teacher pressed into clerical labors – Ulrich Zwingli was as much an inspiration for their churches as Zacharias Ursinus, author of the Heidelberg Catechism. In fact, in some of the earliest historical accounts of the German communion in America, Zwingli functioned as the patron saint of the German Reformed. Still, the local hero for the earliest German Reformed settlers was Boehm. In addition to organizing the first four congregations outside Philadelphia, like Makemie among the Presbyterians he also traveled south to Delaware and Maryland to plant new congregations. His greatest achievement was to establish the framework for the church's government and worship. Boehm's ordinances (approved formally in 1728 by the Classis of Amsterdam) included provisions for the existing consistories' membership, how often church councils should meet, the observance of the Lord's Supper (twice a year), and even how to pay for the bread and wine (by the deacons from the alms). His criteria for admission to the Lord's Supper came directly from the 1618 Synod of Dort. The constitution also specified that the Heidelberg Catechism and the Belgic Confession should function as the doctrinal standards for the immigrant church. Boehm included the instruction that pastors should preach through the catechism "in regular order,"[13] and that they should use the catechism to instruct children. Boehm's constitution not only indicated the ties between the German and Dutch Reformations, but also reflected a strong effort to follow the example of Old World Reformed churches.

Although Boehm's instincts were conservative, as a layman ordained by believers who had no oversight from or membership in a properly constituted communion he was in an incredibly novel situation. These anomalies were glaringly apparent to George Michael Weiss, a Reformed pastor who arrived in Philadelphia in the fall of 1727 with approximately four hundred other German Reformed settlers. The Consistory of Heidelberg had ordained Weiss to be pastor of the colony that accompanied him. The new pastor immediately set about organizing congregations in Philadelphia, Germantown, and Goshenhoppen. Weiss was the pastor-designate of the wealthy leaders of this German colony and had no trouble receiving the appropriate support and calls from the recent settlers. He was not content, however, simply with organizing and ministering to these new German Reformed works. When Weiss became aware of Boehm and his irregular ministerial credentials, the new pastor challenged Boehm, faulted his abilities as a pastor, and, as Boehm wrote in a letter, "sought to force in a violent manner and a shameful way into all my congregations here."[14] One such instance occurred only six months after Weiss' arrival, when he started a rival congregation in Skippack, Pennsylvania, in the home of a church member, the very place where Boehm had been conducting services.

Unable to resolve the conflict, Weiss and Boehm appealed to other Presbyterian and Reformed bodies. Weiss first turned to Jedediah Andrews, the Philadelphia

Presbyterian pastor, to settle the dispute, but Boehm ignored the appeal and continued among the congregations he had organized. Since Weiss had the upper hand of ordination, Boehm's friends responded by questioning Weiss' ministerial credentials. He had a certificate from the Consistory of Heidelberg, but because it was in Latin and the settlers could not read it, they refused to recognize it as valid. Weiss in turn wrote to his consistory for a letter that would satisfy the German-speaking colonists. Upon their receipt of this request, the officers in Germany referred the situation to the Dutch Reformed Synod of South Holland. Before this body could respond, Boehm outflanked Weiss by appealing to the Dutch Protestants closer to home. At roughly the same time that the Dutch church officers were learning from Heidelberg about the situation in Pennsylvania, Boehm, with one of his elders, traveled to New York to meet with Dutch Reformed pastors in the hope that they would either ordain him or recognize his call. The New York pastors responded that they did not have this power but referred the request to the body overseeing them, the Classis of Amsterdam. By June of 1729 the Amsterdam officers had sent letters to the churches in Pennsylvania, the pastors in New York, and to Boehm. They recognized the validity of Boehm's preparation and work, and set the terms for his formal ordination and installation under the oversight of the Dutch churches in Amsterdam. On November 23, 1729, Boehm met with the Dutch pastors in New York for his ordination service. The following day, Boehm and Weiss reconciled; each man forgave the other and agreed to leave the other to the congregations he had established, Boehm retaining the original four congregations outside Philadelphia and Weiss giving up Skippack to work in the Philadelphia and Germantown congregations.

Having averted one early conflict, the German Reformed churches soon experienced two more. The first involved a fundraising trip to Holland. Weiss conducted this appeal with Jacob Reiff, one of the elders from Boehm's original congregations. The colonists were able to secure financial aid (in addition to 130 Bibles), but Reiff misused the funds – purchasing "merchandise" – at the instruction of Pennsylvania church members. During this trip Weiss decided to make a call on a congregation in Huntersfield, New York. The upshot of this episode was that Boehm was left without much-needed financial assistance, and also with the responsibility for Weiss' former congregation in Philadelphia.

The second challenge came with the arrival in 1741 of Moravians in Pennsylvania. Led by Count Nicholas Ludwig von Zinzendorf, these settlers represented a strain of pietistic Lutheranism that made room among traditional Protestant beliefs and practices for individual ecstatic experiences (signs of the Holy Spirit's work) and communitarian forms of Christian brotherhood. Zinzendorf hoped to unite all German Protestants in Pennsylvania: Reformed, Lutheran, and the various pietistic communions (e.g. Dunkers, Mennonites, and

Schwenkfelders), within a united church, or as he called it, the "Congregation of God in the Spirit." To call Zinzendorf the German George Whitefield would be inaccurate. But the Count did come to Pennsylvania partly owing to the English revivalist's request to Zinzendorf to send missionaries to the Pennsylvania Germans. Whitefield had begun evangelistic tours of the British colonies in 1739 and soon realized that he could not communicate with the German settlers. Zinzendorf's mission was to preach the "blood and death of Jesus" without "regard to what will happen to me."[15] With that calling and sense of purpose, he set out to preach in all the German-speaking churches nearby, starting among the Lutherans and Reformed in Philadelphia, and from there visiting the congregations that Boehm had established near the Schuylkill River valley.

Zinzendorf's appeal led to a series of ministerial assemblies, the so-called "Pennsylvania Synod," during the early 1740s which included Reformed, Lutheran, Anabaptists, and other Protestant groups. Boehm responded with a series of critiques, published in book form as a letters to his German Reformed peers. His objections ranged from novel practices, such as administering baptism by pouring water on a child's chest, to faulting a proposed catechism for lacking the chief elements of catechetical training – the creed, Lord's Prayer, and Decalogue. Boehm used material from the Dutch Reformed churches on the errors of the Moravians. He also received support from a retired German Reformed pastor who was living in Bucks County, Samuel Guldin, who also went into print in 1742 against Zinzendorf. Whether or not this opposition was responsible for the Count's return to Europe, Zinzendorf did depart in 1742 after a brief, productive, and controversial stint. The Pennsylvania Synod continued to meet in his absence, with John Bechtel, the German Reformed pastor in Germantown, and Henry Antes, an elder at the Falkner Swamp congregation and one of Boehm's early supporters. By 1748 when the synod disbanded, only Lutherans, Reformed, and Moravians were participating.

Lending a significant hand to Boehm's efforts to organize a Reformed church for German-speaking colonists was Michael Schlatter (1716–90), who arrived in Philadelphia by way of Boston in September 1746 with a mandate from the Classis of Amsterdam to stabilize the Reformed churches in Pennsylvania. A native of Switzerland (St Gallen), Schlatter received his formal training at the University of Helmstedt in the duchy of Brunswick-Wolfenbüttel, and initially found work as a teacher. He entered the ministry and served briefly in Switzerland before moving to Amsterdam and volunteering his services to the classis to work among the German settlers in Pennsylvania. The Dutch church officers were remarkably open to Schlatter's proposal and generous with their concern for the German speakers in the New World. In their commission to Schlatter they gave reasons for undertaking oversight:

Because originally the settlers in Pennsylvania were from the Palatinate and
Switzerland, to which two countries Holland was under the greatest obligations of gratitude, because from them the light of the Gospel first
streamed to Holland.

Because the Pennsylvania congregations are attached so loyally to their time
honored Reformed faith, and

Because Pennsylvania would become thus a safe asylum for the oppressed
brethren of their faith of Europe when driven out by persecution.[16]

By way of introduction to the German Pennsylvanians, the Amsterdam clerics
described Schlatter as a "proper person." He had received a good education in
Hebrew, Greek, German, Dutch, and French, and came from a "good family."
They also encouraged the settlers to give Schlatter a "cordial reception."[17]

What would become decisive for the creation of a German Reformed
communion in North America was the classis' determination to organize a
coetus (in effect a classis) of the Pennsylvania Reformed pastors and congregations. Schlatter was to insure that this body met annually, that its members
subscribed the Heidelberg Catechism and Canons of Dort "with heart and
voice," appointed its own officers, who would rotate regularly, and sent reports
to the Classis of Amsterdam. The call also specified that Schlatter was to function as a "visitor extraordinary," a Dutch church officer who visited congregations, inspected their affairs, and determined the capacity of members and
regular attendees to provide the salary for a full-time pastor. In those towns and
villages where no church existed, Schlatter's task was to see how many settlers
wanted a congregation and how great was their willingness to support a pastor
and construct a meeting house. The Classis of Amsterdam had not forgotten
about the aid it had raised for Weiss and Reiff back in 1742, and wanted Schlatter
to provide a report on how the Pennsylvanians would use Dutch assistance.
Once he had toured the churches and established the coetus, Schlatter was free
to take a call to one of the Pennsylvania congregations.

Boehm could well have perceived Schlatter as simply another challenge to his
own hard-won authority as a legitimate Reformed pastor. But in a letter Boehm
wrote of the new pastor as "an effectual instrument and kind brother and fellow-
work in God's holy service."[18] Schlatter continued to impress Boehm when, after
surveying the German Reformed landscape of eastern Pennsylvania, he brought
the existing pastors together, several of whom had opposed Boehm either during
the days of Weiss or during the failed meetings of Zinzendorf's synods. There the
pastors agreed to put past differences behind them, even shedding, according to
Schlatter, a few "tears of joy." Boehm himself admitted that meeting with his
former adversaries was difficult: "It was indeed hard for me to stand in official

and brotherly connection with men through whom I had to suffer so much affliction." But he followed Schlatter's lead and biblical counsel to throw "all that is past" into "the fire of love."[19] This informal meeting of the four Reformed pastors led to the official gathering of the first coetus on September 29, 1747, which included these same ministers plus twenty-seven elders, at the old meeting house in Philadelphia. At the second meeting in 1748 they appointed officers and elected Boehm president. Although Schlatter's presence undoubtedly contributed to the gatherings' unanimity, the first actions of the coetus also vindicated Boehm's efforts. All except for one minister and one elder affixed their signatures to the Heidelberg Catechism and Canons of Dort, as Boehm had originally proposed two decades earlier. The coetus also approved a constitution and used the one that Boehm had drafted for the churches soon after his ordination.

The Philadelphia Coetus would soon lose the leadership of both Boehm and Schlatter, and that deprivation undoubtedly accounted for the institutional drift among the German Reformed for the rest of the colonial era. Boehm died in 1749, only a year after presiding over the coetus. Schlatter, meanwhile, sailed back to Europe in 1751, to raise funds and recruit ministers, for the Reformed churches in Pennsylvania. His report of thirty thousand members, scattered among forty-six congregations and sharing only six ministers, succeeded in persuading the Swiss, Dutch, and German Reformed churches to give to the cause. In 1752 Schlatter returned not only with much needed finances but also with six additional pastors. So persuasive was he about the conditions in the New World that a pastor to the English congregation in Amsterdam decided to raise funds in England and Scotland for charity schools in Pennsylvania among the German settlers. This plan drew opposition from the Pennsylvanians because the fliers for this endeavor, at least from the North American perspective, portrayed the Germans as illiterate, destitute, and semi-barbarous. The Pennsylvania Germans also wanted to preserve their language, and the new schools were designed to spread English among the immigrants. Back in Pennsylvania, Schlatter worked with the coetus' blessing as the superintendent of these schools. But by 1754 German Reformed opposition to the schools became so strong that, at the request of the Classis of Amsterdam, the Philadelphia Coetus dismissed Schlatter to work exclusively as a teacher. For the remainder of his life, Schlatter never attended another meeting of the coetus that he had organized; instead, he split his time between the schools and serving as a chaplain in the British military.

The German settlers continued to expand throughout Pennsylvania, Maryland, and Virginia, and with the growth of congregations among the extended communities also came obstacles to maintaining ecclesiastical ties. Over time, however, with an influx of new ministers, and after enduring the hardships of the French and Indian War and the War of Independence, the

German Reformed ministers sought independence of their own from Dutch oversight and formed their own synod. The primary reason for independence from the Dutch church was the lack of pastors. In 1793, at the time of the German Reformed church's first synod, the communion consisted of roughly 15,000 members, 178 congregations, and 22 ministers.[20] If the coetus were to oversee the expanding German settlements, it would need more pastors. But the process of ordination was arduous thanks to the need for approval from both the Philadelphia Coetus and the Classis of Amsterdam. Another reason the Pennsylvania Germans gave for independence was language. The German Reformed in the United States also wanted to establish a school to train pastors, but the Dutch classis had refused to authorize the creation of a seminary. Consequently, in 1793, the members of the Philadelphia Coetus declared their independence from the Netherlands at the same time as forming a synod.

Clashes over the introduction of English into predominantly German-speaking congregations, where to locate a seminary, and whom to hire for its faculty would dominate the German Reformed Church at a corporate level for the next fifty years. But an expression of Reformed Protestantism from the Palatinante and southern Germany had taken root in a nation that would provide most Protestants with ecclesiastical freedoms seldom known in Europe. The translation of German Protestantism into the British colonies and then into the American republic was neither smooth nor straightforward. Indeed, owing to ethnic and cultural differences, German Calvinists would never rival the influence in North America of Anglo-American churches like the Presbyterians and Congregationalists. But German Reformed churches kept alive the heritage of the Palatinate. In so doing, they once again demonstrated the advantages of the New World for rejuvenating Reformed Protestantism.

The Novelty of the New World

The immigrant Presbyterian and German Reformed churches in North America broke the mold for Protestant church planting that had prevailed since the 1520s. Granted, no Reformer had a plan for church growth in the early decades of the sixteenth century; the Reformed churches that took root emerged from a variety of unpredictable circumstances. But the Reformed churches of the New World took unpredictability to a new level. With the exception of Protestant refugees in England and the empire after the 1540s, who by necessity met underground and established congregations independent of civil authorities, the start of a Protestant communion throughout Europe had depended on the patronage and protection of city councils, princes, and kings. The new Protestant pastors not only depended on civil authorities for their livelihoods but also for their lives. In contrast, in North America the immigrant churches developed virtually on their own, without any encouragement from the state. To be sure, colonial governments, especially those that implemented policies of religious toleration like Pennsylvania, provided an environment where pastors and church members might practice their faith without fear of punishment. Still, beyond the legal assurance that Protestants had the freedom of assembly and worship, Presbyterians and German Reformed started new communions virtually independent of the state.

As different as the origins of immigrant Reformed churches were from the communions launched throughout Europe two centuries earlier, the experience of Presbyterians and German Reformed was typical for most immigrants to British North America. The pattern involved a group of Europeans from one of the state churches migrating to North America for improved economic opportunities and political maneuverability. With the settlers came pastors or men of learning who might function as ministers. Immigrants located wherever they could support themselves, not always regarding a central point for worship as a high priority. Scattered populations consequently created the need for many pastors, but at the same time for one minister who would organize dispersed communicants into a semblance of order. Without the watchful eye of the magistrate, efforts to organize a communion beyond the local congregations could breed competition and division. A further complication was the need for pastors, and the inability of New World clergy to ordain ministers on their own. Some of these conflicts stemmed from personal ambition, and others from novel understandings of Reformed Protestantism. Such controversies usually prevented the entire immigrant population from joining the emerging new communion, and other smaller and borderline sectarian groups started. But over time a consensus would emerge, and leaders like Makemie and Boehm would reap the rewards of a New World church that combined New World accidents and Old World substance. Perhaps the most peculiar feature of these new communions was their existence and viability; these churches defied the order and rationality typically associated with Calvinism.

The Presbyterian and German Reformed examples of church planting in the New World, however, do reveal one important difference that sometimes affected all immigrant churches, namely, the formal relationships between the European communions that immigrants had left behind and the new churches they joined. Although Francis Makemie had a commission from his presbytery to minister to Presbyterians in the Chesapeake Bay region, he conducted the work of church planting and staging the first presbytery without oversight or approval from a mother church in the Old World. Whether it was his intention, the independence of Makemie's branch of Presbyterianism from European churches was striking, especially compared to the difficulties that John Philip Boehm experienced as a result of his lacking ministerial credentials. Had Boehm arrived in Philadelphia as a pastor with ties to the churches in Heidelberg, he might have been able to follow Makemie's example and avoid oversight from the Classis of Amsterdam. Since Boehm's status became a matter of dispute, the German Reformed Protestants of Pennsylvania, in effect, became wards of the Dutch Reformed churches. This dependence extended beyond rules for ordination and church order to the question of finances. Whether owing to a trait of self-sufficiency or a streak of rebellion, the Scots and Scots-Irish Presbyterians had less trouble going it alone than did the German Reformed.

Whatever these immigrant communions may have revealed about national or cultural character, they did blaze a trail for the beginnings of practically all Protestants churches in the modern era. Even before the epoch-making revolutions of the late eighteenth century in the North American British colonies and France, which shattered the formal ties between magistrates and clergy, Protestants such as Makemie and Boehm had to figure out how to start churches with no backing from civil rulers. A church sustained by personal choice and private finances would become common in the nineteenth century, when Reformed churches developed the notions of denominationalism or adopted the "free church" model. But in colonial North America, well before either the American or French revolutions that would upend Christendom's model of ecclesiastical establishment, Presbyterians and German Reformed had taken the novel step of fashioning voluntary churches, thereby teaching the rest of the Calvinist world an important lesson.

CHAPTER SEVEN

AN EXHAUSTED EUROPE

IN 1726, ONLY THREE years before the Presbyterian ministers who were trying to establish a Reformed communion in North America determined to adopt the Westminster Confession of Faith as the doctrinal standard for their church, Geneva's Company of Pastors decided to abandon their practice of subscription. Fifty years earlier that same body had adopted the Helvetic Consensus to stop the spread and even weed out defective theology that had grown in the wake of controversies over Arminianism and Amyrauldianism. The architect of that creed was François Turretini (1623–1724), a theologian who preserved the convictions of the early Reformed churches in the idiom of scholastic theology. Not only had Geneva's pastors adopted the Consensus, but the city's Council of Two Hundred had also done so. In fact, all the Reformed churches in Switzerland embraced Turretini's formula of orthodoxy. But within a generation the churches in Geneva (and elsewhere) had grown uncomfortable with the Reformed Protestantism that had dominated religious life in places like Zurich, Bern, and Basel.

A generation is generally shorter than fifty years and the Geneva pastors' desire to abandon the requirement of creedal subscription was emerging well before the vote in 1726 that removed the Helvetic Consensus as the doctrinal standard. In fact, Turretini's son Jean-Alphonse (1671–1737) was responsible for leading the charge. But he was not alone. Even his supposed theological adversary, Benedict Pictet (1655–1724), Jean-Alphonse' cousin and colleague at the Academy at Geneva, favored revoking the doctrinal oath. Their successor at the Academy, Jacob Vernet (1698–1789), did a better job of preserving the younger Turretinis and Pictet's outlook than either Jean-Alphonse or Pictet had in following the senior Turretini. Vernet continued a pattern of theological deviation that Reformed scholastics like François Turretini had hoped to forestall.

The changes in Geneva did not simply involve doctrinal requirements for ordination. Turretini and Pictet were also influential in introducing a new catechism. Jean-Frédéric Ostervald, professor of theology at Neuchâtel, participated in the adaptations that Turretini had led, particularly by updating the churches' ministry and witness in ways that would be more flexible than in Calvin's day. As early as 1701, Ostervald had written to Turretini about the need for a new catechism. Until then, Reformed churches in Switzerland used either the Genevan or the Heidelberg Catechism, depending on the language of the congregation. Ostervald's teaching aid employed the Church of England's Book of Common Prayer and the Nicene Creed. His hope was for a simple statement of the "foundations of religion."[1] Some churches rejected the new catechism; the pastors in Bern, for instance, regarded its statements not only to be too simple but also wrong about important doctrines such as justification. But by 1735 it had become widely popular in the churches and the dominant form of instruction within Geneva and the surrounding region. Part of the reason for its success was its simplicity of expression, brevity, and encouragement of lay participation in the churches.

Indeed, a desire to involve the laity in worship was another factor that contributed to the new tone and the substance of Reformed churches in Switzerland. The pastors in Geneva approved the introduction of hymns – compiled by Pictet – into worship, an innovation that accompanied a revision of the psalter which excised the imprecatory Psalms for their impropriety. New forms of congregational singing were only one part of the liturgical reforms. Complaints about an overly long benediction led to the use and official adoption in 1719 of a shorter version. Turretini, Pictet, and Ostervald all favored a liturgy that followed the Church of England more than the austere order of service from Calvin's day. This form of worship would not only assist efforts to unite Reformed Protestants, Lutherans, and Anglicans but also encouraged church members to assume a proper attitude toward God in worship. These changes in the Sunday services began gradually in the 1710s. With them came a new midweek service of prayer and Scripture reading, comparable to the service of morning or evening prayer in the Church of England. In Geneva this prayer service soon replaced the midweek preaching assemblies – three per week – that Calvin had implemented to instruct and edify Geneva's citizens. One reason for the change was the obvious appeal to pastors who were overworked; without having to preach as much, ministers could conceivably devote their attention to other aspects of pastoral work.

Alterations to church life in Geneva, a model for Reformed churches throughout Europe 150 years earlier, were indicative of eighteenth-century developments among the European state churches that traced their roots to the Swiss Reformation. Whether these changes were welcome or lamentable depends greatly on one's point of view. If the era of Reformed orthodoxy represents the ideal, the eighteenth-century churches of Switzerland, Germany, the Netherlands, and Scotland departed widely from the mark. If, on the other hand, the criterion is one of adapting to social realities that saw the modernization of Europe's political order, the Reformed churches persisted successfully. Even so, the difficulties confronted by Reformed state churches, contrary to the thesis that Calvinism was an engine of modernity, signaled that to retain their position within the new social order, Reformed churches could not maintain their original teachings while retaining their status within the political establishment. In some cases, politics forced recognition of this conundrum on Reformed pastors and bodies. In other cases, church officials themselves were responsible for pursuing a course of toleration and moderation in the church and larger society. No matter how it happened, what transpired throughout the eighteenth century was the abandonment of convictions that had initially sparked church reform and guided the articulation of Reformed orthodoxy.

Constraints on Europe's church contrasted all the more with the creativity and vitality of New World Calvinism. If the transplanted Reformed churches would produce a greater harvest than the original vines of Europe, their success owed much to a soil uncluttered by rocks left by the Old World's entrenched structures. Despite Calvinism's uncanny record of adapting to new environments, the setting posed by the Reformed churches' original home turned out to be the hardest challenge of all.

The Curse of Magisterial Reform: Germany

At the start of the eighteenth century the Reformed churches of the Palatinate faced a severe crisis of leadership. In 1697 John Lewis Fabricius, a professor of theology and rector of Heidelberg University, died. A native and citizen of Schaffhausen, Switzerland, Fabricius began his duties in Heidelberg in 1660, and even in that climate, which was more favorable for the Reformed churches, was vigilant for the integrity of Protestantism. He successfully added qualifications about the religious character of Heidelberg University to an offer of a teaching position made to Spinoza by the electors; the Dutch philosopher declined the job. But the potential disruption that Spinoza's philosophy might pose to the university was weak compared to the threat that the French exhibited during the last two decades of the seventeenth century. Thanks to Louis XIV's designs on German territories, between 1688 and 1694 the Reformed churches in the Palatinate experienced opposition that echoed the French monarchy's dealings with the Huguenots. As James Isaac Good described it, the hundred years that ran from Louis XIV's depredations of Heidelberg to the 1789 Reign of Terror in Paris was a "century of night" that began with "five years of midnight."[2]

During this time, however, the light of Reformed Protestantism did not go out, although sometimes it was little more than a flicker. The man who held the candle most successfully was Fabricius, who not only tried to keep the university from being subject to Roman Catholics but also served on the consistory of Heidelberg even when it had dwindled to two officers. In 1689 he used connections with his home town to escape the grasping French military and avoid prison, stopping first in Frankfurt and then taking what amounted to a victory tour of Protestant Switzerland, with stops in Schaffhausen and Zurich where he received tributes from local authorities. The Antistes of Zurich even compared Fabricius' flight from Heidelberg to the apostle Peter's escape from prison. Despite calls from other Protestant universities, including one to Leiden and another to Vienna, Fabricius remained loyal to the Reformed churches in the Palatinate and sought to preserve legal protections that would at least give Protestants the opportunity to worship and retain the faculty at Heidelberg University. During the second French invasion of 1693–94 he was largely responsible for preserving the university's archives. When asked if he would return to Switzerland after the wars with the French to finish out his career in a measure of tranquility, he wrote that he wanted to devote himself to the Reformed church of the Palatinate, "however dejected it may be, lest it fall into the power of the monks."[3]

Once Fabricius died the Reformed churches in the Palatinate were at the mercy of unreliable electors. Early in the eighteenth century, though, prospects for Reformed Protestants brightened. Through the machinations of the empire, they recovered freedoms that the French and Roman Catholic electors had abrogated. In 1705 Francis Joseph I established policies that allowed children of mixed marriages to remain in their homes (rather than be forced to grow up in Roman Catholic families), ended the requirement for all people to kneel during the consecration of the host during the Mass, restored the Protestant faculty at Heidelberg University, and resumed Reformed worship among Protestant churches. These provisions were a setback in the overall scheme: Protestants lost congregations that had been Reformed, two-sevenths of their funds went to pay for Roman Catholic parishes, and they no longer controlled the university. But the emperor did grant freedom of worship to Reformed and established institutional integrity for their churches. For the next decade Protestants and Roman Catholics co-existed uneasily in the former German Reformed territory.

The situation changed significantly under a new elector, Charles III Philip, who in 1716 took charge of Heidelberg. He had been reared a Roman Catholic and was headed for a career in the church. But by the age of twenty-three he had switched to a career in the military and in 1712 became a governor in Innsbruck. Charles Philip's initial policies indicated his unwillingness to accommodate

Palatinate Protestants. In fact, his first acts revealed an agenda to secure Heidelberg's Church of the Holy Ghost for Roman Catholics.

In 1719 he fired a shot at Reformed Protestants by forbidding the use of the Heidelberg Catechism. This pedagogical device was objectionable not only because of its Protestant teaching but also owing to its explicit anti-Catholic polemic. For instance, the eightieth question asks pupils about the difference between the Lord's Supper and the Mass. The pithy answer issues a matter of fact response affirming that the Lord's Supper bears witness to the "full pardon" of sin that comes with the sacrificial death of Christ, accomplished "once for all" on the cross, and that by the work of the Holy Spirit participants "are ingrafted into Christ" through the sacrament. In contrast, the Mass "teaches" that Christ's death on the cross is insufficient "unless [he] is also daily offered" for believers by the priests. The Mass also depends, the catechism continues, upon the notion that Christ is physically present in the bread and wine, thus making the elements fit objects of worship. This simple set of contrasts vividly set apart Reformed and Roman Catholic teaching and practice on the sacrament. The polemics were sharp with the answer's conclusion: "the mass, at bottom, is nothing else than a denial of the one sacrifice and sufferings of Jesus Christ, and an accursed idolatry." If Protestants and Roman Catholics were to co-exist in the Palatinate, the Catechism was not the most diplomatic form of teaching (though plenty of dogmatically controversial assertions informed literature on both sides of the divide). What proved to be decisive for the elector's decision, and stemmed from special pleading by the Jesuits, was the fact that the 1718 edition of Heidelberg was published with the elector's coat of arms on the title page, along with the phrase, "By order of his Electoral Highness."[4] The elector imposed a fine of ten florins on anyone who continued to use the Catechism. To add insult to injury, Charles Philip confiscated the Reformed churches' Bibles and psalters.

Reformed pastors called a synod to respond to the elector's decision but were unable to halt the momentum of Charles Philip's policies. Quite sensibly, the pastors noted that not once had Heidelberg been an object of censure throughout all the warfare and antagonism of the sixteenth and seventeenth centuries, and that none of the elector's Roman Catholic predecessors had banned the Catechism's use. They also pointed out that Heidelberg's language did not have in view the Roman Catholic faithful, but the church's teaching. Furthermore, the language of Heidelberg was hardly more inflammatory than the decrees of the Council of Trent, to which Reformed Protestants had never objected during the years of co-existence between Roman Catholics and Protestants in the Palatinate. Even the logistics of printing appeared to favor the Reformed pastors' argument: the printer who had published Heidelberg was himself a Roman Catholic. Not only were these arguments ineffective, but in some districts Reformed Protestants lost access to the Catechism; worse yet, in some cases they had to observe the Mass and Rome's liturgical calendar of feast days, and Reformed men marrying Roman Catholics had to rear their children as Catholics.

Such hostility to the German Reformed faith was part of Charles Philip's design on the Church of the Holy Ghost, not only for Roman Catholic worship but as his own burial place. At the start of the elector's rule, Roman Catholics already had access to the church's choir for their services. But Charles Philip ordered the Reformed consistory to yield the nave as well. He argued that the church was part of his court's jurisdiction since it housed the remains of the Palatinate's princes. The consistory countered that the elector's co-opting of the church was unfair because Roman Catholics, who were only one-third of the territory's population, already had access to five of the Palatinate's seven churches. To Reformed Protestants the Church of the Holy Ghost was indeed a symbol of the German Reformation, but they also maintained that it was a church not for the prince but for the city. Reformed church officers claimed further that the church's Protestant and public character had been established as part of the treaties for Protestant and Roman Catholic co-existence, going back to the end of the Thirty Years War. These arguments were ineffective. On September 4, 1719, Reformed Protestants locked and barricaded the church to prevent a hostile occupation, only to find that Roman Catholic officials were entering through the tower and descending by ropes to force out the Protestants and let in Roman Catholics. For good measure, the elector also positioned Tyrolese soldiers at the doors as guards to keep Protestants from re-entering.

The elector's anti-Protestant policies provoked other princes and rulers to plead the case of the German Reformed. Ambassadors from Prussia, Hesse-Kassel, England, and the Netherlands traveled to Heidelberg to persuade Charles Philip to abandon his dogmatic partisanship. But the elector remained firm, and some staff among the ambassadors' entourages also experienced first-hand the policies that required all people to kneel during the procession of the Host through Heidelberg's streets. To retaliate, the rulers of Prussia, Hesse-Kassel, and England closed Roman Catholic chapels and churches in their respective territories. The emperor even threatened to issue a decree against Charles Philip's policies. Only in February of 1720 did the Palatinate's elector relent and allow Reformed Protestants back into the Church of the Holy Ghost. Reformed services resumed in the nave, and craftsmen reinstalled the wall that separated the Protestant nave and Roman Catholic choir. Reformed pastors also resumed their use of the Heidelberg Catechism as long as they explained that the language of question eighty referred not to Roman Catholics as people but only to doctrine. In what looked like a spiteful response to outside pressure, Charles Philip in 1720 relocated the capital of the Palatinate to Mannheim, oversaw the construction of a new residence and redesigned the city. This change in territorial administration meant that Reformed pastors would need to hold consistory meetings in the new capital; the distance of roughly ten miles made the regular meetings of consistory virtually impossible. Although the Reformed churches were able to carve out a niche for their worship and ministry, they were on the margins politically despite their demographic majority.

The burden of rule by Charles Philip was borne by others as well as Reformed Protestants, but developments in the early eighteenth century were a reminder – as if they needed it – that the days of the Reformation's success were behind and that Rome was fast making up for sixteenth-century setbacks. The Palatinate also had a sizeable body of Lutherans but Charles Philip left them out of the distribution of state appropriations for churches. Although Roman Catholics were probably only one-third of the population, their churches received five-sevenths of the funding for religion. This left Reformed Protestants with the remainder of revenues and Lutherans with nothing, even though the latter were almost as numerous as the Roman Catholics. A Reformed synod convened in 1736 responded to the Lutherans' plight by pledging 15,000 gulden to support the other Protestants' ministers and congregations; the hope was to raise this funding from charitable contributions by Protestant princes and landholders in other countries. The plan was a failure since the funds never materialized, but the gesture did facilitate warmer relations among German Protestants. Meanwhile, restrictions on religious practice in the Palatinate were responsible for many German Protestants leaving Europe for a new life in the North American colonies. This demographic disruption was part of the reason behind the Heidelberg's Consistory's 1727 decision to send George Michael Weiss to Pennsylvania to work among the Palatinate's former residents.[5]

When the Heidelberg Company of pastors delegated Weiss to minister among the Pennsylvania Germans, the city's consistory still enjoyed a measure of authority. But the pastors' insignificance increased during the remainder of Charles Philip's rule and during that of his successor Charles Theodore, a descendant of the House of Wittelsbach. The latter ruled from 1742 until 1799 and was unpopular, partly because he was less interested in politics then in fine arts and women. Neither of these outlets directly threatened the Reformed churches. When the elector meddled with the composition of the consistory, however, Charles Theodore's reign took on a decidedly anti-Protestant character. No one died, but pastors now realized that the magistrate's blessing in reforming the church could readily turn into the curse of deformation.

The Consistory of Heidelberg was a civic and church institution and as such, although derived from Reformed church polity, oversaw spiritual life for Roman Catholics and other Protestants. Consequently, its membership included

Reformed pastors and Jesuit priests. Under Charles Theodore, Rome's clergy successfully enlarged its membership. The part of the consistory that oversaw civic life expanded from four members to eighteen. The body charged with spiritual affairs went from six members (two for each religious group: Reformed, Roman Catholic, and Lutheran) to twenty-eight. Since these were paid positions, the larger bodies required greater financial provision from the elector's court – from 6,500 florins in 1706 to 33,000 in 1775. By increasing expenses, Jesuits hoped to prompt the court to abolish the consistory. The other complication for Reformed pastors was the control the consistory exerted over the appointment of pastors and teachers: a body no longer dominated by Reformed clergy often refused appointments in the churches and schools to qualified Reformed men. Meanwhile, those who did receive posts often went without their full salary, thanks to the consistory members' appropriation of court funds for their own interests; this situation, in turn, bred the practice of simony. Candidates for positions would sometimes pay as much as 500 florins for one office (and frequently those with sufficient funds would gain more than one appointment). A venerable institution of Reformed church practice thus became one more piece of state apparatus and political aggrandizement.

The magisterial Reformation of the church was proving to be more of a curse than a blessing, with the atmosphere in eighteenth-century German Reformed churches tending decidedly toward bitter rather than sweet. The classes in towns near Heidelberg protested the practice of simony, but Charles Theodore retaliated by forbidding these church bodies to meet. The only encouragement to the Reformed pastors came in 1773, when the Jesuits overextended their activity and the elector drove the order out of the Palatinate. Finally, pressure from Emperor Joseph II of Austria forced Charles Theodore to accede to ministerial calls for the convening of a synod. Reformed pastors met for two days in 1789, just prior to the emperor's death, the first meeting for the German Reformed churches in over fifty years. But the loss of a kindly-disposed emperor was less of a problem for German Protestants than was the political instability within Europe at large. Following the French Revolution of 1789 and given the ambitions of the French Emperor Napoleon, all Christians in Europe would need to adjust their ministry to the new and allegedly enlightened policies of the empire.

The Path of Moderation: Scotland

After the Glorious Revolution finally put an end to the tumultuous rule of the Stuarts, King William faced a decision about the identity of Scotland's religious establishment. Three parties – only two of them serious – vied for control of the Church of Scotland: Presbyterians, Episcopalians, and Covenanters. The latter, also known as Cameronians,[6] were still committed to the principles of the Solemn League and Covenant, refusing to take part in any religious establishment that did not include a covenant among the crown, parliament, and people to defend and maintain the true religion. Presbyterians were strongest in the Lowlands and the extreme north, and their approach to church life appealed most to the middle ranks of Scottish society. Episcopalians in contrast were strongest in the Highlands, where social patterns of feudalism persisted and where nobles saw greater affinity with a hierarchical church. Both sides pled with William to make their position the established one within Scotland's state church. The Presbyterian exiles to Holland who portrayed Scotland to William as solidly on their side may have been persuasive because of uprisings during the winter of 1688–89 in which moderate and covenanting Presbyterians tormented and expelled Episcopalian curates from parishes in the south of Scotland. Even so, when William made Presbyterianism the official polity of Scotland's church, he expected the General Assembly to pursue a uniform polity with the Westminster Standards as the Kirk's accepted doctrine. When the assembly added to its work the further ousting of Episcopalians, even from Scotland's university faculty, William and the Kirk collided to the point where the king in 1695 forbade the assembly to convene. Undeterred, the assembly continued its meetings and in 1699 proclaimed that Jesus Christ was "the only Head and King of this Church."[7]

This manner of Presbyterian vigor characterized the Scottish Kirk once it was reinstituted in 1690 and would continue to do so for almost a generation before the realities of Scottish politics set in. The austere piety that prevailed among Reformed Protestants and that dominated Puritan and Presbyterian conceptions of a godly society was evident as early as 1694, when the General Assembly confessed its many sins on behalf of the nation:

God is dishonored by the impiety and profaneness that aboundeth ... in profane and idle swearing, cursing, Sabbath-breaking, neglect and contempt of Gospel ordinances, mocking of piety and religious exercises, fornication, adultery, drunkenness, blasphemy and other gross and abominable sins and vices.

To remedy these woeful conditions the church called upon ministers to announce the "threatened judgements of God against such evil doers, to bring them to a conviction of their sin and danger." Sessions were instructed to discipline offenders. The assembly also called for visitations in the homes of parishioners to insure that family worship was regular and wholesome, and that parents were rearing children in the faith. In public worship churchmen complained about declining standards of reverence: the people too often fidgeted, lolled, and gossiped during services and sang psalms poorly. Along with encouraging pastors and elders toward the goal of better ecclesiastical supervision of worship and conduct among the people, the assembly regularly called for days of fasting to avoid divine judgment for rampant wickedness. In 1705, for instance, the assembly lamented the way people profaned the Sabbath by idly walking in the streets. Again, in 1710 the commissioners called for humiliation and fasting in response to "immoralities of all kinds" committed by a "professing people in a reformed land."[8]

By the second decade of the eighteenth century the Kirk was beginning to lose its zeal, with substantial assistance from Lords and Members of Parliament in London, who now had authority over Scottish affairs thanks to the Union of 1707. Presbyterian support for union itself involved the dexterity of a scratch golfer. On the one side, Jacobites who pined for a restoration of the Stuarts appealed to Presbyterian churchmen on the basis of seventeenth-century experience with English rule, which had replaced presbyterianism with episcopacy. The attempt was to frighten the General Assembly with the specter of rule by English officials. This approach was less than convincing since the Scottish kings Charles II and James II had supported episcopal over presbyterian clergy after the Restoration. On the other side, Presbyterians witnessed episcopal clergy in Scotland who regarded a United Kingdom as a welcome development for the prospects of an Episcopalian Church of Scotland. The commission appointed by the General Assembly to deliberate on the merits of union followed a middle path, and in so doing, with the help of Scotland's parliament, gained protection for the Kirk with the Act of Security (1704), a law that established Presbyterianism as Scotland's official religion and that gave the General Assembly freedom to regulate its own affairs.

As beneficial to the Kirk as the terms of union may have been – given the alternatives – the pursuit of political moderation may have also committed Scotland's Presbyterians to spiritual equivocation. In some cases, the new political order forced Presbyterian pastors to soften their zeal for a truly Reformed Kirk. The case of James Greenshields, for example, demonstrated this pattern. An episcopal priest, he started to hold services in 1709 in Edinburgh using the Book of Common Prayer. The presbytery convicted him of introducing worship contrary to the pure religion of the Scottish Kirk, and the magistrates imprisoned Greenshields when he refused to conform to the church's demands. But he appealed to the House of Lords, which in turn overturned Scottish law regulating worship and paved the way for the Toleration Act (1712), a bill that secured for episcopalians in Scotland the freedom to minister according to non-Presbyterian standards. Although the Act of Security had specified that the Scottish Kirk would be free from English control and that parliament could not meddle in its business, the realities of the United Kingdom indicated otherwise. As historian William Ferguson comments, this accommodation of episcopalian non-conformists directly undermined the capacity of presbyteries to enforce the discipline for which their General Assembly had called once the Kirk had been re-established. More significantly, the Act "recognised that the old ideal of one national church brooking no rivals was at odds with the facts."[9]

At almost the same time, the Kirk faced a further challenge to its integrity when parliament passed the Patronage Act (1711). This granted Scottish lairds the same prerogatives in appointing clergy that they had enjoyed prior to the ecclesiastical order of the 1690s. It was also responsible not only for prompting opposition to the Union of 1707 but also for nurturing hope for a restoration of the Stuart monarchy. From the perspective of the Covenanters, the condition of the Kirk within the United Kingdom was proof that they had made the right decision in not entering Scotland's religious establishment. After 1712 the Covenanters convened prayer societies that attracted some members of the established church, to pray for religious conditions in Scotland and to protest the imposition of toleration and patronage. Although these meetings were popular in parts of the country among the laity, the ministers of the Kirk generally accepted new laws to retain Presbyterianism's privileged status. According to the nineteenth-century historian William Maxwell Hetherington, British policies regarding the Kirk had so "vitiated" the established church that "instead of a faithful assertion and bold defense of Presbyterian principles," the most the General Assembly could muster was a "faint remonstrance," a "half apologetic statement of rights and privileges," or a "feeble and tame petition for redress."[10]

Whether the martyr spirit of a Knox or Melville could have established a better course for a national church constrained by its own Scottish peers and distant English state officials is a matter of conjecture, but the middle route charted by the Kirk's leaders left the General Assembly in an awkward position to respond adequately to a series of theological challenges. The first of these arose from the teaching of John Simson, a professor of divinity at Glasgow University. The son of a Presbyterian pastor, Simson studied at Edinburgh and Leiden before receiving a call to minister in southwest Scotland in the Galloway region in 1705. By 1708 he had received an appointment at Glasgow and within four years his efforts to make Reformed theology intelligible had prompted suspicions that Simson was guilty of Arminianism and Pelagianism. James Webster, a minister in Edinburgh, had corresponded with the Glasgow professor about his views and then alerted the General Assembly to the dangers of Simson's teaching. Committees volleyed the matter between General Assembly and presbytery for the better part of five years, a further indication of the Kirk's lack of resolve. In 1717 the affair concluded with Simson secure in his teaching post and receiving counsel from the assembly to avoid opinions unnecessary to his subject and unsound language used by opponents of Reformed Protestantism.

But this was only the Kirk's first round with Simson. A decade later the assembly heard another set of charges accusing him of Arianism and Socinianism. In 1726 the Presbytery of Glasgow tried to discover the accuracy of these accusations, but Simson, who was well connected through familial ties to patrons and former students, refused to subject himself to the Glaswegian officers. Then in 1727 the Simson affair went to the General Assembly, which looked into the professor's teaching over the better part of two years. Although Simson's defense relied upon vagueness, his opponents may have also overinterpreted his affirmations. Either way, the assembly could not let the situation rest and so in 1729 they took the middle way by suspending Simson from teaching and his office in the church but allowing him to retain his salary (which he received until his death in 1740).

Simson's case cannot, of course, be isolated from contests for control of the Kirk any more than his views were independent from an emerging Enlightened understanding of social order and political stability. In this sense, Simson and the clergy who defended him (harbingers of the Moderate Party) resembled the English Latitudinarians, who promoted a moralistic and tolerant understanding of the Church of England as way to avoid controversy and promote unity. Simson himself, who studied at Leiden where the equivocations of Reformed faculty paved the way for important features of the Scottish Enlightenment, sacrificed doctrinal precision for biblical fidelity. The aim was to find a Christian ethic that could form a better basis for a common morality than strict adherence to Calvinism. Although he promoted the Bible over creeds, Simson also praised the capacity of reason to arrive at a proper understanding of Scripture. A reasonable interpretation of the Bible yielded a God less vengeful and more merciful than Calvinism's predestinarian deity. At the same time, Simson and like-minded ministers in the Kirk adopted a view of church–state relations that tipped the balance in favor of the magistrate, again largely for the sake of order and stability. Because the state had maintained and protected the Kirk, it could also reasonably regulate the temporal aspects of ecclesiastical affairs. For this reason, whatever Simson actually thought or taught, he nurtured attitudes and assumptions that for a generation of students would bear the fruit of Enlightenment in the nation's universities and foster moderation in the Kirk. The dividends of this approach, as Robert L. Emerson writes, "would come in a happier and more peaceful social world inhabited by better, happier, more productive people."[11]

For Simson's conservative opponents, his case was indicative of the Scottish church's lack of resolve and a spur to recover the glories of Knox and Melville. One sign of conservative opposition came in 1717, when the Presbytery of

Auchterarder began to question prospective ministers on the implications of their doctrinal positions. No longer would agreement with the Westminster Standards be sufficient, since Simson himself had appealed to the Westminster Confession of Faith. Instead, additional information was necessary to evaluate a candidate. This presbytery began to ask young men about the relationship between faith and works for salvation. The so-called Auchterarder Creed consisted of the following proposition: "I believe that it is not sound and orthodox to teach that we must forsake sin in order to our coming to Christ, and instating us in covenant with God."[12] One ministerial candidate, William Craig, who failed to answer the presbytery's questions satisfactorily appealed to General Assembly. In 1718 the Auchterarder Creed received the assembly's verdict of antinomianism. The proposition would encourage believers, the divines concluded, not to follow God's law.

As poorly worded as the Auchterarder Creed may have been, it represented the concerns of Scottish ministers who believed the Kirk, in both the Simson and Auchterarder affairs, was losing the capacity to affirm basic Reformed teaching. These conservatives also feared the harmful effects of patronage on the Kirk: by devising sermons to please wealthy patrons, pastors were neglecting the spiritual needs of ordinary members and the sobering parts of Scripture. Among the leaders of this group of ministers was Thomas Boston (1676–1732), a pastor in the small town of Simprin in the southeastern part of Scotland. He recognized corruptions in the Church of Scotland (as did the Covenanters) but believed that if Christ could participate in the synagogue of his day despite the hypocrisy of religious leaders, contemporary pastors had no warrant to separate from the ecclesiastical establishment (as had the Covenanters). Boston regularly critiqued the compromises that came with the union of Scotland and England; he followed the Simson case closely and protested the assembly's 1728 refusal to depose the Glasgow professor. Boston's most important contribution to eighteenth-century Scottish church history, though, was his work as an editor.

In 1718 Boston had recommended to a fellow minister the seventeenth-century work *The Marrow of Modern Divinity*, often attributed to Edward Fisher and written in London at the time of the Westminster Assembly. This tip led to the republication of *Marrow* in 1718, which in turn launched a pamphlet battle over the place of assurance in true faith, the efficacy of Christ's death (e.g. universal atonement), and whether fear of punishment and hope of reward were proper motives for good works. Also known as the Marrow Controversy, this dispute revealed a legalistic strain (neonomian) within the majority of the Kirk's pastors, and an antinomian impulse among the Kirk's critics.

The Marrow Controversy lasted publicly only two years but the resolve of the Marrow ministers lasted much longer. In 1720 the General Assembly condemned the *Marrow of Modern Divinity* as an expression of antinomianism and forbade six propositions – the antinomian paradoxes – such as "a believer is not under the law, but is altogether delivered from it."[13] Ironically, the assembly's action gave publicity to an obscure book and to the ministers who defended it. Twelve ministers appealed this ruling to the 1721 General Assembly, arguing that the Kirk had in effect condemned the truths of the gospel by endorsing legalism; the Marrow men believed that to retain an incentive for good works the Kirk had resorted to the penalties and sanctions of the law. The assembly deliberated over the appeal, and in 1722 upheld its previous condemnation of the Marrow teaching. The ministers who sympathized with Marrow received rebukes but were able to retain their charges. Their reputation followed them and prevented appointments to larger or wealthier parishes; the Marrow teaching also functioned as a test during ministerial examinations such that licentiates needed to repudiate Marrow Doctrine to be ordained.

Despite this opposition, the Marrow men, led by Boston, and the brothers Erskine (Ralph and Ebenezer) continued in their opposition to the neonomianism that they believed characterized the Kirk. Adding to their discontent were the increasing prerogatives given to patrons in the call of ministers. Not only did the patron at Kinross in 1726 refuse to accede to the congregation's call of Ebenezer Erskine (1680–1754), but in 1732 the assembly gave greater power to land owners and presbyteries than to the laity in the appointment of clergy. The 1732 deliverance provoked opposition; two thousand signed a petition of protest and forty-one ministers issued similar objections over their signatures. As moderator of the Synod of Perth and Stirling, Ebenezer also preached a sermon against the assembly's action in the fall of 1732. In it he said, "I can find no warrant from the word of God to confer the spiritual privileges of His house upon the rich beyond the poor; whereas by this Act, the man with the gold ring and gay clothing is preferred unto the man with the vile raiment and poor attire."[14] Erkine's sermon offended a majority of the synod's pastors and they rebuked him for harsh judgment. When the assembly of 1733 upheld the synod's rebuke and asked for Erskine (and three supporters) to apologize for defying it the minister refused. At this point, the assembly evicted Erkine and his advocates from their churches and prohibited all ministers of the Kirk from communing with the protesters. In response, Erskine led in the formation of the Associate Presbytery, which met in late 1733 at Gairney Bridge (near Kinross). Their Testimony of the following year explained their secession – the assembly's usurpation of presbyteries' powers, toleration of doctrinal error, and refusal to hear legitimate protests – and a desire to commune with all like-minded Presbyterians in Scotland. When the assembly attempted to heal the division in 1734, by restoring the four leading Associate pastors to their parishes – the

Synod of Perth and Stirling even re-elected Erskine as its moderator – the Seceders refused. Erskine's own comment explained their resolve: they would not be fooled by the "great difference between a positive reformation and a stop . . . given to a deformation."[15] By 1736 the Associate Presbytery established its own powers of jurisdiction and continued to spot deformities in the Kirk, at which point the breach was irreparable. Although a small communion, in 1745 the Associate Presbyterians numbered forty-five congregations and their testimony, in the words of historian William Ferguson, was little more "than a cogent summary of the tensions of the previous forty years."[16]

Although the Seceders shared a similar estimate of Scotland's ecclesiastical establishment, they were not of one mind in interpreting threats to their status. The Burgher Oath (1744) revealed these strains. Citizens in Edinburgh, Glasgow, and Perth vowed to endorse the religion professed in Scotland, and in return their pledge secured privileges to participate in commercial enterprises. The problem with the Oath, from the Seceder perspective, was what kind of religion it approved: the moderate Kirk of the eighteenth century or Reformed Protestantism as understood when Scotland condemned Roman Catholicism. By 1747 the Seceders had split between the Burghers (those who interpreted the Oath as an affirmation of Protestantism) and the Anti-Burghers (those who regarded it as an endorsement of the Kirk). Not even the leadership of the Erskines, who argued for the Burgher position (the Associate Synod) could stay the "breach" with the Anti-Burghers (the General Associate Synod). The Associate Presbyterians would remain divided for the rest of the eighteenth century.

The contentious character of Presbyterians outside the Kirk – from the Covenanters to the Seceders – made the Church of Scotland appear moderate by comparison. But moderation, a pejorative term in Scottish church history, was not simply a default position for a communion unwilling to endorse conservative views. Moderation also became a characteristic of Kirk officers and professors who were willing to tolerate the 1690 settlement as the price of doing church business in Scotland. Moderates in particular went along with both the hardships of patronage and the necessity of subscribing the Westminster Standards for ordination. Not only did Moderates refuse to object to threats to the rights of the Kirk from civil authorities, but they tolerated departures from the Confession of Faith, which many felt was theologically severe and the product of a different era. At the basis of the Moderate outlook was the belief that the Scots needed religion, but not the faith of Knox-era Presbyterianism.

Although a moderate position was clearly emerging before 1750, in 1751 it blossomed into a definite ecclesiastical policy. The installation of unpopular ministers within the presbyteries of Dunfermline and Linlithgow – following the wishes of patrons against those of parishioners – not only forced the General Assembly to depose ministers who protested these actions but also led to the emergence of a distinctly Moderate leadership within the Kirk. The deposed ministers would eventually form another Presbyterian denomination in Scotland in 1761 – the Relief Church – a communion created to allow congregations to call their own pastors. The leader of the Moderate Party was William Robertson (1721–93), pastor at Borthwick, Midlothian. He had served in 1751 on the riding committee – one sent to an assembly to seat a regularly appointed minister against popular sentiments – to install the contested pastor in the Presbytery of Linlithgow. He would go on to be principal at the University of Edinburgh, chaplain at Stirling Castle, and royal chaplain, in addition to excelling as a historian. But as the leader of the Moderate Party, Robertson worked to shape an orderly church within a well-ordered Scotland. Within the church, Moderates sought to avoid factionalism, especially in the form cultivated by the Popular Party, which was generally in synch with Reformed orthodoxy and opposed to the imposition of pastors through the system of patronage. Within Scottish society the Moderates sought to cooperate with the civil authorities as much as possible to maintain the Kirk's capacity to shepherd the collective soul of Scotland.

After 1780, the leadership of the Moderate Party passed to George Hill (1750–1819), who guided the Kirk through a period when democratic revolutions in France and America were prompting debates among Scottish Presbyterians and when Moderates were said to be "little more than the Dundas interest at prayer."[17] Hill held a number of ecclesiastical and academic posts but was less effective than Robertson in maintaining a middle course, if only because of his dependence on the lord advocate's patronage. That vulnerability created more room for protests from the Popular Party, and the last two decades of the eighteenth century witnessed renewed contests over patronage and doctrinal regularity. The celebrated Leslie Controversy brought to a close the period of Moderate hegemony and revealed the degree to which the Kirk's intimate involvement with the state had shaped the major ecclesiastical factions. John Leslie was an accomplished scientist, and was a candidate for a chair at Edinburgh in 1805. Moderates favored another candidate who was also a minister in the city. In fact, the patronage system had allowed ministers to hold university posts and receive income from both benefices. To this system the Moderates had no objections as long as they could encourage the right kind of cleric into academic and ecclesiastical life, but the Popular Party was opposed to the abuses inherent in joint appointments.

In this setting, Leslie became the cause célèbre of the Popular Party – his would have been a single appointment to the university – even though he had issued favorable remarks about the heterodox views of David Hume. Leslie's views about Hume became an item of public interest because Moderates, to promote their own candidate for the academic chair, tried to prove the heterodoxy of Leslie. Thus, the less than orthodox Moderates were now in the position of defending orthodoxy, and their opponents, the Popular Party, were promoting an academic whose theology was unreliable – both sides flip-flopping from their ideals in order to score points in a contest over patronage.

In the end, Leslie received the appointment and the defeat of Moderate arguments brought to a close an era of Scottish Presbyterianism when the social standing of the Kirk stole attention away from those teachings and practices that had absorbed earlier generations of Scotland's clergy.

Further Decline: the Netherlands

The victory of Reformed orthodoxy over Arminianism at the Synod of Dort (1618–19) was arguably the brightest spot in Dutch Reformed church history after the initial national independence. In the aftermath of Dort, the Dutch Reformed divided into factions while the state itself, through ad hoc policies of religious and intellectual freedom, presented few incentives for doctrinal rigor within the national church. The dominant division was between the followers of Johannes Cocceius (1603–69) and those of Gisbertus Voetius (1589–1676), two Reformed academics who dominated Dutch universities and by implication the major theological developments of the national churches. Most of the differences between the two parties were formal – whether to use precise categories of logic or to attempt to employ concepts derived from biblical theology, for example, or the viability of Cartesian methods for theological training – with both sides also claiming important theological consequences for either the adoption or rejection of these methods. But this academic antagonism also played out within the churches. For instance, the Coccejans' biblical theology led in the direction of a less rigorous observance of Sunday as the Christian Sabbath, since the development of covenant theology taught that the original prohibitions for a day of rest had ceased with Christ's fulfillment of the covenant of works. Voetians, in contrast, maintained a view of Sunday observance closer to the Puritans, with the entire day given over exclusively to rest and worship. In politics, the Coccejans were more inclined to support the States General and so pray for them in public worship, while the Voetians favored the House of Orange and prayed accordingly. The differences even extended to male grooming: Voetians cut their hair short, and if bald wore simple black caps, but Coccejans wore shoulder-length hair and supplemented their locks with wigs.

Civil authorities sometimes warned against polemics on both sides, but such even-handed caution only intensified animosity. On the theological left were thinkers such as Balthasar Bekker (1634–98), a minister who finished his career in Amsterdam. His book, *Die Betooverde Wereld* (1691) was an important polemic against witchcraft, sorcery, and the spirit world. But because Bekker also questioned the existence of the devil and demons, his effort to explain phenomena on natural grounds drew fire from the orthodox. Adding to the opposition was Bekker's use of Cartesian methods and the separation of spirit from matter. As one of the first published Dutch Divines to question the practice of interpreting developments in nature or history as signs of divine favor or judgment, Bekker was important for later efforts to appropriate science for theology. His arguments also helped to bring an end to judicial charges against alleged witches. But during his own time hostility to his views led to his eviction from the ministry in 1692, though he retained his salary until his death.

If Bekker embodied developments on the left within the Dutch Reformed, from the zealously pious right came additional expressions of discomfort with the ecclesiastical establishment. Jean de Labadie (1610–74) gave voice to one strain of a desire for greater holiness. A Frenchman and former Roman Catholic priest of Jansenist persuasion, he converted to Protestantism in 1650 and found his way to Utrecht, where Voetius welcomed him in 1666 as an ally. After taking a call to a Reformed church in Middelburg, de Labadie grew uncomfortable with the presence of unbelievers within the church and began to restrict access the Lord's Supper to those with a credible profession and outward devotion. When de Labadie refused to sign the church's confession and order, his peers deposed him from the ministry. Undeterred he established his own congregation, which persisted beyond his death into the early eighteenth century. Though the membership of de Labadie's church was small, his concern for greater purity within the established churches gained a following among the regular clergy.

Jacobus Koelman (1632–95) was one of those Reformed pastors who while rejecting de Labadie's call for a pure church also desired greater reform within the Dutch ecclesiastical establishment. He argued that de Labadie was wrong to restrict church membership to the elect – the church would always have wheat and tares – but he also believed that the established churches were in need of reform. Koelman was part of the Dutch Nadere Reformatie – Second Reformation – which sought to purge the church of corruption in ways similar to English Puritans. He preached particularly against entanglements between church and state that compromised ministers' ability to impose moral standards on civil authorities. Koelman also opposed the use of prescribed forms and liturgies within the church. His failure to preach on the designated themes of church holidays – Christmas, Easter, etc. – forced the civil authorities to depose him in 1675.

Instead of establishing his own congregation, Koelman continued to regard himself as part of the Dutch church and to conduct services, but did so in house congregations or conventicles. These small gatherings had always been part of the Protestant experience in the Netherlands. Going back to the upheavals of the sixteenth century, gathering for preaching in small groups had been the only option for some believers. Then, with the Synod of Dort's instructions for catechetical training in homes and among families, the Voetians used conventicles to meet separately from Coccejans. Over the course of the seventeenth century, small groups could either follow the order of a regular worship – like the ones that Koelman conducted – or they could facilitate the more mystically inclined who sought fellowship and inspiration through informal conversations, study of Scripture, and prayer.

Throughout these disputes, the Dutch churches floated along without recourse to a national synod that could address these difficulties. The calling of a national synod remained the prerogative of the civil authorities, and divisions between the House of Orange and the States General prevented the Dutch Republic from taking sides beyond proclamations, such as the one in 1694 that mandated the "conservation of rest and peace in the churches."[18] By the middle of the eighteenth century those calls were also coming from church officials who had grown weary of strife. Johannes Mommers, a Voetian, argued in *Eubulus of Goede Raad* (1738) for both sides to put aside their differences, at least to the point of letting parties within the church exist separately. Mommers also hoped for greater unity with Lutherans, and this may have explained why his proposal generated more rancor.

But just as provocative was William IV of Orange's request, as stadtholder, for the faculty at Leiden to produce articles of reconciliation for a church dispute at Zwolle. One of the city's ministers, Anthonie van der Os, had created a vigorous dispute by denying the received interpretation of certain texts regarding the deity of Christ (Micah 5:1; Psalms 2:7; John 5:26). For good measure, van der Os also questioned the relationship between justification and faith within the stages of private experience (e.g. *Ordo salutis*). In their response to the controversy, Leiden's faculty determined that the minister was neither orthodox nor heretical. That pronouncement did not save van der Os' post. In 1755, the provincial and church authorities deposed him. Despite the action against van der Os, two ministers, Alexander Comrie and Nikolaas Holtius, used the Leiden faculty's performance to denounce the spirit of tolerance within the university and the church at large. They wrote a series of pamphlets during the 1750s, *Examen van het Ontwerp van Tolerantie*, which saw in the steady calls for moderation an abandonment of the Synod of Dort and an opening for Pelagianism and Arminianism. The faculty appealed to the States General, which responded by informing the critics of toleration that ministers should abstain from forming or promoting a party spirit within the church. Instead of cultivating harmony, the incident exacerbated differences: churches in some provinces adopted the position that Dort's formulations were infallible because of their agreement with Scripture, while other regional bodies opposed such efforts to repristinate Reformed orthodoxy. Even so, Prince William IV's remark, "Doctrines need to be taught, but most of them must be considered mysteries, of which we human beings, can form no idea," captured the disposition of late eighteenth-century civil and ecclesiastical authorities toward religious life.[19]

If internal developments within the Dutch Reformed churches were not sufficient to alter the character of the nation's religious outlook, political reforms toppled the tottering church order. In the 1780s, revolutionary impulses from North America and France found sympathizers in the Netherlands who hoped to abolish the not so *ancien régime* of the Dutch Republic. Joan van der Capellen tot den Pol's pamphlet, "To the People of the Netherlands," tapped these revolutionary sentiments, which included doing away with the corruptions of the stadtholder and recognition of the new republic in America. The desire for a liberal and modern nation also included abolishing the ecclesiastical order. The emerging political conflict pushed the advocates of the church and its orthodox past to support the House of Orange, while the revolutionary Patriots advocated a separation of church and state. With help from Prussia the stadtholder William V held out until 1793, when France's war against Prussia and Austria also led to a French invasion of the Netherlands. By 1795 the original Dutch Republic had become the revolutionary Batavian Republic. Out went the House of Orange and the States General; in came a national assembly, elected by all males who were twenty years or older.

Out also went the established church. The new constitution severed state support for Reformed churches and placed them in the same status as all other communions that the old polity had tolerated: Lutherans, Roman Catholics, Mennonites, and others. It also relegated theology professors, who were responsible for training pastors, to the philosophy faculties at Dutch universities. Because the Reformed churches, like the Dutch Republic itself, had been organized along provincial lines, a response from ecclesiastical officials to the proposed constitution was slow to materialize. When it did, the pastors did not object to the separation of church and state but did petition the new government to preserve the Lord's Day, maintain church buildings, and continue paying the salaries and pensions of existing ministers. The most visible form of clerical defiance came when eighteen pastors refused to take an oath of allegiance to the new government. These protestors, despite the separation of church and state, lost their ministerial credentials. Meanwhile, churches outside the ecclesiastical establishment favored the new arrangement. Roman Catholics in particular favored French occupation, despite the adversity that Rome had experienced at the hands of France's radicals. One Dutch Roman Catholic official compared the older ecclesiastical establishment to a Muslim marriage, with the husband (state) espousing one denomination as wife and living with other religious communions as concubines.

French influence had a brief upside for the Dutch Reformed churches when Napoleon modified the revolutionary constitution in favor of oligarchic rule. Laws implemented in 1803 required all Dutch citizens of fourteen years of age or older to register with the denomination of their choice so that the state could allocate funds for the churches on a per capita basis. Owing to the historic strength of the Reformed churches, and because church members were not used to looking for a communion agreeable to their own personal convictions, this provision provided the Reformed pastors with needed financial assistance. By 1809 Reformed Protestantism still claimed the lions' share of citizens, with 55 percent of the population amongst its faithful. Roman Catholics accounted for 38 percent, while Lutherans, Mennonites, Remonstrants, and Jews comprised less than 3 percent each. Still, the French Revolution and its aftermath ended the Reformed churches' privileged legal position within the old order of the Dutch Republic.

Reformation on Hold

Eighteenth-century European state churches confronted significant pressure to decrease doctrinal and liturgical norms if they were to retain the favor of their political patrons. Reformed churches were too young to qualify for inclusion in the category of the *ancien régime*. Still, their position within an elaborate set of European civil institutions that were financially and legally dependent on political rulers – whether in cities like those in Switzerland and the Holy Roman Empire, or within nations like Scotland and the Netherlands – placed Protestants in a situation comparable to Roman Catholics. European Christians – Reformed, Lutherans, Anglicans, and Roman Catholics – had more to lose than to gain from political reform or adjustments to the social order. For this reason, Reformed churches, like their Christian competitors, adjusted to demands for toleration from rulers who wanted both to avoid the religiously motivated warfare of the seventeenth century and to open service to as wide a swath of the population as possible. Of course, this was not true in parts of Roman Catholic Europe such as Spain and France, where persecution of heretics persisted and supplied intellectuals with grist for the mill of reason as a better guide than faith for the affairs of state. But in Protestant sectors – especially where unity was advantageous for withstanding Roman Catholic powers – reducing differences among the various branches of the Reformation was a virtue. As such, the moderation of the Church of England became a model for some rulers and churchmen, and explains why George I of Great Britain and Frederick William I of Prussia would actually intervene to prevent the Reformed churches in Switzerland from re-imposing the Helvetic Consensus in 1722. By the mid-1720s Geneva, Neuchâtel, and Basel had disavowed that late seventeenth-century standard of Reformed orthodoxy. Zurich and Bern retained the Consensus for a few more decades, but after 1745 Reformed synods ceased to affirm it at all.

The difficulty that Reformed churches faced in a post-confessional environment was one of determining the boundaries of correct teaching and erroneous belief. Since the creeds were attempts specifically to explain – often to magistrates – what the churches believed and what the rulers were endorsing if they decided to back Protestants, the loss of these statements as norms left pastors and assemblies with seemingly arbitrary standards. What often happened was that ministers and synods let the civic purpose of serving the city or nation determine the churches' policy and doctrinal firmness. But the dangers of following public demands for enlightened tolerance looked as foolish to Christianity's eighteenth-century critics as did Protestant or Roman Catholic orthodoxy. Jean-Jacques Rousseau's description of the Geneva church, in *Letters Written from the Mountain* (1764), exposed this difficulty graphically:

> It is asked, he says, of the citizens of Geneva, if Jesus Christ is God. They dare not answer. It is asked if He is a mere man. They are embarrassed and will not say they think so. They are alarmed, terrified, they come together, they discuss, they are in agitation and often earnest consultation and conference. All vanishes into ambiguity, and they say neither yes nor no. O Genevese, your ministers are in truth very singular people. They do not know what they would wish to appear to believe. Their only manner of establishing their faith is to attack the faith of others.[20]

Ironically, adjusting to the realities of political establishments did not prepare the Reformed state churches for the changes that spilled from France to the rest of Europe after the French Revolution, however. The case of Switzerland illustrates the point. As early as 1781 some of Geneva's population began to chafe at the existing political structures, but the city called for assistance from France's Louis XVI. This intervention saved the city's aristocracy but also made more likely a violent reaction to Geneva's ruling elites, which occurred in 1792 when the city experienced its own revolution. This break led to democratic elections and a new constitution that gave the middle class and natives of the city greater access to the political process. By 1798 France annexed Geneva and made the city an administrative center of its Léman district. The Reformed cities of Bern, Basel, and Zurich avoided revolution but not French intervention. Between 1795 and 1797 each city attempted to hold off egalitarian uprisings by force. These tactics only drove those who hoped for greater liberty and equality into the arms of the French. For some it was a hostile occupation, while for others it amounted to liberation. In 1798 the cities of Bern, Basel, and Zurich, along with several other cities and cantons, formed the Helvetic Republic. These dramatic alterations upended the established position of the Reformed churches. The new constitution removed all privileges from the nobility and clergy, and established freedom of religion and the press. As one early twentieth-century historian, James I. Good, and not the most conservative, put the changes in Switzerland with particular regard to Geneva:

> How great was the descent from Calvin to this. Geneva, the city that, under Calvin had been a city set on a hill, whose light could not be hid – the model city, the wonder of its day – had fallen into an abyss. The church which so successfully had resisted all the pots of Romanism for centuries was finally captured by its opposite, rationalism. For two centuries and more Geneva had held to its Calvinism; but half a century had undone it all.[21]

To be sure, Reformed theologians and ministers in Geneva and elsewhere were also adapting to important developments in natural science and philosophy that challenged the content and methods of Reformed scholastic theology. Still, the rationalism that surfaced during the eighteenth century among Reformed Protestants was arguably as much a response to political realities as to intellectual innovation.

Having benefited from the helping hand of the magistrate, Reformed churches during the eighteenth century saw a different side of the state. After the revolutions in France and America, and the rise of a form of politics independent from theology and church life, the question for most Reformed Protestants would be how to recover the vitality of their faith without the aid of civil authorities. The colonial churches had already given one answer. Another would be a form of Calvinism that could be practiced anywhere – no matter what civil authorities, church officers, or colonial administrators did.

CHAPTER EIGHT

REFORMATION REAWAKENED

ITINERANT PREACHING WAS A major source of controversy and a vehicle for disseminating new ideas and practices in places like North America, where social and ecclesiastical life was unsettled. George Whitefield, the Anglican priest of Calvinistic persuasion who became the North American British colonies' first celebrity during the contentious First Awakening (1739–43), crossed the Atlantic ocean seven times during the course of his life, and his voice, manner, and public relations contributed to his fame. Meanwhile, his methods as a preacher and self-promoter created controversy among Presbyterians in both Scotland and British North America.

Whitefield traveled with only a small party of assistants but Count Nicholas Ludwig von Zinzendorf moved with an entire congregation. That was at least the case in the winter of 1741 when he arrived in Geneva with his son Christian, who wanted to study at the Academy. Zinzendorf figured he would also take the opportunity to communicate the character and message of the Moravians to the Company of Pastors. Accompanied by his family, the count arrived in early February and over the course of the next four weeks a retinue of Moravians followed. By early March Zinzendorf's household comprised between forty and fifty. To locals, no matter how pious, the Zinzendorf residence must have seemed an odd place: as one of his biographers notes, the household was essentially a congregation of faithful. This "wandering congregation" attracted much attention because it was divided into choirs and the services were constant:

Each choir held first its own matins. The whole church then came together, and the Count generally gave them an address. At eight o'clock in the evening they again assembled, and edified each other with singing: on which a Bible lesson followed with some of the learned brethren, at which others were also present. Afterwards the brethren and sisters assembled, who divided the hours with each other, from four in the morning till midnight, for intercession and converse with the Lord. At the same time, there was an evening service for those who were not of that company; and from twelve till four o'clock, there was a night-watch for prayer, which was held by the brethren in turns. Besides this, the members of this domestic assembly were divided into little companies, according to their sex, and the choirs to which they belonged, for the purpose of promoting their love to each other, and their advancement in the divine life.[1]

Zinzendorf had arrived under a cloud of suspicion, thanks to the novelty and directness of his piety. Even if the practices of his household were odd, the reception by Geneva's pastors was polite. Zinzendorf presented a letter to three professors, appointed as a delegation to meet with him. They responded by expressing the honor of hosting a bishop of the Moravian church. At one such encounter, one of the professors spoke of his own faith in Christ. So eager was Zinzendorf for this kind of personal expression that he "rose up, fell on [the professor's] neck, and thanked him most cordially for it."[2] Although both sides followed the conventions of decorum, the visit was diplomatically a "disastrous failure." Zinzendorf had hoped to mitigate divisiveness within the Moravian ranks and curb reports that the brethren were disrupting the established churches, but W. R. Ward concludes that "[t]he religion of reason and morality now dominant in Geneva was abhorrent to the count" and that "his understanding of grace and spirit was abhorrent to the Genevans."[3]

Soon after Geneva, Zinzendorf journeyed across the Atlantic among German settlers to the New World. In December 1741 he traveled only with one of his daughters and several Moravians functioning as servants and assistants. He spent a few days in New York before arriving in Philadelphia, and preached widely among the churches of the German settlers. By then revivalism was a sensation, and Zinzendorf, like Whitefield, was attracting non-churchgoers. But the appeal also crossed denominational lines, especially among German Protestants. This interdenominational following had limits, however. As his biographer writes:

Besides the Lutherans and Reformed, there were nine different sects amongst the Germans in Pennsylvania; all of whom were so bigoted to their own opinions, that they not only preferred their own way to every other, but spoke harshly of those who differed from them. They despised the Lutherans and Reformed in particular; not only because there was so little animation in their meetings, but also because there was so much of what was objectionable in their life and conduct.[4]

Friction between pietistically inclined Protestants and those drawn to the forms and order of the confessional churches was responsible for much of the opposition that Zinzendorf would eventually encounter. Zinzendorf remained in the area for a while and began to preach for a Lutheran congregation in Philadelphia at a building shared by both Lutherans and Reformed. When Zinzendorf's plans for a union of all Protestants in Pennsylvania included German Reformed congregations abandoning their ties to the Classis of Amsterdam, John Philip Boehm, the leading German Reformed pastor, published a tract against the count's views. Boehm's objections were printed in installments and ranged from a historical narrative of Zinzendorf's antics to lists of the count's strange practices. Boehm's strongest words for the Moravians, however, came from the Reformed churches of the Netherlands:

> We Reformed members, standing under the Church Order, approved of and instituted by the Classis of Amsterdam, recognize no one as a member, much less as a minister of our Church, who contaminates himself with the Moravian soul destructive doctrine, until his total repentance of his serious lapse and return to our doctrine and Church, based upon God's Word.[5]

Zinzendorf published a defense, but, like other itinerants on fire with the gospel, he had other places to go and left Pennsylvania a year after his arrival.

The count's encounter with Reformed churches on both sides of the Atlantic suggests that Reformed Protestants were suspicious of the innovative devotion associated with pietism. As true as that implication may be in the case of the Moravians, it is not a fair estimate of Reformed Protestantism more generally, because as early as the 1590s Reformed ministers began to explore subjective and informal expressions of devotion that prefigured the sort of experiential Protestantism that was to develop among German pietists and that spawned the Awakenings of the eighteenth century. Indeed, frustration with the limits of reforming the state church had prompted some Puritans at the end of the sixteenth century to explore personal and extra-ecclesiastical methods for carrying out the Reformation. If the established church could not be reformed adequately, then the lives of Reformed Protestants could.

This outlook would prove to be particularly attractive to Reformed and Presbyterian pastors in various locales and circumstances, especially after magistrates, who had initially encouraged reformation, became obstacles to further reform. Starting in the 1720s and 1730s through the efforts of Evangelicals such as Jonathan Edwards in New England and John and Charles Wesley in England, revivals on a small and local scale gained the attention of many observers. Edwards was particularly important for calling attention to the Awakenings through his 1735 book, *A Faithful Narrative of A Surprising Work of God*, a text widely circulated on both sides of the Atlantic and responsible for raising hopes for continuing divine outpourings. With Whitefield's first preaching tour in 1739 in North America, the smaller strands of revival came together in the Great Awakening, thanks to the evangelist's remarkable skills as a communicator, knack for publicity, and sheer physical stamina. His revivals produced numerous conversions, imitators, growth in church membership, and noticeable spiritual earnestness. The Great Awakening also generated controversy and church splits. By the late 1740s the ecclesiastical scene on both sides of the Atlantic had basically returned to pre-Awakening levels of devotion. Reformed Protestants preferred Whitefield to Zinzendorf because Calvinism had generated its own brand of fervent devotion to counter the equivocation that afflicted the established churches. Ministers and laity hoped for a vigorous faith that could flourish on its own and they found one that was personal and private, one that did not depend on the sanction of civil authorities. The irony is that the new form of Reformed piety, if followed carefully, did not depend on ecclesiastical authorities either. This was personal and private reformation, independent from church reform.

The Dutch–English Pietist Connection

In January of 1720 the Dutch Reformed church members of New York City greeted the new pastor in town, Theodorus Jacobus Frelinghuysen, recently ordained by the Classis of Amsterdam, to minister among the settlers in New Jersey's Raritan River valley. Born in 1692 to a German Reformed pastor and his wife in Hagen, Germany, Frelinghuysen adopted the distinct ways of Dutch Reformed Protestants at the age of nineteen, when he studied first at the Gymnasium of Hamm and then at the University of Lingen. At the time the Dutch churches were divided between the Coccejans and Voetians, but from each side Frelinghuysen found teaching and practices to encourage personal piety and the zealous pursuit of holiness among church members. From the Coccejans he learned the importance of gathering people in conventicles for catechetical instruction and informal fellowship among the saints. Among the Voetians Frelinghuysen witnessed the importance of preaching on the necessity of conversion and adapting sermons to the spiritual condition of worshippers. After ordination by the Classis of Emden in 1717 he ministered in East Frisia briefly before taking a post as Latin instructor at a school in Enkhuizen in West Frisia. But on his way to the new position he heard about the need for pastors in the New World and presented himself to the Classis of Amsterdam. The Amsterdam pastors approved his credentials and by the end of 1719 he was on board a ship headed for New York.

Upon his arrival, Frelinghuysen encountered another conflict among the Dutch Reformed. On one side, Henricus Boel maintained strict adherence to Reformed teaching and customs, apparently out of fear that if the Dutch churches veered from their established forms the English governors of the colony would renege on their agreement to support the Dutch Reformed pastors. On the other side, the pastor Guilliam Bertholf, who had been a follower of Jacobus Koelman's efforts in the Old World to reform the national church, flouted many of the Dutch churches' conventions – such as conducting services on prescribed church holidays – in favor of intimate methods such as meeting for prayer, fellowship, and worship in conventicles. Frelinghuysen himself indicated which side he favored by the way he conducted his first service in the New World. His ministry prompted a heated dispute with Boel. The older pastor objected to Frelinghuysen's "howling" prayers and failure to use the Lord's Prayer. The newcomer regarded liturgical forms as inferior to heartfelt spontaneous prayers. But Frelinghuysen's performance was equally offensive to Bertholf, who found the new pastor's prayers to be ostentatious.

After upsetting his clerical colleagues, Frelinghuysen proceeded to alienate members of his assigned congregation in New Jersey. He had decided to examine prospective participants of the Lord's Supper whether they had prepared adequately to receive the elements. When he found some of the members wanting, he barred them from the Supper. Some of the spiritually inferior were prominent members of the community, and in turn opposed their new pastor. They won over Boel, who proceeded to prepare a 150-page complaint against Frelinghuysen for the Classis of Amsterdam. The catalogue of errors included presumptuous judging of church members' spiritual conditions, ignoring membership certificates from other Reformed churches, preaching God's law to produce a conversion experience, and public denunciations of fellow clergy in New York.

The controversy over Frelinghuysen would last almost fifteen years thanks to the distance separating the New World churches and the authorities in Amsterdam, but his methods soon produced the conversions for which he had hoped and the first signs of revival in the New World. Soon he met another experientially inclined pastor, this time a Presbyterian by the name of Gilbert Tennent, who in 1726 took a call from a congregation in nearby New Brunswick, New Jersey. Frelinghuysen's methods of preaching and ministry appealed to Tennent, who had experienced a conversion three years earlier, while in the initial stages of a law career. But the effects on church members were equally impressive. According to Tennent:

I had the Pleasure of seeing much of the Fruits of his Ministry: divers of his Hearers with whom I had the Opportunity of conversing appear'd to be converted Persons, by their Soundness in Principle, Christian experience and pious Practice: and these Persons declared that the Ministrations of [Frelinghuysen] were the means thereof . . . . I [then] began to be very much distressed about my want of Success; for I knew not for *half a Year* or more after I came to *New Brunswick*, that any one was converted by my Labours, altho' several Persons were at Times affected transiently.[6]

Soon, however, Tennent was leading the first revivals among colonial Presbyterians by preaching the terrors of the law. This form of sermon reminded hearers of the judgment that awaited them for sin and called for repentance and faith in Christ. That some of the people sitting under such preaching were already members of the church did not trouble Frelinghuysen or Tennent because, at least in part, the state churches of Europe were filled with hypocrites – church members by virtue of citizenship. A similar sort of revival broke out a few years later in Massachusetts under Jonathan Edwards. His "Sinners in the Hands of An Angry God," exhibited a casebook example of terrifying preaching designed to produce conversion and sincere faith.

Over the course of the 1730s these revivals divided Presbyterians, Reformed Protestants, and Congregationalists. The chief point of division was the relationship between the subjective and objective, or internal and external aspects of the gospel and Christian duty. In the case of Tennent's Presbyterian colleagues, revivals drove a wedge between the Old Side Presbyterians, who insisted on strict subscription to the Westminster Confession of Faith and Catechisms, and Tennent's own New Side Presbyterians, who required a narrative of conversion not only from church members but also from prospective pastors. Adding to the dispute was the revivalists' refusal to obey synodical rulings in favor of their own direct calling by the Holy Spirit. The Synod of Philadelphia tried to keep both sides together, and in 1738 even created a separate presbytery (New Brunswick) for the revivalistically inclined. But such moderation could not pacify either side. Meanwhile, Tennent himself contributed directly to the split through his 1740 sermon, "The Danger of An Unconverted Ministry," in which he labeled opponents of revival as unconverted, and implored church members under such pastors to abandon their congregation and find a true one. By 1745 the colonial Presbyterian church had divided into two synods, the pro-revival New Side (New York), and the anti-revival Old Side (Philadelphia).

Not all pro-revival Presbyterians were as vituperative as Tennent, even if the sense of being filled with the Spirit could nurture self-righteousness. New Side Presbyterians also benefited from the labors of Jonathan Dickinson (1688– 1747) and Samuel Davies (1723–61). The former, a graduate of Yale College, hailed from Massachusetts and originally ministered in a Congregationalist church in Elizabethtown, New Jersey. Dickinson persuaded his congregation to switch to the Presbyterian communion, and for the last thirty years of his life he was a prominent figure in colonial Presbyterianism. His stature owed in part to theological writings such as *The Reasonableness of Christianity* (1732) and *Five Points: The True Scripture-Doctrine Concerning Some Important Points of Christian Faith* (1741). Among colonial pastors, only Jonathan Edwards had a wider readership internationally than Dickinson. His theological acumen and support for revival led to his appointment as the first president of the College of New Jersey (still named Log College), which met initially in Dickinson's home. This college's trustees would also employ Davies, the son of Welsh immigrants to Delaware. He studied with another New Side minister before serving as the Presbyterian church planter in Virginia. After the College of New Jersey's founding, Davies traveled with Gilbert Tennent to England and Scotland in 1753 to raise funds for the new school. Davies earned a reputation as a gifted preacher especially among the Scots. Five years later the college appointed him as president. Like Dickinson and Jonathan Edwards, Davies died while presiding over the college.

Although revivalism had moderate advocates, controversy bedeviled the colonial churches where the Awakenings occurred. Beyond the occasional itinerant evangelist who might come to town, new music punctuated worship services and often indicated which side a pastor or congregation was on. Indeed, the Great Awakening was a watershed in the history of Protestant hymnody. Not only did the eighteenth-century revivals unleash a torrent of new songs, particularly the hymns of Charles Wesley and Isaac Watts; the Awakening also popularized the new hymnody in a fashion then ended the dominance of metrical psalmody, at least for Presbyterians in the American colonies (and their descendants). Congregations that promoted the revivals were among the first to introduce Watts' *The Psalms of David Imitated*, originally published in North America in 1729 by Benjamin Franklin. These were adaptations of the Old Testament Psalter that added themes from the New Testament about Christ's death and resurrection. Another Watts publication, *Hymns and Spiritual Songs* (1707), became a favorite of George Whitefield at his services, and by 1752 Samuel Davies had also introduced hymns into Presbyterian worship. The logic behind the use of hymns was their compatibility with the religious experience that revivals promoted. The potential for enthusiasm was a reason for Old Side ministers to stick with the metrical psalter produced by Francis Rous and approved by parliament at the time of the Westminster Assembly. Whatever the motivations, the triumph of religious experience through the Great Awakening broke the exclusive hold of psalmody that had gripped Presbyterians in the New World.

Aside from revealing tensions among colonial Presbyterians over authentic religious experience and proper forms of ministry, the Awakenings also showed the lasting presence of Puritan practical divinity and its mode of transmission from sixteenth-century England all the way down to eighteenth-century Presbyterian and Reformed churches in the New World. The zeal for personal holiness and assurance that characterized Puritanism did not begin in earnest until the 1580s, when English Reformed efforts to establish a national church closer in structure and teaching to what prevailed on the Continent failed. This shift was particularly evident in the writings of three English Protestants, Lewis Bayly (d. 1631), Richard Baxter (1615–91), and John Bunyan (1628–88), for whom the quest for personal godliness became almost an obsession.

Bayly was educated at Oxford and served a series of positions within the Anglican church, including Bishop of Bangor, but controversy marked his ministry thanks to his Puritan-inspired agitation against Stuart religious policy. His greatest achievement came with *The Practice of Piety* (*c.*1612), a book that went through several reprints in England and the Netherlands over the course of the seventeenth century and may have been the most popular Puritan work if not for John Bunyan's *Pilgrim's Progress*. Bayly's book was not lacking in doctrinal precision, even if it was designed to encourage personal piety. It included a large section of traditional Reformed teaching on the Trinity and redemption, before providing average believers with guidance on Bible reading (entirely and annually), prayer, meditation, family worship, and wholesome thoughts. Bayly did provide counsel on preparation for public worship but the overarching character of the book was personal and private, such that a reader could find instruction for the pursuit of godliness from the time of rising early in the morning until placing one's weary but devout head upon the pillow at night. Not to be missed were Bayly's methods for goading believers to such daily rigor. He described the torments that afflicted unbelievers both in this life and in the world to come, contrasted the life of the unregenerate with the blessed estate of believers, and warned the regenerate of unwholesome attachments to the world. By contrasting the lives of saints and unbelievers in their daily routines, Bayly was decisively transferring the evidence of reformation from the outward and corporate life of the church to the private and personal lives of believers.

While Bayly spoke to the needs of Puritans during the reigns of James I and Charles I, Richard Baxter articulated the ideals of Reformed-minded pastors who after the Restoration were unwilling to accept the Act of Uniformity (1662). Born in 1615, Baxter was a rare Puritan Divine to achieve such stature without the aid of a university education. He initially served as a schoolteacher in Dudley, where he also preached and was struck by the lack of moral discipline among professing Christians. By 1641 Baxter had become a pastor at Kidderminster and would continue there (minus service as a chaplain in Cromwell's army) until 1662, at which time he joined the ranks of the Nonconformists. Throughout his life, Baxter hoped to counteract the twin dangers of antinomianism and sectarianism. His most important contribution to practical divinity came in 1649 with *The Saints' Everlasting Rest*, in which he encouraged meditation on heaven, along with careful examination of the heart in the light of these spiritual realities. Baxter also advocated catechetical training in the family as a means of improving both the church and the godly commonwealth. In his *Christian Directory* (1673), Baxter wove together the themes of personal godliness and national righteousness to produce a comprehensive understanding of Christian motivation at all levels of society. What was crucial to this broad view was the characteristic theme of Puritan practical divinity, an urgent plea for individual reformation upon which institutional reforms depended.

This turn toward personal devotion received reinforcement from seventeenth-century Puritan reflection on the *Ordo salutis* (i.e. order of salvation). William Ames' (1576–1633) *Marrow of Theology* (1627) explored in great detail the stages of the Christian life that began with election and proceeded through effectual calling, justification, sanctification, and glorification. Ames had studied under William Perkins (1558–1602) at Cambridge, and taught there before controversy, which dogged his career, took him to the Netherlands. There he ministered to English settlers, engaged in theological disputes over Arminianism, and eventually taught theology at universities in Franeker and Rotterdam. Ames' attention to the inner recesses of spiritual development was supposed to help believers achieve a full measure of assurance about their faith and eternal status. But when Ames described the actual stages of development in the heart, such as the depths of torment that should accompany conviction of sin and repentance, he could leave readers wondering if their experience had been sufficiently profound. In effect, this strand of Puritan reflection took received doctrinal categories of Reformed Protestantism, such justification and sanctification, and directed them inward.

The personal nature of practical divinity was responsible in part for the popularity in seventeenth-century England of journal-keeping that charted the diarist's own experience and progress in holiness. Thomas Goodwin (1600–80), a Puritan pastor, theologian, chaplain to Cromwell, and member of the Westminster Assembly, kept just such a journal that revealed his own attempts to chart his soul's development. Of his childhood, he wrote:

> I began to have some slighter workings of the Spirit of God from the time I was six years old; I could weep for my sins whenever I did set myself to think of

them, and had flashes of joy upon thoughts of the things of God. I was affected
with good motions and affections of love to God and Christ, for their love
revealed to man, and with grief for sin as displeasing them.[7]

But as a young man Goodwin experienced doubts and lustful temptations that
he attributed to a rebellious heart. He finally experienced relief through
conversion:

> ... this speaking of God to my soul, although it was but a gentle sound, yet it
> made a noise over my whole heart, and filled and possessed all the faculties of
> my whole soul. God took me aside, and as it were privately said unto me, Do
> you now turn to me, and I will pardon all your sins though ever so many, as I
> forgave and pardoned my servant Paul, and convert you unto me ...[8]

Aside from the popularity of journal-keeping, alertness to upswings and down-
turns in spiritual development became a characteristic mark of Puritan identity.

Even more indicative of the widespread appeal of practical divinity and its
subjective earnestness was John Bunyan's allegory *Pilgrim's Progress* (1678). He
too lacked a formal education and worked for much of his life in Bedfordshire as
a tinker (pot repairer), with a brief stint in the Parliamentary Army during the
English Civil War. After the war Bunyan married a woman (her name is
unrecorded) with ties to Puritan circles, who had in her library Bayly's *Practice
of Piety*. Bunyan soon began to worship with a Nonconformist group of believers
and underwent a conversion experience. He would eventually preach for this
group, and by the time of the Restoration such activity had landed Bunyan in
jail, where he was to conceive of the allegory that would make him famous. Like
formal Puritan theology, *Pilgrim's Progress* explored the order of salvation within
the convert's experience, from effectual calling to glorification. This meant that
the pilgrim's journey was hardly finished once he gained assurance of forgive-
ness; the pilgrimage had just begun, and it involved mortification (dying to
sinful desires) and vivification (living for God). The account of the protagonist
Christian's ongoing struggle with sin and desire for holiness made Bunyan's
allegory appealing to readers well beyond Calvinistic circles; it would become
a devotional staple among Arminians and Wesleyans. But for English
Nonconformists it became an appealing guide to the nature of religious devotion
outside the established church and on the margins of respectable society.

Puritan practical divinity spread immediately outside the British Isles to the
Netherlands where English Protestants had, at least since the days of William
Tyndale, ventured to escape religious policies in their native land. Aside from the
theological affinity between the English and Dutch, William Perkins was an

important conduit of experimental Calvinism. Equally influential was Willem Teellinck (1579–1629), a Dutch pastor often credited with spearheading the Nadere Reformatie (Second Reformation) among the Reformed churches in the United Provinces.[9] In Teellnick's case the transmission of practical divinity traveled less through English proponents in the Netherlands than through a Dutchman in England. He had originally aimed for a legal career and secured an apprenticeship in the English town of Banbury, where Puritan forms of devotion were prominent. So impressed with the English Protestants was Teellinck that he changed plans and decided upon the ministry. What struck him in particular about the excellence of Puritanism were the Sunday routines of worship, both public and private, and complete cessation from worldly activities. After studying theology at Leiden, where he avoided taking sides in the Arminian Controversy, he pastored in several churches, most notably at Middelburg, until his death. He followed the Puritan example of trying to institute strict observance of the Sabbath, which resulted in a controversy that embroiled the Dutch Reformed churches for most of Teellinck's life. The only synod to approve his proposals was Zeeland.

Teellinck's influence extended beyond church affairs to the publication of edifying literature. From the earliest days of his ministerial career he translated into Dutch various works of English practical divinity. According to one estimate, Teellinck was responsible for translating sixty different English works between 1598 and 1622; the 114 different editions of these titles accounted for more than half of all works in practical piety published in the Netherlands during the first two decades of the seventeenth century. Teellinck made his own contributions. One of his earliest works, *The Christian Report* (1608), called upon the Dutch magistrates to implement and enforce laws that upheld public standards of righteousness. He also wrote manuals for devout families, one a commentary on the Heidelberg Catechism, to be used as part of family worship, and another practical guide on Christian living. His most popular book, *The Path of True Godliness* (1621), functioned for the Dutch Reformed in the way that Bayly's and Baxter's books did for Puritans. In a detailed and exhortation-filled approach, Teellinck presented guidance and motivation for a godly life. This included instruction on Sunday practices, family worship, prayer, fasting, and daily conduct. Throughout, Teellinck appealed to the glory of God and the believer's participation in that glory through a life of godliness, contrasting such devotion with the shameful nature of a life lived in rebellion against God or in pursuit of worldly pleasures and accomplishments. Teellinck had learned the lessons of Puritan instruction on personal reformation well. This form of devotion placed the believer's daily existence before the very face of God.

The appeal of English practical divinity extended not simply to Dutch pastors but also to university professors, including most notably Gisbertus

Voetius (1589–1676). One of the leading defenders of Reformed orthodoxy against theological (e.g. Arminius) and philosophical (e.g. Descartes) challenges, Voetius was also a great proponent of Puritan forms of devotion, thus indicating that precision in doctrinal matters could lead to similar rigor in personal conduct. As much as Voetius established his reputation through polemics, he also advocated a life of holiness and relied upon patterns established by the Puritans. As a student at Leiden he had become acquainted with the practical divinity transmitted through Ames. Later Voetius would add his name to the list of Dutch pastors responsible for translating works of English divinity into Dutch, in this case Bayly's *Practice of Piety* (to which Voetius added commentary in the margins). When he joined the faculty at Utrecht in 1634, Voetius spoke in his inaugural lecture specifically about the importance of uniting knowledge and devotion. His later conflict with Cocceius stemmed not simply from the latter's apparent disregard of scholastic theology, but also concerned the practical matter of Sabbath observance. Because Cocceius' interpretation of biblical covenants highlighted discontinuity between Israel and the church, the Puritan practice of pressing Old Testament rigor upon Christians was a function of misinterpretation. But for Voetius and other leaders of the Nadere Reformatie, raising questions about the believer's Sabbath duties was to undermine a chief component of real piety.

In the classroom Voetius combined instruction in technical theology and holy living, as the career of one of his more illustrious students, Wilhelmus à Brakel (1635–1711), indicated. À Brakel spent his entire career in the pastorate, achieving his greatest notoriety at Leeuwarden (1673–83) and at Rotterdam (1683–1711). At Leeuwarden, where he was one of six pastors at the city church, he became frustrated by the social stratification of clergy and laity, and his convictions on the importance of eliminating hypocrisy and cultivating godliness led to the founding of a conventicle where à Brakel conducted services among a select group. This was a Reformed instance of cultivating piety in settings similar to the *collegia pietatis* (i.e. schools of piety) started in Germany by the so-called father of Pietism, Philipp Jakob Spener. To channel his ministry into public settings, the consistory established a forum for à Brakel to conduct catechetical instruction. He entered into another controversy when he allowed and defended Jacobus Koelman, known for opposing formalism in the Dutch churches, to preach at Leeuwarden. When the provincial authorities disapproved, à Brakel resorted to the anti-Erastian position that Christ was head of the church and that the state had no authority to intervene. Another indication of à Brakel's affinity for experimental divinity was his public opposition to the Cocceian views of another pastor, David Flud van Giffen, whose interpretation of the Old Testament apparently threatened Sabbath observance.

À Brakel's most lasting contribution was a lengthy systematic theology that, as its title indicated – *A Christian's Reasonable Service* (1700) – combined Reformed orthodoxy with detailed practical guidance. One sign of the author's interest in godliness was his organization of topics. Although à Brakel covered the major points of dogmatic theology in the first volume, he addressed the church in the next, while the contours of salvation and Christian experience filled the other four volumes. These included instruction on the Decalogue and the Lord's Prayer, and extended to fasting, family worship, and spiritual meditation. One revealing section was à Brakel's effort to distinguish true Pietists from false ones. The crucial distinction was between a piety that stemmed entirely from natural causes and one whose origin was spiritual. "This is the crux of the matter," he wrote, "salvation or condemnation is contingent upon this." He concluded that anyone to whom salvation matters should "know this distinction, reject that which is natural, and practice what is spiritual, rather than embrace immediately whatever has the appearance of spirituality."[10] Not only was this a warning against hypocrisy, but à Brakel's distinction, although designed to reassure believers, could generate as many doubts as it quelled.

Because the English and Dutch had contributed so heavily to the literature, language, and practice of Reformed Pietism, the rise of revivalism in the North American colonial context over a century later through the preaching of Frelinghuysen was a fitting culmination. But the capstone of experimental Calvinism was arguably the book that set the standard for sifting the chaff from the wheat of spiritual authenticity: Jonathan Edwards' *Religious Affections* (1742). Like Frelinghuysen and Tennent to the south in New Jersey, Edwards (1703–58) conducted local revivals in Northampton that were forerunners of the transatlantic Awakening that George Whitefield would lead after 1739. The son of a prominent minister in East Windsor, Connecticut, Edwards had studied at Yale twice (once as an undergraduate and later for a Masters' degree). He had ministered at churches in New York and Connecticut before accepting a call to Massachusetts, where he labored with his grandfather, Solomon Stoddard, before succeeding him as the senior pastor. In 1733 and 1734 Edwards began to notice signs of spiritual interest among the young people and a greater zeal for religion among adult members after the untimely deaths of people in the community. In his *A Faithful Narrative of the Surprising Work of God* (1737), Edwards did indeed express surprise over the reinvigoration of his congregation. Unlike Frelinghuysen, who had preached with the intent of awakening individual Christians from spiritual lethargy, Edwards experienced a change of heart without any deviation from his regular preaching. Even so, his *Faithful Narrative* circulated widely and established the benchmark for genuine conversion and spiritual awakenings.

Although Edwards did not alter his methods for the sake of revival, his ministry was of a piece with the practical divinity that Puritans had established at the beginning of the seventeenth century in England and that New England descendants brought with them to the New World. When Edwards composed his most important book on revival, *A Treatise on Religious Affections* (1746), he was contributing at one level to an older body of literature, prevalent among the English and Dutch, that inspected the soul for marks of genuine faith. A prolific author, Edwards did not limit his intellectual interests to revival or Christian experience but produced important works (several published posthumously) that combined European philosophy with Puritan doctrine to defend important facets of Calvinism, such as *Freedom of the Will* (1754), *The Nature of True Virtue* (1765), and *Original Sin* (1758). He was also addressing the needs of the hour among proponents of the Great Awakening who hoped to rescue authentic conversions from spurious enthusiasm. Critics of the revivals during the 1730s and 1740s had regularly charged that the antics accompanying the Awakenings – fits, spells, fainting, weeping – were the telltale signs of enthusiasm: the revivals were all passion devoid of reason. But Edwards wanted to defend revivals and the movements of the spirit that accompanied them while still condemning enthusiasm. He did so by arguing that religious affections were an inherent part of genuine faith. Instead of pitting the heart against the head, Edwards insisted that affections and the intellect were intimately connected in genuine piety. In effect, affections were a form of intimate or felt knowledge. The image he used to describe such understanding was one he drew from John Locke: one may know that honey is sweet, but fail to understand such sweetness until tasting and experiencing it.

As much as Edwards defended revivalism, he was adding another chapter to practical divinity's exploration of the interior and private side of faith. The Massachusetts pastor conceded that many improprieties had accompanied the Awakenings but did not believe that the entire phenomenon could be discredited simply because of abuses. If conversion was marked by humility, love, joy, a desire for the glory of God – Edwards' list of wholesome signs ran to a total of twelve – instances of physical excitement, though unnecessary, could be tolerated. By the mid-eighteenth century these distinctions were conventional, even if Edwards himself had taken the exploration of personal piety to a new level by employing Enlightenment thought for spiritual zeal. As one historian has written, with the Puritans (especially after 1660), the older Reformed quest for an external reform of ecclesiastical and social life yielded to a "concern with the inward religious life," marked by a change of heart: "the will and affections convicted, converted, and sanctified by the predestining grace of God."[11] In other words, once the avenue of reform that the godly magistrate had originally opened proved to be a dead end, English practical divinity took the path of personal and inward reformation. At which point the best indication of reformation was not the form, polity, or teaching of a particular congregation or communion, but was to be found in the believer, with a self-denying way of life, Bible-laced speech, and frequent attendance at small groups of pious believers for meditation, prayer, and encouragement. It was a long way from Calvin's *Ecclesiastical Ordinances*.

Scottish Seasons of Devotion

A different variety of Reformed zeal arose among the Scots from the one that informed the "hotter" sort of Puritanism or the introspective piety of the Dutch Nadere Reformatie. The political circumstances in all these cases were similar; civil authorities no longer sided with church reformation as they had in the sixteenth century. In which case, Presbyterians of Scottish descent considered, and in some cases were forced to explore, alternative forms of devotion for nurturing the true religion, as had Puritans in England and Reformed Protestants in the Netherlands. But for Presbyterians in Ireland and Scotland, the turn toward religious experience depended less on a program of individuals or godly parents reading manuals of edification than it did on communal responses to church rites. In particular, a form of piety emerged among Reformed Protestants from Celtic backgrounds that featured the observance of the Lord's Supper.

At the outset of the Kirk, John Knox had prescribed that the sacrament of the table be celebrated once a month, but political struggles with episcopacy as well as poverty (in the Highlands) sometimes limited the observance of the Lord's Supper to once a year. Owing in part to infrequency, administration of the sacrament assumed great significance and Communion Seasons became the means for marking the Supper's import. Ministers would conduct a series of services during the days leading up to the sacrament, and people from miles around would attend the services, which needed to be held outdoors so as to accommodate the crowds. John Livingstone (1603–36), a minister in Scotland, observed in his diary an unusual response to his sacramental preaching during the 1620s in towns to the north of the River Forth. The chief novelty in Livingstone's practice was to move from manuscript to extemporaneous preaching. Whether this accounted for the revivals he witnessed, the Awakening forged a link in Scottish Presbyterianism between revival and sacrament. These gatherings also encouraged a variety of non-religious activities, such as commerce, carousing, and other forms of secular sociability. Robert Burns gave the name "Holy Fairs" to these Communion Seasons. Although this way of administering the Lord's Supper functioned as an outlet for revelry, it also encouraged forms of spiritual intensity, as preachers used these closely connected series of services to arouse zeal for godliness.

At roughly the same time, the Scots took these observances with them to Ireland, where Communion Season-styled revivalism led to the creation of the first Irish presbytery. Early in the 1620s a handful of Presbyterian ministers began to preach regularly, among them James Glendinning, Robert Blair, Josiah Welch (grandson of John Knox), Robert Cunningham, and even Livingstone, who had first recorded the new forms of piety connected with the Lord's Supper. Glendinning's preaching achieved the greatest notoriety and sparked an awakening later known as the Six Mile Water revival. What made Glendinning so effective was the terror he aroused. Ministers who eventually persuaded him to leave for a rural parish heard complaints that Glendinning never pointed the way toward comfort but only harped on God's wrath for sin. Whether or not he was preaching at Communion Seasons, the other Presbyterian pastors were producing their most evangelistic sermons in connection with the observance of the Lord's Supper. The popular response created expectations for calls to faith and repentance in preparation for the sacrament. In the 1630s, English authorities cracked down on these stirrings, which in the long run forged sentiments behind an Irish Presbyterian church.

The phenomenon of Communion Seasons and revivalistic preaching continued in Scotland through the 1640s and 1650s, but after the Restoration became a defining practice of the Covenanters, those Scottish Presbyterians most resolute in holding onto the National Covenant and most critical of the Kirk. One of the most notable of these occasions took place in 1678 in East Nisbet, south of Edinburgh near Scotland's border, under the ministry of John Blackadder (1615–86). A Covenanter pastor who gained a large following through itinerant preaching, Blackadder's experience highlighted the plight of resolute Presbyterians after the resumption of the British monarchy and the Covenanters' reliance upon Communion Seasons for spiritual sustenance. He lost his parish after refusing to comply with the Rescissory Act but continued to preach as an itinerant. Civil authorities forced Blackadder into hiding several times (once he fled to Rotterdam). In fact, the legendary Communion Season at East Nisbet took place when he was an outlaw. But his account of the event indicated how popular the observance of the Lord's Supper had become. According to Blackadder, in addition to the regular preaching and conversions, the East Nisbet Communion Season brought together over 1,500 participants. What helped him keep count was the use of two long tables, each seating about a hundred communicants, at which the converted received the sacramental meal. Blackadder estimated that the ministers had served fifteen or sixteen tables that Sunday. Within three years of the revival at East Nisbet, the authorities finally caught up with Blackadder and sent him to the island penitentiary of Bass Rock, where he died.

If intense religious experience akin to revivalism attended the Covenanter practice of Communion Seasons during the seventeenth century, in the eighteenth century Awakenings began to spread beyond the Covenanter context and raised questions about the relationships between Presbyterian convictions and an enthusiastic sort of piety. For the Seceders, led by Ralph and Ebenezer Erskine, the revivals conducted by George Whitefield and John Wesley on both sides of the Atlantic appeared initially to share the Associate Presbytery's desire for a doctrinally correct presentation of the gospel and stress upon faith, as opposed to good works. When Whitefield heard about the concerns of the Erskines and their run-in with the Kirk's authorities, he saw in the Associate Presbytery another instance, comparable to the controversy between Old and New Side Presbyterians in North America, of ecclesiastical authorities obstructing the work of gospel-motivated preachers. In 1739 he initiated correspondence with Ralph Erskine which led to an invitation for the premier revivalist of the eighteenth century to visit Scotland. But Erskine attached strings to the invitation. He hoped that Whitefield would join with the Associate Presbytery, and "dreaded" the consequences if the revivalist failed to do so.[12] Whitefield replied that he could not because he was an "occasional preacher . . . to all that are willing to hear me, of whatever denomination."[13] Ebenezer Erskine prevailed to achieve a compromise between his brother and the evangelist, but the results were disastrous, at least for the Seceders. When Whitefield arrived in Scotland in the summer of 1741, he met with the Associate Presbytery at Dunfermline and learned that he needed to come under their oversight if he were to preach in their services. In Whitefield's words, he had reached an "open breach" with the Erskines.[14] Obviously, the Seceders were not Whitefield's only option. He found evangelistic Presbyterians within the Kirk who were more than willing to host him. But for some like the Seceders who insisted upon the Westminster Confession and Presbyterian polity, Whitefieldian revivals were a threat to reformation despite an apparent stimulus to wholesome piety.

One of the congregations where Whitefield experienced a more favorable reception was in Cambuslang, a congregation in the Church of Scotland where members, elders, and different pastors had balked at Scotland's ecclesiastical system of patronage and where the tradition of covenanting still resonated among the laity. In 1731 the local duke presented William McCulloch to the parish as its pastor. He was sympathetic to the Covenanter's convictions, as well as the Seceders' critique of the ecclesiastical establishment. But McCulloch was also an avid reader of reports about revivals in England and North America and became an editor of one of the newspapers that Whitefield established, *The Weekly History*, which reported on the evangelist's exploits. News of revival nurtured a desire among McCulloch's parishioners for week-night lectures and small-group pastoral counsel. He began to preach daily, and despite his unexceptional powers of public speaking drew crowds that were larger than normal church attendance. These meetings took place in February 1742, and by the time of Whitefield's arrival four months later the gatherings had soared to as many as twenty thousand. Since Whitefield's preaching coincided with the Lord's Supper, the high numbers reflected older Scottish patterns of piety as much as the revivalist's fame. Even so, the revival at Cambuslang spilled over to the surrounding area, and soon James Robe was leading revivals at his parish in nearby Kilsyth, which in turn sparked Awakenings throughout the area. The appeal was not simply a personal one of greater spiritual zeal; these revivals also tapped discontent within the Kirk.

As much as revivals in Scotland provided an outlet for discontent with the Kirk and tapped Scottish Protestant sacramental piety, they proved inadequate for recovering the heady days of reformation. The Kirk's faculties of theology and pastors continued to orient their reflections to the philosophy and ethics of the Scottish Enlightenment. Patterns of patronage prevailed in most established congregations, such that even in Cambuslang and Kilsyth the call of successors to McCulloch and Robe produced significant conflicts. As W. R. Ward concluded, "Like the revival in New England to which it was so closely linked, the revival in the Lowlands bloomed but for a day." And when it came to recovering the convictions of the original Kirk, the revivals were even less successful. Ward adds that the eighteenth-century Awakenings did little to establish "confessional solidarity." Instead, they assimilated the converted into "a broad fellowship" of "unconfessional and international revival."[15] In 1751, when evangelicals in the Kirk eventually invited the Arminian John Wesley to preach in Scotland, their action had no precedent in the world of Scottish Presbyterianism.

Geneva Gets Religion

When revival came to Geneva during the second decade of the nineteenth century the links between practical divinity and Protestantism of a distinctly Reformed variety had become negligible. The experience in Switzerland of the Scottish evangelist Robert Haldane (1764–1842) illustrated the trajectory that most Awakenings had followed during the eighteenth century: as the fervor of devotion waxed, attachment to the forms of Reformed Protestantism waned.

Haldane was born in London to James Haldane, a pious Scottish sea-captain who died when Robert was four, just after the birth of his brother James, a

collaborator in the work of revival. Robert studied in Scotland and graduated
from the University of Edinburgh, at which point he joined the navy. He served
until 1783, soon thereafter married, and settled at the family estate, Airthrey
Castle in Stirling. Although born into a devout home, Haldane did not become
an ardent believer until 1795 when he experienced a conversion through the
Congregationalist David Bogue, pastor of the Independent church at Gosport in
the south of England. Prior to his conversion, Haldane, like Bogue, had looked
favorably upon the radical politics of the French Revolution and hoped that
France's abandonment of arbitrary power would characterize future social developments. After his conversion Haldane hoped that a zealous form of Christianity
might provide an alternative to France's secular radicalism. Haldane's own
itinerant evangelism and plans in 1796 for a mission to Bengal looked sufficiently threatening to the religious status quo in Scotland that he needed to
explain to authorities that his religious interests were not politically subversive.
A year later, Haldane became frustrated with the coolness of the Kirk and sold
the family estate to fund the Society for Propagating the Gospel at Home, an
organization, founded by Haldane's brother, that enlisted a number of Kirk
pastors to challenge the unbelief dominating the established church. The Society
functioned as an alternative to the Kirk, with its own preachers, evangelists,
teachers, and programs – including Sunday school, catechesis, and private Bible
studies. This was another indication to Scottish officials of Haldane's subversive
plans. To counter this impression, he wrote the *Address to the Public Concerning
Political Opinions* (1800) and tried to reassure his audience that his intentions
were not radical but evangelistic. Until 1808, when he became convinced that
infant baptism was wrong, Haldane and his brother supported the spread of
Congregationalism in Scotland.

After 1808 the Haldanes supported Baptist causes, but Robert's work
transcended any single denomination. In addition to engaging in a series of
theological debates – the authority and inspiration of Scripture, the running of
trains on Sundays, and the British and Foreign Bible Society's decision to
include the apocrypha in the Bibles it circulated to Roman Catholic countries
– Haldane traveled extensively throughout the United Kingdom to encourage
the development of alternative religious structures to the established churches.
By the second decade of the nineteenth century, Haldane had set his sights
on the Protestant churches of Europe. In October of 1816, Haldane left
Edinburgh to conduct a missionary tour of the Continent. His first stop was
Paris but he soon found his way to Switzerland, first explaining the gospel to a
Reformed pastor in Bern and then seeking to do the same in Geneva. What
Haldane found in the old bastion of Reformed Protestantism was "deplorable
darkness":

Calvin, once its chiefest boast and ornament, with his doctrines and works, had been set aside and forgotten, while the pastors and professors were in general Arians or Socinians. Some exceptions . . . who held the divinity of our Lord Jesus, and, I believe, loved and served him according to their light; but that light was so obscure – they were on the whole so ignorant, so incapable of rightly dividing the word of truth, that their preaching was without fruit. They preached neither law nor Gospel fully, and their doctrine did not seem to affect the consciences of their hearers.[16]

The only spiritual life that Haldane found was a small prayer meeting of fervent Protestants who had been hoping for an instructor. According to Haldane, they told him that his arrival was an answer to prayer. The Scotsman did not necessarily see the situation the same way; he and his wife judged Geneva to be so decrepit that they would take their labors elsewhere. But an unexpected meeting with a divinity student at the university gave Haldane an opening with the young scholars in the city. He discovered that they knew more about "heathen" philosophy than the gospel. Haldane now had an opening for his missionary labors.

Coincident with Haldane's presence in Geneva was a mild controversy over the divinity of Christ between theological students and the city's pastors, but for the better part of six months the Calvinistic Baptist worked out of public view. A trail of students came to his rooms and he proceeded to teach a course on the Epistle to the Romans. Despite the private nature of this instruction, Haldane could not resist pointing out the deficiency of instruction at the university and preaching in city churches. By his own admission, he wrote, "It was not . . . by avoiding controverted subjects, and simply dwelling on truths common to the professing Christians . . . that I labored to raise up the fallen standard of the Gospel at Geneva." Instead, his aim was to "declare the whole counsel of God . . . by dwelling on every doctrine of the Bible" no matter how repulsive to "the carnal mind." This included "confronting" all objections to his teaching from Geneva's pastors and professors.[17]

Haldane's teaching, as well as his following among the students, drew opposition precisely from those he confronted, faculty and pastors. In the spring of 1817, Geneva's pastors attempted to limit Haldane's influence on the students. On the one hand, they expressed reservations about an understanding of salvation that appeared to encourage antinomianism: Haldane's Calvinistic doctrine so stressed divine sovereignty and human wickedness that it seemed to undermine incentives for virtue. On the other hand, the Scot's teaching was a throwback to Genevan orthodoxy in the era of Calvin and Turretini and was no longer plausible in the light of modern thought. To quell controversy and encourage tolerance the pastors attempted to halt all discussions of the deity of Christ, original sin, effectual calling, and predestination. Instead of silencing Haldane the threat only gave him a larger student following. What is more, Geneva's authorities could not penalize Haldane too harshly for fear of alienating the students. As a result, Geneva's academic and ecclesiastical officials took no formal action against Haldane. But his own decision to leave Geneva in May 1817 on conclusion of the public controversy could be interpreted as a victory for the city's establishment.

At the same time, Haldane's stay did influence a number of students who would go into the ministry in Geneva and contribute to a revival (i.e. the Réveil) of Calvinistic Protestantism in Switzerland and Europe more broadly. Among those students who heard Haldane's lectures were: Gabriel Louis James, ordained in 1818 and a pastor to the French congregation at Breda in the Netherlands; Jules Charles Rieu, who pastored an awakened Protestant congregation in Frederica, Denmark; and Jean-Henri Merle d'Aubigné. D'Aubigné was a pastor first at Hamburg to Huguenots and then in Brussels, before returning to Geneva where he led the efforts of Protestants to restore an orthodox expression of the faith. On his return to Geneva, d'Aubigné worked with the Geneva Evangelical Society by teaching church history at its seminary. These organizations sustained dissident pastors and congregations through alternative training for ministers, devotional literature, the establishment of Sunday schools, and evangelistic activity in Switzerland and beyond.

To be sure, Haldane was not alone responsible for the Réveil at Geneva. Before his arrival the influence of Moravians had sparked dissatisfaction with the perceived liberalism and formality of the established churches. The city of Calvin had also emerged under Napoleon's policy as the site for Protestant theological training, at least in French-speaking territories, thus giving orthodox Geneva-trained pastors, though a minority, greater access to other parts of Europe. In effect, Geneva became the center of an awakening amongst European Protestants.

Although encouraging to those sympathetic to Haldane's Calvinistic teaching, these developments were distant from the efforts of previous eras when ministers in Geneva, Zurich, Bern, and Basel strove for a reformation of the entire set of ecclesiastical forms: teaching, worship, and government. In contrast to the older strategy of convincing the magistrates to patronize reform, evangelical pastors now saw political authorities as an obstacle. This recognition led eventually to the establishment in 1849 of the Evangelical Free Church as a Swiss communion separate from the corruptions of the established churches. This communion did not adopt any of the old creeds, used a loose form of Presbyterian government, refused a strict order of worship, and allowed members to decide whether or not to have their infants baptized. D'Aubigné himself became an

Almost thirty years earlier the path to the mission field had passed by the established Reformed churches. The case of Johannes Theodorus van der Kemp (1747–1811) illustrates the point. The son of a Reformed pastor at Rotterdam, van der Kemp studied medicine at Leiden. He left the university in 1764, before completing his degree, and pursued a fifteen-year career in the military. During this time he sired a daughter out of wedlock and took responsibility for rearing her. The Prince of Orange challenged van der Kemp about the impropriety of his personal affairs, and the young father resigned from the army and married the mother of their child. He also returned to the study of medicine, this time at Edinburgh, completing his degree in 1781 before returning to the Netherlands to practice medicine. When his wife and daughter drowned in a boating accident that almost took van der Kemp's life as well, he returned to the faith of his upbringing. His newfound devotion brought him into contact with Moravians at Zeist, who in turn informed van der Kemp about the recently formed London Missionary Society, a non-denominational organization created in 1795 by Nonconformists and evangelical Anglicans at the inspiration of the famous English Baptist missionary to India William Carey. In 1798 van der Kemp founded the Dutch equivalent, the Netherlands Missionary Society. When he left for South Africa as a missionary, he did so under the aegis of the London body. Van der Kemp worked for the rest of his life among the native populations in South Africa, the "Hottentots", and established a station at Bethelsdorp designed to civilize and evangelize the non-Europeans. His marriage as a sixty-year-old to a teenage native girl, with whom he had four children, was only one of many incidents that drew criticism from Dutch colonists. But such infelicities might have been the price of the conversion of all peoples, particularly since the established Reformed churches were uninterested in missions. The only alternative was an agency without oversight or connection to the church.

At roughly the same time that van der Kemp began his career in missions, Protestants in Scotland like Robert Haldane were also promoting the work of propagating Christianity among non-believers. Non-denominational missionary societies sprang up in Glasgow and Edinburgh, and their existence prompted some within the Kirk, particularly the synods of Fife and Moray, to petition the General Assembly to add its support. But the Moderate Party, still in control, rejected the proposal. According to George Hamilton, one of those to speak against the motion, as desirable as spreading the gospel among "barbarous and heathen nations" was, before the work of evangelism could transpire the uncivilized peoples needed first to be civilized: "Philosophy and learning must, in the nature of things, take the precedence." Another objection stemmed from the difficulties that even the civilized Scots experienced with Reformation teaching. He wondered what would happen if natives learned that not good works but faith alone was responsible for salvation. "We have too much experience of the difficulty of guarding our own people against the deplorable misapplication of this principle," Hamilton asserted, "to entertain a rational doubt, that the wild inhabitants of civilized regions would use it as a handle for the most flagrant violation of justice and morality."[1] Others added further reasons for not supporting foreign missions. Some thought that in the future the conditions might be favorable, but that for the present the Scottish church had enough to do simply in extending the influence of Christianity within Scotland itself. Consequently, one of the first proposals before a Reformed church to establish an agency dedicated to foreign missions went down to defeat.

The difference between 1796, when Reformed missionaries needed to work with independent agencies, and 1825, when the Scottish church became the first Reformed church to commission a foreign missionary, reveals that missionary societies set the pace for churches, and that churches sponsored missionaries reluctantly. Prior to the late eighteenth century, Christian missions – Protestant and Roman Catholic – were invariably an offshoot of colonialism. Portuguese, Spanish, French, Dutch, English, and Scottish enterprises included priests or pastors who first ministered to colonists and later considered evangelizing native populations. With the exception of Lutheran King Frederick IV of Denmark, who in 1706 sent missionaries to India with the express purpose of evangelization, Protestant state churches would not commission pastors for the dedicated purpose of converting non-Europeans until the nineteenth century, when humanitarian ideals combined with pietistic zeal to nudge the established communions to engage in overseas missions. In other words, the push for foreign missions came not from a logic within Reformed Protestantism itself but from an experiential piety spawned by revivalism. Of course, Reformed churches had supported missionary-type efforts well before Alexander Duff's arrival in Calcutta, but only as a subtext of colonialism.

After 1800, Reformed missions would continue to depend on avenues paved by European commercial and political interests. But as the experience of van der Kemp illustrates, a new form of mission developed. By bringing a new zeal for converting "heathen" peoples to the stability of church structures, foreign missionaries would take Reformed Protestantism beyond its comfort zone in the transatlantic world of European exploration to exotic peoples and places. Discomfort arose specifically from the experience of missionaries who confronted the possibility of an expression of Reformed Protestantism independent of a European outlook. Could Calvinism make sense to people who had no experience with popes, emperors, priests, and sacraments? Equally pressing was whether Calvinism made sense outside a European context. The expansion of Reformed Protestantism through foreign missions was the greatest challenge to Calvinism's powers of adaptation.

The David Brainerd Effect

That the formation of mission societies occurred at the same time as the expansion of European commercial enterprises around the world was no accident. An interest in Christianizing peoples outside the reach of European culture depended on more than the new awareness of the diversity of the planet's population. It also took root thanks to the success of Pietist versions of Protestantism, both Lutheran and Reformed, which encouraged evangelism. To be sure, before the rise of Pietism and revivalism Protestants had known about texts in Scripture, like the end of Matthew's gospel, which spoke of making disciples of all the nations with Christ's teaching. But not until the middle of the eighteenth century did such texts become the justification for widespread missionary endeavors in lands completely unfamiliar with Christianity. The rationale for evangelism was so compelling that it no longer depended on the institutional church. As the example of Robert Haldane indicated, voluntary societies, along with church officers and lay people, needed to support and engage in the work of evangelism and humanitarian assistance. These good works were the necessary evidence of true faith.

David Brainerd (1718–47) illustrates aptly the missionary mindset that grew among Protestants during the eighteenth century on both sides of the Atlantic. The child of Connecticut farmers, Brainerd early in his life desired to serve in the ministry of the colony's churches and in 1739 enrolled at Yale College. He soon became a convert to the religious zeal made popular by Jonathan Edwards and George Whitefield. When this newfound devotion prompted an untoward remark from Brainerd about the piety of one of his tutors – "he has no more grace than a chair" – Yale's president Thomas Clap expelled the student, not simply for the impropriety but also for refusing to apologize publicly. This setback did not deter Brainerd from pursuing the ministry. In 1742 the Society in Scotland for Propagating Christian Knowledge (SPCK) commissioned Brainerd to work among Native Americans in North America. The chief design of the Scottish SPCK was to propagate Presbyterianism among the Highlanders in Scotland, but its mandate to evangelize "Popish and Infidel parts of the world" provided the warrant to employ ministers or aspiring ones in Boston and New York to work among Native Americans.[2] By 1744, pro-revival Presbyterians in the Synod of New York had ordained Brainerd to evangelize natives in the Lehigh and Delaware valleys. A lifelong fight with tuberculosis combined with a propensity to regard suffering as a test of holiness took Brainerd's life a few years after his arduous labors among the Native American tribes.

Brainerd's premature death made his life all the more compelling for those converted in the revivals who sought to lead lives of holy sacrifice. Jonathan

Edwards in particular, who had known Brainerd at least since the missionary's student days at Yale and had approved the engagement between Brainerd and his oldest daughter Jerusha, was alert to the virtues of this young minister. In 1748 Edwards decided to write a biography of Brainerd that would include large sections from the missionary's journals. At the time Edwards was concerned about the decline of vital Christianity in Northampton and New England more generally, and sensed that Brainerd's account might be a remedy. As Edwards explained in the appendix to *The Life of David Brainerd* (1749), "We have here opportunity . . . in a very lively instance, to see the nature of true religion; and the manner of its operation when exemplified in a high degree and powerful exercise." Edwards added that Brainerd's "religion differed from that of some pretenders to the experience of a clear work of saving conversion wrought on their hearts; who depending and living on that, settle in a cold, careless, and carnal frame of mind, and in a neglect of thorough, earnest religion, in the stated practice of it." If Edwards hoped to provoke the religiously listless to a more godly form of devotion, he also offered remarks on the work of missionaries that would inspire converts to link evangelism to personal holiness. "We learn from the life of holy Brainerd the value and honor which we ought to put upon the missionaries of Christ," Edwards declared. Missionaries demanded "our admiration," claimed "our sympathy," needed "our prayers," and demanded "our support."[3] Above all, missionary enterprise was a sign of the progress of redemption for which Edwards hoped and prayed:

> [Brainerd] was but the morning star of a missionary day. The twilight has now passed away, the morning dawns, the star gives place to the glorious sun, and that sun shall enlighten the whole globe at one and the same moment: the earth shall be full of his glory, and it shall be a glory of grace and truth, of right-eousness and peace.[4]

Edwards' *Brainerd* was more than a spur to godly zeal; it was also a progressive and optimistic reading of the Great Awakening and its cosmic consequences.

Brainerd was Edwards' most popular book, and has never gone out of print. Its wide circulation inspired many of the first English-speaking missionaries during the eighteenth century and beyond. William Carey (1761–1834), an Anglican who changed his denominational allegiance to the English Baptists while he was a teenager, became the first Baptist missionary of the modern era and worked in India for most of his religious career. In 1792, he wrote a book on behalf of missions, *An Enquiry into the Obligations of Christians, to Use Means for the Conversion of the Heathens.* Not only was this work inspired by Brainerd's experience among the natives in colonial North America, but it also prompted the establishment in 1793 of the London-based Baptist Missionary Society. Carey regularly employed the example of Brainerd to answer objections to foreign missions and also upheld the Connecticut native as an example of someone who had given himself "wholly to the work of the Lord."[5]

The combined influence of Brainerd, Edwards, and Carey popularized the cause of missions amongst English dissenters, and in 1795 gave the impetus for the creation of the London Missionary Society. One of the proponents of the LMS was David Bogue, who had been an important influence on Robert Haldane's missionary efforts (both the failed attempt in Bengal and the successful revivals in Geneva). So influential was Brainerd, whether mediated through Carey or not, that he became the benchmark for most of those engaged in religious work among non-Europeans. Henry Martyn, a chaplain for the East India Company in the early nineteenth century, turned to Brainerd for a godly example. So too did Samuel Marsden, a Church Missionary Society (Anglican) chaplain to New South Wales, who described Brainerd's success among Native Americans as a testament to the same power that could awaken the "ungodly sinners to whom I am about to carry the words of eternal life."[6]

As appealing as Brainerd's example was, his evangelistic endeavors faced a formidable obstacle in the shape of officers of established Reformed churches, who were responsible for allocating resources and deciding on missionary works outside the nations they served. In Scotland, independent mission societies consolidated and coordinated activity overseas well before the Kirk, as the example of Alexander Duff indicated. In 1796, at the same time that the General Assembly declined to sponsor foreign missions, evangelistically minded Presbyterians formed both the Edinburgh Missionary Society (later Scottish) in the east and the Glasgow Missionary Society in the west. The model for these societies was the London Missionary Society, and one of the chief proponents was John Erskine (1721–1803), a leader of the Evangelical Party within the Church of Scotland and a cordial correspondent with Jonathan Edwards.

These societies in Scotland's largest cities were by no means the only expression of interest in foreign missions. The news of missionaries such as Carey and publications such as Brainerd's journals nurtured among the laity a thirst for information and a willingness to support evangelism overseas. Approximately sixty additional local mission societies emerged in Scotland during the first three decades of the nineteenth century. The student mission societies at Aberdeen (1820), Glasgow (1821), St Andrews (1824), and Edinburgh (1825) were further evidence of a foreign mission groundswell. These societies circulated information, raised funds, and generated enthusiasm for evangelizing native populations in foreign lands. None of the Scottish churches – the Relief Church, Anti-Burghers, Burghers, or Kirk – would commit funds for the societies. They might establish committees of correspondence, but across the board they saw the conduct of the mission societies as a threat to procedures of Presbyterian order. One consequence of these organizations was the decline of the Scottish Society for the Propagation of Christian Knowledge, the older independent institution created to plant churches in the Highlands and the North American colonies. Officers in the Kirk continued to endorse the SPCK, but the new mission societies had most of the organizational momentum.

By 1829, however, when the Kirk took steps to send its first missionary, Duff, to India, the Reformed churches began to catch up and in some cases surpassed the independent mission societies. In 1835, for instance, the Scottish Missionary Society could no longer support its three missionaries in India and ceded them to the oversight and support of the Kirk. The work of the Church of Scotland continued to be educational, following the pattern established by Duff. At the close of the 1830s the Kirk had established colleges in Calcutta, Madras, and Bombay. It also sent missionaries to South Africa, where a theological college in Lovedale, created in 1841, became the center for five Scottish mission stations.

Although encouraging to Scotland's missions-minded Presbyterians, the Disruption of 1843 – which saw the establishment of yet another Presbyterian communion in Scotland, the Free Church – jarred the Kirk from its missionary course.[7] In India, the Kirk's missionaries, including Duff, transferred their credentials to the Free Church, which began its existence with a young but established missions endeavor. Although Duff aligned with the Free Church, his college remained an operation of the Kirk. In South Africa the Kirk's missionaries also shifted their allegiance to the Free Church. This left the Free Church, which relinquished state subsidy as part of its free status, with a substantial financial burden, but church members responded vigorously and supported their new missionaries in India and South Africa. According to one Free Church publication, the new Scottish communion more than doubled comparable donations to foreign missions by a larger Presbyterian body in the United States ($1.1 million compared to $442,000). No doubt, the cause of evangelism in foreign lands added to the luster of the Free Church's identity.

The Free Church received assistance for its missionary work through participation and even union with other Scottish Presbyterian communions. In 1876, for instance, the Reformed Presbyterian (Covenanters) missionaries in New Hebrides came under the auspices of the Free Church. Almost twenty-five years later, when the Free Church merged with the United Presbyterian Church (a body formed in 1847 by a union of one of the Associate Presbyterian denominations – the United Secession Church – and the Relief Church), its foreign missionaries extended to works in the West Indies, China, and Japan. The United Free Church, the new name for the union of the United and Free

Presbyterians, by the end of the nineteenth century counted 330 missionaries, 56,000 students at the various colleges and academies, and 41,500 communicant church members among different native populations, making it one of the most active Reformed and Presbyterian missionary agencies in the heyday of denominational foreign missions.

Not very far behind the Scottish Presbyterians in establishing church-based missions were Presbyterians in the United States. Here the evangelistic and devotional fervor that had sparked the formation of independent missionary societies in England also set the tone for Americans. The first indication of an interest in evangelism overseas occurred in 1810 in New England among students at Andover Seminary and Williams College. The famous "Haystack Revival" at the latter institution led several Williams graduates to pledge their lives to foreign service. The question was how to organize and fund the enterprise, since the only institutions then available were ones dedicated to missionary endeavors (i.e. church planting) in such exotic places as the Ohio Country of the United States' Northwest Territory. In response, New England Congregationalists formed the American Board of Commissioners for Foreign Missions (ABCFM) which at first relied on the London Missionary Society to support workers overseas. The ABCFM's first missionary was Adoniram Judson, a graduate of Andover Seminary who had become convinced of the case for foreign missions. He was the first evangelist from North America and became a Baptist on his way to Burma, where he remained for the entirety of his career.

Because of an agreement with the Congregationalist churches to cooperate in planting churches in the Northwest Territory, the Presbyterian Church in the USA (PCUSA) initially also cooperated with the ABCFM to send out Presbyterian missionaries. But theological conflicts surrounding the revivals popularized by Charles Finney, as well as demographic changes within the PCUSA, nurtured a renewed commitment to Presbyterian order. In 1837 the Old School party within the PCUSA broke ties with Congregationalists and those Presbyterians who had retained alliances with the New England churches. Not only did this decision lead to the split of the PCUSA into the Old School and New School branches, which would last until after domestic peace provided by Appomattox,[8] but a rejuvenated sense of Presbyterian identity prompted the Old School denomination to form its own Board for Foreign Missions, the first such in North America. Although creating a distinct organization, American Presbyterians did not veer from paths already worn by the English, Scots, or New Englanders. The Presbyterian Board sent missionaries from 1837 on to India, China, and Africa, though it was the first to send workers to Japan.

Other than the Presbyterian denominations on both sides of the Atlantic, during the first half of the nineteenth century the rest of the Reformed churches were slow to establish foreign mission organizations. The reason had as much to do with conditions in the churches as with any reservations about missions. In the Netherlands, the Netherlands Missionary Society continued to be the chief vehicle for Reformed Protestants to support evangelism among natives in foreign lands. The Dutch Reformed churches themselves, having lost their privileged status under French rule within the Batavian Republic, were doing the best they could to maintain their own congregations, ministers, and witness, though some of the churches did funnel support to the independent society. Even then, resources within the Netherlands were meager, as the case of Joseph Kam (1769–1833) illustrates.

Kam holds a reputation as one of the great Dutch Reformed missionaries, second only to van der Kemp. Although reared in the Dutch Reformed world, like van der Kemp, Kam's zeal for missions came through Moravian contacts at their outpost in Zeist in the province of Utrecht. In 1808 Kam applied to work with the Netherlands Missionary Society and underwent training at the organization's center in Rotterdam. Unable to travel because of war between England and France, the Society eventually smuggled Kam into London where he affiliated with the London Missionary Society. He received further training from the English, was ordained as a priest in the Church of England, and in 1814 traveled to and settled in Batavia (Jakarta). In 1815 he started religious work among the Moluccas, which led to an indigenous congregation. For eighteen years he performed the duties of a pastor and executive. In addition to preaching, establishing a church order, and leading worship, he also trained pastors and teachers, distributed Bibles, hymnals, and Christian literature, and even helped construct buildings for meetings. Over time he persuaded the mission society in the Netherlands to send additional workers, whom he supervised. Although Kam himself remained Calvinistic – even opposing the Baptist views promoted by William Carey's son Jabez – Reformed churches in the Netherlands decided to support their own missionaries instead of Kam. One reason related to ecclesiastical divisions in the Netherlands,[9] while others came from a perceived broad-church tendency within the Netherlands Missionary Society. By 1859, almost two decades after Kam's death, leaders within the Dutch Reformed churches had founded three other societies, one under the direct auspices of the church, the other two independent societies, similar in structure to the original voluntary organizations that had arisen at the beginning of the nineteenth century.

Elsewhere in Europe, members of Reformed churches needed to work through independent societies if they were to venture into foreign fields. Notable French and Swiss missionaries from the nineteenth century were Eugene Casalis (1812–91), François Coillard (1834–1904), and Adolphe Mabille (1836–94). Casalis was a descendant of the Huguenots, and had been born at Orthez, France. He converted through Swiss-led revivals initially instigated through Haldane's visit to Geneva; at the age of fifteen he decided to become a missionary and trained at the Paris Evangelical Missionary Society's school. In 1833 he went to South Africa as one of the Paris society's missionaries. For the rest of his life he worked among the native population and was so successful that the Paris society and the London Missionary Society appointed him as head of a school to train missionaries. One of those Casalis directed was François Coillard, another Frenchman of Huguenot descent. He had studied at the Protestant school of Asnières and then at the University of Strasbourg before applying to the Paris society to become one of their missionaries to South Africa. He trained with Casalis and worked for almost his entire career in Basutoland (modern-day Lesotho). Coillard's efforts to evangelize the natives and plant indigenous churches involved political intrigue between local kings and European powers, sometimes catching the French missionary up in political rivalries that he was ill prepared to handle. But his work, publicized through letters he wrote to the Paris society and later published, made him a hero to European supporters. Assisting Coillard in Basutoland was Adolphe Mabille, a Swiss-born Protestant from Vaud who taught French in the Netherlands and England before applying to work under the Paris society. He married Casalis' daughter Adèle, and hoped to go to China. But his father-in-law assigned Mabille to Basutoland in South Africa, where he worked from 1860 until his death.

German Protestants interested in foreign missions found the Netherlands Missionary Society the most feasible outlet. Two missionaries of note to Indonesia reveal the ongoing affinities between German and Dutch Protestants. Johann Friedrich Riedel (1798–1860) acquired an early interest in overseas evangelism and trained first at the mission school in Berlin that had its roots in experiential Awakenings among Lutheran churches during the late eighteenth century. He pursued a second course of preparation at the mission school in Rotterdam after which in 1831 the Netherlands society sent him to Indonesia. His base was Tondano, Minahasa, and he worked among the native people as a schoolteacher, preacher, and even physician. By the end of his career as many as two thousand people attended his worship services. Working with Riedel in Minahasa was Johann Gottlob Schwarz (1800–59), a Prussian who converted at the age of eighteen and attended the same mission school in Berlin that Riedel had. He also went to Indonesia in 1831, but started his work in Kakas. Three years later the society sent him to assist Riedel, where he collaborated in evangelizing and establishing indigenous churches. Schwarz introduced a Reformed church order, likely supplied by the colonial pastors among the Dutch settlers in Indonesia. After his death Schwarz's letters and diaries were published as part of an anonymous biography, which proved instructive to missionary trainees on

the subject of evangelizing native populations. But aside from working in proximity to the Dutch Reformed churches in Indonesia, Riedel and Schwarz did
more to promote a generic or experiential Protestantism than to transplant
Reformed Protestantism to non-European environments.

After the initial surge of foreign missions, the Reformed churches that
embraced the enterprise were Presbyterian communions in Britain and North
America, a further indication of the flexibility that reigned in voluntary church
settings. In Europe, however, the only viable players were the independent societies, staffed and funded by Protestants of all stripes. Since the Reformed
churches on the Continent were in many cases no closer to their theological and
ecclesiastical heritage than individual missionaries who sought the support of
the independent evangelistic societies, the predominance of non-ecclesiastical
organizations made sense. What may have been perplexing to missionaries, their
homeland supporters and administrators, and the administrators of the colonial
governments was why so many missionaries were duplicating the efforts of other
church-based and independent societies in places like Indoneia and South
Africa. In these colonies, Dutch and British governments already had churches
that could have evangelized the non-European populations. The emerging theories of foreign missions by Reformed spokesmen would provide an answer, even
if they did not stop the redundancy.

To Civilize or Christianize?

When the Kirk's General Assembly decided in 1796 not to start foreign missionary
activity, its reason – that indigenous peoples needed to be educated before being
able to appropriate Christianity – highlighted what would be the fundamental
dynamic of missionary theory for the next two centuries. In fact, three decades
later when Alexander Duff sailed to India as the Kirk's first missionary, the original
reasons for not sending missionaries had become the very rationale for Presbyterian
missions. That Duff established a school that provided a western education to
native Indians testified to the priority of civilization to religion no matter how
many evangelistic sermons Duff preached. Nevertheless, Duff's approach, sanctioned by the Kirk, was not the last word on missionary methods. By the end of
the nineteenth century, as Presbyterianism began to take root in East Asia (particularly Korea), another understanding of the best way to evangelize native peoples
called the Nevius method had emerged. It stressed the priority of indigenous
peoples and their ways, in effect making European culture of secondary importance to church life in its own right. Because foreign missionaries depended politically on the expansion of European colonization, however, separating the European
character of missions from the Christian nature of the enterprise was never easy.

The Kirk's mission to India followed generally the method earlier employed by that of the Scottish Society for the Propagation of Christian Knowledge in the Highlands. These efforts included preaching and teaching, and the creation of schools, libraries, and churches. The Kirk's rationale reflected the Christian-friendly character of the Scottish Enlightenment: civilization was the preparation for conversion, and culture found its fulfillment in Christ. The General Assembly's decision to start a mission to India, and its selection of Duff, followed directly from this understanding of religion and culture. The assembly called Duff to the position of headmaster at an academy in India that would do for the natives what the SPCK had done for the Highlanders.

After a decade of work in India, Duff elaborated the links between education and evangelism in the 1839 charge he gave to Thomas Smith, another missionary sent by the Kirk to India. One part inspiration, one part job description, and one part analysis of India, Duff's charge explained what would be the dominant Scottish Presbyterian approach to foreign missions for the next century. The inspirational part of Duff's remarks repeated the thoughts made popular by pietistic Protestants since the early eighteenth century. For instance, the Scottish missionary sanctioned the outlook that had divided Presbyterians a century earlier when he spoke of conversion as a necessary qualification for a person engaged in foreign missions. Granted, the critics of revivalism had not favored unconverted ministers or evangelists. What they questioned was an equation of regeneration with a certain kind of conversion experience (instead of a life-long pattern of faith and repentance) that had become the norm in the days of George Whitefield. According to Duff:

> When the sinner is powerfully awakened to an alarming sense of his sin, and guilt, and danger; – before, a fiery lake ready to consume him; behind, the dark mountain of unforgiven sin, ready to crush him into perdition; within, the scorpion sting of an accusing conscience, ready to be changed into the worm that never dies; above, the thick clouds surcharged with Divine vengeance! – pale with horror, and speechless with despair, his eyes are turned to the wondrous cross! Who can describe his emotion, when there he beholds the storm of Divine vengeance exhausted, and even death and hell actually swallowed up and devoured? Can he confine to himself the bursting expression of his joy, when the sense of pardon, reconciliation, and love, comes streaming through his inmost soul? Impossible.[10]

From the intensity of this experience it followed that a missionary who was going to preach "repentance and remission of sins" and call "men from darkness to light, from sin to holiness, from Satan unto God" must be himself a convert, "effected by a specific operation of Divine grace." Without a conversion experience, all other gifts "are but as sounding brass or a tinkling cymbal."[11]

With this understanding of Christian experience went the idea of the church as chiefly a vehicle of evangelism instead of an institution that nurtured and instructed the faithful. Duff took his cues from the end of the Gospel of Matthew, where Christ commissions his followers to go throughout the world and make disciples. This biblical warrant indicated that the "chief end" of the church – "the supreme function which she is called on to discharge" – was to be an "an evangelist to all the world."[12] Duff was smart enough to recognize that foreign missions comprised a fairly new enterprise for Protestants, and consequently that the Reformation did not exhibit the evangelistic activity that was supposed to characterize a true church. He conceded that the Reformers did not think much about the pagan world. But Duff was harder on the Presbyterian descendants of the Reformers, who neglected to be good stewards of the treasure given them, and whose "highest ambition" was "to have her own privileges fenced in by laws and statutes of the realm – to have her own immunities perpetuated to posterity by solemn leagues and covenants."[13] The Reformation itself, he explained, was a "grand evangelistic work" that rescued the Bible and emancipated believers from "idolatrous Rome" for the end of resuming "the great evangelistic function" of preaching the gospel to all nations.[14] This gloss may have been responsible for Duff's failure to recognize that the Reformers may have cultivated "unholy jealousies, and ungodly rivalries" that divided Protestants in Scotland. He hoped, in fact, that missionaries to India would leave behind such enmity and work together on the basis of "universally acknowledged fundamental principles of Christianity," which alone could "lay the foundation for real concord on earth."[15] Whether he knew it or not, Duff identified a central tension between the project of reformation and the work of evangelism – between consolidation and expansion – that would bedevil Reformed churches throughout the modern era.

Having exonerated Knox, even at the expense of scorning Samuel Rutherford and the Erskines, Duff turned to the task of modern missions, a topic that involved description of the work in India. To reach the "teeming millions of India," the Church of Scotland had chosen education, specifically creating a school whose pupils would be "men who, from being habituated to the climate, from their vernacular acquaintance with the languages, from their knowledge of the manners, customs, feelings, sentiments, and prejudices of the people, would possess unrivaled facilities in bringing the Gospel of salvation within reach of the millions of their benighted countrymen!" The graduates of such a school would then become the preachers, teachers, catechetists, translators, and tract distributors for spreading the "light and life" of Christianity throughout India.[16]

Key to the school was the cultivation of the English language. Missionaries would be expected to learn the indigenous language in as many dialects as possible, but the amount of religious and pedagogical material available in English made it the unsurpassed medium for teaching. English would be the only vehicle for "the full stream of European knowledge." The West's learning "tends to whet the faculties, sharpen the intellect, and expand the whole sphere of mental vision." Ultimately, such instruction in literature and science, combined with native religion, would plant a mine that after detonation would "shatter the whole hideous fabric of Hinduism into atoms." In sum, the arts and sciences provided "external evidences of Christianity" and furnished converted Indians with "a magazine of weapons, offensive and defensive, in conducting the mighty warfare with idolaters, Pantheists, and infidels of every kind."[17]

The theme of intellectual aggression continued when Duff responded to the allegation that believers should have nothing to do with natural science. Since the heavens declared the glory of God, Duff believed it strange to avoid such a large domain of divine works. He also told his audience that missionaries should assume "the highest and most commanding position" with regard to science by informing students that they had no "valid right, or title" to contemplate natural wonders as "unpardoned" rebels and enemies of God.[18] The capstone of instruction was the Bible and theology, including "the *entire* system of revealed truth," from creation to the final judgment. But at all times and everywhere the missionary as teacher should cultivate "the holy art of converting every fact, every event, every truth, every discovery, into a means, and an occasion of illustrating or corroborating sacred verities."[19]

Finally, Duff analyzed India's demographics to insure that the missionary's educational program would be the most effective. He divided the native population into four classes. The first and most numerous was a group completely immune to education. Their "reason is in fact laid prostrate" and their minds are impregnable to the arts, sciences, or the gospel. The only way to reach them was through improved "infant and juvenile" schools but this was impossible for adults; the best way to reach adults was through Indians who had received instruction in the mission school. The second class consisted of educated Brahmins, another difficult case because of their status as "despotic lords not of opinion merely, but of the very souls of men."[20] Here Duff cautioned against direct polemics and advised the cultivation of simple arguments for Christian truths. The third class involved a liberal or westernized Hinduism that attempted to combine Hindu beliefs with Christian learning. This group of Indians was so supple in its danger to the missionary that Duff could only count upon "the keenest weapons which the armoury of heaven can supply."[21] Finally, there was a fourth group of natives, familiar with English and a western education and often holding positions of responsibility in the colonial government. These were the people most likely to be receptive to Christianity and who would function in turn as credible voices to the other Indian groups. The mission school was best equipped to reach the nations.

Duff expected that the results of his mission school would be slow, though he spoke of the "momentous transformation" occurring almost as suddenly as the dawn that follows the darkest part of night.[22] Despite opposition from the East India Company, which saw no advantage to their commercial interests in supplanting the natives' Hinduism, Duff received support from the English colonial government, which supported the advancement of schools and colleges from the mid–1830s on along the lines proposed by the Scottish mission. Not even the mutiny of 1857, which witnessed the sepoys of East India Company's army rebel against their English authorities, and which resulted in the deaths of dozens of western missionaries in northern India, altered Duff's aims or the means by which he executed them. Even so, the strong identification between Christianity and western learning raised the question – not addressed for another century – of whether conversion required cultural reorientation in addition to spiritual illumination. Although Duff believed that denominational differences should not define the foreign missionaries' endeavors, ironically he was much less inclined to ignore civilizational differences, which were as much a part of the West as its ecclesiastical history.

In a markedly different context and later era emerged another approach to foreign missions, pioneered by John L. Nevius (1829–93), an American Presbyterian missionary of Dutch descent. A native of western New York, Nevius studied at Union College, in Schenectady, and then at the Presbyterian church's premier and oldest seminary in Princeton, New Jersey. After being ordained and married to Helen Coan, in 1853 he sailed with his bride to China where he joined the American Presbyterian mission. Protestant missionaries had next to no access to China prior to the first Anglo-Chinese (Opium) War, 1839–42, in which the British forced the Chinese to open their ports and markets to opium produced in India, the chief commodity of the East India Company. As missions historian Gustav Warneck writes with pronounced understatement, "We have here one of the most striking examples of the manner in which commercial and colonial politics are at one and the same time a pioneer and a hindrance to missions." Such a co-mingling of empire and faith cast "a dark shadow" on Protestant missionaries from the beginning of their work in China.[23]

Treaties between China and western nations signed during the 1840s included access for foreign missionaries, both Protestant and Roman Catholic. By the time Nevius arrived, in 1853, American Presbyterian missionaries were establishing works in the coastal ports of Canton, Ningpo, and Shanghai, the places from which the European presence in China would grow. American Congregationalists, Baptists, and Episcopalians were also present, along with workers from the London Missionary Society. In contrast to the emphasis on education by Scottish Presbyterians in India, American Presbyterians sponsored a variety of humanitarian and evangelistic initiatives. In Canton they established colleges and a hospital, and medical missionaries were also active in Ningpo. A second Anglo-Chinese War between 1856 and 1860 complicated life for foreign missionaries, but, as was the case with the 1857 mutiny in India, the hostilities between Chinese rulers and British colonial administrators did not disrupt the Presbyterian missions. Ultimately, the war's outcome opened China to a larger western presence, both commercial and religious, than had existed prior to 1856.

Nevius experienced few hardships as a direct result of the conflicts between European colonists and the Chinese, but the impropriety of western dealings with the native population was an important factor for rethinking missionary methods. In *The Planting and Development of Missionary Churches* (1899), Nevius adapted the "three-self" ideals of veteran missionaries Rufus Anderson (American Congregationalist) and Henry Venn (Church of England) – self-propagating, self-governing, self-supporting – and devised a "new" plan for foreign missions that would correct the "old" methods. According to Nevius, the difference between the two systems was not so much the goal of establishing a native church; he conceded that both systems endeavoured ultimately to see the establishment of indigenous churches that were not merely clients of European Christians. Instead, the real difference was when to start the process of indigenization. Both used native workers and these were crucial for weaning the new churches away from European oversight, but the question was whether to pay these workers or encourage them to remain in their ordinary occupations and eventually raise their own support from like-minded native Christians. Nevius explained:

> ... the Old System strives by the use of foreign funds to foster and stimulate the growth of the native churches in the first stage of their development, and then gradually to discontinue the use of such funds: while those who adopt the New System think that the desired object may be best attained by applying principles of independence and self-reliance from the beginning. The difference between these two theories may be more clearly seen in the their outward practical working. The Old uses freely, and as far as practicable, the more advanced and intelligent of the native church members in the capacity of paid colporteurs, Bible agents, evangelists, or heads of stations; while the New proceeds on the assumption that the persons employed in these various capacities would be more useful in the end by being left in their original homes and employments.[24]

Nevius believed that the new method actually followed the example of the apostles but he also scored points on questions of practicality. If missionaries were to tempt natives with the possibility of an income, he asked, were they not then giving a financial incentive to conversion? Nevius felt that the employment model established a "mercenary spirit" and produced the unwelcome phenomenon of "mercenary Christians." He commented on his own experience, in which natives would show little interest in Christianity until the possibility of working for the mission emerged. Some of these were adept at feigning the proper knowledge and loyalties for the sake of compensation, only to leave a native congregation when employment ceased.[25] Nevius was smart enough to recognize that his argument could also be turned on himself: he believed that the apostle Paul had taught that evangelists and preachers should receive financial support from their congregations. Nevius also knew that the apostle was willing to forego compensation and work with his own hands while engaged in planting churches, and the American hoped that he himself would be willing to forsake compensation if necessary. Still, behind his "employment" was a missions board that had examined his calling and character, and found him sufficiently "tested and proved" to avoid abusing missionary service for the sake of "worldly advantages." In point of fact, Nevius was simply asking for the same standard for native converts, which meant a time of testing before using them in the formal paid work of missions.[26]

Adherence to professed biblical norms in executing missions also extended to Nevius' model for "church organization." Although he was reluctant to say that the New Testament revealed a single pattern of church government, Nevius was not bashful in declaring the need for elders and bishops in establishing native congregations. He also showed no hesitation in maintaining that the various forms of government among the western churches were not cultural but scriptural. At the same time, Nevius understood that he was a Presbyterian missionary and was not ashamed of his calling: "We are Presbyterians, and our churches should be organized from the first on Presbyterian principles."[27] This did not mean that missionaries could enter a foreign land and establish a full-blown system of presbyteries and synods. It did mean, though, that missionaries should avoid establishing congregations where one pastor was the leader of all the people; instead, elders (unpaid) needed to be cultivated to provide oversight for the entire congregation, and all church members needed to be involved in establishing networks of congregations. Nevius actually feared that western cultural norms and a growing professionalization of the clergy were responsible for a model of ecclesiasticism in the mission field where the work of evangelism, teaching, and edification fell to paid workers.

As it turned out, Nevius' model for foreign missions owed less to the animosities between Europeans and Chinese than to his own frustration with his labors in Shantung:

I commenced itinerating work in Central Shan-tung about fifteen years ago, my previous tours having been in the eastern part of the province, knew the language and had the advantage of seventeen years of experience elsewhere . . . making long tours over the same ground every spring and autumn, but for five years had not a single convert. . . . Why these methods proved fruitless for so long at time is impossible to say. In looking back over my experiences during the first five years of work in this field, it appears made up chiefly of failures and disappointments. Men for whom I had watched and labored for years, who seemed almost persuaded to be Christians, went back and were lost sight of. Associations of co-religionists were at different time on the point of entering the Church in a body with their leaders. From them all I have realized little else than wasted time and labor, with no doubt the acquisition of some valuable experience.[28]

This remarkably candid assessment was likely not what members of Nevius' Presbyterian missions board wanted to hear or see circulating among potential supporters. But it was refreshing for avoiding the sugar-coated inspiration that often linked the success of foreign missions to either the mysterious work of God or the glorious advance of the West.

Nevius' experience and attention to methods would pay dividends beyond his own lifetime. By the end of his life he had emerged as an offbeat missionary guru and his mission board gave him the chance to instruct missionaries to Korea. From 1890 on, American missionaries, both Presbyterian and Methodist, implemented his method and the contrast with China was dramatic. By 1935 the number of Korean Christians had exceeded the total number of Chinese believers, even though the missionary presence in China was almost five decades older. To be sure, Nevius' model alone cannot account for the apparent success. Korea was smaller and travel was easier than in China. Korean churches needed to negotiate with only six mission boards by 1920, compared with the 130 agencies that vied for supervision of Chinese churches. Meanwhile, the politics of Korea meant that converts faced vigorous persecution from Japanese imperialists and Communists, which increased devotion by identifying Christianity with Korean independence and nationalism. Whatever the factors, Nevius' method was responsible in some way for the remarkable success of foreign missions to Korea.

From Northern Europe to the World

Among the varieties of Protestantism to emerge in the sixteenth century – Lutheran, Reformed, Anglican, and Anabaptist – the Reformed churches had the widest presence, from Lithuania in the East to Scotland in the West. That scope of influence owed partly to the circulation of ideas, the flexibility of Reformed structures of governance, and the adaptability of Reformed churches themselves. By the end of the sixteenth century, however, Reformed Protestantism was strongest and most stable in four European contexts: the Protestant cantons of Switzerland; the German-speaking territory of the Palatinate; the Dutch Republic; and Scotland.

Three centuries later, Reformed Protestants had taken their faith and churches to every corner of the habitable world. Colonialism and migration had accounted for the transplanting of Reformed Protestantism to North America, and small parts of Africa and Asia during the seventeenth and eighteenth centuries. But the period of greatest growth territorially came in the nineteenth century, owing to the efforts of foreign missionaries, colonists, and the pastors who ministered in European colonies. As a result, while the Reformed churches in northern Europe struggled for viability amid compromises required from both civilian authorities and learned elites, their counterparts in Asia, Africa, North America, South America, and Australia grew and in some cases thrived.

Presbyterianism in Korea represents the Reformed church least dependent on European sources. Its origins go back to the 1870s when Scottish Presbyterians founded a mission in Manchuria to evangelize Koreans, as Korea had denied entry to foreign workers. Several Korean nationals converted, among them So Sang-Yoon, who in 1883 organized one of the first Protestant congregations in Korea. These efforts also included Korean translations of the Bible. As a result, Protestantism had begun in Korea even before the arrival of foreign missionaries in 1882 thanks to a treaty between the United States and Korea, which opened the country to workers from Australia, Canada, and the United States. American Presbyterians took the lead in cooperating with and organizing indigenous activity. Horace Allen, a medical missionary, successfully treated an ailing Korean prince, which enhanced the reputation of missionaries; Horace G. Underwood, the first ordained missionary, produced the first Korean hymnal; and Samuel A. Moffett led in the establishment of the first presbytery and theological seminary. By 1907 Korea had its first presbytery and in 1912 its own General Assembly. The Korean church was even sending missionaries to China.

Of course, the presence of Reformed Protestantism in Asia predated Korean developments and goes back to the colonialism of the Dutch in Indonesia. As was the case in South Africa and North America, colonial governors – this time from the Dutch East India Company – sent pastors from the Reformed churches to serve the settlers and administrators in the East Indies, Java, and Sumatra. By 1816, when the Dutch state made Indonesia a colony, the original Reformed churches devolved into a state institution, the Protestant Church of the Indies, which received government funding and served Reformed, Lutheran, and sundry other Protestants. With Indonesia firmly open to Europeans, a variety of Protestant missionaries established works in Indonesia, including those sponsored by the Netherlands Reformed Church. Most of these churches formed along tribal lines.

Over time, three types of churches emerged in Indonesia. The first was a string of churches that grew out of the established church. For instance, the Protestant Church in the Moluccas began through the efforts of Joseph Kam, whom the established church drafted to promote Christianity among the natives in Maluku. For most of their history these churches, like the one established by Kam, would be spokes in the hub of the established church until they gained autonomy in the twentieth century. A second type of church emerged in the nineteenth century when European missionaries associated with independent missions societies, many from Germany and the Netherlands, established congregations outside the state church. For instance, the Karo Batak Protestant church, a communion that loosely followed a Reformed church order, began in the 1890s through the labors of missionaries from the Netherlands Missionary Society. It remained tiny until the 1940s, when native pastors established autonomy from European direction and assumed leadership of the church. The last type of church in Indonesia, the one most zealous of following older Reformed standards, stemmed from the efforts of conservative Reformed missionaries from the Netherlands, who in 1892 had seceded from the national church and formed the Reformed Churches of the Netherlands.[29] For instance, the Christian Church of Sumba began when the new seceding Dutch church in 1892 assumed responsibility for a work begun by a conservative missionary operating within one of the independent missions societies. The model for the mission was to establish a church that would confess the Heidelberg Catechism, Canons of Dort, Belgic Confession, sing psalms, and follow Reformed church order. After years of European domination, in 1940 the Christian Church of Sumba became an indigenous communion and adapted the conservative ideals of its Dutch patrons to its Indonesian members and officers.

With the exception of South Africa, where Reformed Protestants had been part of the colonial order since the seventeenth century, Reformed churches took root on the continent of Africa through a combination of European colonialism, independent mission societies, and Reformed and Presbyterian missionaries. The oldest Reformed churches were those started for Dutch colonists in South Africa. In most cases these communions resisted evangelistic overtures to the black population. Where Dutch Calvinists did minister to native populations the result was an order of communion that remained separate from European bodies, an ecclesiastical version of apartheid. From the 1820s Presbyterian missionaries also operated in South Africa thanks to the initial presence of Scottish soldiers in the initial British settlement. The efforts of Scottish Presbyterians led to the formation of the Presbyterian Church of South Africa, which held its first General Assembly in 1897; at the time it had thirty-three congregations, ten of which ministered primarily to Africans. By the early decades of the twentieth century this Presbyterian body had expanded into Zambia, Zimbabwe, and among the Bantu people. Missionary efforts amongst Africans eventually prompted the formation of indigenous churches, such as the Presbyterian Church of Africa in 1898, led by James Phambani Mzimba, which initially included four congregations and two presbyteries.

Throughout the rest of Africa, the establishment of Reformed and Presbyterian churches would await the nineteenth-century arrival of missionaries from independent societies. Ghana witnessed the establishment of the two oldest Presbyterian churches on the continent outside South Africa. The Presbyterian Church of Ghana stems from the efforts of the Evangelical Missionary Society of Basel, which in 1828 started work among the Ashanti people. About a decade later the Bremen Mission Society of Germany also initiated evangelistic activities in Ghana that led in 1847 to the formation of the Evangelical Presbyterian Church, Ghana. The British presence in West Africa took root in Nigeria, where the Scottish Missionary Society in 1846 sent Presbyterian missionaries who provided a range of religious and humanitarian services for the rest of the nineteenth century and well into the twentieth. Only after World War II did the Presbyterian Church of Nigeria become an independent communion.

The last major Reformed or Presbyterian missionary project in Africa took place in Kenya in the last decade of the nineteenth century, when independent missionaries from Scotland established a mission in British East Africa. The East Africa Scottish Mission eventually absorbed this work and conducted services for both Church of Scotland members laboring in Nairobi and for native blacks. Over time, some of the congregations in Kenya affiliated with the Church of Scotland as the Overseas Presbytery of Kenya. An independent church for native Kenyans also took root, the Presbyterian Church of East Africa. Kenya was also home to Dutch settlers in the early twentieth century who in 1909 established the Reformed Church of East Africa, a communion that remained separate from the native African population.

As much as the efforts of foreign missionaries, whether working for established churches or independent societies, assisted the expansion of Reformed Protestantism around the world, the older pattern of European migration continued to be a factor in the expansion of Reformed churches. The migration of people of Scottish and Irish descent produced the greatest number of Presbyterian denominations around the world, and the unwitting patron of these churches was the British Empire. In the British colonies north of the United States, Associate Presbyterians (Seceders) began in the last two decades of the eighteenth century to form congregations and presbyteries in the Maritime Provinces, even replicating the ecclesiastical divisions that in 1747 had split the Associate Presbyterians into the Burgher and Anti-Burgher factions. At the beginning of the nineteenth century, the Maritimes also received an influx of Scots associated with the Church of Scotland. The presence of the Kirk also made itself felt in the provinces of Upper and Lower Canada. At the time of the 1843 Disruption in Scotland that led to the formation of the Free Church (see Chapter Ten), tensions within the mother country also led to a split among the Church of Scotland bodies in Canada. Only in 1875 did these three streams of Scottish Presbyterianism put aside differences to form the Presbyterian Church of Canada.

In Australia and New Zealand Scottish settlers again followed the path paved by English colonialism. In the case of the former, a Presbyterian congregation began as early as 1809 but ministers from the Church of Scotland did not arrive until the 1820s, and by 1840 they had established the Synod of Australia, a body connected with the Church of Scotland. The controversy that led to the formation of the Free Church of Scotland also produced two Presbyterian bodies in Australia, the Presbyterian Church of Eastern Australia (1846) and the Free Presbyterian Church of Victoria (1846), both of which were independent but shared close ties to the Free Church in the mother country. A similar pattern prevailed in New Zealand, with the organization in 1840 of the Presbyterian Church of Aotearoa New Zealand. This communion stemmed from Church of Scotland pastors who ministered to Scottish immigrants. But again, the Disruption of 1843 provoked the formation in 1844 of Free Church Presbyterianism in New Zealand. In this case the Free Church of Scotland took responsibility for formal oversight of congregations and a presbytery.

Almost coincident with the realignment among Presbyterians in Canada, Australia, and New Zealand thanks to 1843 Disruption, Presbyterianism also took root in Brazil. Ashbel Green Simonton (1833–67) was the first Presbyterian missionary from the United States. In 1859 he organized the first Presbyterian congregation and presbytery, both in São Paulo. He was also instrumental in the conversion of a Roman Catholic priest, José Manoel da Conceição, who would become the first Brazilian Presbyterian pastor. Green had help from other missionaries, but the greatest assistance came from Presbyterians in the American South, who in 1869 began to send missionaries to Brazil for sustained efforts throughout the country. Adding to the southerners' interest in Brazil was the migration of disaffected citizens of the southern United States, who either took their slaves or who refused to accept the new political order in their homeland.

Brazil was hardly a colony of the United States, but Presbyterianism grew in South America from circumstances comparable to its emergence elsewhere, namely, from the migration of European populations, who settled, mixed, and gradually included the native peoples in their churches.

To coordinate the Reformed and Presbyterian churches around the world, in 1877 church leaders in the United States established the Presbyterian Alliance. At first, its membership was almost exclusively from the English-speaking world, with forty-nine member churches. In 1880, for instance, continental Europe accounted for fourteen separate Reformed communions, the United Kingdom nine, North America ten (nine from the United States), Africa two, Australia four, New Zealand two, and Asia one. Over time, as the appeal of ecumenism spread in the West and among foreign missionaries, the Alliance attracted a wider membership and attempted to establish guidelines for the practical and social problems confronting the churches. The temptation at these international gatherings was to attribute the scope and influence of Reformed Protestantism to superior theology or strategic planning by visionary church leaders and missionaries. The reality that quickly upended any self-congratulation was that Reformed Protestantism had spread largely by adapting to demographic, economic, and political currents that carried the churches along, often unwittingly and sometimes reluctantly. Still, for all of the Reformed churches' dependence on colonialism and migration, they had by the end of the nineteenth century gone from being one of Europe's confessional churches to a global faith that included the uneasy mix of state churches in Europe, denominations with direct ties to the West, and indigenous churches that were developing an ethos independent of European assumptions. Identifying what was distinct about Calvinism in all of these settings became increasingly difficult, beyond formal membership in an international association of churches that called itself Reformed.

CHAPTER TEN

KIRK RUPTURED AND CHURCH FREED

BETWEEN 1834 AND 1843 Reformed churches around the world experienced upheavals that were indicative of adaptations to new social and political circumstances. The Dutch were on the front lines of these developments in 1834, with the formation of churches outside the state's established communion as a protest against the perceived corruption of church establishment. Three years later Presbyterians in the United States participated in a split between Old and New School Presbyterians that stemmed from debates over adapting Reformed convictions to the enterprise of constructing a Christian civilization in the new nation. Finally, in 1843 the Church of Scotland witnessed the departure of one-third of its ministers and half of its laity over the historically contested issue of patronage. Had Friedrich Schleiermacher, the most formidable of German-speaking Reformed theologians, not been such an advocate of the union of Reformed and Lutheran churches in Prussia (and had he not died in 1834), the German Reformed churches in the mid-1830s might have joined their confessional Lutheran counterparts – the neo-Lutherans – and sought to create congregations that remained distinctly Reformed in teaching and practice. Even so, during the second quarter of the nineteenth century, Reformed Protestants were coming to terms with the political circumstances that had both nurtured and then disappointed their hopes and endeavors.

Before the 1830s and 1840s, of course, Reformed and Presbyterian pastors had protested the state's or prince's religious policies and opted out of the ecclesiastical establishment, at least informally. The rise and cultivation of experimental divinity among English Puritans early in the late sixteenth century was one response to frustrations with state-run church reform. Throughout the seventeenth century Dutch Reformed ministers sometimes chose to meet with their flocks in conventicles rather than accept the breadth of doctrine and worship in the national church. The Covenanters and later the Seceders

(Associate Presbyterians) also objected to the ecclesiastical arrangements with civil authorities and formed separate communions to preserve the church's independence under the lordship of Christ. Even the phenomena of revivalism, Pietism, and the creation of independent mission societies reflected discontent with formal structures instituted by the ecclesiastical establishment.

Nevertheless, the disruptions of the nineteenth century were markedly different from these earlier developments, if only because of their size and scale. They drew clearly upon the lessons of the seventeenth and eighteenth centuries. At the same time, they represented an informal international consensus, discerned through local rather than global circumstances, on the limitations and even dangers of the church's participation in political establishments. To be sure, differences of ecclesiastical and civil polity would produce diverse accounts of the church's spiritual autonomy from the state and responsibility for public morality. Still, the events of the first half of the nineteenth century among the Reformed churches yielded a widespread recognition that the pact made with civil magistrates at the time of the Reformation, as valuable as it had been for reforming Europe's churches, had reached the end of its usefulness. From now on, if churches were going to pursue the kind of reform conceived by the first Calvinists, the Reformed and Presbyterian communions would need not greater cooperation with but increased autonomy from the magistrate.

Scotland's Disruption was the first of several waves that would crash on the Reformed churches of greatest influence, which included Dutch Calvinists, Presbyterians in the United States, and German Reformed Protestants. By 1970 when these waters had calmed, the world of Calvinism would be divided between two groups: the ecumenically minded churches that still aspired to establishment status; and conservative denominations that forsook cultural or political privilege for theological authenticity. Awareness of these divisions is essential to understanding how modern Calvinists appropriated their Reformed heritage.

Establishment Recovered and Lost

On May 18, 1843 commissioners to the General Assembly of the Scottish Kirk gathered at the cathedral of St Giles in Edinburgh for their annual meeting. Although part of the ordinary proceedings of the assembly, the 1843 meeting had attracted more than the usual pastors, elders, lords, and royal commissioners; it also packed the streets of Edinburgh with ordinary Scots who hoped to witness a resolution to a decade-long controversy within the Kirk. As William Maxwell Hetherington wrote only a few years afterward, all that Scotland could produce of aristocratic grandeur, and civic authority, and legal dignity, and clerical aspiration, and ministerial worth, and upright integrity, and fervent piety, and eager curiosity, thronged the ancient capital, and poured their countless multitudes along her streets, and to every point of peculiar importance.[1]

If the crowds had come hoping to be spectators at a day filled with debate, they were sorely disappointed, even if what they observed was no less dramatic. Dr David Welsh convened the assembly by stating that proceedings were illegal, so the officers could not actually convene. He declared:

Fathers and brethren, according to the usual form of procedure this is the time for making up the roll. But in consequence of certain proceedings affecting our rights and privileges, proceedings which have been sanctioned by her majesty's government and by the legislature of the country; and more especially in respect that there has been an infringement on the liberties of our Constitution, so that we could not now constitute this court without a violation of the terms of the union between Church and State in this land, as now authoritatively declared, I must protest against our proceeding further.[2]

Welsh explained his decision by reading from a protest, signed by 203 members of the scheduled assembly. He then led roughly 400 protesters out of the church to Tanfield Hall where Thomas Chalmers became the moderator of the Free Church of Scotland's first General Assembly. The new moderator's opening address praised the protesters for choosing to sacrifice "worldly possessions" instead of principle, and offered comfort that despite the "wide ocean of uncertainty" on which they had embarked, they also possessed a "great and generous certainty which is apprehended by the eye of faith."[3] What Chalmers did not recognize fully at the time was how certain support for the Free Church was. Of the 1203 ministers in the Kirk in 1843, 752 remained and 451 seceded. The numbers of elders and lay members who followed was also approximately one-third of the total within the Kirk. For this reason, historians and commentators have opined that the 1843 Disruption was the most significant episode in nineteenth-century Scottish history.

By all accounts, Chalmers was the dominant and most charismatic Scottish churchman in the events of 1843 and his involvement in establishing the Free Church demonstrate a remarkable transformation in his life. Since 1816 when he had successfully opposed George Hill, the leader of the Moderate Party within the Kirk, over the practice of plurality (i.e. whether ministers should hold appointments beyond their parish duties), Chalmers had functioned as leader and example of the Evangelical Party. Some of this owed to his own remarkable skills as an orator, and more to his ability to reconceive the nature of the Scottish parish in response to the dilemmas posed by industrialization and urbanization. As much as the Disruption of 1843 revolved around the perennial struggle over patronage in the established church, the dynamics of the nineteenth-century debates were distant from those that had driven the Erskines to secede from the national church and form an Associate Presbytery. Chalmers was no Erskine. Neither were nineteenth-century patrons defenders of lairds' and heritors' ancient rights.

For the first third of his career, Chalmers appeared to be more an example of the Kirk's defects than a harbinger of reform. The son of a merchant in the shipping business in the coastal town of Anstruther, his early life was that of a conventional middle-class boy. He attended the parish school in town and by the age of eleven had received the requisite training to matriculate at St Andrews University, one of Scotland's oldest institutions but also one that was affordable for families of moderate means such as the Chalmers. The dominate figure at the University during Chalmers' studies was George Hill, professor of divinity and the leader of the Kirk's Moderate Party, who aligned the university closely to the Tory outlook of Henry Dundas, Viscount Melville. Insufficient training in Latin at school prevented Chalmers from excelling in his studies prior to the third and fourth years at university, when he distinguished himself in the fields of politics and mathematics. After graduating, Chalmers remained at St Andrews to study divinity. He listened to Hill's lectures, which followed without great affect the contours of Reformed theology; he was underwhelmed, and questioned Hill's authenticity.

During preparations for the ministry Chalmers accumulated first-hand resentments that nurtured emerging Whig political dispositions. A tutorship with a wealthy family went badly, partly because the parents indulged the children and did not back the tutor's attempts at discipline, and partly owing to Chalmer's own suspicion of hierarchy and privilege. But when the family's social rank did not aid Chalmers in securing a church position, he begrudged his employers all the more. Chalmers' father had professional ties to Sir John Anstruther, who possessed six patronages in eastern Fife. Out of respect to his father, Anstruther had promised one of these charges to the young Chalmers. But the unexpected death of Sir John left the promise to be carried out by his widow and sons, none of whom were familiar with the elder Chalmers: the position went to another preacher, and Thomas' sense of the gentry's arrogance festered.

Eventually, after assisting instruction in mathematics at St Andrews, Chalmers received a church appointment to the Kilmany parish. To help his father, he took

responsibility for supporting two sisters and a younger brother, and to supplement his income Chalmers continued to teach mathematics. Within the Kirk at
the time it was common for pastors to hold a teaching post in addition to
pastoral responsibilities. Chalmers' father and presbytery would eventually
question whether the Kilmany pastor gave adequate attention to the spiritual
needs of his parishioners. But he was eager for a university appointment and in
1805 sought the chair in mathematics at Edinburgh, which ended up going to
John Leslie, exposing both the hypocrisy of the Kirk's Moderate Party and the
Tories' weakness (see Chapter Seven). Chalmers was a small player in the
controversy, even though he did write one of his first treatises at this time, a
defense of ministers' capacity for mathematics. Again, he was too far removed
from the corridors of power either in the church or state where such appointments became final, but for Chalmers it was further proof of the "putrid system
of interest" that dominated Scottish life. After a trip to London, where he
observed the "grossness of a mercantile age," Chalmers wrote another treatise,
published at his own expense, on economics and national stability, which advocated the agricultural and communal values of Scotland's past and argued for
increased taxation on the wealthy to undermine privileged interests.[4] Almost
thirty, Chalmers was both part of a system he believed to be corrupt and frustrated that the system did not pay members appropriate dividends.

Personal circumstances – deaths in his family and a life-threatening bout of
consumption – provoked in Chalmers a religious conversion around 1810 that
drew him into the circle of the Kirk's evangelicals. William Wilberforce's defense
of evangelical piety was particularly effective. Once Chalmers recovered and
resumed pastoral duties, his preaching changed dramatically and started to
attract crowds along with invitations to preach and write in wider forums. At
first, the newfound evangelical faith dovetailed with the methods of English
evangelicals who worked outside or were indifferent to the ecclesiastical establishment in their promotion of voluntary societies, for Bible reading and education, moral reform, and evangelism and foreign missions. In Kilmany Chalmers
organized an auxiliary branch of the British and Foreign Bible Society, and he
promoted the cause of various missionary societies. In so doing, Chalmers also
discovered a rationale that drew upon his lifelong attachment to the communal
ideal of the godly Christian commonwealth: by supporting the work of foreign
missions, wealthy patrons would inevitably also respond to the needs of their
impoverished neighbors and townspeople.

The communal dimension of Chalmers' arguments was anomalous among
evangelicals but it tapped a growing interest among Kirk clergy in the ideal
parish. For too many pastors during the eighteenth century, their call was little
more than a sinecure that provided both a living and a credential for additional

appointments – hence the problem of plurality faced by ministers who also served as university faculty or government administrators. But at the beginning of the nineteenth century came a wave of interest in reviving the traditional responsibilities of a minister in his parish, from education to poor relief. Chalmers was part of this parochial groundswell and began to experiment within the parish of Kilmany. He instituted educational programs, including the evangelical model of Sunday schools, and sought a reformation of morals through visitation in parish homes. The most absorbing part of his work in the parish was poor relief; Chalmers received gifts from wealthy residents in Kilmany that he distributed to various needy families without following state laws that governed such welfare. This was a pivotal development for the rest of his career; for Chalmers the church needed to be at the center of Scotland's response to industrialization, poverty, civic morality, and ultimately of efforts to create a godly society. The role of the minister in his parish was especially important to Chalmers' opposition to pluralities. How could a minister carry out all that a parish required if he also prepared lectures or ran a bureau?

In 1815 Chalmers took his experiment with the ideal parish to a very different Scottish setting: the Tron parish in Glasgow. Here the gap between rich and poor was widening and the parish system was dysfunctional, from the insufficient number of churches for the burgeoning urban population (and no parish schools) to the Kirk's abandonment of poor relief altogether. Chalmers oversaw the revival and enlargement of the work of elders, particularly in home visitation. He also responded to the parish's need for education by instituting Sunday school programs. His most important initiative was to reform the laws governing poor relief, an effort that gave Chalmers a savory whiff of political activism. At this time, he wrote in opposition to poor laws and advocated an alternative: a church-based system of poor relief that would abolish all extra-parochial welfare institutions, locate assessment of need within the parish's session, and solicit private contributions to stretch church-based welfare. Chalmers faced considerable opposition, even from fellow evangelicals both within and outside the Kirk. But after a brief flirtation with an appointment to a chair in natural philosophy at Edinburgh, in 1819 Chalmers instituted phase two of his plans to reactivate the Kirk's parish system. In this case, town officials in Glasgow approved the creation of a new parish – St John's – in which Chalmers would minister along with a set of elders from the Tron parish. For four years he devoted himself to all facets of the parish – spiritual, diaconal, and educational – and achieved results that were longer on good intentions than they were in relieving urban poverty. But he also burnt himself out. Although Chalmers had never given up on achieving the prestige of a university appointment, his tireless work in Glasgow made the relief afforded by an 1823 appointment to teach moral philosophy at St Andrews seem all the more attractive. He would hold this position until 1828 when his peripatetic career took him to Edinburgh as professor of divinity.

At St Andrews Chalmers hardly hid in his ivory tower from important developments both in the Kirk and Scottish society. He taught and wrote on moral philosophy, a discipline that opened a wide canvas for Chalmers' activism and idealism. He also dabbled in civil legislation, intervened in faculty politics, and spoke out on matters within the Kirk, most of the time on all these fronts, as his own man with a knack for estranging allies. But the major issue to which Chalmers devoted his energies was the sustainability of the ecclesiastical establishment in Scotland. He was particularly intent on preserving the Kirk's privileges in a manner that recognized the hardships experienced by dissenting Protestants and even Roman Catholics (Chalmers did argue for the latter's emancipation). His creative defense of the Kirk's status and authority made a dent in the 1830s debates over patronage and anti-patronage by elevating evangelical arguments from the obscurity of a few conservative ministers into a celebrated campaign in which the health and future of Scotland was at stake.

Parliament's consideration of Roman Catholic emancipation in 1829 coincided with increased demands from Protestant dissenters in Scotland for an end to ecclesiastical establishment. Since the eighteenth-century squabbles over patronage, the Kirk had lost about one-third of the churchgoing population either to Presbyterian Secession churches or to Baptists and Congregationalists. Presbyterian dissenters had generally held to the propriety of ecclesiastical establishments and were resolved to reconnect with the Kirk once the system of patronage ended. But debates about the status of Roman Catholics in the United Kingdom bred hostility to establishment altogether. Entanglement with the state, the argument went, was inherently corrosive of the church's capacity to carry out her mission. Voluntaryism, the flip side of disestablishment, became a plank in the platform of liberal reform. It would allow for greater responsiveness to the people's convictions and it would extend private initiative into the religious world. Voluntaryism also stood for an enlightened approach to church life. Protestants did not need coercion to defeat false religion; they could triumph through the power of their own ideas.

In 1833 the Kirk began to respond to the dissenters' challenge with the formation of the Glasgow Society for Promoting the Interests of the Church of Scotland, which in turn published the *Church of Scotland Magazine*, a publication designed to answer the *Voluntary Church Magazine*. The debate threw into greater relief the disparity between the liberal social outlook that went with voluntaryism and the ideal of the Christian commonwealth that undergirded the establishment position. At the same time, the Kirk looked for ways to reform the system of patronage so that the appointment of ministers would be responsive to popular will. Chalmers, in turn, came into his own as the leading critic of liberal economic theory, defender of the parish system within the Christian common-wealth, and wise opponent of privilege within church and government. On the strength of his appeal, the 1832 General Assembly elected him moderator. Chalmers himself was not convinced that abolishing patronage would improve the system and did not use his growing stature to add to the opposition. Still, he was a symbol of the establishment principle and of the Kirk at its best as the soul of the Scottish nation.

By 1833 support for anti-patronage proposals throughout Scotland had become so strong that the British government, run by the Whigs, asked the Kirk to reform its patronage system. This direction was an important catalyst for the eventual approval by the Kirk in 1834 of the Veto Act, which gave the majority of male heads of households within a parish the authority to disapprove the presentation of an unpopular minister. The irony of the situation was remark-able. By instructing the Kirk to reform its ways, the British government set into motion a conflict in which church reform would infuriate the state. Meanwhile, it also exposed the very point the voluntaryists were keen on making: that political entanglements were corrupt. Even so, the situation again played to one of Chalmers' strengths, his ability to portray the established order as truly repre-sentative of the Scottish people. Unlike the voluntary system of church life, which would appeal to the middle and upper classes who could afford to sponsor their own congregations and pastors, the Kirk was "the poor man's church," since it could underwrite congregations even where voluntary contributions could not sustain them.

Still, the new mood prompted by Protestant dissent and Roman Catholic emancipation required the Kirk, at Chalmers' prodding, to fight voluntaryism with establishmentarian voluntaryism. On the one hand, Chalmers headed the Church Accommodation Committee, which conducted a study to determine how many churches the Scottish population needed. On the other hand, he also supplied the rationale for the Church Endowment Committee's plans to fund the new churches that Scotland needed. He called for an "internal Voluntaryism," an idea that called upon the wealthy members of Scottish society to help pay for the creation of new parishes (along with the attendant bills that buildings and pastoral stipends rendered). In fact, part of the argument determined that state funds for the Kirk should only go to the congregations that were most successful at raising voluntary contributions. In 1835, Chalmers became the head of the Church Extension Committee, which consolidated the Endowment and Accommodation committees into a single body. The Extension Committee took over the administration of generating new parishes. Adding to the Kirk's growth and responsiveness was the Chapels Act of 1834, which allowed independent chapels, formerly designed as institutions outside the establishment where parishes were non-existent, to become officially part of the Church of Scotland. Although the chapels relied upon voluntary donations, their pastors and elders through this Act had the same status as Kirk officers and would be permitted the same legal standing at presbyteries, synods, and assemblies as other church officers. In addition to the chapels-of-ease which ran to well over a hundred in number, the Kirk grew between 1834 and 1841 with the addition of 222 new parishes (a 20 percent increase).

The Church Extension Committee functioned as Chalmers' own fiefdom within the Kirk, and ecclesiastical and civil officials grew critical of his power and vision for Presbyterianism in Scotland. An 1835 dispute over the moderatorship of the General Assembly allowed critics of Chalmers and the Evangelical Party to voice their objections through support for John Lee, a moderate in the Kirk and a supporter of the Whig government. Chalmers weathered the storm from within the church but British politicians posed a much greater obstacle. Thanks to church extension plans and the need for a larger endowment for the Kirk, the religious situation in Scotland was an important piece of business for British officials during the 1830s. A royal commission tasked with inspecting Scotland's religious needs – a much-contested body thanks to fears within the Kirk that the study was a means for dissenters to achieve their goal of disestablishment – found in 1838 that the number of churches was inadequate for Scotland's needs, but the royal body provided no mechanisms for financing new churches beyond meager support for the Highlands. As bad as this news was, worse was the 1839 decision by Court of Session to uphold the rights of patrons and heritors in two parishes over the powers granted to the laity and pastors through the Veto Act and the Chapel Act of 1834. The Court's ruling pulled the rug out from under Chalmers' Church Extension Committee, put a stake through the heart of his communal parish ideal, and threw the Kirk in its evangelical phase into crisis.

These state rulings occurred at the same time that Scottish Presbyterians were celebrating the bicentennial of the Solemn League and Covenant (1638), so Kirk leaders were not predisposed to receive passively the British government's slight. On the one hand, the 1838 assembly passed a resolution (183 to 42) that affirmed the Kirk's spiritual independence. It also contained a resolution to appeal the Court of Session's ruling to the House of Lords. The appeal was an indication of how upset the Kirk's leaders were since it also conflicted with the resolution regarding spiritual independence: why would the church need to appeal to Caesar to confirm its own authority? It was also a tactical blunder because the House of Lords not only upheld the Court of Session's ruling, thus upending the power of the laity to veto an unpopular pastor; the

Lords also rejected any attempt to give the people a voice in the call of a minister. Still, the most important part of the Lords' decision was its renunciation of the Kirk's affirmation of spiritual independence. From the perspective of parliament, synods and assemblies were subordinate to civil courts even in spiritual matters.

Chalmers, who had not been a commissioner at the 1838 assembly, was present the following year and responsible for crafting the Kirk's response. He relied on a distinction between the temporal and spiritual aspects of the church's affairs. Into the former went church buildings, manses, and ministerial stipends. Chalmers argued that the civil courts had legitimate authority to dispose of these matters, but that the civil government had no such authority over the spiritual or internal affairs of the church, which included the standards and conditions for ordination. Chalmers also lobbied for the principle of non-intrusion, which he believed was part and parcel with the Scottish Reformation. According to this notion, no agency or person should impose a minister in a parish against the will of the congregation. Chalmers was persuasive: the assembly of 1839 approved his response by a vote of 204 to 155.

Although Chalmers was successful, the crisis of the 1830s revived the Moderate Party, which regarded the state as the sovereign authority and the creator of the established church. In turn, the Evangelical Party increasingly identified with the Veto Act and opposed patronage by appealing to popular will. Meanwhile, the principle of spiritual independence was an abstraction. Two more patronage disputes concluded in 1839, one from the presbytery of Dunkeld and the other from Strathbogie, with the Court of Session siding with patrons against each congregation's lay members. The latter case was especially contentious since it involved a presbytery submitting to the Court of Session as its superior body rather than the General Assembly. Seven ministers in particular – the Strathbogie Seven, who had been suspended by the General Assembly from conducting services owing to their insubordination – were able to keep their parishes. The reason was an interdict from the Court of Session that forbade any minister from the Kirk from holding any religious service in the contested parishes without the approval of the infamous seven Presbyterian clerics.

For the next few years, a committee appointed by the General Assembly worked with parliament in London on a political compromise, but the genuine drama continued to play out north of the English border. Chalmers was an important member of the assembly's committee and again he proved to be hamfisted in the give and take of negotiation, sometimes vacillating on the Veto Act, and at other times letting differences become personal. At the same time, Chalmers had little room to negotiate since both the Whigs and Tories were unwilling to concede on the matter of the church's spiritual independence: each party wanted the civil government to have ultimate authority in ecclesiastical affairs. Even so, while Chalmers was unable to find a way around the Kirk's impasse with parliament, the most pressing matter before the General Assembly was the situation in Strathbogie Presbytery. The Strathbogie Seven, despite being suspended by the assembly, went ahead in January of 1841 with the ordination of a contested minister, John Edwards, whom the laity had vetoed. They could act so defiantly because of the Court of Session's ruling in their favor. When the assembly convened in May, the commissioners proceeded to depose the seven pastors by an almost two-to-one majority (222 to 125), even though the assembly spent twelve hours in debate before casting its votes. When the Court of Session sent its messenger-at-arms to block the suspension, the assembly would only admit him if he left the court's document outside the door. The deposition of the Strathbogie Seven stood, and the Disruption became a fait accompli. The issue was whether the church or civil government was sovereign over the Kirk's spiritual affairs.

The last two years before the Disruption saw each side harden its position. In 1842 the assembly passed one motion that abolished patronage altogether, and another, the Claim of Right, that asserted the Kirk's spiritual independence. Some ministers wanted to wait for the government's response to the Claim of Right before disrupting the bond between church and state, so that the Kirk would have the satisfaction of the state's recognition even if spiritual independence were rejected. Others wondered how the Disruption would plausibly affect their own livelihoods. To that end, the Evangelical Party employed a form of voluntaryism by establishing local associations to raise funds for salaries, manses, church buildings, and schools. Meanwhile, the British government continued to uphold the rights of patrons and heritors in contested ordinations. As many as thirty-nine lawsuits were pending on the eve of the Disruption. A further indication of the government's refusal to budge was the decision, conveyed in a "Queen's Letter," not to consider the Claim of Right. By the time of the 1843 General Assembly, the only question was how many ministers would leave. The 454 who entered the Free Church were disproportionately ministers ordained between 1830 and 1840, those from the Highlands, and those who staffed the chapels-of-ease.

The Free Church's protest stated succinctly the chief cause of the Disruption when, while recognizing the "absolute" jurisdiction of the civil courts in any of the church's civil matters or temporal affairs, it declared:

the Church Courts, – do, in name and on behalf of this Church, and of the nation and people of Scotland, and under the sanction of the several statutes, and the Treaty of Union herein before recited, Claim, as of Right, That she shall freely possess and enjoy her liberties, government, discipline, rights, and privileges, according to law, especially for the defence of the spiritual liberties of her people, and that she shall be protected therein from the foresaid unconstitutional and illegal encroachments of the said Court of Session, and her people secured in their Christian and constitutional rights and liberties.

But this protest, Free Church leaders believed, was also significant for Reformed churches around the world that held "the great doctrine of the sole Headship of the Lord Jesus over his Church." The new body pleaded with other Reformed Protestants in other countries to pray that God:

> would give strength to this Church – office-bearers and people – to endure resignedly the loss of the temporal benefits of an Establishment, and the personal sufferings and sacrifices to which they may be called, and would also inspire them with zeal and energy to promote the advancement of his Son's kingdom.[5]

The ministers and laity who left the Kirk did indeed experience hardship, and their sacrifice for the sake of principle was so impressive that the Edinburgh politician Henry Cockburn, Solicitor General for Scotland, could only marvel:

> Whatever may be thought of their cause, there can be no doubt or coldness in the admiration with which all candid men must applaud their heroism. They have abandoned that public station which was the ambition of their lives, and have descended from certainty to precariousness, and most of them from comfort to destitution, solely for their principles. . . . It is the loss of station that is the deep and lasting sacrifice, the ceasing to be the most important man in the parish, the closing of the doors of the gentry against him and his family, the altered prospects of his children, the extinction of everything that the State had provided for the decent dignity of the manse and its inmates.[6]

Lord Cockburn was no fool. As much as the Free Church clung to the establishment principle, the reality was a Free Church without the blessing of the establishment.

From Establishment to Voluntaryism

Despite Chalmers' insistence on the establishment principle, even before his death in 1847 the Free Church was living up more to the voluntary part of its name than to its kirkly aspirations. To be sure, one of the reasons for the broad appeal of the Free Church was its ability to raise funds for the fixtures that went

with an ecclesiastical establishment, such as ministers' stipends, church buildings, schools, and even a college at Edinburgh University. The Free Church's
New College, designed by the well-known Edinburgh architect William Henry
Playfair, would be the setting for the final years of Chalmers' career as a professor
of divinity and college principal. Had the Free Church not been able to establish
local societies and build support for its institutions – a program that drew
directly on Chalmers' indefatigable capacity as an administrator and his vision of
the godly commonwealth – the new communion would not have attracted as
many Scots as it did. Earlier secessions, after all, had failed to take root in the
Highlands and Islands – places of Free Church strength – precisely because
the populations were too sparse to sustain a minister and building. This was the
problem of the voluntary principle: whether people could afford to pay for religious services without a patron's subsidy. But the Free Church not only proposed
a church that would duplicate the national establishment, but also delivered,
through a variety of mechanisms for personal generosity, an institution with
resources that could assist a parish in poor and sparsely populated places. By
1847 the Free Church's institutional edifice was impressive, even if its church
buildings were initially humble. Only four years into its existence the Free
Church had 730 churches, roughly 600 ministers receiving an annual dividend
of 122 pounds, 513 teachers responsible for 44,000 pupils, and a church college.

At the same time, the logic of the appeal for voluntary contributions soon
nurtured an outlook within the Free Church that was closer to the voluntary
principle than Chalmers' vaunted establishment ideal. Church–state debates
encouraged among younger ministers a willingness to see the church as distinct
from the state and to sympathize with the Covenanters and the original Seceders.
An outbreak of revivals, centered in Kilsyth in 1839, also encouraged those in
the Free Church who supported these Awakenings to regard the church as a
gathered body set apart from wider society. Consequently, Free Church communicants began to question Chalmers' ideal of a national, territorial church. They
wondered why the services of the Free Church should be rendered for all of
Scotland when only a part of the nation was supporting the new church. In other
words, by leaving the establishment behind and adopting voluntary mechanisms, the Free Church was implicitly becoming the kind of a voluntaryist
communion that Chalmers had opposed.

The voluntary character of the Free Church was much easier to spot outside
Scotland, where the controversies in the Kirk also played out in colonial settings.
In Canada the Disruption in the mother country contributed to a similar split
among Presbyterians despite a very different set of religious and political
circumstances. Early on, the Associate Presbyterians (Seceders) dominated
Presbyterian life in the British territories north of the United States and were

particularly strong in the Maritime Provinces. Only in 1825, with the formation of the Glasgow Colonial Society, did the Church of Scotland begin to establish a presence in Canada. This society was one of the many independent missionary societies to arise in the early nineteenth century but its mission, in addition to "promoting and assisting the moral and religious interests of Scottish settlers in British North America" included sending out only ministers who had been ordained by the Church of Scotland.[7] The Society's first missionary went to Canada in 1829, and by 1844 a total of twenty-eight were ministering primarily in the provinces of Upper and Lower Canada. In 1831 the first ecclesiastical organization affiliated with the Kirk emerged, the Synod of the Presbyterian Church in Canada in Connection with the Church of Canada. The rules, procedures and personnel for this Canadian body all came from the Church of Scotland but the New World synod had no official standing within the Kirk. It was both dependent and "quasi-autonomous."[8]

This ambivalent relationship between Canadian Presbyterians and the Kirk was even more noticeable at the level of finances. Canadian Presbyterian ministers, whether in the case of the Associate Presbyterians or the Kirk, depended largely on voluntary contributions for their salaries or stipends. Some of this came from gifts to missionary societies in the Old Country. Some came from the collection plate in each congregation, though an 1867 statistical report on the Presbyterian Church in Canada indicated that each parishioner was giving on average one cent per Sunday, a sum that hardly covered the expenses of salary, building, and manse. Scottish ministers from the Kirk could also receive funding from the Clergy Reserves established by the British government to underwrite the established clergy in the Canadian colonies. The natural expectation was that these revenues would go to priests from the Church of England. But because Kirk ministers were also part of a British ecclesiastical establishment, they too petitioned for support from these reserves. Prior to the secularization of the Clergy Reserves in 1854, Presbyterian ministers received a portion (disproportionately smaller than the Anglican share) of their stipend from these funds. Still, the church in Canada had no battle with patrons, vetoes, and state intrusion the way the Kirk did. Protestantism in colonial Canada resembled far more the denominational structures of the United States than the establishment-versus-dissenters pattern of the United Kingdom.

Despite these formal differences, the Disruption played out in Canada almost exactly as it had in Scotland. The composition of the ministers in the Canadian Synod by 1840 was generally sympathetic to the Evangelical Party in the Kirk thanks to the age and associations of Canadian ministers, most of whom had been ordained in the 1830s and had ties to missionary societies. Also important for convincing Canadian ministers and lay people to sympathize more with the Free Church than the Kirk were the Free Church's overt appeal to Canadians, the start of a pro-Free Church newspaper, and a legal dispute that many interpreted along the Free Church lines of an Erastian government interfering with ecclesiastical affairs. The Temporalities Bill of 1842 proposed the construction of seven-member committees in each congregation to manage its property. But because this legislation appeared to be a state-appointed committee, Presbyterians already inclined to affirm the church's spiritual independence were ready to interpret it as an attempt by the civil government to dictate legal terms to the church. In 1843, with the example of the Scottish Disruption in full view, some ministers seceded independently from the Canadian Synod. But the rest of the Canadian Church debated the situation in Canada, as well as their synod's relationship to the two bodies in Scotland, for another year. Some ministers were hoping to avoid a split by arguing that the Canadian Synod was already independent from the Kirk, thus making disruption unnecessary.

In 1843 the Canadian Synod passed a motion that was essentially neutral on the Scottish Disruption. It clarified that the colonial church was technically not connected to the Kirk, specified that it would receive ministers from any Presbyterian body who could comply with its doctrine and polity, and expressed willingness to forego the synod's claim to Canada's Clergy Reserves. This passed, at 56 to 40. But this moderate resolution was insufficient for some. The following year at the Canadian Synod, twenty of the ninety-one ministers present signed a protest that took the synod to task for failing to repudiate the Kirk and its abandonment of the spiritual independence of the church under the lordship of Christ. These dissenters formed the Canadian equivalent of the Free Church, with two distinct synods of operation, one in Nova Scotia and the other covering the provinces of Upper and Lower Canada.

Without the same political dynamics that had prompted the Scottish Disruption, maintaining separate Presbyterian bodies in Canada was difficult, especially when the British colonies in North America formed a Canadian Confederation. By 1861 the synods of the Free Church in the Canadas and Nova Scotia had merged with the Associate Presbyterians. A force behind the union of Nova Scotia Presbyterians was George Munro Grant (1835–1902), a native of Nova Scotia who had studied for the ministry at the University of Glasgow before returning to Canada as a missionary of the Church of Scotland to gather congregations in the Maritimes. Over time Grant became a settled pastor, revamped Dalhousie College as a provincial university, advocated political confederation, and still had time to seek the union of Canadian Presbyterians. In 1875 the three main strands of Presbyterianism in Canada, the Seceders, the Kirk, and the Free Church, put aside their differences to form the Presbyterian Church of Canada. In their preamble these communions made no mention of the formal considerations that had either led to divisions in Scotland or separate denominations in Canada. They affirmed that each body held "the same doctrine, government and discipline." The new church would be "independent of all" other churches in its jurisdiction, and under the sole authority of Christ, "the Head of the Church, and Head over all things to the Church . . ."[9] Meanwhile, congratulations came from Presbyterian churches on both sides of the Atlantic and even the Pacific: From Irish Presbyterians, the Presbyterian Church in the USA, the Presbyterian Church of Victoria, Australia, and the Free Presbyterian Church of Scotland. Perhaps the voluntary status of Presbyterian churches outside of Scotland – and even for some within – accounts for the absence of good wishes from the Presbyterian establishment in the Church of Scotland.

In Australia, which became the home of thousands of Scots during the 1820s and 1830s, a similar pattern emerged to the one in Canada, where ecclesiastical divisions in the motherland shaped colonial ecclesiastical dynamics.[10] As in Canada, Australian Presbyterians had no experience with overbearing patrons, Erastian legislators, or hallowed memories of a godly commonwealth. Presbyterian ministers came to distinct colonies within continental Australia – New South Wales and Victoria were the most receptive – and brought their own associations and convictions from the Old World. The first three pastors each represented a distinct strain of Scottish Presbyterianism. Archibald Macarthur, who settled in Tasmania in 1822, came from a Secession background. John Dunmore Lang, who began his labors in 1823 in New South Wales and became arguably the chief force in the colonial Presbyterian church, was sympathetic to the Evangelical Party in the Church of Scotland. John McGarvie, who also landed in 1826 in New South Wales, was more at home with the Moderates in the Kirk. Ministers received compensation from a combination of civil government funding and voluntary contributions. Still, the events that had led to the Disruption in Scotland also split Australian Presbyterians, even if the circumstances of establishments and voluntaryism were markedly different.

Unlike Canada, Presbyterianism in Australia developed prior to the establishment of strong assemblies, thus encouraging an alignment in the colonial church along the lines of the Scottish Disruption once that breach took place. The one exception to this organic extension between Scotland and Australia was Lang, whose zeal and energy usually outran his Scottish ministerial peers and prompted him to find a place for his hyperactivity within his own synod, which had loose connections to the United Presbyterians (Seceders) in Scotland. Although the aftershock of the Scottish Disruption would vary from colony to colony in Australia, the case of New South Wales illustrates the general dynamics that confronted colonial Presbyterian ministers with ties – both professional and personal – to the churches in Scotland. Thanks to the distance between Glasgow and Sydney, news of the 1843 split in the Kirk did not reach Australia for the better part of a year. In October of 1844 the Synod of Australia received a motion from one of its ministers calling upon Australian Presbyterians, in language redolent of Free Church convictions, to affirm the headship of Christ and the spiritual independence of the church. It also asserted the synod's freedom "from all transmarine control" in terms that followed the Declaratory Act of 1840 approved by the Kirk's assembly. This legislation had devolved authority over Presbyterian affairs in the colony to the Synod of Australia and obligated the Australian church to follow the Scottish church's confession and polity, while implementing its procedures "in so far as they are applicable to the circumstances of the colony."[11] Subsequent debate on this proposal outlined three options: Australian churches could side with the Free Church; they could retain their status as a church "in connection" with the Kirk; or they could simply retain their own status as an independent and neutral body. The majority of presbyters favored a policy of practical neutrality and refused to identify officially with either of the Scottish churches.

The news of the Australian body's attitude did not please either the Kirk or the Free Church. The former's response, characterized by one historian as "bitter," interpreted the Australian church's position as a rejection of the statutory relationship between Australia and Scotland.[12] The Kirk also determined that ministers and elders in Australia would no longer be regarded as or have the privileges of officers in the Church of Scotland. The Free Church did not react as dismissively but was no more inclined to view the Australian position of neutrality as courageous.

Presbyterians in New South Wales continued to evaluate their relationship to Scottish Presbyterians for the next several years. Although the Free Church's frustration with Australia was milder than the Kirk's, in 1846 the Synod of Australia nevertheless decided to reaffirm its connection to the Church of Scotland (which was a reversal from an 1844 motion that had revealed a substantial majority in favor of the Free Church). Whatever the reasons for this decision, it also split the Presbyterian churches in New South Wales. In 1846, four ministers from the Synod withdrew on grounds that resembled the Free Church's protest. Three of them formed a Free Church body, the Synod of East Australia. The other, Andrew Hamilton, left his charge, which included a comfortable salary and manse, departed for the interior, and proceeded to establish the Free Presbyterian Church of Australia Felix. Although an opponent of voluntaryism, Hamilton also acknowledged after several years of dependence upon contributions from his parishioners that the voluntary principle was not sufficient to sustain "a Gospel ministry even in the interior."[13]

As the experience of Canadian Presbyterians taught, if time did not heal all wounds it did at least provide room for colonial Presbyterians to recognize the merits of church union. Redrawing the lines of Australian colonies combined with the end of government grants to the churches encouraged Australian Presbyterians within a decade of their disruption to consider a united Presbyterian church. The union did not occur until 1865, thanks both to lingering questions about how to handle the indefatigable Lang and to dissent from Free Church immigrants who had come from the Scottish Highlands where Free Church convictions ran deep. Still, the United Presbyterian Church of Australia was an indication that the dynamic of voluntaryism versus establismentarianism was of little relevance in political circumstances far removed from Scotland.

It was even beginning to wear thin back in Scotland, for instance when the Free Church had to decide whether to recognize the united Australian church. In 1861, as Australian authorities were combing the fine print of union plans, the Free Church voted to recognize the proposed ecclesiastical incorporation even though it meant approving colonial Free Church Presbyterians' acceptance of voluntaryism. That only a minority of Free Church delegates voted against their colonial peers was a sign that the Free Church of Scotland was in for a battle over its own union talks. But for the majority of Free Church Presbyterians, both in Scotland and in the colonies, the differences between them and other Presbyterians who had seceded from the Kirk seemed much less signifi-cant than they had at the time of the Disruption. The original Free Church was merely the last of the disrupted communions to unite with Presbyterians outside the Kirk.

The Free Church of Scotland contemplated mergers with three Presbyterian communions between 1860 and 1900. The most prominent was the United Presbyterian Church, a communion formed in 1847 from the original Seceders of 1733 and the Relief Church of 1761. Another was the Original Secession Church, a body formed in 1842 from Associate Presbyterians who had split almost a century earlier over the Burgher Oath, and united in a commitment to the establishment principle and a restoration of the national covenants. The last was the Reformed Presbyterian Church, the communion that embodied the convictions of the Covenanters. The Free Church had no significant objections to either the Original Seceders or the Reformed Presbyterians, and in 1852 the Free Church merged with the Seceders. Negotiations may have taken longer with the Covenanters since the older body had existed practically on a voluntary basis, even if it was not a champion of voluntaryism. But in 1876 the Free Church and Reformed Presbyterians also merged. In contrast, the United Presbyterian Church included a provision in its founding documents that spoke of the importance and value of charitable giving, thus signaling sympathy with voluntaryism. For this reason the Free Church balked at merging with the United Presbyterians. Even if Free Church Presbyterians were dependent on the mechanisms of voluntaryism, they were still committed to the establishment principle as part of their status as a Scottish church.

Free Church leaders divided over such explicit voluntaryism but other factors were also at play. The anti-unionists, led by James Begg (1808–83), Chalmers' right-hand man and a strict constitutionalist, refused to accept that under no circumstance should the state establish and endow a particular church. He continued to believe in and defend the establishment principle even after parliament abolished patronage in 1874. Leading the advocates of union was Robert Rainy (1826–1906), a vigorous church politician who also led Free Church Presbyterians in supporting the disestablishment of the Kirk once parliament had ended patronage. For Rainy, voluntaryism was an equitable way for Scotland's churches to have the greatest influence on the nation, and union was a way to make such influence effective. The contrast between strict anti-unionists and loose unionists may be too simple, but questions over worship – whether to sing psalms only – and over theology, specifically the higher critical views of William Robertson Smith's biblical scholarship, reinforced the image of Begg and his allies as rigid and Rainy and company as equivocal. But once Begg died in 1883, those opposed to union lost their only substantial check upon Rainy. Although the proposed union took the better part of four decades to achieve, in 1900 the Free Church overcame its original objections to voluntaryism and united with the United Presbyterians to form the United Free Church.

Disruption Again

The union of the Free and United Presbyterians was hardly smooth. In fact, seven years before the Free Church had experienced its own disruption, a division that greased the wheels for a union. In 1893, Free Church traditionalists, upset over the Declaratory Act of 1892, which granted latitude in subscribing to the Westminster Confession, withdrew to found the Free Presbyterian Church of Scotland, thus confirming McMurphy's law of Presbyterianism that with every ecclesiastical merger comes at least one new communion. Historians of Scottish Presbyterianism regard this as one of the rare instances of a split based on theological dispute. As many as fourteen thousand members left the Free Church. But this was not the only division prompted by church union. In 1900, at the assembly when the Free Church voted by an overwhelming majority – 643 to 27 – to join with the United Presbyterians, the minority refused to submit and continued with the meeting, claiming that the majority had "lawfully ... withdrawn from membership of the Free Church."[14] To the majority such tenacity was laughable. But United Free Church leaders were less inclined to merriment when the legal claims of the minority went first to the Scottish courts and then to the House of Lords.

Scotland's Court of Session quickly dispensed with the case and sided with the majority of the Free Church, now the United Free Church. But the minority was resilient, and in 1903 its appeal went before the House of Lords. The continuing Free Church case hinged on three points: first, the establishment principle, which was essential to its being the Free Church; second, the Declaratory Act of 1892, which indicated a departure from the Free Church's creed; and third, a change in ordination vows to accommodate United Presbyterians from the original Free Church constitution. The House of Lords surprised most of the United Kingdom by vindicating the Free Church minority as the lawful instantiation of the 1843 Disruption. Had the disparity between the numerical size of the minority and the Free Church's property and trusts not been so great, the matter would likely not have gone before the courts. But the lawful Free Church could not use all of its legal possessions and the United Free Church wanted access to property its leaders thought belonged to their communion. Meanwhile, the United Free Presbyterians invoked the spiritual independence of the church to protest the Lords' ruling. That Free Church conviction rang a bit hollow when United Free Presbyterians also swayed the British government to appoint a commission to allocate the Free Church's assets equitably. The civil authorities agreed to do so a few years later. One newspaper editor could not resist noting the irony that "the last outcome of the long protest against Erastianism is that the funds and property of the Free Church of Scotland should be vested in a Parliamentary Commission."[15]

Ironies aside, between the Disruption of the Kirk in 1843 and the disruption of the Free Church in 1900, Scottish Presbyterianism had tested the premise that a Reformed Protestant church could be serious about its theology, worship, and polity while also retaining its status as an agency of the civil government. Even when the Free Church, whose evangelical convictions situated it to the theological right of the Moderate Party, but not as far as the Erskines or Knox, relinquished its formal ties to the state, it persisted in adhering to the propriety and even the necessity of an established church. In the end, however, establishmentarianism and theological strictness could not co-exist in an increasingly pluralistic modern setting. The legal Free Church turned out to be a small slice of Scottish Presbyterianism, characterized by Reformed orthodoxy. Although it was strong in the provincial Highlands, it remained several steps removed from a national church or a body with wide-reaching influence in Scotland. Meanwhile, the United Free Presbyterians inherited the original Free Church's claims about establishment (even if they compromised the United Presbyterians voluntaryist conviction) when in 1929 they united with the church they had left almost ninety years earlier: the Church of Scotland. The Articles Declaratory (1921) that provided the legal foundation for this union affirmed the national status of the Kirk, the traditional Church of Scotland position, and the spiritual independence of the church, a Free Church principle. As a result, the established church embraced all of the legal considerations that had vexed Scottish Presbyterianism for eight decades, while the legal Free Church became simply a small Presbyterian denomination.

The old and original ideal of one Kirk, binding together people and nation, was gone. One part, the Church of Scotland, still held on to the nationalist spirit of the Scottish Reformation but needed to dispense with much of its doctrinal heritage for the sake of its public status. The Free Church, the other part of the Scottish ideal, preserved the theological tradition of Scotland but in doing so necessarily became small and institutionally isolated. This was the choice that confronted most Calvinists once nation-states abandoned the confessional aspect of their authority.

CHAPTER ELEVEN

THE NETHERLANDS' NEW WAY

ALMOST A DECADE BEFORE the Free Church of Scotland took leave from the Kirk, Reformed Protestants in the Netherlands were engaged in similarly disruptive efforts. The Dutch Secession of 1834, however, lacked the drama and publicity that attended the Scottish Disruption. The difference had little to do with the actual issues at stake. As in the case of Scotland, Reformed ministers in the Netherlands were upset with compromises they believed had infected the ecclesiastical establishment. Also, Dutch Reformed pastors were as interested as the Free Church leaders in recovering the golden age of their national church. Even so, the Dutch Secession of 1834 sounded more like a whimper compared to the bang of Scotland's Disruption, thanks to significantly different political and religious circumstances.

The Secession of 1834 – the Afscheiding – was chiefly confined to one town and one man. The minister who headed the split was Hendrik de Cock (1801– 42), who until he became the pastor at the national church in Ulrum, a town near Groningen, was indistinguishable from most other Netherlands Reformed church ministers. He grew up in the state church – his grandfather had been a Reformed minister – and studied for ecclesiastical service at the University of Groningen. He served at two other Dutch congregations before taking the call to Ulrum, where he found a congregation much more conversant in the discourse of Reformed orthodoxy than he was. His parishioners encouraged him to re-examine the teachings of Reformed Protestantism through the Canons of the Synod of Dort and Calvin's *Institutes*. De Cock's preaching changed dramatically. It also acquired a millennial flavor thanks to the Belgian revolt against Dutch rule, beginning in 1830, which de Cock interpreted as a judgment from God against the nation. De Cock soon developed a large following among the laity in the region.

The popularity of this zealous preacher soon created problems for the national church. Not only did de Cock question the established ministers' integrity, but he also cultivated a similar sensibility among like-minded lay people and pastors. Members of other congregations, believing that their ministers were unconverted, brought their children to de Cock for baptism. When he rejected the rules of church order that should have prevented such irregularities, the Classis of Middelstum initiated disciplinary proceedings against him. Enhancing his notoriety was the zeal that he provoked among other conservative ministers. When Hendrik P. Scholte, who attracted thousands and castigated the state church's ministers, preached to the congregation in Ulrum, the classis barred the guest pastor from returning to preach the afternoon service. The incident precipitated a minor riot that police had to quiet. Meanwhile, Scholte, with de Cock's backing, defied the ecclesiastical authorities and preached outside the church in the evening to a large crowd. De Cock formalized such defiance when on October 13, 1834 he issued a statement, "The Act of Secession and Return," to the Classis of Middelstum, which declared the Nederlandse Hervormde Kerk (NHK), the state church, to be apostate and himself free from its oversight. Thereafter de Cock worked as an itinerant preacher in the region and established several congregations identified with the Secession, or Afscheiding.

The events of 1834 tapped local expressions of lay frustration with the established church, but such discontent would take almost forty years before it could blossom into a communion that could vie with it for national prominence. By then the remarkable figure Abraham Kuyper would emerge as the voice of traditional Dutch Reformed Protestantism and would add a new communion to the various churches that had arisen to lament the health of the Dutch national church. But even Kuyper's genius as an institution builder and statesman could not consolidate all the Reformed Protestants outside the state church into a single ecclesiastical entity. The reason for the lack of consensus among Dutch Reformed traditionalists (compared to the relative unity of Free Church Presbyterians) owed as much to conditions within the Dutch national church and its sponsoring civil government as to the character of conservative church leaders. Even so, developments in nineteenth-century Dutch Reformed Protestantism, the second episode in the post-1800 transformation of Calvinist centers, demonstrated (as they had in Scotland) that the path to recovering the insights of the original Reformers required the difficult task of extricating the spiritual work and mission of the church from the patronage of the civil authorities.

Ecclesiastical Disorder in the Dutch Kingdom

The Dutch Republic emerged from almost twenty years of French control in 1815 as a kingdom ruled by William I, son of the last stadtholder, William V,

Prince of Orange. The House of Orange fell in 1795 after the invasion of French revolutionary armies. After 1813, as Napoleon's empire began to shrink, Dutch patriots established a provisional and indigenous government which in turn called William I as their sovereign. At the Congress of Vienna William introduced himself as the king of the United Kingdom of the Netherlands, a title that included rule over Belgium, the historically Roman Catholic sector of the Low Countries. The new constitution granted broad powers to the king, established a two-chambered States-General, and attempted to give equal representation to the northern and southern provinces even though the South (Belgium) outnumbered the North at least three to two, an allotment that Belgians resented.

Religion was another source of resentment. Ruling over the Reformed Protestant North and the Roman Catholic South put William I, a proponent of the Reformed church, in a position where he could satisfy neither side. The constitution separated church and state and guaranteed protection to all religions, but the king was a Protestant, and he supported the Reformed churches by distinguishing between the doctrine and polity of Reformed Protestants. The state would promote and maintain the organization of the Reformed churches but leave doctrinal questions to the churches. The resulting church–state relationship was obviously unacceptable to Roman Catholics, but it was equally objectionable to zealous Reformed Protestants. They wanted the king to return to the order and teaching of the Synod of Dort (1618), where the state was not a neutral bystander to a variety of religious practices but promoted the true religion and suppressed idolatry and blasphemy.

Also offensive to conservative Reformed Protestants was the overhaul of the synodical system that the Reformed churches had used to achieve a modicum of order. The king recognized that the Reformed churches went about their affairs fairly autonomously, according to the governing synods within each of the Netherlands' provinces. This spirit of independence among the provincial churches was one factor in the failure of the Dutch Reformed churches to convene a general synod since that of 1618 at Dort. In order to facilitate a general synod that would ratify and then enforce church order, William I revised rules that governed participation in such a church assembly. Instead of functioning as a representative body that drew from each of the provincial synods, the General Synod of 1816 was a small body of ministers appointed by the king. William I's control of the church, as friendly as it was to the Reformed churches, was unacceptable to many conservative officers and church members, who pined for a Dutch society where the Reformed church was solely responsible – in theory if not in practice – for shaping spiritual and moral norms.

The Secession of 1834 tapped these frustrations with the post-Napoleonic ecclesiastical establishment. Dutch Reformed Protestantism had a long tradition of dissent and these dissenters invariably found ways to remain within the structures of the Reformed churches, resorting to conventicles that encouraged the kind of piety and holiness lacking in the established churches. The devout could remain connected to the national church through the local congregation while receiving spiritual guidance within the pious conventicle. What made the situation different in the 1830s was a growing division between the Dutch elite and the rural commoners, made all the more stark by the disruptions in trade that damaged local farmers and by changing financial and political administration that allowed urban dwellers to prosper. But unlike other Pietists in Protestant lands, some of the most prominent Dutch seceders generally tied their zeal and pursuit of holiness to the official teachings and worship of the Dutch established church, though differences would emerge as the Afscheiding debated its own mission.

The initial leaders of the 1834 Secession were a small band of young ministers. In addition to de Cock and Scholte, a group of theology students at Leiden, influenced by Scholte, also decided to minister outside the national church. These included Anthony Brummelkamp, Simon van Velzen, Albertus Van Raalte, Louis Bähler, and George Gezelle Meerburg. In 1836 they attempted to adopt a church order, but the churches in the southern regions rejected it. By 1844 this group would form its own denomination under the name Gereformeerde Kerk order het Kruis (i.e. Reformed Churches under the Cross). Significant to this division was the nature of church reform that Secession leaders desired. In the North, where de Cock and van Velzen held sway, the hope was for a restoration of Dort's theology and church order with a synod sufficiently powerful to insure uniformity. In the South, however, where Brummelkamp and Van Raalte were influential, the hope was for greater autonomy and authority in local congregations in which members could share warm and experiential forms of Christian devotion. Scholte was the least predictable of the group, and eventually espoused millennialist beliefs about the direction of modern history and the imminent return of Christ to judge decadent Dutch society.

Despite internal divisions, the Afscheiding grew, thanks in part to missteps by the king and the national government that allowed the Secession to become a vehicle for the frustrations of the Dutch people. The government imposed fines on some ministers, expelled others, and employed an old law from the Napoleonic Code that prohibited public gatherings of more than twenty people without prior approval from the civil authorities. Initially, the king and his government refused to recognize the legal status of the Afscheiding on the grounds that the religious dissenters undermined and sowed distrust of the established ministers. Despite the constitution that granted liberty to all faiths, the Afscheiding would have to wait until 1838 before the government began to recognize individual congregations and grant them the legal status to conduct worship. The conditions for legal recognition of a congregation were: submitting a petition for freedom of assembly; rejection of membership by the national church; taking care of its own poor; being entirely self-sufficient; adopting a church order different from Dort's; and submission to the government. These terms indicated that the Afscheiding would have no basis for claiming continuity with the national church (NHK) or for trying to reform the established body. In 1838, when Scholte's group of congregations had adopted the name Christian Seceded Church, the civil authorities forbade Scholte from using the word Reformed in its title. Still, Scholte kept a loyal following. In 1847, to escape a variety of economic and political hardships, Scholte led nearly nine hundred church members to found a colony in Pella, Iowa.

Although Scholte's appeal ran largely in the direction of the Dutch folk piety, his training at the University of Leiden also suggests an elite reaction against the political and religious changes in the Netherlands that paved the way for the Secession. The first intellectual of note to object to the new Dutch order was Nicolas Schotsman (1754–1822), a pastor in the state church at Leiden, whose convictions grew out of the influence of the Réveil that Robert Haldane had instigated in early nineteenth-century Geneva. In 1819, the bicentennial of Dort's conclusion, Schotsman celebrated the anniversary with two published sermons that reaffirmed the orthodox theology of the seventeenth-century Dutch churches and promoted the church polity that had prevailed before the recent constitution. Schotsman's views prompted sharp criticisms from enlightened defenders of the new political order, which in turn drew Willem Bilderdijk (1756–1832) into a pamphlet war with Schotsman's critics. Bilderdijk, the foremost Dutch poet of the time, directed and taught at a theological school in Leiden. Like Schotsman, he regarded the doctrine and polity of Dort as foundational to traditional Dutch society. For Bilderdijk, in fact, traditional Reformed Protestantism represented a bulwark against rationalism, utilitarianism, and revolutionary ideology. His defense of Schotsman persuaded few of the pastor's critics, but it did attract a following that included: Guillaume Groen van Prinsterer (1801–76), secretary of the Cabinet, archivist of the royal records, and an eventual member of parliament; Isaac da Costa (1798–1860), a Jewish poet who had converted while studying law and philosophy in Leiden; and Abraham Capadose (1795–1874), a physician who also converted from his ancestral Jewish faith to Protestantism under the sway of Bilderdijk. These Dutch intellectuals practiced their own form of elite conventiclism, meeting together privately for Bible study, devotion, and reflection on Dutch history and the conditions of their society.

Unlike the Seceders, the peculiar combination of Reformed orthodoxy and Dutch political theory that informed these elite believers was not as threatening to the social order as was the prospect of setting up a rival to the national church. On the one hand, opposition to the philosophy of the Enlightenment led Bilderdijk and Capadose to regard the newer forms of medicine as a deformation thanks to their roots in anti-Christian ideas. This outlook led Capadose to write pamphlets in opposition to vaccinations, a medical discovery that had originated at a time when the false philosophy of the French Revolution was dominant. The medical profession in the Netherlands took great exception to Capadose's arguments, particularly because the critique of vaccinations undermined a concerted effort to wean the Dutch people away from a religious mistrust of science. On the other hand, such opposition to the Enlightenment was welcome news to King William, especially because Bilderdijk's interpretation of Dutch history espoused a divine-right theory of monarchy, including the place of the House of Orange in the glory of the Netherlands, and refuted social-contract theories that laid the basis for democratic society. Da Costa applied his mentor's teaching in a dissertation at Leiden in which he argued that any effort to limit the monarchy's authority was a form of rebellion against God himself. As useful as such an argument might have been for William, however, he frowned on it so as not to alienate the Belgians.

While the arguments of Bilderdijk and his followers generated intellectual sparring, the Réveil circle never contemplated a break with the Netherlands' established institutions; such a division would have been radical, the very stance that Bilderdijk opposed. Groen's attention to the Secession was indicative of the differences between the two groups of Reformed Protestant conservatives. His initial reaction in 1834 was that the Seceders were wrong to leave on the mere suspension of one minister, but after observing the legal penalties inflicted on the Seceders, Groen doubted the merits of the new ecclesiastical order. In 1837 he wrote a memorandum to the king that was published as a separate tract, *The Measures Against the Seceders Tested Against Constitutional Law*. Groen still maintained that the Seceders commended "themselves neither in content nor in tone," but also believed they had a plausible point about the new constitution and its potential for abuse.[1] On the one hand, he argued that the Seceders were correct to detect faults in the new order of the Reformed churches. Changes in the formula of subscription had theological repercussions that truly compromised the integrity of the new church. He also maintained that the people were well within their lawful duties to desire a church that taught sound doctrine. On the other hand, Groen argued that the application of Dutch law to the Seceders – restricting their freedom of assembly – was unconstitutional. His conclusion was to argue not for the soundness of their separation but for their fair treatment before the nation's laws governing religious freedom.

Thanks to Groen's defense, pressure mounted within the national church to restore traditional standards. In the early 1840s Groen himself led a select group of parliament's members in petitioning for stricter rules governing subscription and ordination. Seceders watched these developments carefully and wondered if reform of the established church would obviate the Afscheiding, but efforts to impose greater doctrinal rigor on the Dutch church ultimately failed. The greatest changes came a decade later in 1852, when the king granted the state church independence to govern its own affairs. This revision did little to encourage conservative ministers, because theologically suspect personnel in the synods and at the universities were still in positions of authority. But another change to the church order in 1852 was more significant: the synod gave congregations the power to appoint elders and call ministers. Because this revision appeared to cede too much ground to the democratic spirit of the age, again the orthodox were not as encouraged by reforms as they might have been. Still, over time the greater involvement of congregations in the selection of officers provided room for reformers to nurture a following among average church members and to establish a base for resisting the dominant liberal theology of the synod and the universities.

The rise of a conservative Reformed faction within Dutch Protestantism unleashed forces that would disrupt the Dutch ecclesiastical establishment and prompt a recovery of the Netherlands' historic faith. Because these conservative movements involved definite ideas about the ideal social order at a time when the Netherlands was in flux politically, the Afscheiding and Réveil failed to add up to a coherent set of either religious or political convictions. They were definitely opposed to the French Revolution and the rationalistic philosophy that undergirded it; they also viewed Reformed Protestantism as the source of the Netherlands' original greatness and knew that a return to the old theology was key to the nation's renewal. But they were open to a variety of doctrinal and devotional innovations that did not line up with the ways of the old Dutch Calvinists; especially missing from these conservative developments was a single voice or institution builder that could capitalize on the new circumstances. Conservative Dutch Reformed Protestants in the United Kingdom of the Netherlands were for the most part committed to the theology of the Reformation but were susceptible to innovations coming from pietistic and millenarian Protestantism in other parts of Europe. This combination of recovering traditional Dutch Calvinism and opposition to the French Enlightenment added a strong dose of nationalism to conservative Protestantism. Absent from the Afscheiding and Réveil was anything resembling consensus.

Abraham Kuyper and Neo-Calvinism

The person who came remarkably close to establishing order among the devout Dutch Reformed Protestants was Abraham Kuyper (1837–1920), who was no less remarkable for disentangling the church from the state while also taking over the Netherlands politically, however briefly. Kuyper was the son of a moderately orthodox minister in the national church (NHK), Jan Frederik Kuyper, who had supported the pietistic Dutch Religious Tract Society. The father had a string of pastorates before settling for the bulk of his career at Leiden. His son was born in Maassluis, near Rotterdam, but by the age of twelve was living in Leiden, where in 1855 he enrolled at the university with designs on becoming a pastor. Kuyper studied divinity in Leiden at a time when the university was establishing its own distinct theology, a blend of Friedrich Schleiermacher's stress upon the religion of the heart and higher critical methods for biblical study. This outlook dismissed the old orthodoxy of Dort as rigid and assumed the need for a vital, critical, and modern understanding of Christianity. As an impressionable student Kuyper followed the path trodden by his professors, but he was still pliable. He read a novel, *The Heir of Redclyffe* (1853) by Charlotte M. Yonge, a supporter of the Oxford Movement, which had the effect of producing a conversion experience. While he was still a student, Kuyper completed a dissertation in which he compared the ecclesiology of John Calvin and Jan Laski and found the Polish reformer's views to be more agreeable than the rigid approach of the Frenchman. He left the university to pastor a congregation in Beesd without a grasp of historic Dutch Reformed convictions.

Like de Cock in Ulrum, Kuyper began to acquire a better understanding of traditional Protestantism through the tutelage of his congregation, who knew more conservative theology than their pastor. Some of the malcontents, as they were known, refused to attend Kuyper's services because of their opposition to liberalism in the national church. The pastor wanted to understand these critics better and began to visit them regularly. Over time he recognized a form of Calvinism that was not merely a piece of history, but much more vital and profound than any of the university faculty could imagine. Kuyper's exposure to these devout Dutch Protestants was his first-hand introduction to some of the believers who adhered to the traditions of Dort outside the established church structures, by means of informal conventicles. Meanwhile, Kuyper gained acquaintance with the leaders of the Réveil through his ongoing research on Laski, which had obliged him to request access to the royal archives through the office of Groen van Prinsterer.

These influences paid dividends apparent in Kuyper's next ministerial appointment in 1867 to the Domkerk in Utrecht, a city identified historically

with Reformed orthodoxy and for Kuyper himself a "Zion of God."[2] Kuyper's
newly invigorated preaching, which began to assume the shape of traditional
Reformed theology, drew large crowds and also sharp criticisms from the
moderate and liberal quarters of the national church. He also took an active
interest in the nature and scope of state education, and worked further with
Groen to promote the work of the Dutch Society for Christian Education.
Kuyper's brief against the state schools bore the marks of the Réveil's opposition
to the French Revolution. For Kuyper, the state could not assume a position of
neutrality on questions of faith and unbelief – a philosophical and religious
impossibility. The solution was to create more space for private Christian
schools where faith could permeate the curriculum.

Kuyper lasted only three years in Utrecht, where he became disappointed by
the lack of support from conservative ministers. He took another ministerial call
to a congregation in Amsterdam, where he faced the dilemma that confronted
French farmers after seeing Paris: how to return to the work of a pastor once he
had seen the opportunities of the city. Indeed, the young pastor's tenure in the
Dutch capital gave access not simply to larger audiences but also to the means to
create a whole set of institutions that would nurture his neo-Calvinist outlook.
The first piece of his emerging empire came in the field of journalism. In 1872
he founded the daily newspaper *De Standaard*, which he edited along with
De Heraut, a religious weekly. Both publications became popular and effective
vehicles for propagating the anti-revolutionary principles that Kuyper had
learned from Groen and other Réveil leaders. In contrast to the French
Revolution's ideals of liberty, equality, and brotherhood, the anti-revolutionary
movement countered with "God, the Netherlands, and the House of Orange."
The Netherlands in view for Kuyper and Groen was always the one that traced
its origins to the Protestant Reformation and its codification at the Synod of
Dort. The success that Kuyper enjoyed through his editorials and articles
prompted Groen to cede leadership of the anti-revolutionaries to his younger
colleague, which in turn prompted Kuyper in 1874 to run for parliament. He
won decisively in the district of Gouda and became the second youngest
member of the Second Chamber in The Hague, leading him to resign from his
office as a minister of the Dutch Reformed Church.

Two years into his labors as both editor and minister of parliament Kuyper
suffered a nervous breakdown, but the incident did not diminish his productivity. His collapse came not very long after a trip to England to seek inspiration
from the revival campaigns of Dwight L. Moody and Robert Pearsall Smith, both
of whom taught a version of personal holiness that drew from the perfectionism
popularized by John Wesley during the revivals of the Great Awakening. The
meetings duly inspired Kuyper – as they did delegates from all over Europe and

North America – and he returned to the Netherlands promoting the newfound devotion. But when rumors spread that Smith had been involved in an adulterous relationship during the meetings in England, Kuyper was crushed. His disappointment in Smith was not the sole factor; his non-stop work as an editor and politician also took a toll. Even so, Kuyper later acknowledged that he had mistakenly supported a religious movement that was tainted with Arminianism and that his erroneous support had contributed to his collapse.

After a year in recovery, Kuyper resumed duties in parliament with sufficient strength to tackle one of the wedge issues for the anti-revolutionaries: public education. The dominant liberal party had proposed an educational reform bill that would have consolidated public schools under the oversight of the state and financed them through the government's treasury. The bill drew Kuyper's opposition not so much for the reforms proposed to the existing schools but because it denied any government assistance to private Christian schools. The anti-revolutionaries launched a petition drive against the measure and Kuyper used the bully pulpit of his editorials to solicit support. The petition drew over three hundred thousand signatures, a remarkable figure considering that only half that number were eligible to vote for members of the Second Chamber. In the end, the king signed the bill into law and Kuyper's petition failed, but the effort had popularized the importance of Christian education as an alternative to the state-run schools for devout Calvinists and indicated to anti-revolutionary leaders the kind of success they might enjoy if they formed their own party, which they did in 1879. The school-bill petition also revealed a common area for activism between Protestants and Roman Catholics in defending and seeking support for Christian schools.

As if Kuyper did not have enough to do, he also found time to start a new university. At the start of Kuyper's political career, the Netherlands had three universities: Utrecht, Groningen, and Leiden. The orthodox members of the national church, along with Roman Catholics, lamented the control of the Dutch system of higher education by modernist theology. A new law introduced in parliament and passed in 1876 granted freedom for citizens to establish universities independent of the state, though graduates would still need to pass exams administered by state universities. Two years later, Kuyper participated in a conference sponsored by the Society for Higher Education on the Basis of Reformed Principles. The name proposed was the Free University and its mission was to recover the genius of the Protestant faith that had facilitated Dutch independence from Spain. The proposed institution drew opposition, and some politicians proposed the establishment of chairs of theology at the existing universities that would be dedicated to orthodox professors. But Kuyper again used his journalistic outlets and abilities as a speaker to rally support for the new university, which opened in Amsterdam in the fall of 1880 with Kuyper as its rector magnificus.

Kuyper's opening address was key to understanding most of what he tried to accomplish in the Netherlands, and gave little attention to what the anti-revolutionary principles might mean for Reformed churches. The theme of the address was sovereignty, a subject that touched upon most of the developments in the post-Napoleonic Netherlands. Kuyper appeared to engage in a form of double-speak that came with the territory of elected public officials. But his twofold message, while politically motivated, was an answer to the orthodox demand for a restoration of the Netherlands where Calvinism had flourished and to the realities of a social order and diverse population that was far from a religiously unified nation. On the one hand, Kuyper asserted the lordship of Christ over all aspects of human existence and, true to anti-revolutionary princi-ples, explained the crisis of liberal society as a form of rebellion against Christ the king. The divide between belief and unbelief was all the more poignant with the rise of the nation-state and its sovereign claims over areas of life that belonged only to Christ. "At last the State, embodied in Caesar," Kuyper lamented, "itself became God, the god-State that could tolerate no other states beside itself. Thus the passion for *world* domination." It was also the impulse behind "Hegel's system of the State as 'the immanent God.'"[3]

On the other hand, the proper response to such tyranny was not a rival Christian tyrant but a recognition of the sphere in which Christ had delegated his all-powerful authority, which Kuyper called "the glorious principle of Freedom." Christ's own challenge to "all absolute Sovereignty among *sinful* men on earth" was to divide human existence into spheres. "Just as we speak of a 'moral world,' a 'scientific world,' a 'business world,' the 'world of art,'" he explained, "so we can more properly speak of a 'sphere of morality,' of social life, each with its own domain."[4] Sphere sovereignty would have obvious relevance to the modern university with its various academic subjects and specializations. But it also extended to the social world, such that Kuyper envisioned a real diversity and genuine political liberty in the Netherlands that would nurture, in effect, a Protestant society with its own institutions within the Dutch nation. Instead of asserting the sovereignty of Christ in a way that imposed his authority on all Dutch citizens, Kuyper sought autonomy for Reformed institutions, which in turn would be free to follow their own religious norms. Sphere sovereignty provided a way for Kuyper to contrast the absolute power of the state that did not recognize God as the source of its authority with a Christian understanding of society that protected the freedom and authority of all persons and institutions.

Education was one obvious test for Kuyper's theory, but so was the church. The Free University was a response to alleged liberal neutrality at the level of higher education, but what he and other Anti-Revolutionary Party figures wanted for primary and secondary education was the freedom to establish private schools. The Afscheiding represented a similar form of independence in the sphere of religion, but the Christelijke Gereformeerde Kerk (CGK) of de Cock was too radical and too far removed from the levers of power to be an option for Kuyper. Still, the appeal of sphere sovereignty would finally push him to address his own relationship to the national church. After his journalistic, political, and educational initiatives, Kuyper eventually tackled the problems posed by a national Reformed church that was as complacent about orthodoxy as it was comfortable with its status in the liberal Dutch political order.

The occasion for this phase of Kuyper's career was his appointment in 1882 by the Electoral Commission in Amsterdam to the office of elder as part of the city's consistory. At first his many other duties and his health problems impeded active attendance. But this did not prevent him from establishing what was in effect a conventicle for the city's ecclesiastical administrators where they could gather for fellowship and discussion. The setting also became a place to develop strategies for the formal business of the consistory. One of the first matters requiring attention was another change in the state church's formula of subscription. Already the orthodox party, including the Afscheiding, had objected to the formula legislated in the 1816 Constitution. Instead of subscribing to the Three Forms of Unity (i.e. the Belgic Confession, Heidelberg Catechism, and Canons of Dort) *because* they summarized Scripture, the new language required subscription *in so far as* the doctrinal standards agreed with the Bible. But in 1883 the state church adopted a form of subscription that abolished fidelity to the historic doctrinal statements of the Dutch churches altogether. Now aspiring ministers needed simply to vow "to promote the interests of the Kingdom of God in general and especially those of the State Church."[5] Here was an issue that Kuyper could use to expose the compromised nature of the state churches and to promote a reconfiguration of Reformed Protestants in the Netherlands.

In the spring of the same year, Kuyper organized a conference limited to those officers who expressed hearty agreement with the Three Forms. At this meeting participants resolved a course of action should the National Synod fail to reform the national church. Because the ecclesiastical order of 1816 had subjected the church to the sovereign of the Netherlands instead of to its true king Jesus Christ, the only responsible plan for orthodox congregations who desired to honor their spiritual lord was to sever ties to the state church. Secession was a possibility, but for the time being conference participants determined to appoint acceptable elders and deacons within "grieving" (i.e. Doleantie) congregations, which would wait and hope for reform of the state church.

Thus far in the dispute the historic decentralization of the NHK, no matter the formal authority of the national synod, had worked to Kuyper's advantage. The Consistory of Amsterdam was initially able to act with relative autonomy. The spirit of independence advanced another step on December 14, 1885 – still with no retribution from the national authorities – when the Amsterdam Consistory made adjustments to its church order so that if irreconcilable conflicts arose between the local body and the higher church authorities (either classis or synod), the regional and national jurisdictions would have to recognize the conservative consistory as the true and legal entity, not a set of officers appointed by state officials. This resolution underlined 1869 polity revisions that had authorized the Amsterdam Consistory to administer its properties and finances independently from regional and national oversight. The problem for Kuyper and other conservatives was the presence on the consistory of ministers and elders who were either liberal or indifferent to Kuyper's proposals. Some unconvinced church members also preferred the status quo, occasionally approaching liberal pastors to ask for admission to the national church membership.

This declaration of Amsterdam's independence finally drew fire from higher church authorities. Only a day after the consistory's determination of its own legitimacy the Classical Board for the region met and asserted its sovereignty over the city's congregations. It insisted that the consistory send within two weeks (by January 1, 1886) a copy of its constitution, transcripts of its recent proceedings, and the names of those officers who had voted for the changes in administration. With such a small window in which to respond, the consistory informed the Classical Board that it would supply the requested information but not by the deadline. The board interpreted this response as a further act of defiance, and on January 4, 1886 suspended five ministers, forty-two elders, and thirty-three deacons (out of a total of twenty-six pastors, fifty-three elders, and fifty-seven deacons).

The Classical Board's formal reproach of Kuyper and the other conservatives set off a year-long controversy in which both sides – Kuyper's followers in the Doleantie (grieving churches) and the Classical Board – dug in their heels while appealing their respective cases before the National Synod. In Amsterdam the traditional devout recourse to private conventicles became the vehicle for Kuyper and company to meet for instruction and encouragement without having to participate in the state churches' public worship services. Meanwhile, less patient conservative ministers decided to secede before any verdict. In all, seven congregations declared their independence from the state church, many with ministers who had trained at Kuyper's Free University and most located in the traditional conservative provinces of Frisia and Gelderland. Meanwhile state authorities lined up against Amsterdam's conservatives. On July 1, 1886 the Provincial Board overseeing the Amsterdam churches deposed the city's rebellious officers, and finally, on December 1, 1886, the General (i.e. national) Synod ratified the decision of the Provincial Board.

Kuyper was now deposed but had yet to abandon the hope of reforming the state church. The word "Doleantie" was key to the group's self-identity. The reforming officers and congregations of Amsterdam were not a secession church. They still claimed to belong to the NHK and their departure was provisional for the time being. But they grieved over the state of the national church and were committed to doing as much as possible – especially educating other conservative members – to restore the health of the Dutch church. This stance also included a financial incentive, maintaining property rights and stipends that were part of belonging to the state church. During the first two years after being deposed, Kuyper's conservative peers sponsored a number of conferences and even took steps to put into place a rival synodical body. But this non-seceding strategy became impossible to maintain once the Netherlands' Supreme Court judged Kuyper and his followers to be a separate denomination and therefore lacking all legal claims to church property. The Doleantie churches numbered approximately a hundred thousand members in two hundred congregations.

Because the new communion was committed to the theology and church order of the Synod of Dort, the very same convictions maintained by the CGK (Afscheiding), almost as soon as the Doleantie congregations lost their legal fight leaders from both groups began explore a merger. Despite shared commitments, each church had reasons for remaining separate. The CGK had a longer history, and its leaders believed that Kuyper and his followers should have left the national church earlier, as the Afscheiding had. The CGK had also struggled for decades to gain the legal right to call itself a "Reformed" church; the government had required approval of a church order and constitution before the use of this word. To join with the Doleantie would wipe out years of labor. Furthermore, the Afscheiding had established a theological college in Kampen for training ministers. The CGK plausibly wondered if this school would become peripheral should Kuyper's Free University become another option for ministerial training. One last consideration was influence: many in the CGK wondered if they would be relegated to the sidelines in a communion where Kuyper and his institutions were the prime attractions. On the other side, Doleantie leaders regarded the Secession of 1834 as premature, and the CGK as unwise in its decisions first to leave the state church and later to acquiesce to the government's regulations for recognition of the communion.

Between 1888 and 1892 both sides debated the merits of merger within their respective synods and further differences emerged, most of these stemming from Afscheiding reservations about the Doleantie. One was the authority granted to congregations in Kuyper's church. Here the CGK was objecting to the new Dutch church order of 1852 that had democratized the process of calling and ordination of church officers, which the Doleantie followed within their congregations. A couple of reservations also stemmed from the lack of strictness among the Doleantie. On the one hand, the 1886 separation had been tepid compared to the Secession of 1834: the Afscheiding's reason for leaving was not simply that the national church was deformed but that it was false. Some also wondered about the reliability of the Doleantie congregations themselves, which appeared to be a mixed group thanks to their longer association with the national church. The last concern was a fear that Kuyper had introduced among the Doleantie novel and significantly erroneous doctrines, such as baptismal regeneration. None of these issues was a deal breaker, but they did reveal how distinct the strands of Dutch Reformed conservatism had become.

These differences prevented a handful of the CGK congregations and pastors from entering the merger of the Secession and Doleatie bodies. On June 17, 1892, delegates from each church gathered in Amsterdam to participate in a Uniting Synod which would mark the beginning of the new church. All of the Doleantie's approximately three hundred congregations entered the united communion. On the other side, only three of the almost four hundred Afscheiding congregations stayed out of the merger. These dissenters were able to retain their name without legal haggling. The merged church became the Gereformeerde Kerken in Nederland (GKN). This ecclesiastical reformation was hardly the culmination of Kuyper's life and activities. He still had almost three decades to live and by the turn of the twentieth century his success as a politician would move him into the office of prime minister; in other words, within the larger scope of Kuyper's career, his work as a churchman was secondary. Even so, herding the diverse strands of Dutch Reformed Protestantism into a relatively coherent whole took a man with the stamina, energy, and genius displayed by the indefatigable Kuyper.

International Neo-Calvinism

In 1901 Kuyper became prime minister of the Netherlands, a responsibility that lasted until 1905. To make that appointment possible, his Anti-Revolutionary Party had found common ground with Roman Catholics to form a majority coalition. The wedge issues of state funding for private schools and extending the franchise revealed that Protestants and Roman Catholics could overlook older hostilities for the sake of a principled pluralism that recognized the import of families, schools, and voluntary associations. As successful as Kuyper was as a politician – though his government was by no means free from controversy or insoluble difficulties – the statesman's negotiation of Reformed insularity and the diversity of Dutch public life was fraught with tensions that could readily disrupt the neo-Calvinist movement.

In South Africa the closest affinity between the GKN and African Reformed communions was the development of new Reformed churches in the latter half of the nineteenth century outside the original Cape Colony. The reasons for this tie had less to do with Dutch church history than with the competitive relations between the Dutch and English in the economically attractive South Africa. In 1795 the English had assumed control of the Cape Colony, with the blessing of William of Orange, then in exile in England, to prevent French rule in South Africa. Although the English government's tenure was brief – it lasted until 1802 – it did alter the ecclesiastical landscape. The Dutch Reformed churches remained dominant, but the Church of England established a foothold and evangelists from the London Missionary Society also cut into the Dutch monopoly on religion. When the English returned in 1806 to replace Dutch rule entirely, Dutch Reformed ministers and laity had to adjust to new circumstances ecclesiastically and politically. Eventually, the Reformed churches developed from the established religious body into many Protestant denominations. British rule also brought English as the official language, as well as the abolition of slavery.

Afrikaner farmers (Boers) who were descendants of the original colonists, including Dutch, French, Germans, Scandinavians, and Scots, bristled under English rule. After the abolition of slavery, the Boers initiated the "Great Trek" which saw as many as ten thousand Afrikaners and approximately five thousand of their servants migrate into the interior of South Africa to elude English rule and preserve Afrikaner ways, which included a sharp division between whites and blacks. This migration led by the 1850s to the formation of the Transvaal (or South African Republic) and the Orange Free State as independent political units. The historic Dutch Reformed synods in the Cape Colony refused to approve this migration or the Trekboers' desire to establish new churches. Despite disapproval, the Boers went ahead with their own religious institutions. In 1855 the Afrikaners in the Transvaal established the Nederduitson Hervormed Kerk (Dutch Reformed Church), which would function as the state church in the South African Republic. This communion could not avoid internal controversy, and within a few years a conflict over the use of hymns led to the formation in 1859 of a stricter communion, the Gereformeerde Kerk in Suid-Afrika (Reformed Church in South Africa). As these dates indicate, the divisions among the Dutch in Africa had practically no correlation to the Afscheiding or Doleantie. Although these communions would have looked to the Netherlands for ministers and theological instruction – after the establishment of the Free

University in 1880, many of the ministers in the Transvaal and the Orange Free State came from Kuyper's institution – the creation of new African Reformed denominations stemmed from political circumstances that were distant from those in the Netherlands.

But because of the political prominence of neo-Calvinism in the Netherlands and the ongoing rivalry between the Dutch and the English in South Africa, Kuyper's theology was to have appeal in Africa no matter how illegitimate the appropriation. The two Boer Wars were particularly responsible for cementing ties between the Dutch in Europe and Africa. The first, from 1880 to 1881, was a war for Boer independence after the English expanded their South African colony and annexed the Transvaal. After a negotiated settlement that granted the Republic of South Africa and the Orange Free State autonomy in domestic affairs, the peace could not withstand another attempt by the British to consolidate operations in South Africa, especially after the discovery of diamond mines in Witwatersrand in the Transvaal. A second war lasted from 1889 to 1902 and extended to the first years of Kuyper's tenure as prime minister. Even before holding that office, England's policies in South Africa had roused him from Anglophilic slumbers (based in large measure on Kuyper's understanding of Calvinism's political contribution to freedom and order in the Netherlands, England, and the United States).

In 1899 Kuyper wrote a significant article (originally published in French) in which he defended the practical wisdom and spirit of the Boers' protest against English imperialism. Three years later he traveled to London as prime minister and offered to function as mediator between the British and Boers. Even without Kuyper's intervention a peace treaty brought the second war to an end, but along the way the statesman's version of Calvinism, and particularly his ideas about sphere sovereignty, acquired a following among Afrikaners who were looking for doctrinal justifications for their political and religious independence. The idea that each portion of the created order should follow structural principles divinely given could readily justify the separateness of the Boers from the English. It also underwrote the rationale for apartheid, as the theology of J. D. du Toit (1877–1953), which leaned heavily on Kuyper, revealed. Except for expressing the sort of European superiority that was common in an age of European imperialism and western chauvinism Kuyper himself did not endorse the theology that underwrote the racial segregation practiced in South Africa. But his name and that of Dutch Reformed Protestantism often ran together in the development of conservative Reformed churches and an African social order profoundly divided by race.

In North America, Kuyper's influence would follow the lines laid out in the Netherlands, even if the capacity of his vision to unify disparate conservative forces was to be limited. In 1846 Albertus van Raalte (1811–76) led a group of Dutch immigrants to the United States, where a year later he founded a colony in western Michigan named Holland. Van Raalte was a member of the Afscheiding churches even though his father was a minister in the national church and he had tried diligently to follow in his parent's footsteps. The reasons for the migration were largely economic, but the religious liberties available in the United States also made the journey attractive. By 1848 van Raalte had established a classis that had nine congregations, six ministers, and close to a thousand members.

Conditions on the frontier may have been better than those in the mother country, but the immigrants also sought support from fellow Dutch-Americans, both financial and ecclesiastical. This search led van Raalte to engineer a union between his classis and the Reformed Protestant Dutch Church (later named the Reformed Church in America or RCA), the Reformed communion with roots in the original North American Dutch colony. This merger did not last, owing to the different histories of the two Dutch groups. The older denomination still had harmonious relations with the mother church in the old country, though the American and French revolutions had contributed to important differences among the Dutch Reformed on both sides of the Atlantic. Even more germane for van Raalte's group was the American denomination's lack of familiarity with the Afscheiding. Owing to the differences among Reformed practices – particularly over whether or not to sing hymns, and the importance of Christian schools (Afscheiding concerns) – a significant number of van Raalte's colony in 1857 left the Reformed Protestant Dutch Church to form a separate denomination, the Christian Reformed Church (CRC), despite the founder's disapproval and decision to remain with the older American communion. The first Dutch denomination in the United States could not accommodate the recent Dutch Reformed migration, which combined strict orthodoxy with sober conversion.

The CRC remained a small operation in western Michigan among committed Reformed Protestants who maintained ethnic ties that were as strong as doctrinal convictions. As long as the church remained isolated and grew only through immigration from the Old World – many of its ministers received their training at the Afscheiding seminary in Kampen – its members and pastors worried about accommodations to American society. But between 1885 and 1895 the CRC's membership went from 21,156 to 47,349. Responsible for this increase was an influx of Dutch-Americans from the RCA over the propriety of membership in the Freemasons (the CRC was opposed, as were Dutch Seceders) and new arrivals from the Netherlands. This surge of membership prompted the CRC to reckon with the problem of assimilation. The influence of neo-Calvinists from Kuyper's GKN, along with a heavy dose of the Calvinistic consciousness that Kuyper taught and nurtured, helped the CRC to find its place in the new world. Although American neo-Calvinists had trouble in establishing and nurturing the layers of institutions that Kuyper had created in the Netherlands, the importance of cultivating a Reformed worldview in the young through catechesis and Christian day schools became crucial to the CRC's ethos and success.

Neo-Calvinist models proved to be incapable of binding together Dutch Reformed Protestants in the New World, however, as debates within the CRC after World War I revealed. These debates mirrored the tensions between the Afscheiding and Doleantie that even the accomplished Kuyper had failed to bridge in the Netherlands. As the church that received the bulk of Dutch Reformed immigrants after the 1840s, the CRC held together awkwardly the pious isolation of the Afscheiding and the activist engagement of the Doleantie. That awkwardness became apparent in 1920, when Roelof Janssen, an Old Testament professor at the CRC's Calvin Seminary who had received a PhD from the University of Halle, became the object of scrutiny. His accommodation of critical views of the Hebrew scriptures was objectionable to the orthodox, not simply for questioning the authority of Scripture, the biblical accounts of miracles, and the religious and cultural uniqueness of the Hebrews, but also because his teaching prompted a reconsideration of Kuyper's idea of common grace.[6] According to his critics, Janssen's teaching revealed how common grace could blur the lines demarcating grace and nature, orthodoxy and unbelief, or divine revelation and autonomous reason. The CRC Synod of 1922 deposed Janssen, but since his critics were also increasingly hostile to the doctrine of common grace the controversy over Janssen extended to a debate over the validity of Kuyper's distinction between special and common grace.

One of the most vocal critics, and the prosecutor in the Janssen trial, was Herman Hoeksema, who while writing as editor of the church magazine continued to denounce Kuyper's recognition of the goodness of people and creation apart from special or redeeming grace. By the notion of common grace, Kuyper only meant that common humanity enjoyed the benefits of creation and divinely instituted restraints upon human depravity. This was gracious in the sense of restraining the devastation of human wickedness, not in the sense of redeeming unbelievers. But Hoeksema regarded this outlook as a threat to the uniqueness of salvation. He also believed it was responsible for Kuyper's peculiar notion of presumptive regeneration, the idea that baptized children ought to be counted as Christian until they acted to the contrary. This disagreement tapped an older controversy in the Netherlands that divided theologians along supralapsarian and infralapsarian lines (i.e. whether God chose the elect before or after the Fall). For Kuyper and those who followed his teaching (supralapsarian), regeneration of the elect occurred before creation, and the church and sacraments were means of confirming this eternal decree. For critics like Hoeksema (infralapsarians), many of whose roots were in the Afscheiding tradition where devotion was experiential and personal rather than formal and corporate, regeneration took place in one's lifetime and church members always needed to make their election sure through rigorous piety. Also fueling this debate was the difference between the separatist impulse of the original Afscheiding and the positive engagement advocated by Kuyper and the Doleantie. Those from Afscheiding backgrounds in the CRC wanted the church to preserve its Dutch and Calvinist heritage through isolation, while the Doleantie were comfortable adapting Reformed Protestantism to the circumstances of the United States.

The CRC Synod of 1924 – called the "Common Grace" Synod – resolved the dispute by backing common grace in a restrained manner. On the one hand, the synod affirmed the truth of divine favor to the saved and the lost, gracious restraint of human wickedness, and the value of unbelievers' civic or external righteousness, not as having redemptive merit but still as desirable qualities for daily existence. On the other hand, the synod withdrew from the United States parent Protestant body, the Federal Council of Churches, because of its captivity to liberal theology. It also condemned worldliness by prohibiting dancing, gambling, and the theater. At the same time, the synod ruled that Hoeksema's criticism of common grace conflicted with the teaching of the Reformed creeds and Scripture. When he and other critics of common grace refused to accede to the 1924 ruling, their classes deposed them from the ministry. In response, Hoeksema with a half-dozen other ministers formed in 1925 the Protestant Reformed Church, a communion that provided an additional outlet in North America and another wrinkle to the Afscheiding's legacy.

The tensions within the coalition that Kuyper patched together would also be evident in his own church, though not until several decades after his death in 1920. The loss of a figure with as much energy, charisma, and accomplishment as Kuyper inevitably took its toll on the GKN, where for some the churchman and statesman's outlook had become the hallowed standard. But for a younger generation in the church, Kuyper seemed increasingly dated compared to the vigor and relevance that Karl Barth was bringing to theological discussions among European Protestants.[7] At the same time, the GKN suffered from internal theological disagreements. One concerned a ruling by the 1905 Synod of Utrecht that affirmed Kuyper's particular teaching on presumptive regeneration. As was the case with the Afscheiding descendants in the United States, their Dutch siblings were not enamored with a doctrinal formulation that took a high view of the church and its ordinances at the expense of personal zeal and striving for holiness. For Dutch Reformed who were partial to the conventicle-based piety cultivated by the Nadere Reformatie or the Réveil, assuming that the children of believers were regenerate was a disincentive to personal effort. Another battle that confronted the GKN, similar to the debates over Janssen in the United States, was the question of higher criticism and biblical authority. At the Synod of 1926 – when delegates debated whether the serpent in the Garden of Eden actually spoke to Eve – the GKN affirmed the older understanding that took the first chapters of Genesis not as myth but as history.

One of the critics of higher criticism at the 1926 gathering, Klaas Schilder (1890–1952), would emerge as a lightning rod in the GKN and add another layer to the legacy of Kuyper's neo-Calvinist coalition. He was born and grew up in the Afscheiding stronghold of Kampen, though originally his parents were members of the state church and joined the GKN only when Schilder was a boy. After studying at a Reformed school, Schilder trained for the ministry at the theological college in Kampen. In 1933 he completed a PhD in philosophy at Erlangen, which would lead to his appointment at his alma mater as a professor of theology. But from 1914 on he occupied a series of pulpits in the GKN, achieving a measure of fame after 1928 with his pastorate in Rotterdam. As an editor of the periodical De Reformatie, Schilder gained a hearing beyond his congregations and also acquired a reputation as a provocateur who showed no reluctance in pointing out the GKN's theological deviations. In addition to the errors of Barth and liberal theology, Schilder was particularly critical of the neo-Calvinist outlook on cultural engagement which, in his view, placed life ahead of doctrine and was responsible for the GKN's doctrinal breadth. Like Kuyper's other critics, Schilder viewed presumptive regeneration as a novel error.

Schilder was an outspoken critic of National Socialism at a time when some within the GKN left the Anti-Revolutionary Party to join the Nazis. This political maneuvering was partly a result of the pro-German and Anglophobic sentiments among the Dutch that went back to the hostilities of the Boer Wars. No matter the source of Dutch friendliness to Hitler, Schilder remained an inveterate opponent, and after the German occupation of the Netherlands, his criticisms landed him in prison. Schilder's philosophical analysis led him to conclude that National Socialism's ideological origins were the same as those of Marx and Engels, thus making Germany as radical and dangerous as Russia. This kind of opposition to the Nazis stood in marked contrast to the rest of the Dutch churches, where caution, submission, and silence prevailed. In 1940 the Germans shut down De Reformatie and arrested Schilder, who remained in prison for over four months. Once released, he went back to teaching at Kampen but the Nazis continued to monitor Schilder's movements and teaching. He finally went into hiding to avoid another arrest, and spent the remainder of the war on a farm in the rural Netherlands; not even his closest friends knew where he was.

To add insult to deprivation, Schilder had to learn about the decisions of the 1942 GKN Synod to address lingering doctrinal quarrels second hand. By a close vote – twenty-seven to twenty-four – delegates reaffirmed the 1905 Synod on baptism and presumptive regeneration. When Schilder learned of the decision he wrote to church authorities to state that he could not submit to the decision. Two years later, the synod voted to depose him for insubordination deemed to be schismatic. Eight days after the 1944 Synod's decision, Schilder came out of isolation to meet in The Hague with likeminded ministers, church members, and seminarians. He read a statement that declared independence from the GKN's oppressive leadership. This formed the basis for another secession church, Gereformeerde Kerken in Nederland (Vrijgemaakt) (GKN (Liberated)). Within two years the new communion had grown from sixty-eight pastors and seventy-seven congregations to 216 churches, 152 ministers, and 77,000 communicants.

For all of the problems that attended the neo-Calvinist movement, it was a testimony to the genius of Kuyper and his organizational abilities. Unlike in Scotland, where conservative Presbyterians were generally unified under the aegis of the Kirk, in the Netherlands loose ecclesiastical structures combined with the tradition of informal devotional gatherings made the possibility of consolidating committed Reformed Protestants in a unified communion difficult. Adding to the challenge were competing theological impulses. For a generation or so Kuyper managed to herd the factions of Dutch Reformed Protestantism into a set of institutions that rivaled the existing ecclesiastical and political structures and gave hope to Protestants who longed for a recovery of the Dutch Reformation. To do this, he needed to free the church from the oversight of civil authorities, a process that required reversing the original dependence of Reformation churches on the magistrate. But Kuyper was not content with a sequestered church. He also desired, as Chalmers did, a communion of sufficient stature to recover the original Reformed churches' social and political influence. This meant that Kuyper was as much an activist as a church reformer. Since neo-Calvinists invariably stumbled over the dilemmas posed by public life, the Kuyperian project of cultural renewal and ecclesiastical reform turned out to be no more difficult than coordinating and consolidating the Netherlands' most zealous Reformed Protestants. Even so, for both the Netherlands and Scotland, the path to rejuvenating Calvinism lay in leaving behind the ecclesiastical establishment.

CHAPTER TWELVE

AMERICAN FUNDAMENTALISTS

PRESBYTERIANS IN THE UNITED States had little trouble extricating themselves from compromising entanglements with the civil magistrate. None of the British colonies in North America that were to become the United States had a Presbyterian ecclesiastical establishment. Neither did the Articles of Confederation or the United States Constitution call for church–state relationships that prevented Presbyterians from exercising their convictions regarding the institution and maintenance of a Reformed communion. Some Presbyterians, like the Covenanters, objected to the silence of United States law about the lordship of Christ and so forbade members from voting, serving in the military, or holding public office in a republic that did not acknowledge Christ. But the main branch of American Presbyterians never originally objected to the new political order of the United States. In fact, the Presbyterian Church in the USA on the eve of its first General Assembly in 1789 revised the Westminster Confession's teaching on the civil magistrate: where the original confession had required civil authorities to protect the true church and punish false religions, the American revision taught that rulers had a duty to protect all religious groups.

The separation of church and state as codified in the United States Constitution and affirmed in the revised Presbyterian Confession of Faith did not mean that Presbyterians in the United States were less inclined than their European counterparts to regard the church as a servant of the nation or the nation as a partner in religious mission. US Presbyterians tended to view the War of Independence not simply as just but also as a conflict between the forces of spiritual light and wicked darkness. They also imbibed the heady mix of political theory and Christian theology sometimes known as Christian republicanism. This melange encouraged many US Protestants to believe that the success of their nation depended upon the spiritual health of its citizens. Such an outlook was partly responsible for the Presbyterian Church USA's 1801 decision, codified in the Plan of Union, to cooperate with the Congregationalist churches of New England in planting churches in the Northwest Territory (later added to the political union as the states of Ohio, Indiana, Illinois, Michigan, and Wisconsin). US Presbyterians also participated significantly in the establishment of the so-called Benevolent Empire, a network of religious and humanitarian voluntary associations that the revivals of the Second Great Awakening inspired. This phalanx of pan-Protestant societies was important for securing moral and social order in the new nation through such initiatives as primary education, temperance, and wholesome literature. It was also responsible for giving Presbyterians a stake in the fortunes of the new nation thanks to the mutually reinforcing tasks of religious outreach and moral reform.

By the second quarter of the nineteenth century, a significant element in the North American church began to question the material and formal aspects of the Second Great Awakening. These Old School Presbyterians, as they became known, took exception to the theology that characterized many of the revivals' supporters. The doctrine of the imputation of Adam's sin was central to these debates, with Old Schoolers arguing that subscription to the Westminster Standards involved adherence to imputation and revivalists contending that such an understanding of human nature would undermine incentives for revival. Old School Presbyterians also began to question cooperation with Congregationalists in the Plan of Union and with other Protestants through the voluntary agencies of the Awakening thanks to a heightened commitment to Presbyterian church government. The defense of federal theology and *jure divino* Presbyterianism led Old School Presbyterians in 1837 to abrogate the Plan of Union, reject interdenominational cooperation, and exscind twenty-eight presbyteries and over five hundred ministers, most of whom were in areas (New York and Ohio) where the revivals had been strongest.

The Presbyterians whom the Old School banished were known, appropriately, as New School. Forceful figures in their ranks included Lyman Beecher, a Boston Congregationalist who became president of the Presbyterian seminary in Cincinnati (Lane), and Albert Barnes, a popular preacher and Bible expositor in New York and later in Philadelphia. Each of these figures held views on the atonement (an example of God's displeasure) and the nature of sin (individual acts versus corporate guilt) that drew fire from Presbyterians who adhered to the Westminster Confession of Faith. New School theology did provide a rationale for the revivals of Charles G. Finney, since he too stressed the power of individuals to choose Christ. This outlook also underwrote the social activism of the Second Great Awakening by encouraging Americans to do all in their power to live lives of holiness. New Schoolers hoped and prayed that, if enough people would freely choose to follow Christ and lead moral lives, the

United States could usher in the kingdom of God. For them, the Old School insistence on the truth of historic Reformed teaching or the necessity of Presbyterian procedure was an impediment to the power of Protestants from all denominations to build a righteous society together.

The collision between these two versions of New World Presbyterianism in the 1830s coincided with controversies in the Netherlands and Scotland that also involved efforts by Free Church Presbyterians and the Afscheiding to extricate the spiritual mission of the church from the social programs of the state. Old School theologians, such as James Henley Thornwell in South Carolina, Robert Lewis Dabney in Virginia, Charles Hodge in New Jersey, and Stuart Robinson in Kentucky, injected into American Presbyterianism a strong dose of self-consciousness. They argued that the church had a unique commission to perform a task that was essentially spiritual in nature. At the same time they contended that to execute this mission the church had specific means through the ordained ministry and oversight of ministers and elders meeting in delegated assemblies.

This Old School sensibility flourished for roughly a generation but became marginal among US Presbyterians after the 1869 reunion of the Old and New School churches. It continued to inform the teaching at different Presbyterian seminaries. When controversies at the beginning of the twentieth century over biblical criticism and evolution drove American Protestants into fundamentalist and modernist camps, the Old School Presbyterian doctrine of the spirituality of the church became a casualty in the polemics that aggravated Presbyterians. But it was a crucial factor in the thought of J. Gresham Machen, a professor of the New Testament at Princeton Theological Seminary, who led conservative Presbyterian opposition to theological modernism. His reliance on and defense of the spirituality of the church and Presbyterian polity provoked another secession among modern Reformed Protestants. It was neither as large as those led by Chalmers or Kuyper, nor did it involve withdrawing from the patronage of the state. It did mean the abandonment of aspirations to be part of an informal ecclesiastical establishment, however, known in the United States as the mainline Protestant churches. Even if Machen's secession added only one more name to the handbook of United States denominations, it was similar to those of Chalmers and Kuyper in displaying a willingness to reject cultural prestige for clarity of purpose.

Reunion and Union

At the beginning of the 1860s, as citizens of the United States were dividing along sectional lines in preparation for civil war, Presbyterians themselves were split theologically and regionally. The New School Presbyterians broke apart first, as a result of an issue that was alienating the northern United States from the southern. In 1857, after repeated efforts by the General Assembly to establish committees to investigate the practice of slavery and its effects on southern Presbyterians, a small minority of the New School resolved to form a separate communion, the United Synod of the Presbyterian Church, for Presbyterians who defended slavery in principle. Four years later, the Old School Presbyterians also divided, and by then the question was whether or not to support the federal government's efforts to maintain the union of the United States and go to war against southern states that had begun to secede from the nation after the attack on Fort Sumter in Charleston, South Carolina. A resolution before the 1861 General Assembly by the New York pastor, Gardiner Spring, called upon the Old School communion to endorse the federal government, a motion that clearly confronted ministers from South Carolina as well as other southern states with the dilemma of ministering in a church whose politics were seditious in the South. To resolve the dilemma, southern Old School Presbyterians withdrew into a distinct communion with 10 synods, 45 presbyteries, 840 ministers and approximately 72,000 communicant members. Consequently, at the beginning of the Civil War, the major branch of Presbyterianism in the United States was divided into four separate communions: Old School and New School, in both the north and the south.

But by the end of the 1860s these divisions were beginning to heal, and the politics of preserving the nation's union were an important ingredient in ecclesiastical cooperation. Southern Presbyterians led the way in 1867, with the Old School communion absorbing the three synods of the New School that had operated within the bounds of the Confederacy. Some Old Schoolers opposed union because of lingering theological suspicions, but the merger prevailed thanks to hopes that a united southern church would give Old School theology the upper hand and eventually extinguish New School sentiments. The united church became the Presbyterian Church in the US (PCUS). In 1869 northern Presbyterians followed suit and overcame theological objections from a minority of conservatives to unite as the Presbyterian Church in the USA (PCUSA).

In the case of northern Presbyterians, the ideals of political integration clearly contributed to the reasons for ecclesiastical union. The report that recommended union of the northern Old and New Schools recognized the nation's need for a unified Presbyterian church:

The changes which have occurred in our own country and throughout the world, during the last thirty years – the period of our separation – arrest and compel attention. Within this time the original number of our States has been very nearly doubled.... The population crowding into this immense area is heterogeneous. Six millions of emigrants, representing various religious and nationalities, have arrived on our shores within the last thirty years; and four millions of slaves, recently enfranchised, demand Christian education. It is no secret that anti-Christian forces – Romanism, Ecclesiasticism, Rationalism, Infidelity, Materialism, and Paganism itself – assuming new vitality, are struggling for the ascendency. Christian forces should be combined and deployed, according to the new movements of their adversaries. It is no time for small and weak detachments, which may easily be defeated in detail. . . . Before the world we are now engaged, as a nation, in solving the problem of whether it is possible for all the incongruous and antagonistic nationalities thrown upon our shores, exerting their mutual attraction and repulsion, to become fixed in one new American sentiment. If the several branches of the Presbyterian Church in this country, representing to a great degree ancestral differences, should become cordially united, it must have not only a direct effect upon the question of our national unity, but, reacting by the force of a successful example on the Old World, must render aid in that direction, to all who are striving to reconsider and readjust those combinations, which had their origin either in the faults or the necessities of a remote past.[1]

The Presbyterians responsible for this report were not guilty of overestimating the effects of their reunion on the rest of the United States, since while the Old School and New School were combing through the fine print of merger plans, other Presbyterians were also involved in establishing closer ties among US Protestants. In 1867 an American branch of the British society, the Evangelical Alliance, attracted Protestants from other Anglo-American denominations to work with it. It had started in London in 1846 – thanks in part to the efforts of the Free Church leader, Thomas Chalmers – to bring greater cooperation among Protestants both within and outside the Church of England. The appeal of and need for the Alliance became apparent to Americans after their Civil War precisely because of the belief that Protestantism was crucial to the preservation of a free and Christian society. The Evangelical Alliance did not sponsor many specific activities beyond supplying American Protestants with information about threats to the character of their nation. The list of perils included materialism, infidelity, and socialism, and extended to specific evils such as the saloon, threats to the home and motherhood, and Sabbath desecration. The subtext for particular vices was Roman Catholicism, and leaders of the Alliance had little trouble in naming Romanism as a threat to Christian civilization as great as atheism. The danger posed by Rome was evident to cooperative Protestants thanks to changing demographics in the United States, where large influxes of immigrants after the Civil War brought waves of Roman Catholics that appeared even more menacing than the arrival of Irish and Germans during the 1840s and

1850s. Beyond the composition of the American population, Rome's threat loomed large after the First Vatican Council in 1870. Here the doctrine of papal infallibility gained formal acceptance among Roman Catholics; for many American Protestants, cooperation and consolidation were necessary if they were to rival Rome's reinvigorated unity and authority.

The support for ecumenicity and Christianizing the social order in the United States drowned out scientific and theological challenges that might have sapped Protestant confidence. During the decades that Presbyterians facilitated interdenominational cooperation they also witnessed heated debates over new ideas in the academy, namely, Charles Darwin's arguments about natural selection and new historical research on the text and reception of the Old and New Testaments (i.e. higher criticism). In the southern church (PCUS), James Woodrow (the uncle of Woodrow Wilson), professor of natural theology at Columbia Seminary in South Carolina, drew fire for efforts to reconcile evolution and Old Testament accounts of creation. Although his presbytery and the synods that controlled the seminary acquitted Woodrow of heresy charges, he lost his faculty post (only to land on his feet at president of the University of South Carolina), even while retaining his credentials as a minister. In response to Woodrow's views, the southern church at its 1886 General Assembly declared by a vote of 137 to 13 that Adam was not a descendant of animals but the direct creation of God.

In the northern church (PCUSA), Presbyterians debated the reliability of Scripture in the light of modern scholarship. Charles A. Briggs, an Old Testament professor at Union Seminary (an institution formed in 1836, which was clearly in the New School camp), denied the verbal inspiration of the Bible and argued for a greater role for reason in theological reflection. Benjamin B. Warfield, a theologian at Princeton Seminary, opposed Briggs by arguing for the inerrancy of Scripture in a way that tried to account for its divine and human aspects by arguing that its divinity made the Bible authoritative and its humanity gave it intelligibility. In response to Briggs, the northern church affirmed the doctrine of biblical inerrancy in 1892, and a year later dismissed him from the ministry. Briggs retained his position at Union thanks in part to the seminary's decision to become a school independent of the church.

Some Presbyterian conservatives who also opposed the most alarming features of Darwinism and higher criticism, such as Warfield, objected to their church's involvements in the wider ecumenical world. Still, leaders of Protestant ecumenism, such as Philip Schaff, a professor of church history at the German Reformed school, Mercersburg Seminary, before joining the faculty at Union Seminary in New York City, helped to create other outlets for cooperation. Many southern Presbyterians who were still resentful over the outcome of the Civil

War resisted cooperation. They also argued that the substance of their doctrinal and ecclesiastical convictions would not allow cooperation with non-Presbyterians. The remedy was the Presbyterian Alliance, founded in 1877 as a Reformed equivalent to the Evangelical Alliance. The Presbyterian Alliance's rhetoric did not differ substantially from the earlier organization but it did signal a desire among ecumenical leaders for a union of Presbyterian bodies as a means toward a unified Protestant communion. One indication of this goal was the 1906 merger of the Presbyterian Church USA and the Cumberland Presbyterian Church. This union took some time to achieve thanks to doctrinal differences between the two communions. The Cumberland church had started in 1810 owing to a rejection of the predestinarian Calvinism and federal theology in the Westminster Confession. In order to overcome this theological chasm, northern Presbyterians spent the better part of the 1880s and 1890s considering a revision of their confession of faith. Once accomplished, with the addition in 1903 of chapters on the Holy Spirit and the Love of God which were designed to soften the hard edges of Calvinism, the merger was possible, thus adding another group of Presbyterians to the widening coalition of united Protestants.

The culmination of postbellum ecumenism in the United States was the formation in 1908 of the Federal Council of Churches. The stated clerk of the Presbyterian Church USA, William H. Roberts, was also the first acting president of the newly formed Council. Another tie to the Presbyterian Church was the use of the Witherspoon Building, a modern high rise in downtown Philadelphia that amounted to the national headquarters for the Presbyterian Church. This structure served as the registration hall for the delegates arriving from roughly thirty different denominations to respond to the need for interdenominational cooperation "for the moral and spiritual welfare of the nation and of the world."[2] Aside from the services rendered by Presbyterians, the initial meeting of the Council in Philadelphia, the nation's first capital, was significant. As E. R. Hendrix, Bishop in the Methodist Church, explained after taking over the presiding functions from Roberts:

> I count it a very suggestive historical parallel that we meet in this goodly city of Philadelphia, where the Liberty Bell rang out with the inscription upon it, "Proclaim liberty through all the land and to the inhabitants thereof." ... I count it a very interesting historic parallel, my brethren, that in Philadelphia there has been already formed, registered and shaped, in large measure, the Federal Union, not of thirteen separate states, feeble in resources and weak in population, but the Federal Union of thirty-three great Christian Churches, aggregating in number of communicants nearly eighteen millions, – six times

the original number of souls gathered together in our American Union more than a hundred years ago.[3]

This was the same city, according to Hendrix, which heard the nation's first martyred president, Abraham Lincoln, say, "God bless all the churches and blessed be God that in this time of peril giveth us the churches." These inspiring and patriotic precedents led Roberts to conclude that if the Federal Council were to be of any value or significance, it would need to proclaim "the manliness of Christ, the 'strong Son of God,'" and so make "this great nation mighty in cooperation."

Thank God, in this assembly to-day the nation through its representative Churches sees eye to eye. No longer any North, no longer any South, but one United Nation, one flag over all. Let it be ours to sustain that flag and to see to it that wherever that flag goes our holy religion goes, in every part of the world.[4]

With such political and religious motivations echoing through Philadelphia's Academy of Music where the Council convened, the delegates turned to the business at hand. Their first act was to create and adopt a new creed. But this was no set of theological or liturgical affirmations; it was in fact a social creed that attempted to show the relevance of a common Protestant faith for the well-being of the United States. The "Social Creed for the Churches" did not descend to the level of policy or legislation. It highlighted, instead, the need for the churches to respond to the social unrest generated by the disputes between big business and organized labor. The new creed was moderate ("gradual and reasonable reduction of the hours of labor to the lowest practicable point, and for that degree of leisure for all which is the condition of the highest human life"), idealistic ("equal rights and complete justice for all men in all stations of life"), and generically religious ("a release from employment one day in seven").[5]

Presbyterians in the United States were no more prone to the excesses of nationalism and civil religion than the other denominations that in 1908 sent delegates to Philadelphia. At the same time, Protestants in the United States were no less tempted to adapt their convictions to the needs of their nation. Indeed, the nationalistic urge among Presbyterians in the United States is all the more remarkable considering that Reformed Churches in Europe modified their teachings and practices in order to retain the support of their governmental patrons and their status as part of the political establishment. Even without the demands from the United States government, the nation's Protestants, according to one historian, "felt responsible for America: for its moral structure, for the religious content of national ideals, for the educative and welfare functions that government would not ... carry out."[6] Questioning the connections between Protestant beliefs and national identity would prove to be almost as difficult as the disentanglements attempted in Scotland and the Netherlands.

The Presbyterian Controversy

J. Gresham Machen (1881–1937) was an unlikely field marshal in the 1920s conflict that would divide American Presbyterians. Since 1906 he had taught New Testament at Princeton Theological Seminary, first as an instructor, and then after 1914, once he resolved doubts about becoming ordained to the ministry, as an assistant professor. Machen's misgivings stemmed in part from his cultural background and previous education. The son of a prominent Baltimore attorney and a graduate of Johns Hopkins University with a Bachelor's and Master's in Classics, Machen saw the ministerial credentials necessary for teaching at a seminary as an awkward barrier to his intellectual interests and social standing. A degree from Princeton and a year of advanced study with some of Germany's leading biblical scholars failed to quell these misgivings. But friendships made at Princeton and associations with former professors helped Machen to resolve his vocational dilemma. Even then, in 1918, during World War I, he took an assignment as a secretary with the YMCA in France, leading Bible studies and running a canteen, out of some frustration with the distance between academic work and active life. He returned from Europe, shaken by the horrors of modern warfare, just in time to prepare lectures for students and faculty at Union Seminary in Richmond. His subject was the title of his first book, *The Origin of Paul's Religion* (1921), a systematic critique of naturalistic accounts of the apostle Paul's ministry.

Machen also returned to the United States in time to hear the proposal that was the culmination of Protestant hopes since the Civil War for a united church and a Christian nation. After the war, Protestant leaders believed that their cooperative activities during the war pointed to the possibility of an organic union of the nation's largest denominations. Unlike a federation, where each denomination retained its own prerogatives, an organic union called for a single Protestant body. Presbyterians again played leading roles and brought the plan to the General Assembly of 1920 where Machen was a first-time commissioner. He was stunned when the president of Princeton Seminary, J. Ross Stevenson, who served on the Committee for Organic Union, presented the plan to the assembly. Although the plan failed (a similar effort among Presbyterians, Anglicans and Methodists in Canada would succeed), the US proposal alarmed conservatives, and the assembly of 1920 planted the seeds of a struggle. The specific issue was whether Presbyterians, thanks to their theology and polity, retained a mission distinct from other Protestant churches, or whether by virtue of a generic Protestantism they could unite with other communions to Christianize America. This question would absorb the Presbyterian Church's energies for the better part of two decades.

American Presbyterians also had several other matters to consider during the tumultuous decade of the 1920s. From the left came objections to dogmatism and intolerance. Harry Emerson Fosdick, a popular Baptist minister who functioned as stated supply at the First Presbyterian Church in New York City, preached a controversial sermon in May of 1922: "Shall the Fundamentalists Win?" His contention – that the doctrines of biblical inerrancy and the second coming of Christ were mere "peccadillos" compared to the weighty problems of international peace – attracted numerous and vociferous objections from conservatives. Eventually, the Presbytery of New York was forced to ask Fosdick to step down from his role at The First Presbyterian Church. New York Presbyterians attributed the problem to the anomaly of a Baptist ministering outside the bounds of his denomination. From the right came objections to Darwinism in the schools and alcohol in the wider society. William Jennings Bryan, an elder in the Presbyterian Church USA, and arguably its most famous church member thanks to three unsuccessful runs for the United States presidency and his role as the lead prosecutor in the Scopes Trial (which resulted in the conviction of a Tennessee public school teacher for teaching evolution) peppered his denomination with proposals to insure that Presbyterian ministers and agencies remained free from the taint of evolution and drunkenness.

Machen wrote critically of Fosdick and was reliable enough for Bryan to invite him to testify at the Scopes Trial (an invitation Machen declined), but his major contribution to the Presbyterian and fundamentalist controversies was his book *Christianity and Liberalism* (1923). Its thesis was as simple as it was provocative: Christianity and liberalism were two entirely different religions, and as such Christians and liberals could not remain together in the same communion. Most of the book was an effort to prove that liberalism departed from historic Christianity by comparing its tenets to those of the church. Machen's outline mirrored the topics of systematic theology: God, man, Scripture, Christ, salvation, and the church. In each case, liberalism departed from any meaningful definition of Christian orthodoxy. But he was no less critical of the utilitarian appropriation of Christianity by Protestant ecumenists for social progress:

> ... religion is discovered after all to be a useful thing. But the trouble is that in
> being utilized religion is also being degraded and destroyed. Religion is being
> regarded more and more as a mere means to a higher end. ... The persons who

speak in this way usually have little interest in religion for its own sake; it has never occurred to them to enter into the secret place of communion with the holy God. But religion is thought to be necessary for a healthy community; and therefore for the sake of the community they are willing to have a church.[7]

Machen's controversial book generated a wide audience, partly owing to the unintended publicity he gained when Henry van Dyke, professor of literature at Princeton University and former United States ambassador to the Netherlands, in reaction to a Machen sermon gave up his pew at the First Presbyterian Church, Princeton, and held a press conference about his decision to do so. The Princeton Seminary professor became a staple among newspaper editors and conference organizers who were looking for the "fundamentalist" side on a given topic. Machen also received favorable comments from some of the nation's leading columnists such as H. L. Mencken and Walter Lippmann for clearly identifying the issues dividing the Protestant churches. But although Machen attempted to write a general account of the source of controversy, *Christianity and Liberalism* spoke directly to the Presbyterian Church USA and the question of whether the church could cooperate or affiliate with other Protestant denominations. The book itself stemmed from a series of talks that Machen gave to conservative Presbyterian audiences while trying to increase opposition to the 1920 plan for organic union. Furthermore, his discussion of the function of creeds in the Protestant churches indicated the chief reason for opposing Protestant ecumenism. The ecumenists (both liberal and fundamentalist) proposed a doctrinal basis for unity that neglected the particular tenets of creedal churches. Whether desirable or not, Machen observed, ordination in the Presbyterian Church required subscribing the Westminster Confession of Faith and Catechisms. This situation put liberal Presbyterians in an admittedly awkward position: "Finding the existing 'evangelical' churches to be bound up to a creed which he does not accept, he may either unite himself with some other existing body or else found a new body to suit himself."[8] At the same time, if the existing creeds exposed the radical character of liberalism, evangelical doctrines also stood as obstacles to interdenominational cooperation.

The publicity surrounding Fosdick's sermon, Machen's book, and Bryan's crusade against Darwinism would not have provoked sustained controversy and institutional deliberation were it not for the Presbytery of New York's ordination of two candidates who could not affirm the virgin birth of Christ. In 1922, two recent graduates of Union Seminary (New York), Henry P. Van Dusen and Cedric O. Lehman, gained approval from the presbytery for ministry, despite their reservations about certain doctrines. This happened at a time when New York was already under close scrutiny.[9] Compounding the problem for New

York Presbyterians was the General Assembly's repeated insistence that the virgin birth was an essential and necessary doctrine within the confession of faith. Going back to debates over higher criticism during the 1890s, the Presbyterian Church had in 1892, 1910, and 1916 affirmed and reaffirmed five doctrines, including the virgin birth, as necessary for holding office. The assembly that met in 1923 was not inclined to change this. In response to the unsettling state of affairs in New York, it again insisted that the virgin birth was non-negotiable. This left one of the most progressive and wealthiest sectors of the denomination, comprised of the Presbytery of New York City and the Synod of New York, on a collision course with the General Assembly, which was by no means controlled by fundamentalists but was quite unprepared for what liberals proposed. "The Auburn Affirmation" (1923), a document written and circulated by ministers and faculty predominantly from the Synod of New York, was indicative of the escalating differences. The Affirmation called for tolerance and charity in the Presbyterian Church by allowing for a variety of interpretations of the confession of faith.

The growing divide between conservatives and liberals came to a head in 1925 at the General Assembly, which saw another Princeton Seminary professor, Charles R. Erdman, selected as moderator. The man who taught practical theology to the students learning the New Testment under Machen was a good barometer for the mind of the Presbyterian Church. He was an evangelical, friendly to the world of revivalism and Bible conferences, but did not follow the church's theological standards rigorously. More important, he was not inclined to force anyone out of the church, whether on the left or the right. When the 1925 assembly voted to reaffirm the virgin birth as an essential and necessary article of the Christian faith – in response to the situation in New York – the commissioners followed Erdman's own convictions about the fundamentals of the faith. But like many other evangelicals in the denomination, Erdman did not want to lose liberals. Consequently, when commissioners from the Presbytery of New York City and the Synod of New York threatened to secede from the denomination, Erdman intervened as moderator. He established a committee, the Special Commission of 1925, and gave it the task of assessing the cause of controversy in the Presbyterian Church and recommending a course of action.

The Special Commission worked diligently over the course of the next year. In an effort to be fair and balanced, the committee interviewed prominent figures on both sides of the controversy. On the right were Machen and Clarence Macartney, a pastor from Philadelphia; from the other side came testimony by Henry Sloane Coffin, a pastor in New York City, and William Adams Brown, professor of theology at Union Seminary (New York). The committee's report followed in two installments, one for the assembly of 1926 and the next at the

subsequent General Assembly. Without naming names, the committee attributed less blame for the controversy to liberals than to conservatives, who were
guilty of issuing "misjudgments and unfair and untrue statements which have
been made in speech and in printed publications." For peace and purity to prevail
in the church, the committee argued, "all slander and misrepresentation must be
brought to an end."[10] The committee's recommendations posed a real threat to
conservatives. "Public expression of hasty or harsh judgments of the motives of
brethren whose hearts are fully known only to God" should be prohibited. Even
beyond the matter or manner of judging others was the committee's desire to
rally the resources of the Presbyterian Church for the advance of God's kingdom
around the world. "With resourceful America on one side of the globe," the
committee's report concluded, "and, on the other, contemplative India and
progressive Japan and seething China, there flame before the faces of men the
signal fires of a Providential purpose."[11] The ideals of cooperation and unity for
the sake of social wellbeing were still dominant among American Presbyterians.

Also pronounced among American Presbyterians was a strong identification
between the health of their nation and the blessings of their faith. One sign of
this relationship was the Presbyterian Church's support for Prohibition. Even
without William Jennings Bryan's constant lobbying – he died in 1925, only days
after the conclusion of the Scopes Trial – the Presbyterian Church regularly
passed resolutions at both the national and local levels in support of United
States law banning the sale and distribution of alcohol. In 1926 the pro-
Prohibition outlook had direct consequences for Machen. The Presbytery of
New Brunswick (New Jersey) where he was a member passed a motion to
support the federal government's policy. Machen voted "no" but did not protest
any further. His understanding of the church was that it could speak only on
matters revealed in Scripture, and because neither bans on alcohol nor the
authority of the federal government were clear from the Bible, Machen opposed
any effort that might turn the church into a political lobby or an agency of the
police. But his doctrine of the spirituality of the church was lost on many of his
fellow Presbyterians. At the General Assembly of 1926, which as part of its business had to review a recommendation from Princeton Seminary to promote
Machen to the vacant chair of apologetics and ethics, commissioners decided to
postpone the promotion. The reason was Machen's vote against Prohibition:
some commissioners wondered how a man who failed to recognize the evils of
alcohol could teach Christian morality.

The decision to postpone Machen's appointment was a product of more than
simply the pious fears of the saloon; it was also an indication of ecclesiastical
political maneuvering at the Presbyterian Church's oldest seminary. Princeton
Seminary had been established in 1812 and was under the direct oversight of the

assembly, unlike other institutions that were the creations of synods. During the 1920s Princeton became a piece of denominational machinery coveted by both sides in the struggle. For conservatives it was the last vestige of the Old School Presbyterian theology taught by the likes of Archibald Alexander, Charles Hodge, and Benjamin Warfield. For liberals and some evangelicals, Princeton became a roadblock to greater unity and more effective outreach by the Presbyterian Church. President J. Ross Stevenson's support for the 1920 Plan of Union and Charles Erdman's establishment of the Special Commission of 1925 indicated that some members of the faculty at Princeton were open to moving the seminary away from its Old School course and onto a moderate road of unity and progress. The decision to delay Machen's promotion at Princeton was a further indication of efforts to bring the seminary into the denomination's mainstream. That effort became explicit when the 1926 assembly also approved the appointment of a committee to investigate the differences among members of the faculty at Princeton. This committee was essentially an extension of the Special Commission of 1925. It eventually recommended an administrative overhaul, which increased the president's power and diluted the authority of the board of directors (a largely conservative body) by merging it with the board of trustees. Legal objections delayed the reorganization for two years but it finally took place in 1929.

By this point, Machen had abandoned Princeton and decided to start an independent Presbyterian seminary in response to the reorganization. He was frustrated by church politics and string-pulling by remote denominational bureaucrats. He also had considerable means to initiate such a venture, despite economic upheaval worldwide, thanks to wealth inherited from both parents. Machen had a following among Presbyterian conservatives and fundamentalist Protestants; during the years after the publication of *Christianity and Liberalism* enrollments at Princeton spiked (though many new students were not from Presbyterian backgrounds). He rallied ministers and presbyteries in southeastern Pennsylvania, a stronghold of conservative congregations, and launched Westminster Theological Seminary from its center-city campus in Philadelphia. As Machen explained at the new seminary's convocation, held at the Witherspoon Building, the very place where delegates to the Federal Council of Churches' first meeting had registered:

Fifty years ago many colleges and universities and theological seminaries were devoted to the truth of God's Word. But one by one they have drifted away, often with all sorts of professions of orthodoxy on the part of those who were responsible for the change. Until May 1929 one great theological seminary, the Seminary at Princeton, resisted bravely the current of the age. But now that

seminary has been made to conform to the general drift.... [T]hough
Princeton Seminary is dead, the noble tradition of Princeton Seminary is alive.
Westminster Seminary will endeavor by God's grace to continue that tradition
unimpaired; it will endeavor, not on a foundation of equivocation and compromise but on an honest foundation of devotion to God's word . . .[12]

The new seminary was the only institutional base for conservative
Presbyterians, but its effectiveness was questionable once Machen embarked on
the second phase of ecclesiastical independence. In 1932 the report from an
interdenominational project, *Re-Thinking Missions: The Laymen's Foreign Missions
Inquiry*, was published. The largest Protestant denominations co-sponsored the
study, while John D. Rockefeller underwrote actual expenses. The report,
written by William Ernest Hocking, a professor of philosophy at Harvard
University, contained the committee's recommendations but could not avoid
objections from evangelical and conservative Protestants. The purpose of the
study was to arrive at a new motive for foreign missions in response to growing
indifference and declining contributions. The committee narrowed its scope to
missions in Asia. Hocking's report highlighted changes in theology and science
over the previous five decades that undercut the old rationale for missions,
namely, saving sinners from eternal damnation. It proposed instead some fundamental spiritual and moral ideals that Christianity shared with other world religions and recommended cooperation between Protestant missionaries and
indigenous religious institutions. The report also addressed the perennial tension
between a western expression of Christianity and the place of indigenous culture
after evangelization. Now that missionaries needed to be concerned less with
questions of heaven and hell than previous generations, they could devote their
energies to those educational, economic, and medical enterprises that would
build a better world. In *Re-Thinking Missions* the liberal Protestant notion of the
kingdom of God advancing through the spread of western civilization was less
Eurocentric than it had been prior to World War I. But Hocking's understanding
of cultural improvement still depended on western notions of civilization.

The report on foreign missions reignited conservative Presbyterian arguments about the dangers of theological liberalism and gave plausibility to their
objections to the indifference of denominational officers. The Presbyterian
Church USA had been a co-sponsor of *Re-Thinking Missions* but was no more
responsible for the report than any of the other participating communions.
Ignoring critics became much more difficult when Pearl S. Buck, the author of
the Pulitzer Prize-winning novel *The Good Earth*, daughter of Presbyterian
missionaries to China, and a woman on the Presbyterian Church's missionary
rolls, welcomed the report's findings. In a couple of magazine articles and public

talks, Buck expressed relief that missions could finally proceed without outdated, crude theological formulas. Opposition to the report and objections to Buck's remarks would eventually force her resignation from the Presbyterian missions board. But the church's officials refused to condemn either her words or Hocking's report to a degree that would satisfy conservatives. Machen was one of the conservatives to take issue with the church's Board of Foreign Missions and drafted an overture in 1933 that called for reform of the agency. The Presbytery of New Brunswick failed to act on this proposal, but the Presbytery of Philadelphia did adopt Machen's overture and sent it to the General Assembly. When the commissioners rejected the proposed reforms, Machen countered with the creation of a new foreign missions agency: the Independent Board for Presbyterian Foreign Missions.

Presbyterian officials may have been reluctant to condemn Buck and Hocking but they had no trouble spotting Machen's errors. The General Council of the General Assembly found that the new missions board was unconstitutional, arguing that contributing to the official agencies of the denomination was as much a requirement for church members as the Lord's Supper. In turn, the General Assembly of 1934 adopted the Council's study of the Presbyterian Church's constitution and ruled that the Independent Board was illegal. It also instructed all presbyteries with members of the board on their rolls to bring those board members to trial. In 1935, the Presbytery of New Brunswick complied and tried Machen in Trenton, New Jersey, before a crowd of his supporters and newspaper reporters. The charges ranged from a violation of his ordination vows and defiance against the church's lawful authority to contempt for his superiors in the church. One of the more amazing aspects of this trial, aside from the irony of liberals conducting an ecclesiastical proceeding that many Americans associated with the Middle Ages, came when Machen's counsel tried to defend the Westminster professor. Before the defense could begin, the Presbytery of New Brunswick's judicial council ruled that it could hear no testimony that questioned the General Council's interpretation of the church's constitution or its determination that the Independent Board was illegal. When Machen told reporters that he had been condemned without a fair hearing, he did not exaggerate.

But while the Westminster professor appeared to be the victim of a miscarriage of Presbyterian justice, his initiatives were nevertheless losing support among conservatives. At Westminster, Machen alienated a majority of the board of trustees when he established the Independent Board. Several high-profile trustees, including Clarence Macartney, judged that the new agency was inflammatory and deemed that its associations with the seminary were preventing graduates from gaining calls within the Presbyterian Church. For Macartney the whole point of starting Westminster had been to reform the church from within by producing a group of conservative young pastors. Rather than force the majority of the faculty who supported Machen and the Independent Board to resign, in 1935 Macartney and some of the other board members resigned from their responsibilities instead. The seminary was also responsible for alienating other conservatives, such as Carl McIntire, a flamboyant and entrepreneurial New Jersey Presbyterian pastor who would go on to be a powerful voice of anti-communism among the Old Christian Right. McIntire inherited many of the conventions of US Presbyterianism, including a form of civil religion and opposition to vices such as alcohol and tobacco. Because the faculty at Westminster included hyphenated Americans (three were Dutch-Americans and one a Scottish-American) who did not follow American expectations, a division developed within the ranks of Machen's followers.

These fractures among conservative Presbyterians left Machen with a small and apparently marginal body from which to form a new communion. The members of the Independent Board who were tried and convicted appealed their cases to the General Assembly of 1936. With little fanfare the assembly upheld all of the convictions. Machen and his conservative peers had already planned their response, which was a new Presbyterian denomination. On June 11, 1936, the Presbyterian Church of America (PCA) became the vehicle for the conservatives who had opposed the spread of liberalism in the Presbyterian Church USA. Its first General Assembly convened in Philadelphia only a few blocks from the campus of Westminster Seminary, and the commissioners elected Machen their first moderator. By the time the assembly convened the following year, Machen was dead, McIntire had decided to leave the new denomination to form another conservative Presbyterian body (the Bible Presbyterian Synod), and the Presbyterian Church USA had brought a civil suit against Machen's communion over the new denomination's name.

Machen's premature death on January 1, 1937 deprived the Presbyterian Church of America of its most celebrated figure but his survival would not likely have stopped the division with McIntire. The immediate cause of his death was a cold that turned into pneumonia during a trip to speak to a small group of conservatives in North Dakota during the week after Christmas, 1936. But Machen had already been suffering from a case of betrayal since McIntire orchestrated a takeover of the Independent Board for Foreign Missions, which had ousted Machen as president. Indeed, differences among conservatives had been mounting during the last months of 1936. Articles from the Westminster faculty that were critical of dispensational premillennialism[13] put some like McIntire (who had sympathies for dispensationalism) on the defensive. The issue that drove an institutional wedge between these opponents of modernism was alcohol: McIntire's wing of the PCA proposed an overture in support of Prohibition within the church and the majority, led by the Westminster faculty, rejected the proposal on the grounds of Christian liberty. Even so, it was a telling debate. The non-native-born faculty members at Westminster came from Reformed backgrounds where drinking alcohol was common. But for a wide swath of American Presbyterians, both liberal and conservative, total abstinence had become the national and Christian norm. When McIntire complained about the direction of the PCA under the influence of hyphenated Americans at Westminster and formed a new church, he was in effect faulting the church that Machen had created for not being truly American. Not only were its leaders like Cornelius Van Til and John Murray from Dutch and Scottish backgrounds respectively, but their theology (of Christian liberty) and their piety (which countenanced beverage alcohol) was foreign to American Presbyterianism.

The civil suit by the Presbyterian Church USA on August 13, 1936, registered a similar complaint, namely, that the PCA could not legitimately present itself by as an American Presbyterian communion. Attorneys argued before the Philadelphia Court of Common Pleas that the name "Presbyterian Church of America" was too close to the "Presbyterian Church in the USA," and would confuse the public and divert support and attendees from the established to the fringe denomination. The defendants countered that the Presbyterian Church USA did not have a monopoly on the word "Presbyterian", since at least four other communions had the word in their names. They also contended that, given all the publicity surrounding Machen and the Presbyterian Controversy, few Americans would mistake the PCA for the Presbyterian Church USA. On June 27, 1938, the judge hearing the case ruled against the PCA on the grounds that the new denomination was confusing, would hamper and impair the work of the plaintiff church, interfere with its orderly procedure, and disturb the resources of support in its field of activity.[14] Two years later, to comply with this ruling, the PCA changed its name to the Orthodox Presbyterian Church.

The reasons for the new name were various, and the record of votes on alternatives was humorous at times, but it captured Machen's opposition to the drift of US Presbyterianism as practiced by the Presbyterian Church USA. He recovered the Old School Presbyterian doctrine of the spirituality of the church and argued repeatedly that either through humanitarian efforts or social activism the Presbyterian Church was turning away from its spiritual mission. Machen's most important statement of this argument came in 1933 before a gathering of political and social scientists who had requested various clergy to address the question of the church's responsibility in the light of domestic and international woes. Machen's response followed closely the logic of Old School Presbyterians:

> ... you cannot expect from a true Christian church any official pronounce-
> ments upon the political or social questions of the day, and you cannot
> expect cooperation with the state in anything involving the use of force.
> Important are the functions of the police. . . . But the function of the church in
> its corporate capacity is of an entirely different kind. Its weapons against evil
> are spiritual, not carnal; and by becoming a political lobby, through the advo-
> cacy of political measures whether good or bad, the church is turning aside
> from its proper mission, which is to bring to bear upon human hearts the
> solemn and imperious, yet also sweet and gracious, appeal of the gospel of
> Jesus Christ.[15]

In the nineteenth century, that understanding of the church had been acceptable even if Presbyterians in the United States had no direct experience with ecclesi-astical establishment. By the time of Machen's trial the spirituality of the church had no plausibility thanks to the overwhelming identification by US Protestants, both modernist and fundamentalist, of Christ's cause with the nation's wellbeing. Even so, it was the motivation behind conservatives like Machen who desired a version of Reformed Protestantism that was both true to the genius of Reformation theology and free from the encumbrance of national destiny. In the setting of a political order that played no favoritism with its religious institutions, Machen's secession was the American version of Chalmers' Disruption and Kuyper's regretful withdrawal. The crucial difference was the absence on Machen's part of an effort to create a shadow religious establishment.

The Princeton Theology Exported

Roughly a decade before his death, Machen received an invitation to become the principal of Knox College, the Presbyterian Church of Canada theological school at the University of Toronto. John Gibson Inkster, pastor at Knox Church in Toronto, was the man who proposed Machen to Canadian Presbyterians at their 1926 General Assembly. As much as this invitation may have tapped Machen's notoriety as an ecclesiastical controversialist, it also reflected natural bonds between the then Princeton professor and Presbyterians in Canada. Inkster himself had frequently invited Machen to occupy the pulpit in Toronto. Machen also regularly sent seminary students for summer internships and guest preaching to assist the church in Canada. The idea of selecting Machen to head the Toronto school was not far-fetched from the Canadian side, even if it made no sense to an ecclesiastical leader who was in the thick of a fight in his own country.

In fact, Machen's nomination made even more sense to Canadians considering the struggle in which Presbyterians had battled just prior to the search for a principal for Knox College. The same variety of ecumenism that had Protestants in the United States consider an organic union of the largest denominations actually succeeded in Canada. The idea of a united church in Canada emerged as early as 1902 with impromptu remarks by William Patrick, the principal of a Presbyterian college in Manitoba, during greetings delivered to a gathering of Methodists. Although Patrick broached the idea of closer cooperation independently, Canadian Methodists interpreted his comments as the formal position of Canadian Presbyterians. The following year the Methodists submitted a formal invitation to the Presbyterians which became the basis for the creation of a committee that soon included Congregationalists as well. By 1906 the proposal had extended to Anglicans and Baptists in Canada. A 1912 vote by Presbyterians on the plan for union revealed that the measure had support from a majority of the church. The vote also demonstrated a sizable opposition party that considered union to be a form of ecclesiastical suicide. In 1915 an organization dedicated to opposing union, the Presbyterian Church Association, started activities with a conference at St Andrew's Church in Toronto and a formal declaration "to maintain and continue the Presbyterian Church in Canada."[16]

World War I stalled union plans but in 1921 the proposal gathered steam, with advocates unwilling to consider any arrangement short of union and opponents charging that the issue was dividing the Presbyterian Church. A chief debating point was the name of the church: union supporters denied that any Presbyterians who remained outside the merger could continue to use "Presbyterian Church of Canada," since union was technically supposed to absorb this ecclesiastical body. On the other side, opponents were adamant in maintaining that they were continuing the witness and work of the Presbyterian Church in Canada. In 1924 the Assembly approved the plan for union and left to each congregation the decision of whether to enter the United Church. Any failure to vote would be interpreted as approval. On June 10, 1925, when the United Church of Canada held its inaugural worship service at Toronto's Mutual Street Arena, the Presbyterian Church in Canada persisted but had shrunk to one-third of its previous size. Of the denomination's 379,762 communicant members, 154,243 voted to remain Presbyterian; the proportion of congregations refusing union was smaller, 302 out of 4,509, with 211 resisting congregations in southern Ontario alone. Such resistance to church union by no means stemmed from the sort of Old School Presbyterian outlook that Machen espoused. But enough affinities existed between conservatives in Canada and the United States that Machen appeared to be a viable leader to opponents of union in Canada.

In Northern Ireland, Machen proved to be a source of inspiration to conservatives who feared the increasing prominence of liberal theology in the theological colleges of the Irish Presbyterian Church. In 1927 he visited Belfast as the guest of a former student, W. J. Grier, an Irishman aspiring to the ministry who had studied for two years at Princeton but needed to complete his course at the General Assembly's theological college in Belfast. After giving a series of lectures in Edinburgh, Manchester, and Liverpool, Machen arrived in Belfast on June 7 at the height of an investigation into the teaching of James Ernest Davey, a professor who taught theology at the General Assembly's college and who had drawn fire from conservatives for questioning the infallibility of Scripture and the reliability of Christ's teachings. The trial of Davey was one in a series of protests initiated by the Presbyterian minister James Hunter, who had led opposition to liberal trends among Irish Presbyterians since 1904 when his assembly passed a resolution expressing sympathy with the House of Lords' decision to remove the property and assets of the United Free Church of Scotland and return it to the smaller Free Church (see Chapter Ten). Hunter believed that siding with the United Free Church against the Free Church put Irish Presbyterians on the wrong side. In Davey's case, the evidence of ambiguity toward, if not outright departure from, the theology of the Westminster Confession was much easier to spot than choosing the correct ecclesiastical allies. In fact, Hunter had access to Grier's own notes from Davey's lectures.

Machen delivered talks he had given elsewhere about the contest between liberalism and historic Protestantism, and preached to a packed church during both morning and evening Sunday service; he estimated as many as 1,700 turned out at night. The large crowds were a function of the publicity surrounding the Davey trial. During Machen's stay, he had lengthy conversations with Grier, Hunter, and other conservatives about the situation. But in the end, the Princeton professor's inspiration and counsel could not alter the willingness of Irish Presbyterians to give Davey the benefit of the doubt. Not helping the conservatives was the revelation that Grier had added comments to his notes on Davey's lectures, raising questions of whether the student had doctored the evidence. By the summer of 1927, the Presbytery of Belfast had already acquitted Davey on all charges. In the appeal to the General Assembly the conservatives lost again: the vote was 707 to 82. In response, Hunter renounced his office in the Irish Presbyterian Church and within four months helped to found the Irish Evangelical Church (later the Evangelical Presbyterian Church). Its original congregations were few and its members often met in small groups within private homes. If the controversy among Presbyterians in Ireland indicated

Machen's appeal to conservatives beyond the United States, the outcome of the affair also presaged how small the actual numbers of militant Presbyterians backing Machen in the United States would be almost ten years later.

One last example of Machen's influence outside the United States for conservative Presbyterians opposed to liberalism and ecumenism comes from Korea. Even though Korean Presbyterianism exemplified a successful case of a church formed by foreign missionaries developing an indigenous identity, it remained wedded to North American norms despite significantly different environments. One of those important differences was political: while Presbyterians in the United States and Canada who sent missionaries to Korea enjoyed unchecked religious freedom, in the first half of the twentieth century the Korean church endured the rule of a hostile and aggressive Japanese Empire. After 1910, when Japan annexed Korea, Japanese policy was designed to extinguish Korean identity and any efforts that might support independence. Japanese control ran from a coercive military presence to such cultural measures as controlling the content of school curricula, requiring the use of the Japanese language, and enforcing the Shinto practice of shrine worship. Christian churches in Korea also came under rigorous Japanese surveillance and indigenous pastors and foreign missionaries experienced imprisonment and deportation respectively if they failed to comply with the regime. An unintended consequence of Japan's treatment of the churches was to make Christianity tremendously popular in Korea, since the faith, especially Protestantism, became closely identified with Korean nationalism. But responses to Japanese rule and Shintoism were mixed. In the 1930s some of the largest Korean Presbyterian synods encouraged church members to participate in shrine worship by concluding that it was simply a political ritual without explicit religious significance. Other synods opposed Shintoism and for their defiance saw their schools and universities closed. In addition to these different responses to Shintoism were theological disagreements among Korean Presbyterians. Here either foreign missionaries introduced liberal theological trends among Koreans, or Korean natives who had studied in North America or Europe brought back the new theology when they returned home.

Hyung-Nong Park (1897–1978) was one of those native Koreans who tried to adapt theological developments in the United States to the situation in Korea. After receiving an undergraduate degree from Geumrung University in China, he traveled to the United States to study at Princeton Seminary during the heyday of Machen's influence. He left Princeton in 1929 with two degrees and enrolled at the Southern Baptist Seminary in Louisville, Kentucky, to pursue a PhD in the New Testament. When he returned to Korea in 1933 he taught at Pyongyang Theological Seminary, from which he opposed liberal theological trends in the Presbyterian Church of Korea, particularly over critical and modern readings of Genesis and initiatives to soften New Testament prohibitions against the ordination of women. This opposition earned him the nickname the "Machen of Korea." In 1938 the Japanese government closed the school and Park went into exile in Manchuria. He taught at Dongbuk Theological Seminary until the end of World War II and befriended Presbyterian missionaries from the United States, among them Bruce Hunt of the Orthodox Presbyterian Church. After the war, Park returned to South Korea to train ministers for the Presbyterian Church of Korea.

Between 1946 and 1959, when the Presbyterian Church of Korea was reconstituted, Park taught at a number of seminaries and was instrumental in a number of church divisions. The first occurred in 1951 when opponents to Shintoism, Park among them, insisted that the church should discipline those who had participated in shrine worship. When these critics themselves split and Park returned to the mainstream Presbyterian Church, another division occurred in 1953 over women's ordination, with the small pro-ordination group founding a separate Presbyterian communion. Finally, another division among the Korean Presbyterians took place in 1959 over the denomination's membership in the World Council of Churches. Park perceived the international body to be a proponent of liberal Protestantism under the guise of ecumenism. He argued for membership in an alternative agency established by Carl McIntire, the International Council of Christian Churches. Because McIntire was willing to assist Park in establishing a conservative seminary, Park's new denomination, the Hapdong Presbyterian Church, initially joined McIntire's council. Membership lasted for only a year, partly owing to McIntire's inability to let affiliated institutions oversee their own affairs. Even so, from the example of the Presbyterian controversy in the United States, Park had learned a theology predisposed to oppose liberalism and ecumenism based on social activism. He also recognized the importance of theological education for the identity and direction of church life. As much as those lessons may have been ill-suited to a church that was trying to establish its own standards and mechanisms of oversight, they illustrated the appeal of Machen's conservative arguments to Presbyterians in small denominations around the world.

The doctrine of the spirituality of the church was not as important in Canada, Ireland, or Korea as it was to Machen's own understanding of Presbyterianism. Even for Machen's followers in the Orthodox Presbyterian Church, the spirituality of the church could be a minor matter compared to fighting liberalism, the Social Gospel, and non-discriminating forms of ecumenism. But the doctrine of spirituality was crucial to Machen's own struggles with utilitarian forms of Protestantism that set aside the particular convictions of Reformed Protestantism for the generic

quest to build just and righteous societies through interdenominational cooperation. The spirituality of the church animated his opposition as much as it under-
scored the distinct character of Presbyterianism. It made him as suspicious of
fundamentalist indifference to distinct parts of Reformed theology and church
order as he was critical of liberalism. As such, Machen's understanding of the
church's spiritual character and mission was one more instance of modern
Reformed Protestant efforts to disentangle the ministry of word and sacrament
from Calvinist assumptions about the church's responsibility for the social order.
For the church to be the church, she would need to abandon old habits that tended
to reduce Christianity to strategies for personal and social wellbeing.

CHAPTER THIRTEEN

THE CONFESSING CHURCH

In 1918, as a devastating European war was coming to an end, Karl Barth (1880–1968) dropped his own theological bomb upon Europe's Protestant churches, namely, the first edition of his famous commentary on the Epistle to the Romans. At the time, the author was an unknown Reformed pastor in the Swiss village of Safenwil (where he had lived since 1910), the population of which barely included 1,600 inhabitants. In fact, so marginal was Barth that he had trouble finding a publisher. "Three well-known Swiss publishers," he confessed, "refused to have anything to do with [the Romans commentary], which was quite understandable at the time . . ."[1] Yet, the Swiss pastor's reflections on the apostle Paul's epistle reflected a break within Barth's own theological outlook and would cast a long shadow over Protestant churches in Europe and beyond.

The new direction in Barth's thinking came from his own study of the Bible. For instance, in 1917 while preparing the commentary, Barth gave a talk about "The Strange New World of the Bible," in which he explained that Scripture opened up a world not of history or morality or religion, not "the right human thoughts about God but the right divine thoughts about men."[2] This theocentric perspective was especially compelling to Barth because of its potential to liberate Christians and the message of the gospel from their captivity to justifying and serving the affairs of nations and progress of civilizations. In a lecture he gave the summer following the publication of the commentary, the Swiss pastor declared that the "wholly otherness of the kingdom of God" was impossible to overemphasize. "The kingdom of God is the kingdom of God," he asserted. "The new Jerusalem has not the least to do with the new Switzerland and the revolutionary state of the future; it comes to earth in God's great freedom, when the time has arrived."[3]

Roughly coincident with Barth's controversial biblical studies, Reformed Protestants in Germany were reeling from revolutionary political developments that disrupted the historic ties among churches, people, land, and rulers. During the closing weeks of the World War I Germany experienced two waves of revolution, first from the organization of socialist political parties that demanded a new form of government, and second from the abdication of Kaiser Wilhelm II. The new regime, the Weimar Republic, replaced the older imperial arrangements with a parliamentary system formed to respond to the demands of industrial workers and introduce a democratic form of government.

The formation of the Weimar Republic was hardly free from conflict, both armed and ideological, but for the nation's Protestant churches the situation was especially unsettling. According to Reinhard Moeller, one of the highest ecclesiastical officials from the old political and religious order, "the splendor of the German Empire, the dream of our fathers, the pride of every German has departed." "Therewith," he added, "the exalted vessel of German power, the ruler, and the royal house that we loved instinctively."[4] In a highly complex arrangement that accommodated Reformed, Lutheran, Roman Catholic, and dissenting or free church bodies, the German monarchy had provided a supportive setting for Protestants to conduct their affairs. But almost overnight, the new political order launched the German churches on a sea of uncertainty. Instead of producing relief from the ongoing meddling of the magistrate, the new order churned up angst over how ministers and congregations would persist without the magistrate's benevolent patronage. On the one hand, the new German government removed the very structures that had provided stability for Protestant churches in favor of a society indifferent to religion, with voluntary churches and secularized state schools. On the other hand, some church leaders saw the democratic ideals of Weimar as an opportunity to make the church more responsive to the German people and thus invigorate a sleepy institution. Either way, Protestant church leaders were hardly willing to consider a church independent from the German state. Practically everyone was looking for a way to transfer the privileges the churches enjoyed under the German Empire to the Weimar government.

Despite differences between Barth's idea of an otherworldly kingdom of God and German Protestantism's nationalism, the Swiss pastor would establish himself as the dominant voice of twentieth-century Reformed Protestant theology from this unstable setting. No doubt, the courageous stands he and other German Protestants would take against the National Socialist regime that emerged in 1933 partly accounted for Barth's eventual prominence. In fact, for Reformed church leaders in liberal theological settings where the advance of western civilization was virtually identical to the coming of God's kingdom, the Swiss pastor's categorical affirmation of divine transcendence was a welcome alternative. The irony was that Barth developed and applied his ideas to an ecclesiastical situation where even his Protestant allies were hard-pressed to abandon the ideal of a German church in the service of a German nation. If Chalmers and

Kuyper recognized the import of giving up ecclesiastical establishment and if Machen saw the problems inherent in cultural hegemony, Barth took the goal of ecclesiastical autonomy to an altogether different level. His appeal was to articulate a Calvinism that was almost mystical, with the sphere of spiritual truth not just separate from politics and culture but even above and beyond the institutional church.

Whither the German Reformed?

In 1921, when Barth accepted an offer to become the honorary professor of Reformed theology at the University of Göttingen, he entered the complicated world of German Protestantism, one that was far removed from the days either when Frederick III had overseen the production of the Heidelberg Catechism or when Reformed Protestants had been forced to heed the demands of the Roman Catholic prince-elector, Charles Philip. An institution founded in 1734 by King George II of England and the elector of Hanover, Göttingen drew inspiration from the intellectual ideals of the Enlightenment. This did not mean a release from the responsibilities that universities had for training ministers of the state churches. Göttingen's faculty pioneered historical and pragmatic approaches to theology and biblical studies while also examining prospective clergy in the ordination process. This was no less true in Barth's day, when university faculty conducted theological exams for the territories of Lower Saxony. This meant that Barth had the task of teaching Reformed dogmatics in a setting dominated by the legacy of the merger of Lutheran and Reformed Protestants in the Church of the Old Prussian Union.

Almost a century before Barth moved to Göttingen, on October 31, 1817, Frederick William III celebrated the tercentenary of the German Reformation. He did so by calling for a union of the Lutheran and Reformed churches in his kingdom. Instead of subsuming one side into the other, the plan was to forge a single evangelical (read: Protestant) church. Although other rulers would imitate Frederick William's proposal – such as those in Nassau, Rhineland-Palatinate, Baden, and Württemberg – the Prussian union blazed a trail for harmonizing Protestants as a means of political centralization and consolidation. The proposed union was not without its critics. The king's own assertion of his unilateral right to interpret the doctrine, liturgy, and church polity of the united bodies, not merely as prince of the realm but also as a bishop of the church, posed a significant hardship when penalties for violations of civil law could also be imposed on those who broke church law. For instance, in 1831 when pastors refused to use the liturgy prescribed by the king, a royal decree called for the prosecution of the offenders with the appropriate punishment of fines and imprisonment. The heavy hand enforcing union was largely responsible for the rise of a neo-Lutheran movement that resulted in attempts to establish free Lutheran churches, the most prominent of which took root in Silesia. But such voluntary churches were initially illegal according to the terms of Protestant union.

The outworking of ecclesiastical union provided the setting for the work of the greatest nineteenth-century German-speaking Reformed theologian, Friedrich Schleiermacher (1768–1834). The son of a Reformed chaplain for the Prussian Army, Schleiermacher came under the influence of Moravians during his teens and prevailed upon his father to permit him to study at the University of Halle, an institution founded by German pietists. He absorbed some of the school's critical methods in the study of Scripture and acquired a love of philosophy that extended to the ancients and moderns, from Plato and Aristotle to Kant. His first pastoral assignment was as chaplain for a Berlin hospital, where he quickly fit in with the city's elite circles. In this context, Schleiermacher authored his first major work, *On Religion: Speeches to its Cultured Despisers* (1799), in which he defended faith not as a specialist or sectarian matter but as a perennial and quotidian human trait. For two years starting in 1802 Schleiermacher took a call to pastor the small town of Stolp (now in Poland). His reputation as a controversialist may account for the variety of posts he held for the next few years, first at the University of Halle as professor of theology, then as pastor in Berlin. But none of Schleiermacher's controversies prevented him from taking part in 1810 in the formation of the University of Berlin. He joined the new institution's faculty of theology and became an officer in the Prussian Academy of Sciences. From this setting Schleiermacher was well positioned to offer advice and shape the reorganization of the Lutheran and Reformed branches of the Prussian church.

Although the Berlin professor supported church union, he also sought ecclesiastical independence from the state. In the mid-1820s Schleiermacher wrote an anonymous tract to oppose the liturgy that the king was imposing on the Prussian churches. Not only had these proposed practices violated Protestant understandings of worship from Schleiermacher's perspective, but royal prerogatives should not extend to church affairs, where the king's status was no different from other church members. Despite objections to the implementation of union, Schleiermacher supplied the theological rationale for merging German Protestants. In 1822 he wrote *The Christian Faith* to summarize the fundamental doctrines that a united Protestant church must affirm and to defend a doctrine of the church that would undergird the Prussian Union.

The real problem with church union as Schleiermacher construed it was not between Lutherans and Reformed but between Protestants and Roman

Catholics. For Protestants the individual believer's relationship to Christ was essential while for Rome the individual's relationship to Christ depended on the Christian's status within the church. In sum, the differences between Reformed and Lutherans on the church were "quite negligible" and were in "no sense traceable to a difference in the religious affections themselves . . ."[5] Even so, a united church did not mean a church beholden to the state. Although Schleiermacher argued for a union of Protestants he also insisted on a church free from state control. He did believe that the church had a responsibility to minister to the state. He also conceived of the civil government taking charge of most aspects of society, including the education of citizens. Nevertheless, a union of Protestant churches in service to the kingdom did not mean the subjugation of the church to the king. Each institution had its proper sphere.

Schleiermacher's understanding of the church and support for union were indicative of German Reformed Protestants' willingness to acquiesce to the monarchy at least until a final church–state policy emerged. Unlike the Lutherans, among whom several pockets of confessionalism developed into secessionist movements, Reformed Protestants were content to go along with the state's policies. The Prussian Constitution of 1850 may have functioned as a catalyst for the German Reformed to recover their heritage. Liberal efforts in the 1840s to democratize Prussia, establish a neutral state, and remove religion from public education failed but did generate reforms that granted the churches greater autonomy than they had enjoyed previously. Still, the 1850 arrangements were by no means a clear victory for the churches to regulate their own affairs. On the one hand, Lutheran, Reformed, and Union churches used a presbyterian-synodical structure that allowed ecclesiastical officers a role in the management of church life and church members a hand in selecting those who sat on administrative committees. On the other hand, the king continued to govern the churches through the Evangelischer Oberkirchenrat (EOK), an executive body appointed by the king, who continued to govern the church in his capacity as *summus episcopus* (highest bishop), and to represent the monarch's sovereign rights over the churches.

Reformed churches within Prussia did not fare well after church union but persisted in other German territories, despite the appeal of the Prussian Union to other rulers. As a general geographical pattern, Lutherans were strongest in the eastern sections of the kingdom and Reformed Protestants dominated the west. Pockets of Reformed Protestant vitality within Prussia persisted in Hesse and Hanover. Outside Prussia, Lippe and Bremen supported self-conscious Reformed churches, as did Huguenot remnants in parts of Lower Saxony, Alsace, and Lorraine. Still, the appeal of union was so strong even outside Prussia that historic centers of Reformed conviction lost their ties to the

Reformation. The German-American historian, James Isaac Good, describes the situation thus: "It is a sad fact to the Reformed that the burial-place of Olevianus at Herborn in Nassau, as well as the burial-place of Ursinus at Neustadt in the Palatinate, do not know either of these men any longer, for they have left the Reformed faith."[6] Good adds that Reformed sympathies in Germany had declined so precipitously during the nineteenth century that the German Reformed from the United States had to intervene to replace a decrepit plaque in the church at Herborn commemorating Olevianus' accomplishments.

After 1850, Reformed Protestants in Prussia and other German territories began in small ways to recover their traditions. After 1873, identifying with a church different from the established one became easier in Prussia thanks to a change in the constitution that made the established church voluntary. Some of these efforts stemmed from a reaction against church union policies. Others, like so many confessional revivals in nineteenth-century Europe, stemmed from anniversaries in Reformation history. As early as 1850, a diet of Reformed pastors, twenty-eight in all, met in Stuttgart to bemoan the state of convictions among Reformed Germans. The initial solution was to found a journal, *Reformierte Kirchenzeitung*, and to sponsor a series of books dedicated to the founders of the Reformed churches (modeled after a similar Lutheran series). The blossoming of Reformed self-awareness during the 1850s and 1860s also spawned several conferences for education and edification. These events took place at Elberfeld, Emden, and Detmold and culminated in an 1863 conference to celebrate the tercentenary of the Heidelberg Catechism. Another wave of conferences and publications refreshed pockets of Reformed Protestant vitality during the late 1870s and early 1880s. *Reformierte Kirchenzeitung*, which had ceased publication, received a new lease on life and accompanying it were two publication societies, one at Barmen and the other at Hanover. Another anniversary in 1884, this time the 400th anniversary of Zwingli's birth, led to another conference. It also generated the formation of the Reformed Alliance (Reformierter Bund), an informal association of congregations (as many as one hundred at the time) dedicated to the recovery of the churches' Reformed heritage. This organization proved to be the most enduring of the Reformed initiatives after 1850. The Alliance continued the work of education and publication and also promoted theological training for pastors by establishing seminaries in Berlin and Halle (though the education was informal rather than traditional).

By the time of the First World War, the ecclesiastical pattern in Germany was highly complex. Lutheran, Reformed, Union, and Roman Catholic churches enjoyed establishment privileges, while even if Germans themselves were free to align or refuse membership with any religious body. Protestant churches continued to be regulated by the state, and with this oversight came the compensation of church taxes raised by the civil authorities to subsidize the churches. The German population also reflected the church's privileged status. The 1910 German census indicated that Protestants in the Union, Lutheran, and Reformed congregations numbered close to 40 million (compared to approximately 24 million Roman Catholics, over 600,000 Jews, and 283,000 "other" Christians). A 1925 census revealed that the German membership of Free Reformed churches was 9,559, only 3,000 more than the Moravians.[7] Degrees of participation in the churches varied. Although membership lists were large, the ratio of pastors to parishioners was even larger; in some German cities the number of church members for each pastor ranged between 10,000 and 14,000. In some of those same cities, the percentage of people attending worship ranged between 5 percent and 16 percent of membership. At the same time, the number of Germans submitting infants for baptism, seeking marriages within the church, and receiving Christian burials remained high: almost universal participation in baptism, three out of four burials within the church, and almost half of all marriages being conducted by ministers or priests. No matter if other western church leaders regarded German universities as a hotbed of infidelity, the churches remained a conservative piece of the German social fabric. The stature of Germany's churches made ecclesiastical leaders reluctant to adapt to the new political order that came with Weimar.

Reformed Awakening and German Doldrums

The Weimar Republic closed a four-century chapter in German church history that had commenced with the Peace of Augsburg (1555). With the abdication of Germany's princes and monarch in 1918, its churches lost the officials that had functioned as *summi episcopi* in each territory. The question that all church officers were asking after 1918 was who would now oversee the churches. This worry was all the more pressing because some of the Social Democrats, who initially controlled the new republic at the national level, called for the separation of church and state and the elimination of religious instruction in public schools. As a result, the pressing ecclesiastical issues for the new government were the place of religion in public education, whether the state would continue to support military, hospital, and prison chaplains, and the legal status of the churches as corporations with powers of taxation and state subsidies.

The first Weimar assembly, dominated by a coalition of Social Democrats, Democrats, and Center Party ministers, received a petition from the German Evangelical Church Committee that pressed these matters and added Sundays and religious holidays to the list of Christian endeavors that the state should protect. The new German constitution, which went into effect on August 11,

1919, quieted many Christians' fears, even if most pastors lamented the replacement of the old hierarchical order with a republican and democratic system of government. The churches received almost everything they wanted, minus the Kaiser: the right of self-government, financial support, and a continuation of religious instruction in primary schools. The constitution also granted religious liberty to citizens, thus maintaining the voluntary model of church membership. But by granting the same liberties to the institutional churches – namely, the power to govern their own affairs – while continuing to subsidize them, the new constitution was not as revolutionary or as threatening as many had feared.

When Barth assumed his teaching responsibilities at Göttingen in February of 1921, the changes introduced by the Weimar Constitution had practically no direct bearing on his duties. His appointment to the newly founded chair of Reformed theology was a joint endeavor that involved lobbying by the Reformed Church of Northwest Germany and approval by the Prussian Ministry of Cultural Affairs. Technically, this made Barth a civil servant. But the political implications of this professorship absorbed few of his thoughts. His immediate challenge was to prepare lectures on Reformed theology, and Barth admitted that he had little acquaintance with Reformed Protestantism's doctrinal features. This deficiency was no great impediment since Bart himself admitted that the Reformed churches in the surrounding territory (Hanover) "were a dwindling and even despised minority."[8] He confessed that the first edition of his Romans commentary was responsible for the invitation from Karl Müller, a professor at Erlangen, and Adam Heilmann, a pastor at Göttingen, to occupy a chair funded in large measure by Presbyterians in the United States. Of his commentary (the first edition), Barth wrote, "one will hardly find [it] distinguished by a particular Calvinistic content." In fact, he admitted that being addressed as a Reformed theologian so often was "a novel experience." Barth did not even have a doctorate, a deficiency soon remedied by the Protestant faculty at Münster, who awarded him an honorary degree for his "many and varied contributions to the revision of religious and theological questioning." What attracted Barth to his German advocates was that, in his own words, "I was passionately concerned with holy scripture."[9]

The Bible may have been the draw, but Reformed doctrine was Barth's assignment in the classroom. This meant becoming familiar with material from the sixteenth century that he had previously ignored. At one point, he admitted he did not own a copy of the Reformed confessions and had "certainly not read them – not to mention all the other terrible gaps in my knowledge." His first lectures in 1922 were an exposition of the Heidelberg Catechism; this course attracted only fifteen students compared to almost sixty for his lectures on Ephesians. Barth's initial approach was to sympathize with the historical context for the catechism and then assess its relevance to contemporary Christians. According to Barth, this twofold task involved "having to approve and disapprove of almost everything." In his second semester he lectured on Calvin, which turned out to be an intellectual feast: "a waterfall, a primitive forest, a demonic power, something straight down from the Himalayas, absolutely Chinese, strange, mythological."[10] Later in 1923 he undertook lectures on Ulrich Zwingli and was deeply disappointed. He had started "full of good will and trust" but found in Zwingli all the problems of modern theology "with a few eggshells from the early church thrown in." Attention to Zwingli led Barth to the debates with Luther over the Lord's Supper. The Göttingen professor believed that Luther had the better of Zwingli but was too persistent. Barth viewed Calvin as the theologian to the rescue: he had lifted the "two carriages" out of the ruts of "an undialectical relationship" and moved them forward. Such exposure to the Reformers and their debates convinced Barth that his eyes were now "properly open to the Reformers and their message of the justification and sanctification of the sinner, of faith, of repentance and works, of the nature and limits of the church, and so on." Barth had "swung into line with the Reformation," not uncritically but with "special attention."[11]

The fruit of this reorientation was Barth's creation of the dialectical school of theology. One outlet for this program was a new journal that Barth co-founded in 1923 (with Eduard Thurneysen and Friedrich Gogarten), *Zwischen den Zeiten* (Between the Times). The predominant theme at the outset was the Bible rather than the Reformed confessions, though Barth's lectures on the Reformation era had cultivated an interest in recovering the formal principle of the sixteenth century, namely, *sola scriptura*. What the editors wanted was "a theology of the Word of God" and the Reformers were a "model" for this project.[12] Another point of departure for dialectical theology was Barth's *Church Dogmatics*, a writing project that he began in 1924 and continued for the rest of his life (in ways that paralleled John Calvin's lifelong project of the *Institutes*). Here again was an emphasis on the word of God but it included a stress upon Christian preaching such that an explication of dogma involved the exposition of Scripture. By the time that Barth started the *Dogmatics*, his colleagues at *Zwischen den Zeiten* knew that he was not merely following a school of theology. Disputes during the first year of publication with Emil Brunner, Ruldolf Bultmann, and Paul Tillich over natural theology, the significance of Christ, and the usefulness of existentialism indicated that Barth's understanding of the word of God was increasingly becoming his own theological trademark.

Barth had begun to sour on older (liberal) Protestant theology at the beginning of World War I when his former theological professors signed a manifesto of German intellectuals in support of Kaiser Wilhelm II and his war policy.

Liberalism, Barth believed, had lost sight of the transcendence and incomprehensibility of God. It treated religious truth more as the culmination of human reason and initiative than as a reality independent of human endeavor and wisdom. This understanding of God was crucial to dialectical theology, which involved juxtaposing conflicting ideas for the sake of positive affirmation. The polarities in Barth's emerging outlook involved the finitude, sinfulness, dependence, and ignorance of human beings on the one side, and the power, holiness, transcendence, and omniscience of God on the other. This dialectic even extended to the work of pastors and theologians whose responsibility was to speak about divinity even though human beings were incapable of knowing God. The only resolution came through Jesus Christ, revealed in the word, who, as God the man, resolved the dichotomies.

Throughout this process Barth categorically rejected natural theology. He taught that human beings were incapable of knowing or reflecting meaningfully about God and Christ apart from faith or divine revelation. The idea of constructing a chain of thought that led from creation to the creator was anathema. It was also, in Barth's view, responsible for the church's all too ready identification with civil authorities and the civilizations they cultivated. Barthianism was emerging not only as a modern reappropriation of Reformation teaching but also as a Christian expression with potential for political protest.

Barth himself gave little sustained attention to German politics, busy as he was in his academic output. When he began teaching at Göttingen his advocates asked him to avoid politics, and Barth was content to comply with this request. He also continued to view Switzerland as his home and was inclined to think of himself as a foreigner in Germany. Still, Barth could not help noticing the political turmoil that afflicted the Weimar Republic. The Germans' political incompetence seemed "boundless." Meanwhile, university professors were "real masters at finding ingenious moral and Christian grounds for brutality." German scholars' opposition to the republic was particularly vexing. When colleagues at Göttingen donned the colors of the old empire in their regalia, Barth felt the old urge "to take up my position on the left wing."[13] Barth could not understand the "attitude of sabotage" toward Weimar that pervaded the German academy. The professors "did not even give [the republic] a fair chance," Barth complained. "They poured scorn on the notion that the year 1919 might have been a liberation for Germany." He saw similar tendencies among the Protestant churches, which cultivated loyalties to the old imperial order and "developed a remarkably pompous self-importance which did not seem to be matched by the content and profundity of its preaching."[14] Meanwhile, in 1925 when Barth presented a lecture to the Reformed Churches of Duisburg-Meiderich on the desirability of formulating a contemporary Reformed confession of faith, one of his justifications for such a creed was its practical significance: it could allow the church to speak to the wider society. Barth conceded that Reformed Protestants and Lutherans differed over the nature of creeds, including whether a confession should address civil authorities. This difference would eventually cost Barth the support of conservative Lutherans.

The appointment in Göttingen lasted until 1925, when Barth moved to Münster – a "nest of priests and rebaptizers" – where his isolation from colleagues and other neo-orthodox interlocutors prompted another move in 1930, this time to Bonn. His time at Bonn coincided with one of the most productive and accomplished periods for the university's Protestant theological faculty and Barth enjoyed his colleagues there more than at Göttingen or Münster. Although he may have found a congenial academic home, Barth's teaching at Bonn also coincided with the end of the Weimar Republic and the institution of the National Socialist regime under Adolf Hitler. These political developments had enormous consequences for the German churches and drew Barth directly into the fray.

Within the Weimar political order, the German Protestant churches – Lutheran, Reformed, and Union – had established an alliance in 1922 for the sake of protecting and representing the common interests of German Protestantism and cultivating a religious and moral outlook for the nation. The governing body of this German Evangelical Church Confederation was the Kirchentag, an assembly of 210 delegates, 150 of whom the various Land churches elected in proportion to their church members. In addition to the Kirchentag, a second layer of governance functioned within a Church Confederation Council (Kirchenbundesrat), a smaller body that allowed one delegate from each of the Land churches and additional representatives depending on membership (one delegate per 500,000). In 1932 these representative bodies became the object of Nazi designs to control the German churches. In particular, the National Socialists determined to exert control over the Old Prussian Union Church, a communion that had expressed opposition to the Nazis on various occasions, such as in a 1931 edict that prohibited the wearing of party uniforms in public gatherings for worship. This group of National Socialists took the name German Christians, and in the 1932 elections within the Union churches gained roughly one-third of the seats. The aim of the German Christians was to promote Protestant conviction within the National Socialist Party and infuse the German churches with the spirit of the German folk. Racial purity was also part of the agenda. Meanwhile German Christians forbade marriages between Christians and Jews, and rejected evangelism to the Jews because it would introduce foreign blood.

When Adolf Hitler assumed power as chancellor he received warm support from most Germans, including church officials. His willingness to defend

German traditions and affirm Christianity "as the basis of our collective morality" was a welcome change from the religious indifference and ambivalence that had prevailed in the Weimar Republic.[15] The new constitution of 1933 recognized that the "inviolable" foundation of the German Evangelical Church (Deutsch Evangelische Kirche) was "the gospel of Jesus Christ, as testified . . . in the Holy Scriptures" and summarized in the "creeds of the Reformation."[16] The new law also fostered greater administrative consolidation at the national level but allowed for diversity among Protestant churches in different territories along confessional lines. At the same time, the new constitutional provisions, along with the new governing authorities, created a climate in which the pro-Nazi German Christians gained the upper hand in church affairs. In the summer of 1933 the German Christians won almost two-thirds of the seats in the national synod. The emergence of a strong Nazi element in the German Protestant churches also resulted in the reorganization of the territorial churches. In September of 1933, for instance, the Evangelical Church of the Old Prussian Union lost its superintendent and senate in favor of a bishop appointed by a Nazi-dominated synod. This territorial church also witnessed the ratification of a new law that restricted the office of clergy to Germans of Aryan descent only.

Opposition to these changes took shape in two forms. The first was the Pastors' Emergency League, instituted in the fall of 1933 under the leadership of Martin Niemöller, a Lutheran pastor of strong nationalist and monarchist convictions. Members of the organization pledged to expound Scripture and the Reformation confessions faithfully and to resist anything that would prevent such faithfulness. Those who joined the League also took an official stand against the laws that restricted ecclesiastical office to Aryans as "an infringement" of the organization's confessional convictions. At the peak of its appeal, the League had just over seven thousand members. But a meeting with Hitler and Nazi church officials in January 1934 placated the fears of some, and the League lost almost one-third of its membership.

With the decline of the League, the second institution to gather opposition to the German Christians was the Confessing Church movement. This was a grassroots initiative of church leaders, gathering in independent (i.e. free) synods, who pledged fidelity to the word of God as the sole source of truth. These free synods initially developed in Reformed circles, with pastor Karl Immer organizing the first meeting in January of 1934 at Barmen-Gemarke. The Confessing Church would eventually include members of the League. Between January and May, free synods met at various locations; the assembly of roughly 25,000 at Dortmund in March was one of the largest. The culmination of the free synods was the First Confessing Synod of the Evangelical Church of the Old Prussian Union, which met on May 29, 1934 at Barmen. This assembly laid the basis for the Confessing Church as a rival organization to the national Protestant church in Germany (EDK).

The Barmen Declaration, proposed and ratified by the Confessing Church at the May meeting, was chiefly the work of Karl Barth even though he was not involved in German church politics. At the time when Hitler came to power, Barth continued to work on his lectures on nineteenth-century theology and understood that his "first priority" as a professor was to persuade students "to keep working as normally as possible in the midst of the general uproar."[17] When he did consider politics, Barth thought about membership in the Social Democratic Party if only to protest Nazi policies that threatened the dismissal of professors from civil service appointments for belonging to another political party. Still, he did bristle over the National Socialist control of the Evangelical Church. In a sermon peached at the end of 1933 Barth provocatively highlighted Jesus' racial identity. He also prompted a discussion of theological first principles in *Theological Existence Today*. Here Barth reaffirmed the biblical injunctions against worshiping false gods and the sufficiency of the gospel in Jesus Christ. The work appeared on July 8, 1934 and circulated widely: 37,000 copies were printed and Barth made sure that Hitler received one. Within three weeks of publication the German government had banned the treatise.

Barth was a natural ally for the Confessing Church movement but remained ambivalent about German Protestantism. He had known the leaders of the Pastors' Emergency League and Confessing synods for some time and appreciated their stance. At the same time, Barth believed that the Confessing synods were voicing objections on grounds that were too narrow: whether or not to remain within the national church. For him, the real question was National Socialism, not simply the status of the German churches in the new government. If the chancellor of Germany were actually saying what Nazi teaching claimed, then the churches needed to recognize, according to Barth, that Hitler was "a god incarnate and offending most seriously against the first commandment."[18] Despite tensions between Barth and the Confessing Church leaders, he participated in the first synod in January of 1934, where delegates discussed his paper on the status and conception of the Reformation confessions within contemporary Germany. Barth may have given the delegates more than they wanted to hear when he reiterated that the problem with German churches was not simply the dominance of the Nazis but centuries of capitulation to German rulers.

The second Confessing synod, which ratified Barth's Barmen Declaration, combined awkwardly the historic conservatism of the German churches and Barth's radical theological affirmations. The fifth article on the state was cautious but did break with older Reformation teaching, which held that the civil magistrate had some responsibility for maintaining the true religion:

Scripture tells us that, in the as yet unredeemed world in which the Church also exists, the State has by divine appointment the task of providing for justice and peace. [It fulfills this task] by means of the threat and exercise of force, according to the measure of human judgment and human ability. The Church acknowledges the benefit of this divine appointment in gratitude and reverence before him. It calls to mind the Kingdom of God, God's commandment and righteousness, and thereby the responsibility both of rulers and of the ruled. It trusts and obeys the power of the Word by which God upholds all things.[19]

With this affirmation came rejections of state power that harbored totalitarian impulses or church power that embodied characteristics of the state. To Barth's later regret, the Declaration did not make the Jewish question "a decisive feature."[20] Barmen's radicalism was evident in its first two articles, which recognized Christ as the only revelation and the Bible as the sole source of the church's proclamation. If the delegates rejected all other "events and powers, figures and truths, as God's revelation," as Barmen indicated, and limited their task simply to proclaiming the word of God, some might wonder about the status of all confessions, even that of Barmen, which used the powers of human reasoning to understand Scripture. Soon after the Synod, Barth issued his famous "Nein!" to Emil Brunner's proposal to recover natural theology. In the context of a dispute over the state's authority as a manifestation of the created order, Barth's heated rejection made sense. But his insistence on the Word of God understood only by the work of the Holy Spirit raised questions about the human aspects of Christian ministry and witness that Barmen failed to answer.

Barth's unique doctrinal convictions were not alone responsible for the lack of unanimity among Confessing Church leaders. His socialist convictions always proved a stumbling block among German church leaders, who were historically conservative and preferred the church's status under the monarchy. At the same time, confessional Lutherans remained wary of the Confessing Church because Barmen seemed to undermine the status of Lutheran confessions. Some Lutherans in particular took issue with Barth's idiosyncratic understanding of Scripture and the church. Beyond Lutheran opposition Barth also differed with Confessing Church leaders on the aims of the movement. While Barth was prepared to abandon the trappings of ecclesiastical establishment altogether for the sake of the church's proclamation, most of the Confessing Church members wanted recognition from the Nazi regime. As a result, when German officials began to investigate Barth's disloyalty to the Nazi government – he refused to take an oath of allegiance to the Führer and to give the Nazi salute before his classroom prayers – he was basically on his own. The Confessing Church would not identify its aims with Barth's, and at one point some of its leaders refused to invite him to their synod. For his part, Barth believed the Confessing Church had "no heart for the millions who suffer unjustly."[21] After a period of being banned from the classroom and public speaking, on June 14, 1935, Barth accepted an offer to teach at the University of Basel.

After his relocation, Barth and the Confessing Church went broadly separate ways, though Barth did continue to monitor the German church and enlisted support for German Protestants among the Swiss. The Confessing Church failed to gain recognition from the German authorities, and after 1936 it and the German Christians were merely two factions within a national church overseen by the Ministry of Church Affairs, which used intimidation and mediation to control clergy. Differences also afflicted the Confessing Church. Lutherans balked at Barmen as a true expression of Lutheran theology. Furthermore, in territories where they had retained control over local church committees Lutherans rejected calls by Confessing Church leaders to contest the regime's ecclesiastical administration. The one issue on which the Confessing Church achieved unanimity was in opposing the government's effort to secularize the nation's schools.

Meanwhile, Barth went back to teaching Reformed subjects and composing the *Church Dogmatics*. In 1937 he delivered the Gifford Lectures at Aberdeen and chose the Scottish Confession (1560) as the basis of his presentation on the knowledge of God. He also started a new series of classroom lectures on the Heidelberg Catechism. Onlookers may have wondered how Barth could continue to study old documents in a context where those confessions made so little difference. And yet, his lectures fit Barth's emphasis on divine transcendence and God's word. They also isolated Barth from Protestants who looked to the state churches as the embodiment of ministering Scripture. This was a theological move clearly in step with the original Reformed protest against Rome's easily abused identification of God's designs with the pope's determinations. But whether Barth would grant God a point of contact with fallen humanity was a question that haunted his breathtaking recovery of church dogma.

Neo-Orthodox Boundaries

After World War II, Barth's reputation and influence expanded thanks to his ongoing intellectual productivity and the increased opportunities for personal exchange and ecclesiastical fraternity that accompanied peace. After the war, he accepted an offer to teach summer semesters at Bonn, where he attracted other opportunities for speaking, preaching, and giving interviews with the media.

Barth also established contacts with former colleagues in the Confessing Church movement. Wherever he taught, whether in Basel for the regular year or in Bonn over the summer, Barth received visits from numerous church leaders from Denmark, Sweden, Poland, Hungary, Czechoslovakia, and Germany. He was not simply the most productive and widely published European Protestant theologian, but was also perceived as a man of political conviction who had stood up to the worst regime in European history.

Barth was readily accessible to German-speaking Protestants, but his reception in the Anglo-American world was delayed. The most important conduit for Barthianism to Presbyterian churches was Scotland, and specifically faculty and students from the New College at Edinburgh, a theological school originally established by the Free Church of Scotland but now part of the University's faculty, thanks to the recent merger in 1929 of the United Free Church and the Church of Scotland.[22] Hugh Ross Mackintosh (1870–1936), who lectured in systematic theology at New College since 1904, originally taught a version of theology that followed the trail established by Albrecht Ritschl. Like Barth, Mackintosh had studied at Marburg with Wilhelm Hermann. But by the 1920s when Barth's writings were circulating, Mackintosh shifted into a dialectical mode, particularly in his posthumously published book *Types of Modern Theology, Schleiermacher to Barth* (1933).

One of Mackintosh's students who played a critical role in the reception of Barth was Thomas F. Torrance. The son of Church of Scotland missionaries to China, Torrance had studied philosophy at Edinburgh as an undergraduate, and then arrived at New College in pursuit of ministerial credentials. Torrance finished his academic training at Basel from 1937 to 1938, where he studied with Barth. Although he did not know German at first, and while struggling with Barth's pronunciation of Latin, the young Scot excelled to the point of becoming one of the Swiss theologian's prized pupils. (Three decades later, when Barth retired, his recommendation was for Torrance to be his successor at Basel.) After a year in Switzerland, one of his professors from New College arranged for an appointment for Torrance at Auburn Theological Seminary in upstate New York, an institution of the Presbyterian Church USA, and the place of origin for the liberal Presbyterian manifesto "The Auburn Affirmation" (1923). Between his missionary background and studies with Barth, Torrance sounded more conservative than the colleagues that the progressive faculty at Auburn were used to. Torrance passed the year teaching systematic theology without any serious incidents, but his experience was an indication of how much more theological (read: dogmatic in the older sense) and churchly were members of European Protestant theological faculties than their peers in the United States.

Torrance turned down offers to teach at the University of Chicago and at Princeton University in 1939, deciding to return to Europe instead and serve as a chaplain in the British military. Throughout the 1940s he served in parish ministry, but in 1950 accepted an appointment at New College where he transmitted Barth's theology in two significant ways. The first was through classroom instruction; the second was to persuade the Scottish publisher T&T Clark to publish an English translation of Barth's *Church Dogmatics*. Torrance served on the two-person editorial team with Geoffrey Bromiley, an English historical theologian teaching at the newly founded Fuller Theological Seminary in California, who performed the bulk of translation.

Torrance was not the sole mediator of Barth to the English-speaking world. Barth's influence in Scotland extended to theologians at Glasgow and Aberdeen where the likes of Ian Henderson, Ronald G. Smith, and John K. S. Reid appropriated Barthian themes into their own teaching and writing, considered by some to embody the best of Scottish neo-orthodox theology. These contributions, however, made no obvious dent on Scottish Presbyterian churches, in part because the communions' Calvinist creeds had prevented liberal theology from dominating ecclesiastical life as it had in Germany. At the same time, the Church of Scotland never came under the same pressure to issue Barmen-like affirmations because the Scottish authorities did not pose a threat to Presbyterianism on the order of National Socialism. This left Barthianism to develop in the classroom, study, and pulpit, depending on the theological interests of a divinity professor or pastor. It did not generate a program of ecclesiastical reform or renewal.

In situations where Reformed confessions as expressions of church teaching held little force – such as England and the United States – Barth's writings had much less influence. Some of this difference owed to the lack of familiarity with – and in some cases hostility to – German theology. But equally important to the reception of Barth in the United States was the presence of a homegrown version of neo-orthodoxy produced by Reinhold Niebuhr (1892–1971). The son of a German-American minister in Wright City, Missouri, Niebuhr studied at his denomination's (Evangelical Synod of North America) college (Elmhurst) and seminary (Eden) before enrolling at Yale for degrees at the Divinity School and in arts and sciences. After graduating from Yale, Niebuhr received a call to serve as parish minister in Detroit, to an Evangelical Synod congregation. This ecclesiastical body was a direct successor of the Evangelical Church of the Prussian Union. When some of its members immigrated to the United States and settled in Illinois and Missouri, they sought pastors from the Old World who upon their arrival in America in 1840 formed German Evangelical Church Association of the West, the Evangelical Synod's original name. This meant that

Niebuhr's lone pastoral experience was in the American offshoot of the Prussian Union church. In 1928 he accepted a teaching post in social ethics at Union Theological Seminary, the most influential liberal Presbyterian school in the United States. By 1934 the Evangelical Synod had merged with the German Reformed denomination, the Reformed Church US, to form the Evangelical and Reformed Church.

Barth's first encounter with Niebuhr occurred in 1947 when the American visited Barth at Basel. The Swiss professor later wondered whether "we would sniff at each other, or lie stretched out peacefully in the sun side by side."[23] By that point, Niebuhr was every bit the spokesman for neo-orthodoxy that Barth was. In fact, in the United States the Yale professor was the preferred option for mainstream Protestant pastors and professors, since Barth's project of producing a church dogmatics was distant from the intellectual habits that prevailed among Americans. Much of this appeal owed to Niebuhr's own efforts as a pastor, when he had tried to apply liberal Protestant ideals to the gritty realities of an urban, working-class neighborhood. He had realized that liberal idealism about the fatherhood of God and the brotherhood of man was powerless to address deep-seated social problems. In 1932 Niebuhr took matters into his own hands and ran for Congress on the Socialist ticket, arguing that only socialism had the rigor to save western civilization. He won 4 percent of the vote. That same year saw the publication of *Moral Man and Immoral Society*, which introduced a strain of ethical realism to mainstream Protestants in the United States. Instead of invoking the ethics of love and self-sacrifice, Niebuhr taught liberal Protestants about the realities of power politics and the ever present reality of self-interest. For liberals to hope that people would embrace selflessness was "stupid"[24]; Niebuhr preferred radical politics to the hypocritical status quo. By 1934 he had repudiated pacifism and rejected the tenets of liberal Protestant progressivism: that education promotes justice, that western civilization was improving, that character was more important than social structures, that appeals to love and justice would overcome selfishness and greed, and that wars are simply the product of ignorance. Although he eventually abandoned socialism, Niebuhr maintained a sober perspective on American and world affairs. This outlook even appealed to secular liberals because of its frank affirmation of the West in the face of Soviet communist tyranny.

When Barth and Niebuhr met again in 1948 at the World Council of Churches inaugural assembly, held in Amsterdam, the former's opening address became the occasion for these neo-orthodox leaders to air their differences. The Council's theme was "The Disorder of the World and God's Design," and Barth argued that "God's Design" should always go before the "World's Disorder." The church's task was to witness that Christ had "robbed sin and death, the devil and hell of their power." He elaborated that the church was not responsible for solving the world's problems; its task was to announce the kingdom of God. As such, "God's Design" for the world was not a kind of "Christian Marshall Plan" but a requirement to trust in and follow the Lord Jesus Christ. To Niebuhr's ears this was typical Barthian fundamentalism, a "sanctified futilitarianism."[25] He challenged Barth for relegating the church to institutional irrelevance and denying Christians any voice in discriminating between better and worse forms of social organization.

The brawl between neo-orthodox heavyweights persisted throughout the 1950s, precisely because the international tensions evident during the initial phase of the Cold War raised the larger question of the church's role in resistance to Communism. For Niebuhr, Barth's insistence that God stood above all polit-ical arrangements, even capitalism and socialism, left vast parts of eastern Europe condemned to totalitarian rule, with no recourse to divinely derived opposition. For Barth, Niebuhr's defense of liberal societies in the West naively ignored capitalism's and democracy's own forms of tyranny. One positive outcome was Niebuhr's recognition of his dependence on liberal theology. In 1960 he wrote: "when I find neo-orthodoxy turning into a sterile orthodoxy or new Scholasticism, I find that I am a liberal at heart, and that many of my broad-sides against liberalism were indiscriminate."[26] Barth had a similar effect on other American proponents of neo-orthodoxy whose ecclesiastical and doctrinal contexts were distinct from Europe.

Confessing Neo-Orthodoxy

Barth's disagreements with Niebuhr did not prevent the Swiss theologian from appearing on the cover of *Time* magazine on April 20, 1962, an indication of how much Americans had incorporated Barth within their reflections about Christianity. The news story coincided with Easter (hence the title, "Witness to an Ancient Truth"), Barth's first visit to the United States where the University of Chicago was granting him an honorary doctorate, and his seventy-fifth birthday. Barth's appeal in the United States was largely enigmatic, according to *Time*'s reporter. On the one hand, no contemporary theologian had ventured as comprehensive a statement of the Christian religion as he had. On the other hand, he had earned political stripes for standing up to Hitler and the Nazis, even speaking of the Führer in terms that echoed American sentiments: "the enter-prise of an evil spirit." But Barth was hardly a household name. The story cred-ited the Swiss theologian with composing theology that "soared across denominational boundaries, affecting the thought of Baptists, Lutherans and Episcopalians as well as his own Reformed Church." This meant that preachers read Barth and used him for weekly sermons, but "laymen hardly know his name." *Time*'s reporter also judged that Barth had "far fewer disciples in the U.S. than either Niebuhr or Tillich; and even in Germany, young theologians find more impact in the Christian existentialism of Rudolf Bultmann."[27]

One Protestant leader of note in the United States, whom *Time* quoted on Barth – "he bestrides the theological world like a colossus" – was John Mackay, the president of Princeton Theological Seminary. A native of the Scottish Highlands and a son of the Free Presbyterian Church, Mackay's interest in Barth owed more to his European than American connections. After studying at the University of Aberdeen, Mackay pursued theological training at Princeton Seminary, thanks partly to ties between his pastor and Princeton's foremost theologian, Benjamin Breckinridge Warfield. At Princeton, Mackay entered the world of mainstream American Protestant ecumenism and became active in the YMCA and Student Volunteer Movement. Between 1916 and 1930, he served as a schoolmaster in Peru under the auspices of the Free Presbyterian Church and then as an evangelist for the YMCA in Uruguay. While on furlough in 1930, Mackay knew that Barth would be teaching at Bonn and relocated his family so that he could hear the Swiss theologian's lectures. Although not without misgivings, the evangelist expressed "deep sympathy" with the dialectical school of theology, precisely because Barth was "rehabilitating in contemporary thought the concept of God held by the great Hebrew prophets as well as that of Jesus Christ."[28] After returning to Latin America, American Presbyterian officials offered Mackay the post of president of Princeton Seminary in 1936. His chief task at Princeton was to heal the controversy that had divided the seminary between conservatives like J. Gresham Machen and evangelicals like Charles Erdman (see Chapter Twelve, above). The selection of Mackay was stroke of genius. As a Scot he came without any of the negative associations that haunted either liberals or conservatives in the American church, and as a Scot with a conservative ecclesiastical background and openness to neo-orthodoxy, Mackay was well equipped to position Princeton to the conservative side of mainstream American Protestantism without becoming extreme (read: sectarian).

Under Mackay, Princeton Seminary emerged as the home for continental neo-orthodox reflection in the United States and an alternative to Niebuhrian realism at Union Seminary in New York City. His selections would not always have pleased Barth but his new faculty did draw from European theological currents, such as the appointment of Emil Brunner for the academic year 1938–39. (Brunner declined a permanent position.) Objections from remaining conservatives in the PCUSA led Mackay to assert that "Princeton is virtually a bulwark of dialectical theology."[29] To back this up, Mackay added a host of biblical and theological scholars from Europe whose ties to the United States were mainly through ecumenical networks. In addition to Brunner, Mackay recruited: Otto Piper, a German theologian who had succeeded Barth at Münster; Josef Hromádka, a Czech theologian who had escaped his homeland after Nazi occupation through ecumenical leaders in Geneva; and two French scholars, Georges Barrois, a philosophical theologian, and Emile Cailliet, an archaeologist. Rounding out Princeton's international faculty were George Hendry, a Presbyterian from Scotland who did advanced work at Tübingen and Berlin, and Edward J. Jurji, a Lebanese scholar of world religions.

Arguably, the most important Princeton faculty member for securing a Barthian presence in North America, Edward A. Dowey, Jr, was one who started as a student soon after Mackay's inauguration as president. A native of Philadelphia, Dowey studied nearby at a Presbyterian school, Lafayette College in Pennsylvania, before enrolling at Princeton in 1940. Dowey was not keen on all members of the European faculty, but he did admire and seek out Mackay, who assisted the seminarian in finding theological resolution through Barth's writings. After service as a chaplain during World War II, Dowey pursued graduate study, first in the United States at Columbia University in philosophy and then in Zurich under Emil Brunner. Despite deep disagreements between professor and student, which echoed the 1930s exchanges between Brunner and Barth, Dowey completed a dissertation on John Calvin's doctrine of the knowledge of God. Upon his return to the United States, Dowey taught briefly at Columbia, then at McCormick Theological Seminary in Chicago, and in 1958 finally returned to Princeton under Mackay, where he taught for three decades.

Soon after joining Princeton's faculty, Dowey received an appointment from the Presbyterian Church USA to chair a committee responsible for drafting a brief summary of the Reformed faith. The occasion for this doctrinal statement was the 1958 ecclesiastical merger between the PCUSA and the United Presbyterian Church of North America – resulting in a twenty-five year period when the northern Presbyterian church was known as the United Presbyterian Church USA. Under Dowey's leadership, the committee received the General Assembly's approval to survey Reformed Protestantism's entire confessional heritage. The culmination was a proposed Book of Confessions and a new Confession of Faith. Between 1965 and 1967 American Presbyterians debated the merits of both documents. The purpose of the former was to enlarge the church's witness beyond the Westminster Confession and Catechisms and to include a range of Christian creeds. These spanned Christian history from the ancient church (the Nicene and Apostles' creeds) to the Reformation era (Scots Confession, Heidelberg Catechism, and Second Helvetic Confession). The proposed book of confessions also included two twentieth-century statements – the Barmen Declaration and the Confession of 1967 – both of which revealed the unmistakable fingerprints of Barthianism.

At the same time, the Barthian influence proved to be the most contested aspect of the new confessional statements. In summarizing the Christian faith – "In Jesus Christ God was reconciling the world to himself. Jesus Christ is God with man" – the Confession of 1967 drew upon the Christocentric teaching that Barth had been developing for the better part of three decades. But when the Confession reserved for Christ the status of "Word of God" (with a capital "w"), Barth's teaching became harder to negotiate. Some conservatives wanted the Confession to affirm that the Bible was also the Word of God. In fact, controversy over the Confession launched two dissenting organizations, Presbyterians United for Biblical Confession and the Presbyterian Lay Committee, a harbinger of the special-interest groups that would torment the Presbyterian Church USA throughout the late twentieth century. The compromise that finally gained approval reserved a special status for Christ while acknowledging the uniqueness of the Old and New Testaments:

> The one sufficient revelation of God is Jesus Christ, the Word of God incarnate, to whom the Holy Spirit bears unique and authoritative witness through the Holy Scriptures, which are received and obeyed as the word of God written. The Scriptures are not a witness among others, but the witness without parallel. The church has received the books of the Old and New Testaments as prophetic and apostolic testimony in which it hears the word of God and by which its faith and obedience are nourished and regulated.

Ironically, at the very moment that Barth's labors gained ecclesiastical approval and confessional standing, neo-orthodoxy's influence was subsiding thanks to the very inspiration that Barth had provided through the Barmen Declaration. The inclusion of Barmen in the American Presbyterian Book of Confessions drew little opposition because many in the church regarded the heroic struggle of German Protestants against the Third Reich as a model for Protestant churches in the United States to speak religious truth to government power. Although Barth had insisted that the church must limit its message to the reconciliation available to the world through Jesus Christ – a point that Niebuhr found indifferent to the "social crisis" – Barmen functioned as a pretext for the church-based social activism that would dominate the Presbyterian Church's assemblies. The Confession of 1967 tapped protests in the United States against racial segregation, the subordination of women, the Vietnam War, and corporate capitalism in a section on "Reconciliation in Society." This included affirmations of the church's opposition to discrimination, war, poverty, and sexual anarchy.

The Presbyterian Church proved what Barth had known since his exchange with Niebuhr after World War II – namely, that the United States' capacity for proclaiming church dogma could not withstand the American predilection for activism.

The American Presbyterian reception of Barth was ironic not simply because a church was incorporating a non-political theological program partly for the sake of social relevance but also because the Swiss theologian's work in Reformed dogmatics turned out to be alien to most contemporary Reformed churches, American Presbyterians included. Compared to Thomas Chalmers, Abraham Kuyper, or J. Gresham Machen, Barth had done more to learn from and appropriate the theology of the historic Reformed churches. However much his philosophical oddities or dialectical method colored doctrines taught by John Calvin or the Heidelberg Catechism, Barth featured those earlier statements of Reformed conviction in ways that surpassed even the best efforts of conservative church leaders in Scotland, the Netherlands, or the United States.

Yet Barth's recovery of Reformed orthodoxy occurred in contexts where the churches were ill equipped to reflect on and benefit from the past. Whether in Germany, where Reformed churches had languished for several centuries under the weight of German politics, or in Switzerland, where civil polity and social order also put limits on the churches, Barth's recovery of Reformation theology was not institutional but depended on individual pastors and theologians, who would imitate Barth's stance and apply his teaching. The United States and its mainline Presbyterian Church was the sole instance of a Reformed church that attempted to appropriate Barth's insights. Even this appeal to Barth, however, turned out to be partial and inconsistent.

Perhaps the failure of Barth's theology to find ecclesiastical outlets owed to his odd blend of themes from continental philosophy and early modern theology. Just as important, if not more so, was the shallowness of the institutional setting in which Barth labored. Without an ecclesiastical program adding the recovery of Reformed confessions to the heroism of social and political protest, the appeal of Reformation theology would depend on the idiosyncrasies of individual theologians' seminars and writing projects. At the same time, Barth's theology dominated twentieth-century Protestant thought and would rival Calvin's teaching for supremacy within academic theology. For pastors, church leaders, and professors who wanted a serious engagement with Reformed doctrine without the stigma of separatism that haunted followers of Chalmers, Kuyper, and Machen, Barth was and would remain the answer.

CONCLUSION

In April of 2010, Sebastian Heck conducted the first worship service of a new Reformed congregation in the city of Heidelberg. A German native, the pastor trained for the ministry at a non-denominational seminary in Germany before pursuing doctoral studies in the United States. His work is part of a church-planting effort overseen and subsidized by a congregation in the Presbyterian Church of America (a denomination formed in 1973 from conservative opposition to liberal and ecumenical trends in the southern Presbyterian Church). In fact, Heck's ministerial credentials come from a presbytery in the state of Georgia. After a year of conducting services, the Independent Evangelical Reformed Church in Heidelberg is small, dedicated, and working to secure an arrangement with city authorities to allow its members to worship in the historic Church of the Holy Spirit. The start of this congregation is indicative of the enormous changes between the sixteenth-century origins of Calvinism and contemporary prospects for Reformed churches. It also demonstrates an important feature of Calvinism's global reach and presence.

When Reformed Protestantism emerged in the 1520s, pastors like Ulrich Zwingli could not rent a room in a center-city facility to conduct Protestant worship services. Instead they needed approval from the city council to meet at all, and once they secured the magistrate's backing they automatically gained access to the city's church buildings. The same was true for the city of Heidelberg some forty years later, even if the form of government differed from Zurich. When Pierre Boquin teamed up with other Reformed theologians at Heidelberg University and instituted reforms of the city's congregations, they did so at the behest and with the approval of Frederick III. To Zwingli or Boquin, the idea of believers meeting on their own and voluntarily supporting a pastor under the jurisdiction of a foreign church body would have been inconceivable.

In early modern Europe churches were woven into the fabric of the social order, and any change threatened both earthly and heavenly powers. That is why the church reforms introduced by Calvinism could not have survived without the endorsement of civil authorities. But in late modern Europe, churches are simply one of many forms of human organization that citizens and rulers may support or ignore, with no direct bearing on the wellbeing of communities or residents. This is why starting Reformed churches in cities like Heidelberg is possible, despite the history and traditions of German Reformed Protestantism that haunt the city, and why these churches may survive without the endorsement of contemporary German rulers. That seismic shift in church–state relations and in modern understandings of religion's importance puts an exclamation point on the challenges that led Calvinists first to deplore the demise of Christendom and then to laud the benefits of differentiating the religious and secular spheres.

The emergence of a conservative Reformed congregation in Heidelberg with ties to a United States Presbyterian denomination also illustrates the international qualities of Calvinism. Reformed Protestantism has been a global faith since the seventeenth century when Calvinist teachings and practices spread throughout Europe and began to surface in new worlds recently discovered by Europeans. Of course, Calvin, who was by no means the defining character for Reformed Protestantism that Luther was to Lutheranism, had no ambitions for a church with global proportions. The early leaders of the Reformed churches were Eurocentric, like most Europeans, and their hope was to restore western Christianity to its biblical origins. But the Reformation coincided with the expansion of European civilization around the world through the efforts of colonial merchants and the migration of peoples. Calvinism was not the driver of this first vehicle of globalization but merely one of the many passengers. By the beginning of the eighteenth century, Reformed churches were holding services in Asia, Africa, and North America. Within the next century, the reach of Calvinism would extend to Australia and South America.

Calvinism and Global Christianity

Reformed churches were by no means alone in the processes that took western Christianity to other parts of the world but recent studies of what has become known as global Christianity have tended to overlook the extensive networks and numbers of adherents for which Calvinism was responsible. In fact, scholarship on contemporary global Christianity has contrasted European or western Christianity with newer expressions of Christian devotion in the southern hemisphere. This contrast includes a sometimes dismissive tone from scholars and journalists toward the formal, cerebral, and somber qualities of European Christianity. Western churches supposedly lack the spontaneity, vitality, and fervency of churches in the global South. According to Philip Jenkins, the author of *The Next Christendom*, the "center of gravity" in the Christian world has shifted from the northern to the southern hemisphere, from Europe and North America to Africa, Asia, and Latin America. Indeed, Latin America and Africa are homes to the largest Christian communities in the world. In contrast, the nations with the most Christians in 1950 – Britain, France, Spain, and Italy – are nowhere on the current lists of religious adherents. These differences have led scholars like Jenkins to predict that within the next century global Christianity will be the dominant version of Christian expression, while the churches that trace their roots to Europe will continue to fade into oblivion. "The era of Western Christianity has passed," Jenkins writes, "and the day of southern Christianity is dawning."[1]

As much as such prognostications blur lines between divine agency and human fertility, they do explain why Calvinism fails to register as an expression of global Christianity. The differences are not simply numerical or historical. Reformed Protestantism can claim communions throughout the civilized world and has done so for at least 250 years. One recent survey indicated that Reformed and Presbyterian churches have close to 550 communions on the six habitable continents. The largest number of Reformed Protestants come from churches in Asia (150 denominations), Africa (132), and Europe (118). North America accounts for thirty separate Reformed communions. But in raw numerical totals, Calvinism lags well behind many of the churches that count as global Christianity's "next Christendom." A 2000 set of data indicated that Reformed and Presbyterian churches worldwide accounted for approximately 26,000,000 members in close to 98,000 congregations. In contrast, Pentecostal and charismatic churches had as many as 38,000,000 adherents in roughly 285,000 congregations. (This does not include independent congregations, which are often more common in developing countries than ones affiliated with a denomination; in 2000, independent Protestants numbered over 190,000,000 members in approximately 1,600,000 congregations.) Reformed church leaders may plausibly have claimed two centuries ago to be a faith on the front lines of global Christianity, but that is no longer the case.

Important for putting into perspective this contrast between contemporary and historic forms of global Christianity is the enduring nature of Calvinism's appeal, even when it was expanding in significant ways beyond western Europe. As Jenkins shows in his study of Christianity in the global South, the animating force in many non-Western churches is a form of devotion that is highly relevant to people in developing societies on the margins of economic and political modernization. Southern Christianity offers a spiritual universe that runs parallel to that of animism and spiritualism. In effect, charismatic and Pentecostal Protestantism is a Christian version of the surrounding native faiths. The importance of the Holy Spirit's power to global Christians is not simply personal or spiritual. In countless urban settings, churches have become vehicles for social services yet to emerge from either governmental or community sources. According to Jenkins, "The churches provide a social network that would otherwise be lacking, and help teach members the skills they need to survive in a rapidly developing society."[2] These resources extend beyond Christian acts of charity; they also include a divine presence that leads to supernatural healings, exorcisms, and miraculous financial provisions. Despite the popular perception that Spirit-filled Christianity is escapist and otherworldly, this global faith is precisely the opposite. According to one Brazilian pastor, the appeal of new southern churches "is that they present a God that you can use." "Most Presbyterians," he adds, "have a God that's so great, so big, that they cannot even talk with him openly, because he is far away. The Pentecostal groups have the kind of God that will solve my problems today and tomorrow. People today are looking for solutions, not for eternity."[3]

However much this comment may caricature the piety and appeal of southern Christianity, it serves as a useful contrast with Calvinism's global presence. Of course, the idea of Calvin's deity as the great welfare agency in the cosmos would have been appalling to the original Reformed pastors. The transcendence of God and the wickedness of humans were truths that prevented most Reformed and Presbyterian believers from ever developing expectations that their God would keep them from experiencing hardships or even spare them from persecution, famine, or death. At the same time, Reformed teaching about God, human nature, Christ, and the Christian ministry did sustain people who were experiencing the initial stages of globalization. Calvinism's God may have been far off and his ways may have been inscrutable, but belief in a transcendent and holy God sustained seventeenth- and eighteenth-century refugees, immigrants, and colonists in conditions not far removed from those in contemporary Lagos, Mexico City, or Jakarta.

Although Calvinism sustained people through a variety of hardships, its appeal, even in its most vigorous and successful phases, was always subdued. In sixteenth-century Europe Reformed Protestantism started well and gained a following in practically every territory, even where penalties for following the new faith were harsh. Congregations met in locales as different as Edinburgh and Sárospatak, and Reformed churches counted as many as ten million adherents across the continent. But by the turn of the seventeenth century, politics, war, and internal declension limited Reformed vitality to Scotland, England, the

Netherlands, Switzerland, and some German-speaking territories such as Brandenburg-Prussia. Even in Reformed strongholds like the Dutch and Scottish churches, the experience of the seventeenth century was beginning to teach lessons about the compromises political patrons would require from ecclesiastical establishments. Outside Europe in colonial contexts, Calvinism gained a foothold in North America and South Africa but Reformed churches lacked freedom to construct a society afresh upon religious convictions. Instead, struggles with governors and settlers were often as difficult – though less bloody – as those in Europe. The expansion of Calvinism through foreign missions came late to Reformed churches, but once it did support was vigorous, even if the results were mixed. Finally, in recent history the efforts of figures such as Chalmers, Kuyper, Machen, or Barth took place as protests from the margins of ecclesiastical and political life. Reformed Protestantism's leaders traditionally liked to think of their history as one of unfolding world dominance, but just as plausible was a narrative that featured as many setbacks as victories.

Of course, no Christian communion has had an easy time adjusting to the conditions of modern society. Reformed Protestantism's challenges may have been greater than other Christian traditions, though, thanks precisely to Calvinism's sternly theocentric piety. Leigh Eric Schmidt summed up this problem:

> What the Reformed Church offered in the place of the old calendar and the traditional festivals was a spiritual life of sustained discipline and devotion.... Day-in, day-out, Sabbath after Sabbath, the Reformed saints were to strive after joyful, harmonious communion with their God and their fellow Christians.... The hope for a community of saints who year-round were diligent, self-controlled, sober, prayerful, and devout within their families and outside them ran up against an older way of organizing devotional life around festal public events. In the traditional society of early modern Europe people could live their lives "in remembrance of one festival and in expectation of the next." The reformers sought to end this cycle, to make life a perpetual festivity with Christ.[4]

As demanding and unrelenting as Calvinism may have been, its genius was a capacity to adapt to diverse settings. What was true of the sixteenth century, when Reformed churches sprang up in various political, cultural, and linguistic settings, also characterizes Calvinism throughout its history. In colonial, missions, and secular contexts, Calvinists have adapted their institutions to new realities. In fact, the churches that had to alter established ways the most – particularly the voluntary communions – became the most successful in perpetuating Reformed norms, while established national communions suffered significant decline thanks to the constraints of serving a diverse public. Presbyterian forms of government, the order that Calvin himself developed as early as the 1540s, deserve much credit for Reformed Protestantism's adaptability. Rule by assemblies that ranged between groups of local churches and national representatives granted to Reformed and Presbyterian churches a responsiveness to particular communities or regions and an outlet for institutional coherence across large territories or nations. Adjusting to theological or intellectual challenges would prove more difficult, and some of the greatest statements of Reformed orthodoxy came in response to doctrinal deviations. Once freed from the patronage of the state and lacking the power to require uniformity, Reformed responses to doctrinal error would usually take the form of secession and the establishment of a rival communion. Even here, the presbyterian model of organization supplied new denominations or churches with a connection to a shared order and heritage.

The power of adaptation has also proven to be a liability in the sense that Calvinism today lacks the international solidarity that prevailed during the controversies and beginning phases of the sixteenth century. In those days, Reformed scholars and churchmen regularly studied outside their native countries and participated in the assemblies of other national churches. Ministers who grew up in one kingdom and served in the Reformed communion of another government were not unusual. Part of this solidarity stemmed from Europe's political circumstances, which required Protestants to rally together against Roman Catholic civil authorities in order to survive. Part also owed to geographical proximity and the shared cultural memory and associations of Christendom. But even in Europe, as states solidified national identities, the respective churches grew isolated. Ministers or church members might move between different communions depending on political realities, but the national churches themselves turned inward and lost connections to an international movement of Reformed Protestantism. Isolation only increased in colonial, New World, and missionary contexts. Geographical, linguistic, and national barriers reinforced the distinct identities of particular communions. Presbyterians in Canada and the United States interacted little. Scottish and Dutch churches went their separate ways. Only the emergence of a heroic figure, like a Chalmers or Kuyper, injected an international awareness among those communions that traced their core convictions back to a celebrated church leader. But even in these cases, the interaction among the Free Church Presbyterians, Dutch neo-Calvinists, conservative American Presbyterians, and Barthians was minimal. Each of the recovery movements from the past two hundred years has cultivated its own sense of identity and traditions. And with this, ironically, has come

ignorance of Reformed tradition and communion before the rise of each movement's courageous institution builder.

The Geography of Global Calvinism

For all the isolation that Calvinist adaptability has encouraged, Reformed
Protestantism over the last century falls into three main groups, which reveal a
measure of coherence despite their diversity. One set might best be described as
ecumenical Calvinists, who have associations through the World Council of
Reformed Communions (formerly the World Alliance of Reformed Churches).
Headquartered in Geneva, the organization includes over two hundred communions (both Reformed and Congregational) from 107 countries, with an estimated (2006) membership of 75 million, and convenes an international assembly
every seven years. The Council's purposes are: to encourage unity among its
members; to appropriate the Reformed tradition; to promote peace, economic
and social justice, and human rights; to protect the environment; to foster an
inclusive community; and to nurture dialogue among Christians and other
religions. The WCRC includes most of the churches that trace their roots to
the original state churches or the colonial communions that maintained a
posture of ecclesiastical establishment. For many of these churches the
Reformation represents a pivotal time in the life of Christian witness, when the
churches were at the forefront of social justice and political activism. Although
this understanding has prompted adjustments, accompanied by liberal theology
and revamped ministry, these ecumenical Calvinists do perpetuate the older
Reformed ideal that churches should be part of the social fabric. To be sure, only
some of the member churches still possess establishment status. Still, ecumenical Calvinism embodies the older Reformation sense of the church serving a
Christian society.

The second group of Calvinists comprise of those who self-consciously reject
the kind of ecumenism that led to the softening or abandonment of historic
Reformed teaching. These committed and, in some cases, militant Calvinists repudiated cooperation to preserve instead the kinds of teaching and forms of ministry
that ecumenical churches abandoned or revised. Some of these Reformed
communions were once members of the Reformed Ecumenical Council, an international body of churches founded after World War II by Dutch neo-Calvinists.
But the Reformed Ecumenical Council gradually abandoned the militancy that
had prevailed among neo-Calvinists and conservative Presbyterians and in 2010
merged with the World Alliance of Reformed Churches. Now many of the
communions that still look to Chalmers, Kuyper, and Machen for inspiration
meet together in the International Council of Reformed Churches, a body of

roughly 700,000 church members in thirty communions (from fifteen nations), formed in 1982, with assemblies held every four years. For these Calvinists the Reformed tradition is primarily theological and their appropriation of the Reformation is largely through the reformers' confessions and ministry. These Reformed Protestants may be nostalgic for the status that Reformed churches enjoyed as part of the European national establishments, but are willing to abandon the church's social influence for the sake of theological clarity.

The last group of Reformed churches comes from communions in Africa, Asia, and South America – places of interest to students of global Christianity – that trace their roots to the church-planting efforts of foreign missionaries. It is impossible to number or trace their formal connections; these Calvinists may be associated with the World Council of Reformed Churches but their understanding of Reformed Protestantism derives less from the pursuit of a Christian society than it does from a sincere personal experience of grace. Here the forms of individual piety cultivated first by the Puritans and Dutch Reformed, and later Calvinistic revivalists, is decisive. Pietistic Calvinists, consequently, appropriate the reforms and teachings of the sixteenth century through the lens of the seventeenth century's practical divinity. This outlook in turn fosters not only an emphasis on personal devotion but focuses the attention of pastors and church officers more on the internal life of a congregation than on the corporate identity of denominations or ecumenical organizations. If some of these churches belong to ecumenical Calvinist organizations, the reasons owe more to the historic ties between European Churches and churches of the global South through foreign missions than to a shared commitment to Reformed Protestantism as an agent of social transformation.

One particular communion, the Protestant Church in the Moluccas (PCM), illustrates the status of non-western Reformed communions that began under European patronage and eventually acquired a separate existence. The Republic of Indonesia, a nation with over two hundred million people who live on the islands (over three thousand) between Southeast Asia and Australia, is overwhelmingly Muslim (87 percent); the Christian minority comprises roughly 10 percent of the population. The PCM has almost 600,000 members, served by almost 800 ministers in 720 parishes. The roots of the PCM go back to 1605, with the original settlement of Dutch colonists employed by the East India Company when Dutch and Protestant hegemony supplanted the Portuguese and Roman Catholicism. As was the case in North America and South Africa, Dutch colonists brought the trappings of European civilization, which included the establishment of Reformed churches. Unlike other instances of Dutch colonialism, the Netherlands remained a force in the archipelago right up 1949, when the Dutch East Indies became the Republic of Indonesia.

The Reformed churches in Indonesia remained part of the colonial enterprise until the early nineteenth century but would not gain independence for another century. Although dominated by Europeans, the churches did translate the Heidelberg Catechism and New Testament (1668) and the entire Bible (1733) into Malay. By 1799, with a change in governance from the East India Company to the Dutch Republic, freedom of religion became the norm and missionaries of all kinds arrived in Indonesia, including Joseph van der Kam.[5] Reformed Protestantism became one of many denominations, and the traditions of an older Dutch Protestantism had to adapt to the fervor of pietistic modern missionaries and their sponsoring societies. Not until 1935 did the PCM achieve autonomy and regulate its own affairs, with its own ministers and elders supervising the communion. Even so, financial support still came from the colonial government. Only with Indonesian independence after World War II would the PCM become generally free from civil authority. Indeed, during the period of Japanese occupation and the early phases of republican government the denomination advocated the separation of church and state to protect its prerogatives. At the same time, autonomy did not mean separation from other churches: the PCM is a member of Indonesian interdenominational church councils and it also belongs to the World Alliance of Reformed Churches. Its church government follows presbyterian models but its confessional status is generic; the PCM affirms the Apostles', Nicene, and Athanasian creeds. It shows the marks of a European past while also striving for an expression of Protestantism true to Indonesia's complicated history. The contours of the ecumenism practiced among theologically broad agencies like the World Alliance are roomy enough to include the PCM. But for fellowship among the stricter Reformed churches, the baggage of colonialism that comes with strict adherence to the Reformed creeds is too much for indigenous communions like the PCM to carry.

Calvinism, the West, and the World

Even if the fingerprints of the West are still evident on indigenous churches like those in Indonesia, this influence is much different from the one that inspired public intellectuals to speak in global categories about Calvinism and the modern world. The older claims made by the likes of Max Weber, Alexis de Tocqueville, or Robert K. Merton on behalf of Calvinism's influence on politics, economics, and science can no longer withstand close scrutiny. Scotland may deserve attention for producing a remarkable number of figures who "invented" the modern world, but the Scots' creativity stemmed less from Presbyterianism's guiding light than from the myriad of developments that accompanied modernization.[6] So too, John Locke's arguments for toleration may have been unthinkable without Geneva's political precedents, but modern societies have discovered any number of religious, philosophical, and political rationales for intellectual freedom and religious diversity other than ones adumbrated by Reformed Protestants.[7] Furthermore, when it comes to the cultural preconditions for the West's extraordinary dominance of recent world affairs, Lutherans, Anglicans, and Roman Catholics deserve as much credit as Calvinists.[8] In fact, contrary to the old Whig view, Calvinism was as much an agent of authoritarianism and intolerance as it was of liberty and popular sovereignty. Even so, Calvinism was one among a kaleidoscope of circumstances that vaulted Europeans into patterns of global dominance that, despite all of their liabilities and failings, evoke wonder and amazement. As William H. McNeill, the gifted world historian and son of Calvinism's first great chronicler, John T. McNeill, puts it: "We, and all the world of the twentieth century, are peculiarly the creatures and heirs of a handful of geniuses of early modern Europe, for it was they who defined the peculiar and distinctive bent of European, presently of Western, and now to a very substantial degree, of world civilization."[9]

Whether this Eurocentric construction of world history is still acceptable, McNeill's acknowledgment of the surprising and unexpected results of human actions is a useful way to conclude. Reformed Protestantism began as a small and beleaguered faith in remote cities, but gained a following and achieved stability thanks to the accidents of early modern European history. Within 250 years, well before scholars used the phrase, Calvinism became a global faith thanks to the energy, vitality, buffoonery, and hubris of Europeans and their colonial cousins. On the eve of its 500th anniversary, Calvinism attracts adherents and inspires churches in settings as diverse as Lausanne, Seoul, San Francisco, Sydney, and Brasilia. None of Calvinism's original leaders could have predicted or planned the outcome of their initial efforts to reform Europe's churches. Even if it is not responsible for the blessings of democracy, liberty, and prosperity, in its own way Calvinism's history qualifies as remarkable.

TIMELINE FOR THE HISTORY OF CALVINISM

1525 – City Council of Zurich abolishes the Mass in its churches.

1536 – Citizens of Geneva vote to follow Scripture and reject papal abuses.

1549 – England's parliament approves the new Book of Common Prayer.

1556 – Jon Laski organizes the first national synod of Protestants in Poland.

1559 – Protestants in France hold their first national ecclesiastical assembly.

1560 – Scotland's parliament abolishes the mass and approves the First Book of Discipline.

1563 – Frederick III of the Palatinate implements the Heidelberg Catechism for religious instruction in his territory.

1572 – Thousands of French Protestants are killed on St Bartholomew's Day.

1579 – The provinces of Holland, Zeeland, Utrecht, Frisia, Gelderland, and the Ommelanden ratify the Union of Utrecht on the way to Dutch independence from Spanish rule.

1581 – Leaders of Reformed churches from France, Hungary, Poland, and the Netherlands produce the *Harmony of Confessions*, published in Geneva.

1598 – The Edict of Nantes grants Protestants limited religious freedom in France.

1612 – Lewis Bayly's *The Practice of Piety* is published.

1618 – The Dutch Synod of Dort rejects the teaching of Jacobs Arminius.

1620 – The Pilgrims arrive in New Plymouth (North America).

1625 – James Glendinning leads revivals in Ireland known as the Six Mile Water revival.

1628 – New Netherland, a Dutch colony in North America, receives its first Reformed pastor.

1630 – English Puritans settle in Massachusetts Bay Colony.

1642 – England's parliament calls for an assembly of church officials at Westminster to create a new church order.

1648 – Ministers to the churches in Massachusetts and Connecticut ratify a congregationalist church government in the Cambridge Platform.

1665 – The Duke's Laws grant religious liberty to the Dutch Reformed church in the English colony, New York.

1665 – The Cape Colony in Africa (Dutch) receives its first Reformed pastor.

1672 – England's Clarendon Code restores the Book of Common Prayer and episcopacy, thus ending Puritanism's influence on the established church.

1673 – Richard Baxter's *Christian Directory* is published.

1674 – Swiss ministers produce the Helvetic Consensus as an answer to theological controversies in the Protestant churches.

1675 – Dutch authorities depose Jacobus Koelman from ministry in the national church.

1678 – John Bunyan's *Pilgrim's Progress* is published.

1690 – The Scottish Kirk is reinstituted as the established church.

1700 – Wilhelmus à Brakel's *A Christian's Reasonable Service* is published.

1706 – Francis Makemie leads the formation of the Presbytery of Philadelphia, the first Reformed ecclesiastical body in the New World.

1707 – Geneva's Company of Pastors admits a Lutheran minister into membership.

1711 – The Patronage Act restores to Scottish lairds the prerogatives they formerly had in appointing clergy within the Kirk.

1718 – *The Marrow of Modern Divinity* is republished in Scotland.

1719 – Charles Philip, elector of the Palatinate, forbids the use of the Heidelberg Catechism.

1727 – Heidelberg's consistory commissions George Michael Weiss to work among Germans in Pennsylvania.

1729 – The Synod of Philadelphia adopts the Westminster Confession of Faith and Catechisms.

1729 – Reformed pastors in New York, with the approval of the Classis of Amsterdam, ordain John Philip Boehm, the first German Reformed minister in North America.

1733 – Ebenezer Erskine leads in the founding of the Associate Presbytery in Scotland.

1737 – Jonathan Edwards' *A Faithful Narrative of the Surprising Work of God* is published.

1741 – Presbyterians in North America split over revivalism between the Old and New Side communions.

1747 – German Reformed pastors in Pennsylvania hold their first coetus.

1749 – *The Life of David Brainerd*, edited by Jonathan Edwards, is published.

1789 – The Presbyterian Church in the USA holds its first General Assembly.

1789 – Reformed ministers in Heidelberg gather at the first synod to meet in fifty years.

1793 – The German Reformed Church in the United States gathers at its first national synod.

1795 – The constitution of the newly established Dutch Batavian Republic overturns the Reformed church order and grants religious freedom.

1798 – The formation of the Helvetic Republic among the cities of Bern, Basel, and Zurich disestablishes the Reformed churches in favor of freedom of religion.

1814 – Joseph Kam, a Dutch Reformed missionary, arrives in Jakarta to work among the Moluccas.

1816 – Robert Haldane arrives in Geneva where he leads a revival among Protestants.

1817 – Frederick William III of Prussia orchestrates the union of Reformed Protestants and Lutherans in the Evangelical Church of the Old Prussian Union.

1830 – Alexander Duff, the first missionary commissioned by a Reformed communion, arrives in Calcutta.

1834 – Hendrik de Cock leads the Afscheiding (Secession) among Dutch conservatives within the national church.

1837 – Groen van Prinsterer, a Dutch official of Reformed convictions, writes *The Measures Against the Seceders Tested Against Constitutional Law* to defend the Afscheiding.

1837 – Presbyterians in the United States divide into the Old and New School denominations over disputes that have arisen from the Second Awakening.

1843 – The disruption within the Church of Scotland yields the Free Church of Scotland.

1846 – Inspired by the Free Church in Scotland, Australian ministers secede from the Synod of Australia to form the Synod of East Australia.

1847 – The Evangelical Presbyterian Church of Ghana is formed.

1847 – Hendrik P. Scholte, a Dutch minister associated with the Afscheiding, migrates to the United States and founds a colony in Pella, Iowa.

1849 – Protestants in Switzerland form the Evangelical Free Church as an alternative to the established Reformed communions.

1850 – German Reformed pastors launch the periodical *Reformierte Kirchenzeitung*.

1853 – The American Presbyterian missionary, John L. Nevius, sails to China.

1857 – Dutch Calvinist immigrants to the United States form the Christian Reformed Church.

1859 – Ashbel Green Simonton, a missionary from the United States, organizes the first presbytery in Brazil.

1875 – Presbyterians in Canada unite to form the Presbyterian Church of Canada.

1886 – Abraham Kuyper, leader of the Doleantie group within the national Dutch church, forms a rival communion, which in 1892 becomes the Reformed Church of the Netherlands (Gereformeerde Kerken in Nederland GKN).

1893 – Traditionalists in the Free Church of Scotland secede to form the Free Presbyterian Church of Scotland.

1908 – Protestants in the United States, with Presbyterians supplying leadership and resources, form the Federal Council of Churches, an important vehicle for Protestant ecumenism.

1912 – Presbyterians in Korea hold their first General Assembly.

1918 – Karl Barth's pathbreaking commentary on the Epistle to the Romans is published.

1925 – Presbyterians in Canada opposed to church union refuse to join the United Church of Canada and retain the name Presbyterian Church of Canada.

1927 – Conservative Presbyterians in the Irish Presbyterian Church form the Irish Evangelical Church (later the Evangelical Presbyterian Church).

1929 – The Church of Scotland unites with the United Free Church of Scotland, the communion that had seceded from the Kirk in 1843 at the time of the Disruption.

1929 – J. Gresham Machen leaves Princeton Theological Seminary to found a rival school, Westminster Theological Seminary.

1934 – German pastors gather at Barmen for the First Confessing Synod of the Evangelical Church of the Old Prussian Union.

1936 – Conservatives in the Presbyterian Church, USA, fearing the triumph of theological liberalism, form the Presbyterian Church of America (later the Orthodox Presbyterian Church).

1936 – Princeton Theological Seminary appoints John Mackay as its president.

1944 – Klaas Schilder leads a group of Calvinists out of the GKN to form the Gereformeerde Kerken in Nederland (Vrijgemaakt).

1947 – Reinhold Niebuhr visits Karl Barth in Basel.

1959 – Led by Hyung-Nong Park, Korean Presbyterians leave the Presbyterian Church of Korea to form the Hapdong Presbyterian Church.

1967 – The United Presbyterian Church USA adopts the Book of Confessions, which includes the Barmen Declaration (1934) and a new creed, the Confession of 1967, one of the first Reformed confessions in almost three centuries.

2010 – The Reformed Ecumenical Council merges with the World Alliance of Reformed Churches.

NOTES

Introduction

1. Bale, quoted in P. Hume Brown, *John Knox: A Biography*, 2 vols (London: Adam and Charles Black, 1895), vol. 1, 195.
2. City council, quoted in ibid., 196.
3. H. L. Mencken, "*Doctor Fundamentalis*," Baltimore *Evening Sun*, January 18, 1937.

Chapter One   City Lights

1. Quoted in Philip Benedict, *Christ's Churches Purely Reformed: A Social History of Calvinism* (New Haven, CT: Yale University Press, 2002), 81.
2. From Walter Schwimmer, *The European Dream* (London: Continuum, 2004), 9.
3. Benedict, *Christ's Churches*, 16.
4. Mark Greengrass, *The Longman Companion to the European Reformation, c. 1500–1618* (London: Longman, 1998), 73.
5. Quoted in Benedict, *Christ's Churches*, 23.
6. Arthur C. Cochrane, ed., *Reformed Confessions of the Sixteenth Century* (Louisville, KY: Westminster John Knox, 2003 (1966)), 36.
7. Bishop Hugo quoted in Steven Ozment, *The Age of Reform, 1250–1550: An Intellectual and Religious History of Late Medieval and Reformation Europe* (New Haven, CT: Yale University Press, 1980), 327.
8. Ibid.
9. The Memmingen Articles (1525) summarized the peasants' concerns and were more economic and political than religious. But the peasants did want the right to choose their own pastors and also appealed to reformers like Luther and Zwingli as figures who could determine whether their demands departed from scriptural teaching. Because Luther unintentionally inspired the peasants with his earlier appeals to Christian freedom, and because he intentionally condemned the revolt and called upon the princes to put it down, the Peasants War had more consequences for the German Reformation than for the Swiss, though the peasants of Klettgau did appeal to Zurich authorities to help settle their grievances. See Ozment, *Age of Reform*, 272–89, and Greengrass, *Longman Companion*, 76.
10. According to Carter Lindberg, *The European Reformations* (Malden, MA: Wiley-Blackwell, 2nd edn, 2010), 240–41, "The Genevan supporters of the Swiss Confederacy were called 'Eidguenots' (Eid = oath; Genosse = associate) and it has been suggested that this name was conflated with that of a Genevan exile, leader Besançon Hugues, to form the name 'Huguenot,' later applied to French Protestants and refugees. The origin of the term 'Huguenot' has long

been debated. Another explanation attributes it to early French Calvinist gatherings near the Hugon Gate in the city of Tours. The derisive diminutive 'little Hughues' was then accepted as a badge of honor."

11. Richard A. Muller, *Unaccommodated Calvin: Studies in the Foundation of a Theological Tradition* (New York, NY: Oxford University Press, 2001).

12. Calvin, quoted in Bruce Gordon, *Calvin* (New Haven, CT: Yale University Press, 2009), 115.

13. John Calvin, "Preface," *Commentary on the Psalms*, Vol. 1, (Grand Rapids, MI: Baker Books, 1979), xlii–xliii.

14. Letters of John Calvin, 1: 141, quoted in Ozment, *Age of Reform*, 365.

15. Letters of John Calvin, 2: 131, quoted in Ozment, *Age of Reform*, 366.

16. From Theodore Beza, *Life of Calvin*, n.1, 25–26, quoted in Ozment, *Age of Reform*, 366.

17. Bruce Gordon, *Calvin*, 209–211.

18. Bishop Hugo, quoted in Ozment, *Age of Reform*, 326–27.

19. Thanks to feuding between the papacy and the French monarchy, the papacy moved to Avignon during the tenure of seven different popes. The Avignon Papacy was a symbol to church reformers of Rome's aspirations for political power and neglect of its spiritual calling.

20. Ozment, *Age of Reform*, 220.

21. Zwingli, *Commentary on True and False Religion*, quoted in Benedict, *Christ's Churches*, 24–25.

Chapter Two   God's Fickle Anointed

1. Gallican Confession of Faith, in Arthur C. Cochrane, ed., *Reformed Confessions of the Sixteenth Century* (Louisville, KY: Westminster John Knox, 2003 (1966)), 144.

2. From Diarmaid MacCulloch, *The Reformation: A History* (New York, NY: Viking, 2004), 455.

3. Bullinger, quoted in Philip Benedict, *Christ's Churches Purely Reformed: A Social History of Calvinism* (New Haven, CT: Yale University Press, 2002), 247.

4. On the Pilgrim expedition, see Chapter Five, below.

5. Polish noblemen, quoted in Benedict, *Christ's Churches Purely Reformed*, 263.

6. MacCulloch, *Reformation*, 184.

Chapter Three   To Rebel and to Build

1. Bullinger, quoted in Philip Benedict, *Christ's Churches Purely Reformed: A Social History of Calvinism* (New Haven, CT: Yale University Press, 2002), 212.

2. Margo Todd, *The Culture of Protestantism in Early Modern Scotland* (New Haven, NY: Yale University Press, 2002), 71.

3. Jane E. A. Dawson, *Scotland Re-Formed: 1488–1587* (Edinburgh: University of Edinburgh Press, 2007), 227.

4. Ibid., 223.

5. James, quoted in Benedict, *Christ's Churches*, 169.

6. Benedict, *Christ's Churches*, 172.

7. Geoffrey Parker, *The Dutch Revolt* (Ithaca, NY: Cornell University Press, 1977), 60.

8. Parker, *Dutch Revolt*, records this observation from Marcus van Vaernewijck, a Ghent chronicler.

9. Ibid., 84.

10. Benedict, *Christ's Churches*, 195.

11. Confession of Dillenburg, quoted in Benedict, *Christ's Churches Purely Reformed*, 217.

12. Berlin crowd, quoted in Benedict, *Christ's Churches*, 224.

13. Compromise quoted in Benedict, *Christ's Churches*, 224.

Chapter Four   Shaking the Foundations

1. See Chapter One, above.
2. Philip Benedict, *Christ's Churches Purely Reformed: A Social History of Calvinism* (New Haven, CT: Yale University Press, 2002), 118.
3. Peter Hall, ed., *The Harmony of Protestant Confessions: Exhibiting the Faith of the Churches of Christ . . .* (London: John F. Shaw, 1842 (1581)), 337–38.
4. Richard A. Muller, *Post-Reformation Reformed Dogmatics: The Rise and Development of Reformed Orthodoxy, ca 1520–1725*, Vol. 1 (Grand Rapids, MI: Baker Academic, 2nd edn, 2003), 28.
5. Technically, the Canons of Dort came in four parts, with the third having two points. The first heading explained election, the second the atonement, the third human sinfulness and the operation of grace in conversion, and the last perseverance.
6. On the influence of English practical divinity, see Chapter Nine, below.
7. On Puritan reactions to James and settlement in the New World, see Chapter Five, below.
8. Benedict, *Christ's Churches*, 349.
9. Diarmaid MacCulloch, *The Reformation: A History* (New York, NY: Viking, 2004), 646.
10. Muller, *Post-Reformation Reformed Dogmatics*, 32.

Chapter Five   Taking the Word to the World

1. These figures and comparison come from Alan Taylor, *American Colonies: The Settling of North America* (New York, NY: Viking Penguin, 2001), 248, 250.
2. Michaelius, quoted in J. Franklin Jameson, ed., *Narratives of New Netherland, 1609–1664*, Vol. 6 (New York, NY: Charles Scribner's Sons, 1909), 124, 126.
3. Bogardus, quoted in Gerald F. DeJong, *The Dutch Reformed Church in the American Colonies* (Grand Rapids, MI: Eerdmans, 1978), 20.
4. In 1660 New Amsterdam had 5,000 colonists compared to New England (33,000), Chesapeake Bay (25,000), and New France (3,000). See Taylor, *American Colonies*, 256.
5. Response from Classis, quoted in DeJong, *Dutch Reformed Church*, 29.
6. Stuyvesant's order, quoted in DeJong, *Dutch Reformed Church*, 35.
7. Reformed pastor, quoted in ibid., 42–43.
8. New Netherland directors, quoted in ibid., 47.
9. English charter, quoted in ibid., 59.
10. Winthrop, quoted in J. William T. Youngs, *The Congregationalists* (New York, NY: Greenwood Press, 1990), 23.
11. Puritan vow, quoted in John F. Cooper, Jr, *Tenacious of their Liberties: The Congregationalists in Colonial Massachusetts* (New York, NY: Oxford University Press, 1999), 15.
12. John Winthrop, "Modell of Christian Charity," *Collections of the Massachusetts Historical Society*, 3rd Series, Vol. 7 (Boston, MA: Charles C. Little and James Brown, 1838), 47, 48.
13. James F. Cooper, Jr, *Tenacious of Their Liberties: The Congregationalists in Colonial Massachusetts* (New York: Oxford University Press, 1999), 101.

Chapter Six   New Communities in the Land of the Free

1. *Life and Letters of John Philip Boehm: Founder of the Reformed Church in Pennsylvania, 1683–1749*, ed., William J. Hinke, (Philadelphia, PA: Publication and Sunday School Board of the Reformed Church in the United States, 1916), 27.
2. Ibid., 28, 29.
3. Robert Blair, quoted in Ron Chepesiuk, *The Scotch-Irish: From the North of Ireland to the Making Of America* (Jefferson, NC: McFarland and Company Publishers, 2000), 43.
4. John Livingstone, quoted in Chepesiuk, *Scotch-Irish*, 55. These figures also come from Chepesiuk, 53.

5. University records, quoted in J. M. Barkley, *Francis Makemie of Ramelton: Father of American Presbyterianism* (Belfast: Presbyterian Historical Society of Ireland, 1981), 9.

6. Francis Makemie, *A Plain and Friendly Persuasive to the Inhabitants of Virginia and Maryland for Promoting Towns and Cohabitation*, reprinted in Boyd S. Schlenther, ed., *The Life and Writings of Francis Makemie* (Philadelphia: The Presbyterian Historical Society, 1971), 142.

7. Anglican criticism, quoted in E. H. Gillett, *History of the Presbyterian Church in the United States of America*, Vol. 1 (Philadelphia, PA: Presbyterian Publication Committee, 1864), 21.

8. Makemie, quoted in Charles Briggs, *American Presbyterianism, its Origin and Early History* (Edinburgh: T. & T. Clark, 1885), 142.

9. Presbyterian Church, *A Collection of the Acts, Deliverances, and Testimonies of the Supreme Judiciary of the Presbyterian Church from its Origins to the Present Time*, ed., Samuel J. Baird (Philadelphia, PA: Presbyterian Board of Publication, 1856), Book I, 4.

10. See Chapter Eight, below, for greater detail on the relationship between Calvinism and revivalism.

11. For more information on eighteenth-century developments in Scotland, see Chapter Seven, below.

12. Joseph Henry Dubbs, *Historic Manual of the Reformed Church in the United States* (Lancaster: n.p., 1885), 145.

13. *Life and Letters of John Philip Boehm*, 167.

14. Ibid., 30.

15. Zinzendorf, quoted in ibid., 90.

16. James Isaac Good, *History of the Reformed Church in the United States, 1725–1792* (Reading, PA: Daniel Miller, 1899), 305.

17. Ibid., 306.

18. *Life and Letters of John Philip Boehm*, 131–32.

19. Ibid., 134.

20. The discrepancy between Schlatter's 1751 figure of 30,000 members and the synod's 1793 number of 15,000 is hard to explain. Schlatter may have been counting all German settlers with potential for membership and the synod's figure may reflect actual membership. Another possibility is the loss of members owing to church splits and independent ministers. But the increase in congregations, from 46 in 1751 to 178 in 1793, suggests a pattern of growth that would also have shown up in increased levels of membership.

Chapter Seven   An Exhausted Europe

1. Ostervald, quoted in Martin I. Klauber, "Family Loyalty and Theological Transition in Post-Reformation Geneva: The Case of Benedict Pictet (1655–1724)," *Fides et Historia*, 24.1 (1992), 65.

2. James I. Good, *History of the Reformed Church of Germany, 1620–1890* (Reading, PA: Daniel Miller, 1894), 244.

3. Fabricius, quoted in ibid., 260.

4. Good, *History of the Reformed Church of Germany*, 286.

5. On George Michael Weiss' ministry in Pennsylvania, see Chapter Six, above.

6. The name comes from Richard Cameron, a Covenanter leader killed in 1680 during armed conflict for refusing to accept Anglicanism in Scotland and for refusing to submit to Charles II as head of the church.

7. General Assembly, quoted in William Ferguson, *Scotland: 1689 to the Present* (New York, NY: Praeger, 1968), 108.

8. General Assembly, quoted in T. C. Smout, *A History of the Scottish People, 1560–1830* (London: Fontana Press, 1990), 230, 231.

9. Ferguson, *Scotland*, 111.

10. W. M. Hetherington, *History of the Church of Scotland: From the Introduction of Christianity to the Disruption* (Edinburgh: John Johnstone, 1844), 588.

11. Roger L. Emerson, *Essays on David Hume, Medical Men and the Scottish Enlightenment: Industry, Knowledge, and Humanity* (Guildford: Ashgate Publishing, 2009), 16.
12. Auchterarder Creed, quoted in Ferguson, *Scotland*, 117.
13. General Assembly, quoted in W. Stephen, *History of the Scottish Church*, Vol. 2 (Edinburgh: David Douglas, 1896), 487.
14. Erskine, quoted in Ferguson, *Scotland*, 123.
15. Erskine, quoted in John M'Kerrow, *History of the Secession Church* (Glasgow: A. Fullarton and Co., 1841), 87.
16. Ferguson, *Scotland*, 123.
17. Henry Dundas (1724–1811), First Viscount Melville and Lord Advocate of Scotland, controlled royal patronage of church and academic life during the last two decades of the eighteenth century. Ferguson, *Scotland*, p. 227.
18. States General, quotes in Gerrit J. ten Zythoff, *Sources of Secession: The Netherlands Hervormde Kerk on the Eve of the Dutch Immigration to the Midwest* (Grand Rapids, MI: Eerdmans, 1987), 16.
19. Prince William, quoted in ten Zythoff, *Sources of Secession*, 18.
20. Rousseau, quoted in James I. Good, *History of the Swiss Reformed Church since the Reformation* (Philadelphia, PA: Publication and Sunday School Board of the Reformed Church in the United States, 1913), 299.
21. Good, *History of the Swiss Reformed Church*, 292.

Chapter Eight   Reformation Reawakened

1. August Gottlieb Spangenberg, *The Life of Nicholas Lewis Count Zinzendorf*, trans. Samuel Jackson (London: Samuel Holdsworth, 1838), 283.
2. Ibid., 285.
3. W. R. Ward, *The Protestant Evangelical Awakening* (Cambridge: Cambridge University Press, 1992), 188–89.
4. Spangenberg, *Life of Nicholas Lewis Count Zinzendorf*, 295.
5. "True Letter of Warning," quoted in John Philip Boehm, *Life and Letters of the Rev. John Philip Boehm, Founder of the Reformed Church in Pennsylvania, 1683–1749*, ed. William J. Hinke (Philadelphia, PA: Publication and Sunday School Board of the Reformed Church in the United States, 1916), 104.
6. Tennent, quoted in J. Milton Coalter, Jr, *Gilbert Tennent, Son of Thunder: A Case Study of Continental Pietism's Impact on the First Great Awakening in the Middle Colonies* (Westport, CT: Greenwood Press, 1986), 16–17.
7. Goodwin, quoted in Ted A. Campbell, *The Religion of the Heart: A Study of European Religious Life in the Seventeenth and Eighteenth Centuries* (Columbia, SC: University of South Carolina Press, 1991), 49.
8. Ibid.
9. See Chapter Seven above on the Nadere Reformatie among Dutch Protestants.
10. Wilhelmus à Brakel, *The Christian's Reasonable Service in which Divine Truths Concerning the Covenant of Grace Are Expounded . . .*, Vol. 2, trans. Bartel Elshout, ed. Joel R. Beeke (Grand Rapids, MI: Reformation Heritage Books, 1993), 694.
11. Campbell, *Religion of the Heart*, 53.
12. Erskine, quoted in Ward, *Protestant Evangelical Awakening*, 330.
13. Whitefield, quoted in Ward, *Protestant Evangelical Awakening*, 331.
14. Whitefield, quoted in Andrew Lang, *A History of Scotland from the Roman Occupation*, Vol. 4, (New York, NY: Dodd, Mead, and Co., 1907), 316.
15. Ward, *Protestant Evangelical Awakening*, 339.
16. Alexander Haldane, *Memoirs of the Lives of Robert Haldane of Airthrey and of His Brother James Alexander Haldane* (London: Hamilton, Adams, and Co., 1852), 377.
17. Ibid., 386.

Chapter Nine Missionary Zeal

1. Hamilton, quoted in W. M. Hetherington, *History of the Church of Scotland* (Edinburgh: John Johnstone, 1842), 694–95.
2. Mandate, quoted in D. E. Meek, "Scottish SPCK," in Nigel M. de S. Cameron, ed., *Dictionary of Scottish Church History & Theology* (Downers Grove, IL: InterVarsity Press, 1993), 762.
3. David Brainerd, *The Life of David Brainerd, Missionary to the Indians: With an Abridgement from President Edwards*, ed. John Styles (Boston, MA: Samuel T. Armstrong, 1821), 245, 242.
4. Ibid., 244.
5. Carey, quoted in John A. Grigg, *The Lives of David Brainerd: The Making of An Evangelical Icon* (New York, NY: Oxford University Press, 2009), 166.
6. Marsden, quoted in ibid., 169.
7. See Chapter Ten, below, on the Scottish Disruption.
8. On the Old School–New School divide, see Chapter Twelve, below.
9. On conflicts among the nineteenth-century Dutch churches, see Chapter Eleven, below.
10. Alexander Duff, *Missions the Chief End of the Christian Church* (Edinburgh: John Johnstone, 1839), 37.
11. Ibid., 36.
12. Ibid., 13–14.
13. Ibid., 22.
14. Ibid., 18.
15. Ibid., 61.
16. Ibid., 67–68.
17. Ibid., 81, 82.
18. Ibid., 91.
19. Ibid., 36.
20. Ibid., 107, 110, 112.
21. Ibid., 121.
22. Ibid., 144.
23. Gustav Warnack, *Outline of a History of Protestant Missions from the Reformation to the Present Time*, ed. George Robson (Chicago, IL: Fleming H. Revell Co., 1903), 293.
24. John Livingston Nevius, *The Planting and Development of Missionary Churches* (Philadelphia, PA: Presbyterian and Reformed Publishing Company, 1899), 8.
25. Ibid., 14–15.
26. Ibid., 20.
27. Ibid, 60.
28. Ibid., 86–87.
29. On this secession in the Netherlands, see Chapter Eleven, below.

Chapter Ten Kirk Ruptured and Church Freed

1. W. M. Hetherington, *History of the Church of Scotland: From the Introduction of Christianity to the Disruption* (Edinburgh: John Johnstone, 1844), 622.
2. Welsh, quoted in W. Stephen, *History of the Scottish Church*, Vol. 2 (Edinburgh: David Douglas, 1896), 487.
3. Chalmers, quoted in Alexander Findlayson, *Unity and Diversity: The Founders of the Free Church of Scotland* (Fearn: Christian Focus, 2010), 32.
4. Stewart J. Brown, *Thomas Chalmers and the Godly Commonwealth in Scotland* (New York, NY: Oxford University Press, 1982), 28, 34.
5. Protest, quoted in Thomas Chalmers, *Memoirs of the Life and Writings of Thomas Chalmers*, Vol. 4, ed. William Hanna (New York. NY: Harper & Brothers, 1857), 531.
6. Cockburn, quoted in Chalmers, *Thomas Chalmers*, 334.

7. William Gregg, *Short History of the Presbyterian Church in the Dominion of Canada* (Toronto: C. Blackett Robinson, 1892), 33.

8. Richard Vaudry, *The Free Church in Victorian Canada, 1841–1861* (Waterloo, Ontario: Wilfred Laurier University Press, 1989), 16.

9. Presbyterian Church of Canada, quoted in Gregg, *Short History*, 190.

10. The pattern in New Zealand highlights the importance of the Free Church disruption to all Presbyterians with ties to the Scottish churches. In 1845 when Scots decided to form a colony in New Zealand, which in 1841 had become distinct from New South Wales as a Crown colony, an independent voluntary association of Free Church Presbyterians saw this new territory as an outlet to practice their convictions. The first Free Church minister did not reach Otago until 1854. But a decade later the Presbyterian Church of Otago and Southland had grown to fifteen ministers, practically all of whom had backgrounds in the Free Church. New Zealand shows that once the Disruption of 1843 was already settled, Presbyterian communions with ties to Scotland did not need to engage in debates that forced ministers to take sides on the questions that had divided the Free Church and the Kirk.

11. Synod of Australia, quoted in Robert Sutherland, *The History of the Presbyterian Church of Victoria: From the Foundation of the Colony to the Abolition of State Aid in 1875* (Melbourne: H. L. Hutchinson, 1877), 58, 59.

12. R. Gordon Balfour, *Presbyterianism in the Colonies* (Edinburgh: MacNiven and Wallace, 1900), 90.

13. Hamilton, quoted in Balfour, *Presbyterianism*, 97.

14. Free Church minority, quoted in Kenneth R. Ross, *Church and Creed in Scotland: The Free Church Case 1900–1904 and its Origins* (Edinburgh: Rutherford House, 1988), 40.

15. Editorial, quoted in Ross, *Church and Creed*, 52.

Chapter Eleven   The Netherlands' New Way

1. Gerritt J. Schutte, *Groen van Prinsterer: His Life and Work*, trans. Harry Van Dyke (n.p.: Publisher's Imprint, 2005 (1976)), 51.

2. Kuyper, quoted in Peter S. Heslam, *Creating a Christian Worldview: Abraham Kuyper's Lectures on Calvinism* (Grand Rapids, MI: Eerdmans, 1998), 35.

3. Kuyper, "Sphere Sovereignty," in Abraham Kuyper, *Abraham Kuyper: A Centennial Reader*, ed. James D. Bratt (Grand Rapids, MI: Eerdmans, 1998), 466.

4. Ibid., 467.

5. Church vow, quoted in Frank Vandenberg, *Abraham Kuyper: A Biography* (Grand Rapids, MI: Eerdmans, 1960), 130.

6. Common grace could be a complicated doctrine, but put simply it was an effort to account for human prosperity and earthly order despite the prevalence of unbelief and sin – the flip side of the problem of evil. According to one of the CRC's theologians, Louis Berkhof, common grace "curbs the destructive power of sin, maintains in a measure the moral order of the universe, thus making an orderly life possible, distributes in varying degrees gifts and talents among men, promotes the development of science and art, and showers untold blessings upon the children of men." See Louis Berkhof, *Systematic Theology* (Grand Rapids, MI: Eerdmans, 1938), 434.

7. On Barth's influence among twentieth-century Reformed churches, see Chapter Thirteen, below.

Chapter Twelve   American Fundamentalists

1. General Assembly, "Report of the Committee on Re-Union," *Minutes of the General Assembly of Presbyterian Church in the U.S.A.* (1868), 670.

2. Elias Benjamin Sanford, *Origin and History of the Federal Council of the Churches of Christ in America* (Hartford, CT: S. S. Scranton, 1916), 245.
3. Hendrix, quoted in ibid., 249.
4. Ibid., 250.
5. "Social Creed for the Churches," reprinted in Harry Frederick Ward, *The Social Creed of the Churches* (New York, NY: Abingdon Press, 1914), 6–7.
6. William R. Hutchison, "Introduction," in William R. Hutchison, ed., *Between the Times: The Travail of the Protestant Establishment in America, 1900–1960* (New York: Cambridge University Press, 1989), viii.
7. J. Gresham Machen, *Christianity and Liberalism* (New York, NY: Macmillan, 1923), 150–51.
8. Ibid., 164–65.
9. The legal counsel for the young ministers was John Foster Dulles, who would later serve as United States Secretary of State and architect of the nation's Cold War foreign policy. One of the defendants, Van Dusen, would go on to preside over Union Seminary in New York during Reinhold Niebuhr's tenure, when theological liberals embraced anti-communism.
10. General Assembly, "Report of the Special Commission of 1925," *Minutes of the General Assembly of the Presbyterian Church in the U.S.A.* (1926), 72.
11. General Assembly, "Report of the Special Commission of 1925," *Minutes of the General Assembly of the Presbyterian Church in the U.S.A.* (1927), 86.
12. J. Gresham Machen, "Westminster Theological Seminary: Its Purpose and Plan," in *J. Gresham Machen: Selected Shorter Writings*, ed. D. G. Hart (Phillipsburg, NJ: P&R Publishing, 2004), 193–94.
13. This popular interpretation of the Bible stressed a pessimistic reading of history – as opposed to postmillennialism – and held that the church would apostacize prior to Christ's return to judge the world.
14. *Presbyterian Guardian*, "Final Decree Entered Against Denomination by Philadelphia Court," *Presbyterian Guardian* 5 (1938), 160.
15. Machen, "The Responsibility of the Church in the New Age," in *J. Gresham Machen*, 375.
16. William Gregg, *Short History of the Presbyterian Church in the Dominion of Canada* (Toronto: C. Blackett Robinson, 1892), 81.

Chapter Thirteen   The Confessing Church

1. Barth, quoted in Eberhard Busch, *Karl Barth: His Life from Letters and Autobiographical Texts* (Philadelphia, PA: Fortress Press, 1976), 105.
2. Ibid., 101.
3. Ibid., 109.
4. Moeller, quoted in Daniel R. Borg, *The Old Prussian Church and The Weimar Republic: A Study in Political Adjustment, 1917–1927* (Hanover, NH: University Press of New England, 1984), 57.
5. Schleiermacher, quoted in Walter H. Conser, *Church and Confession: Conservative Theologians in Germany, England, and America, 1815–1866* (Macon, GA: Mercer University Press, 1984), 43.
6. James I. Good, *History of the Reformed Church of Germany, 1620–1890* (Reading, PA: Daniel Miller, 1894), 568.
7. Ernst Christian Helmreich, *The German Churches Under Hitler: Background, Struggle, and Epilogue* (Detroit, MI: Wayne State University Press, 1979), 36.
8. Barth, quoted in Busch, *Karl Barth*, 130.
9. Ibid., 128, 123.
10. Ibid., 129, 128.
11. Ibid., 142, 143.
12. Ibid., 145–46.
13. Ibid., 148.

14. Ibid., 189, 190–91.
15. Protestant pastors, quoted in Helmreich, *German Churches*, 128.
16. Constitution of 1933 quoted in Helmreich, *German Churches*, 141.
17. Barth, quoted in Busch, *Karl Barth*, 224.
18. Barth, quoted in ibid., 257.
19. Barmen Declaration, reprinted in Arthur C. Cochrane, ed., *Reformed Confessions of the Sixteenth Century* (Louisville, KY: Westminster John Knox Press, 2003 (1966)), 335.
20. Barth, quoted in Busch, *Karl Barth*, 248.
21. Ibid., 261.
22. On Scottish developments after the 1843 Disruption, see Chapter Ten, above.
23. Ibid., 342.
24. Niebuhr, quoted in Gary Dorrien, *Economy, Difference, Empire: Social Ethics for Social Justice* (New York, NY: Columbia University Press, 2010), 30.
25. Niebuhr and Barth quoted in Dorrien, *Economy Difference, Empire*, 40–41.
26. Barth, quoted in Dorrien, *Economy, Difference, Empire*, 40, 41, 44.
27. *Time*, "Witness to an Ancient Truth," *Time*, April 20, 1962.
28. Mackay, quoted in John Mackay Metzger, *The Hand and the Road: The Life and Times of John A. Mackay* (Louisville, KY: Westminster John Knox, 2010), 193.
29. Ibid., 244.

Conclusion

1. Philip Jenkins, *The Next Christendom: The Coming of Global Christianity* (New York, NY: Oxford University Press, 2002), 2, 3.
2. Ibid., 77.
3. Quoted in ibid., 77.
4. Leigh Eric Schmidt, *Holy Fairs: Scottish Communions and American Revivals in the Early Modern Period* (Princeton, NJ: Princeton University Press, 1989), 17–18.
5. For background on Kam, see Chapter Nine, above.
6. See Arthur Herman, *How the Scots Invented the Modern World: The True Story of How Western Europe's Poorest Nation Created our World and Everything in it* (New York, NY: Crown Business, 2001).
7. See, for instance, Friedrich Wilhelm Graf, "Calvin in the Plural: The Diversity of Interpretations of Calvin, Especially in Germany and the English-Speaking World," *Calvin and His Influence, 1509–2009*, ed. Irena Backus and Philip Benedict (New York, NY: Oxford University Press, 2011), 261, 263.
8. See treatments by David Gress, *From Plato to NATO: The Idea of the West and its Critics* (New York, NY: Free Press, 1998), 281–82, and Niall Ferguson, *Civilization: The West and the Rest* (New York, NY: Penguin, 2011), 289.
9. William H. McNeill, *The Rise of the West: A History of the Human Community* (Chicago, IL: University of Chicago Press, 1963), 599.

FURTHER READING

THE LITERATURE ON THE rise of Calvinism in sixteenth-century Europe is vast. Expanding the canvas to include the history of Reformed Protestantism in settings around the world until the late twentieth century only increases chance of readers feeling overwhelmed. What follows is a relatively brief guide to the high points of books in English on topics that bear specifically on the narrative told in *Calvinism: A History*.

General studies of Calvinism

Works on Calvinism are abundant but only a few have attempted to encompass in one volume the history and significance of the Reformed branch of the Protestant churches. Although it covers only the first two centuries of Calvinism's history, Philip Benedict's *Christ's Churches Purely Reformed: A Social History of Calvinism* (New Haven: Yale University Press, 2002) stands head and shoulders above practically all others, thanks to the breadth of coverage and depth of insight into the rise of Reformed Protestantism in early modern Europe. Three additional titles worthy of mention are John T. McNeill, *The History and Character of Calvinism* (New York: Oxford University Press, 1954); Graeme Murdock, *Beyond Calvin: The Intellectual, Political, and Cultural World of Europe's Reformed Churches, c. 1540–1620* (Bosingstoke: Palgrave Macmillan, 2004) and James E. McGoldrick, *Presbyterian and Reformed Churches: A Global History* (Grand Rapids: Reformation Heritage Books, 2012).

General studies of the Reformation and modern church history

Recent scholarship on sixteenth-century Christianity has produced numerous valuable works on the Reformation, including: Diarmaid MacCulloch, *The Reformation: A History* (New York: Viking, 2003); Carter Lindberg, *The European Reformations* (Cambridge, MA: Blackwell, 1996); Hans J. Hillerbrand, *The Division of Christendom: Christianity in the Sixteenth Century* (Louisville, KY: Westminster John Knox Press, 2007); Thomas A. Brady, Heiko A. Oberman, and James A. Brady, eds, *Handbook of European History, 1400–1600: Late Middle Ages, Renaissance, and Reformation, Volume 1, Structures and Assertions* (Leiden: Brill, 1994); and Thomas A. Brady, Heiko A. Oberman, and James A. Brady, eds, *Handbook of European History, 1400–1600: Late Middle Ages, Renaissance, and Reformation, Volume 2, Programs and Outcomes* (Leiden: Brill, 1999). Steven Ozment, *The Age of Reform, 1250–1550: An Intellectual and Religious History of Late Medieval and Reformation Europe* (New Haven: Yale University Press, 1981) still provides a useful orientation to the medieval context of sixteenth-century ecclesiastical reforms.

For general treatments of Christianity since 1600, with attention to important themes such as secularization, religion and the Enlightenment, and confessionalization, readers should consult the following: S. J. Brown and T. Tackett, eds, *The Cambridge History of Christianity, Volume 7,*

Enlightenment, Reawakening, and Revolution, 1660–1815 (Cambridge: Cambridge University Press, 2006), S. Gilley and B. Stanley, eds, *The Cambridge History of Christianity, Volume Eight, World Christianities c.1815–c.1914* (Cambridge: Cambridge University Press, 2006); Dana L. Robert, *Christian Mission: How Christianity Became a World Religion* (Malden, MA: Wiley-Blackwell, 2009); Jaroslav Pelikan, *The Christian Tradition, Volume 4, Reformation of Church and Dogma, 1300–1700* (Chicago: University of Chicago Press, 1985); Jaroslav Pelikan, *The Christian Tradition, Volume 5, Christian Doctrine and Modern Culture since 1700* (Chicago: University of Chicago Press, 1989); Hugh McLeod and Werner Ustorf, eds, *The Decline of Christendom in Western Europe, 1750–2000* (Cambridge: Cambridge University Press, 2003); Alister McGrath, *Christianity's Dangerous Idea: The Protestant Revolution – A History from the Sixteenth Century to the Twenty-First* (New York: HarperOne, 2007); Michael Burleigh, *Earthly Powers: The Clash of Religion and Politics in Europe, from the French Revolution to the Great War* (New York: HarperCollins, 2007); Steve Bruce, *God is Dead: Secularization in the West* (Malden, MA: Wiley-Blackwell, 2002); Mark A. Noll, *A History of Christianity in the United States and Canada* (Grand Rapids, MI: Eerdmans, 1992); and Sydney E. Ahlstrom, *A Religious History of the American People* (2nd edn; New Haven, CT: Yale University Press, 2004).

Switzerland, France, and the Netherlands

Readers have many important works to explore in studying the rise and spread of Calvinism, including: Bruce Gordon, *The Swiss Reformation* (New York: Manchester University Press, 2002); Robert M. Kingdon, *Geneva and the Consolidation of the French Protestant Movement, 1554–1572* (Madison, WI: University of Wisconsin Press, 1967); Irena Backus and Philip Benedict, eds, *Calvin and His Influence, 1509–2009* (New York: Oxford University Press, 2011); W. J. Torrance Kirby, *The Zurich Connection and Tudor Political Theory* (Leiden: Brill, 2007); John B. Roney and Martin J. Klauber, eds, *The Identity of Geneva: The Christian Commonwealth, 1564–1864* (Westport, CT: Greenwood Press, 1998); Natalie Z. Davis, *Society and Culture in Early Modern France* (Stanford, CA: Stanford University Press, 1975); Mark Greengrass, *The French Reformation* (Oxford: Blackwell, 1987); Brian G. Armstrong, *Calvinism and the Amyraut Heresy: Protestant Scholasticism and Humanism in Seventeenth-Century France* (Madison, WI: University of Wisconsin Press, 1969); Philip Benedict, *The Faith and Fortunes of France's Huguenots, 1600–1685* (Burlington, VT: Ashgate, 2001); Michael Wolfe, *The Conversion of Henry IV: Politics, Power, and Religious Belief in Early Modern France* (Cambridge, MA: Harvard University Press, 1993); Phylis M. Crew, *Calvinistic Preaching and Iconoclasm in the Netherlands, 1544–1569* (New York: Cambridge University Press, 1978); Benjamin J. Kaplan, *Calvinists and Libertines: Confession and Community in Utrecht, 1578–1620* (Oxford: Clarendon Press, 1995); Jonathan Israel, *The Dutch Republic: Its Rise, Greatness and Fall, 1477–1806* (New York: Oxford University Press, 1995); and Geoffrey Parker, *The Dutch Revolt* (Ithaca, NY: Cornell University Press, 1977).

Germany and eastern Europe

Although Reformed Protestantism did not take root in central and eastern Europe the way it did in other parts of the continent, the history of Calvinism in these regions is covered in several good treatments, including: James I. Good, *The Origin of the Reformed Church in Germany* (Reading, PA: D. Miller, 1894); Bodo Nischan, *Prince, People, and Confession: The Second Reformation in Brandenburg* (Philadelphia: University of Pennsylvania Press, 1994); Heinz Schilling, *Civic Calvinism in Northwestern Germany and the Netherlands: Sixteenth to Nineteenth Centuries* (Kirksville, MO: Sixteenth Century Journal, 1991); R. Po-Chia Hsia, *Social Discipline in the Reformation: Central Europe 1550–1750* (London: Routledge, 1989); Derk Visser, ed., *Controversy and Conciliation: The Reformation and the Palatinate, 1559–1583* (Allison Park, PA: Pickwick Press, 1986); Karin Maag, ed., *The Reformation in Eastern and Central Europe* (Brookfield, VT: Ashgate, 1997); and Graeme Murdock, *Calvinism and the Reformed Church in Hungary and Transylvania c. 1600–1660* (New York: Oxford University Press, 2000).

England, Scotland, and Northern Ireland

Although the study of Puritanism has dominated treatments of Calvinism in the British Isles, historians have produced substantial works on British Protestantism that reveal the breadth of Reformed Protestantism's appeal, such as: Patrick Collinson, *The Elizabethan Puritan Movement* (Berkeley, CA: University of California Press, 1967); Andrew Pettegree, *Marian Protestantism: Six Studies* (Aldershot, England: Scolar Press, 1996); Diarmaid MacCulloch, *Thomas Cranmer: A Life* (New Haven, CT: Yale University Press, 1996); Margo Todd, *The Culture of Protestantism in Modern Scotland* (New Haven, CT: Yale University Press, 2002); Jane E. A. Dawson, *Scotland Re-Formed, 1488–1587* (Edinburgh: Edinburgh University Press, 2007); J. D. Douglass, *Light in the North: The Story of the Scottish Covenanters* (Grand Rapids, MI: Eerdmans, 1964); Robert T. Kendall, *Calvin and English Calvinism to 1649* (Oxford: Oxford University Press, 1979); John Coffey, *Politics, Religion, and the British Revolutions: The Mind of Samuel Rutherford* (New York: Cambridge University Press, 1997); Robert S. Paul, *The Assembly of the Lord: Politics and Religion in the Westminster Assembly and the "Grand Debate"* (Edinburgh: T&T Clark, 1985); Peter Brooke, *Ulster Presbyterianism: The Historical Perspective, 1610–1970* (2nd edn, Belfast: Athol Books, 1994); St John Drelincourt Seymore, *The Puritans in Ireland, 1647–1661* (Oxford: Clarendon Press, 1969); and Crawford Gribben, *God's Irishmen: Theological Debates in Cromwellian Ireland* (New York: Oxford University Press, 1997).

The literature in English on Reformed Protestant developments after 1700 is not as extensive as the studies of the Reformation era, though the variety of Reformed expressions outside of Europe (especially in North America) has attracted substantial attention.

North America

On Presbyterianism in the United States, readers should consult: James H. Smylie, *A Brief History of the Presbyterians* (Louisville, KY: Geneva Press, 1997); Ernest Trice Thompson, *Presbyterians in the South*, 3 vols (Richmond, VA: John Knox Press, 1963–1973); D. G. Hart and John R. Muether, *Seeking A Better Country: 300 Years of American Presbyterianism* (Phillipsburg, NJ: P&R Publishing, 2007); George P. Hutchison, *The History Behind the Reformed Presbyterian Church, Evangelical Synod* (Cherry Hill, NJ: Mack Publishing Co., 1974); Ray A. King, *A History of the Associate Reformed Presbyterian Church* (Charlotte, NC: Board of Christian Education, 1966); Leonard J. Trinterud, *The Forming of An American Tradition: A Re-Examination of Colonial Presbyterianism* (Philadelphia, PA: Westminster Press, 1949); Paul K. Conkin, *The Uneasy Center: Reformed Christianity in Antebellum America* (Chapel Hill, NC: University of North Carolina Press, 1995); George M. Marsden, *The Evangelical Mind and the New School Presbyterian Experience: A Case Study of Thought and Theology in Nineteenth-Century America* (New Haven, CT: Yale University Press, 1970); Mark A. Noll, *Princeton and the Republic, 1768–1822: The Search for a Christian Enlightenment in the Era of Samuel Stanhope Smith* (Princeton: Princeton University Press, 1989); Bradley J. Longfield, *The Presbyterian Controversy: Fundamentalists, Modernists, and Moderates* (New York: Oxford University Press, 1992); and Milton J Coalter, John M. Mulder, and Louis B. Weeks, eds, *The Presbyterian Presence: The Twentieth-Century Experience*, 7 vols (Louisville, KY: Westminster John Knox Press, 1990–92).

For the history of Reformed churches in North America, the following books are helpful: Randall Balmer, *A Perfect Babel of Confusion: Dutch Religion & English Culture in the Middle Colonies* (New York: Oxford University Press, 1989); James D. Bratt, *Dutch Calvinism in Modern America* (Grand Rapids, MI: Eerdmans, 1984); Jon Butler, *The Huguenots in America: A Refugee People in New World Society* (Cambridge, MA: Harvard University Press, 1983); Gerald F. DeJong, *The Dutch Reformed Church in the American Colonies* (Grand Rapids, MI: Eerdmans, 1978); Joseph Dubbs, *A History of the Reformed Church, German* (New York: Christianity Literature, 1895); D. G. Hart, *John Williamson Nevin: High Church Calvinist* (Phillipsburg, NJ: P&R Publishing, 2005); John R. Muether, *Cornelius Van Til: Reformed Apologist and Churchman* (Phillipsburg, NJ: P&R Publishing, 2008); Robert P. Swierenga and Elton J. Bruins, *Family Quarrels in the Dutch Reformed*

Churches in the Nineteenth Century (Grand Rapids, MI: Eerdmans, 1999); and W. W. J. Vanoene, *Inheritance Preserved: The Canadian Reformed Churches in Historical Perspective* (Winnipeg: Premier Printing, 1975).

The literature on Puritanism is vast but its institutional history in the form of Congregational church history is less well known. For an introduction, readers should examine Louis H. Gunnemann and Charles Shelby Rooks, *The Shaping of the United Church of Christ: An Essay in the History of American Christianity* (Cleveland, OH: United Church Press, 1999); Daniel L. Johnson and Charles Hambrick-Stowe, eds, *Theology and Identity: Traditions, Movements, and Polity in the United Church of Christ* (New York: Pilgrim Press, 1990); Edmund S. Morgan, *The Puritan Dilemma: The Story of John Winthrop* (Boston: Little, Brown, 1958); J. William T. Youngs, *The Congregationalists* (Westport, CT: Praeger, 1998); and Barbara Brown Zikmund, ed., *Living Theological Heritage of the United Church of Christ*, 7 vols (Cleveland, OH: Pilgrim Press, 1995–2005).

The history of Presbyterianism in Canada is accessible in the following accounts: Keith N. Clifford: *Resistance to Church Union in Canada, 1904–1939* (Vancouver: University of British Columbia Press, 1985); Brian J. Fraser, *The Social Uplifters: Presbyterian Progressives and the Social Gospel in Canada, 1875–1915* (Waterloo: Wilfrid Laurier University Press, 1988); Michael Gauvreau, *The Evangelical Century: College and Creed in English Canada from the Great Revival to the Great Depression* (Montreal: McGill-Queen's University Press, 1991); William Gregg, *History of the Presbyterian Church in the Dominion of Canada from the Earliest Times to 1834* (Toronto: Presbyterian Printing and Publishing Company, 1885); William Klempa, ed., *The Burning Bush and a Few Acres of Snow: The Presbyterian Contribution to Canadian Life and Culture* (Ottawa: Carleton University Press, 1994); David B. Marshall, *Secularizing the Faith: Canadian Protestant Clergy and the Crisis of Belief, 1850–1940* (Toronto: University of Toronto Press, 1992); John T. McNeill, *The Presbyterian Church in Canada, 1875–1925* (Toronto: General Board, 1925); and Richard Vaudry, *The Free Church in Victorian Canada, 1844–1861* (Waterloo: Wilfrid Laurier University Press, 1989).

Modern Europe

Books on Calvinism in Europe since 1750 are not as extensive as those on North America, but they feature a number of important contributions, including: Andrew Drummond, *The Church in Victorian Scotland, 1843–1879* (Edinburgh: St Andrew Press, 1975); Andrew Drummond, *The Scottish Church, 1688–1843: The Age of Moderates* (Edinburgh: St Andrew Press, 1973); R. Tudor Jones, *Congregationalism in England, 1662–1962* (London: Independent Press, 1962); Horton Davies, *The English Free Churches* (London: Oxford University Press, 1952); Karel Blei, *Netherlands Reformed Church, 1517–2005* (Grand Rapids, MI: Eerdmans, 2006); K. L. Sprunger, *Dutch Puritanism: A History of the English and Scottish Churches in the Netherlands* (Leiden: Brill, 1982); Gerrit J. Ten Zythoff, *Sources of Secession: The Netherlands Hervormde Kerk on the Eve of the Dutch Immigration to the Midwest* (Grand Rapids, MI: Eerdmans, 1987); John W. Beardslee, *Theological Development at Geneva under Francis and Jean-Alphonse Turretin* (New Haven, CT: Yale University Press, 1956); Peter Brooke, *Ulster Presbyterianism: The Historical Perspective, 1610–1970* (2nd edn, Belfast: Athol Books, 1994); and Andrew R. Holmes, *The Shaping of Ulster Presbyterian Belief and Practice, 1770–1840* (New York: Oxford University Press, 2006).

Australia and New Zealand

Books on Calvinism in this region are not numerous but reliable. They include: Aeneas MacDonald, *One Hundred Years of Presbyterians in Victoria* (Melbourne: Robertson and Mullens, 1937); Robert J. Scrimgeour, *Some Scots Were Here: A History of the Presbyterian Church of South Australia, 1839–1977* (Adelaide, Australia: Lutheran Publishing House, 1994); Rowland S. Ward, *The Bush Still Burns: The Presbyterian and Reformed Faith in Australia, 1788–1988* (St Kilda, Victoria: Presbyterian Church of East Australia, 1989); H. R. Jackson, *Churches and People in Australia and New Zealand* (Wellington, New Zealand: Allen and Unwin, 1987); and John Rawson Elder, *History of the Presbyterian Church of New Zealand, 1840–1940* (Christchurch, New Zealand: Presbyterian Bookroom, 1940).

South America, Africa, and Asia

Historical study of Calvinism in these continents is very thin, but readers will nevertheless find the following to be worthwhile: James Bear, *Mission to Brazil* (Nashville, TN: PCUS Board of World Missions, 1961); Paul Pierson, *A Younger Church in Search of Maturity: Presbyterianism in Brazil from 1910 to 1959* (San Antonio, TX: Trinity University Press, 1973); Darcy Ribeiro, *The Brazilian People: The Formation and Meaning of Brazil* (Gainesville, FL: University Press of Florida, 2000); Adrian Hastings, *The Church in Africa, 1450–1950* (New York: Oxford University Press, 1994); Robert Macpherson, *The Presbyterian Church in Kenya* (Nairobi: Presbyterian Church of East Africa, 1970); J. W. Hofmeyr and G. J. Pillay, eds *A History of Christianity in South Africa* (Pretoria: HAUM, 1994); Harvey J. Sindima, *The Legacy of Scottish Missionaries in Malawi* (Lewiston, NY: Mellen Press, 1992); Gerdien Verstraelen-Guilhuis, *From Dutch Mission Church to Reformed Church in Zambia* (Frankener, Netherlands: T. Wever, 1982); Geoffrey Johnston, *Of God and Maxim Guns: Presbyterianism in Nigeria 1846–1946* (Waterloo, Ontario: Wilfred Laurier University Press, 1988); Samuel Hugh Moffett, *A History of Christianity in Asia: Volume 2, 1500–1900* (Maryknoll, NY: Orbis, 2005); G. Thompson Brown, *Earthen Vessels and Transcendent Power: American Presbyterians in China, 1837–1952* (Maryknoll, NY: Orbis, 1997); Gerald F. DeJong, *The Reformed Church in China, 1842–1951* (Grand Rapids, MI: Eerdmans, 1992); Xi Lian, *The Conversion of Missionaries: Liberalism in American Protestant Missions in China, 1907–1932* (University Park, PA: Pennsylvania State University Press, 1997); In Soo Kim, *Protestants and the Formation of Modern Korean Nationalism: A Study of the Contribution of Horace G. Underwood and Sun Chu Kil* (New York: Peter Lang, 1996); and Mo Hee Yim, *Unity Lost-Unity Regained in Korean Presbyterianism: A History of the Division in Korean Presbyterian and the Role of the Means of Grace* (Frankfurt-am-Main: Peter Lang, 1996).

Biography

Some of the best work on the history of Reformed Protestantism may be in the genre of biography. The most useful include the following: G. R. Potter, *Zwingli* (Cambridge: Cambridge University Press, 1976); William J. Bouwsma, *John Calvin: A Sixteenth-Century Portrait* (New York: Oxford University Press, 1988); Bruce Gordon, *Calvin* (New Haven, CT: Yale University Press, 2009); H. Eells, *Bucer* (New Haven, CT: Yale University Press, 1931); Bruce Gordon and Emidio Campi, *Architect of Reformation: An Introduction to Heinrich Bullinger, 1504–1575* (Grand Rapids, MI: Baker Academic, 2004); Derk Visser, *Zacharias Ursinus, the Reluctant Reformer: His Life and Times* (New York: United Church Press, 1983); Emidio Campi, *Peter Martyr Vermigli: Humanism, Republicanism, Reformation* (Geneva: Librairie Droz, 2002); W. S. Reid, *Trumpeter of God: A Biography of John Knox* (New York: Scribner, 1974); Diarmaid MacCulloch, *Thomas Cranmer: A Life* (New Haven, CT: Yale University Press, 1996); and Robert S. Paul, *The Lord Protector: Religion and Politics in the Life of Oliver Cromwell* (London: Lutterworth Press, 1955).

A selective list of biographies of important Reformed figures in the modern era is as follows: Stewart J. Brown, *Thomas Chalmers and the Godly Commonwealth in Scotland* (New York: Oxford University Press, 1982); Frank Vanden Berg, *Abraham Kuyper: A Biography* (Grand Rapids, MI: Eerdmans, 1960); Milton J. Coalter, Jr, *Gilbert Tennent, Son of Thunder: A Case Study of Continental Pietism's Impact on the First Great Awakening in the Middle Colonies* (Westport, CT: Greenwood Press, 1986); Richard Wightman Fox, *Reinhold Niebuhr: A Biography* (San Francisco: Harper & Row, 1987); D. G. Hart, *Defending the Faith: J. Gresham Machen and the Crisis of Conservative Protestantism in Modern America* (Baltimore: Johns Hopkins University Press, 1994); Boyd S. Schlenther, *The Life and Writings of Francis Makemie* (Philadelphia: Presbyterian Historical Society, 1971); T. H. L. Parker, *Karl Barth* (Grand Rapids, MI: Eerdmans, 1970); and Eberhard Busch, *Karl Barth: His Life from Letters and Autobiographical Texts* (Minneapolis, MN: Fortress Press, 1976).

INDEX